THE WICKET MEN

Also by Tony Hannan

Underdogs: Keegan Hirst, Batley and a Year in the Life of a Rugby League Town
On Behalf of the Committee: A History of Northern Comedy
Being Eddie Waring: The Life and Times of a Sporting Icon
Slouching Towards Blubberhouses: A Guided Tour of Yorkshireness
Tries and Prejudice: The Autobiography of Ikram Butt, England's First Muslim Rugby International

Twitter: @AJHannanEsq
Website: www.tonyhannan.co.uk

THE
WICKET
MEN

The Last Rites of
Minor Counties Cricket

Tony Hannan

Scratching Shed Publishing Ltd

Cover and other illustrations: Mark Eastbrook
Photography by Tony Hannan unless otherwise stated

A catalogue record for this book is available
from the British Library.

Typeset in Minion
Printed and bound in the United Kingdom by
Page Bros (Norwich) Ltd
Mile Cross Lane, Norwich, Norfolk NR6 6SA
Telephone 01603 778800

Page
Bros
Group

For Albie and Violet

CONTENTS

The flannelled fool at the wicket,

In a frivolous pastime may revel;

But the khaki-clad brave in the thicket,

Is playing the game of the Devil.

For the battle that's fought out in cricket,

Is ever a friendly strife,

And I think that to take a man's wicket,

Is better than taking his life.

Verse by Sir Wilfrid Lawson, 1901

'In a short time, this will be a long time ago...'

Slow West, **Dir. John Maclean, 2015**

PROLOGUE

Fourth Ashes Test, Trent Bridge – August 27, 2005. Ricky Ponting, gimlet-eyed at the non-striker's end, is surely the man for the job. One of the greatest international batsmen of all time, if anyone can turn a tricky situation Australia's way it is their skipper.

England in high summer. Dry and bright, but there's an early evening breeze. The hosts need a win to claw their way back into a series that began with an alarmingly heavy defeat at Lord's. Come Edgbaston they drew level, courtesy of the narrowest margin of victory in Ashes history – two runs. The Third Test at Old Trafford finished all-square, England denied by a single wicket, Ponting making 156. For holders Australia, a drawn series would retain the legendary urn, so no cause for panic. But if England captain Michael Vaughan and his teammates are to stay in contention, they need one more win at least, a second defeat too painful even to contemplate.

Destiny though is on England's side. A series capturing eyeballs by the million on terrestrial television – and that some are already describing the greatest ever – will climax in an astonishing 2-1 home triumph to end years of Aussie dominance. It will earn the English heroes a memo from HM the Queen and a notorious bus ride from Mansion House to Trafalgar Square, provoking more Antipodean temper tantrums than there are grains of sand on the Nullarbor Plain. But for the moment no-one is aware of any of that.

Overcoming the loss of a chunk of day one to the Nottingham

rain, England began strongly, forging a hefty first innings total of 477 by tea on day two, by the end of which Australia tumbled to 99 for 5, Ponting falling lbw to Simon Jones, for one. A flurry of boundaries woke the visitors up on day three but, out for 218 by lunch, Vaughan looked to the sky and enforced the follow-on, a first for the Australians since Pakistan had done likewise in Karachi, seventeen years before. Openers Justin Langer and Matthew Hayden made a steady half-century before the latter's fall on 26, cue for Ponting's second coming. And the new partnership had been going well, England struggling to press their advantage. That pair battled on to 129, before Langer was caught out during the evening session, whereupon in came Damien Martyn.

The pendulum, if finely balanced, now appears to be swinging Australia's way. England have wasted a couple of chances, a catch and a stumping, while Ponting's first-innings nemesis, Jones, has gone to hospital for an ankle scan. Andrew Flintoff, buzzing after a maiden Test century against the Aussies on day two, tosses one up to Martyn, comfortable line and length, easily playable. Australia's number four prods forward, pushes the ball to the off-side and calls for a single. Ponting isn't sure but, hey, it's the batsman's call, so off he scampers. Neither knows much – if anything at all – about Jones's replacement fielder, to whom the ball is on its way. And in fact the same could be said for almost everyone outside the England party.

Whoever does notice the 12th man?

As it happens, the lad in question is of confident – you might even say 'cocky' – stock. Consumed by cricket since childhood, he's the type to have practised forward-defensive strokes in the womb. Shirt billowing, he tears in from the covers, collects it on the hoof and instinctively takes a shy at the wicket. Bails fly, a nation roars and after a video replay – 'quick, quick,' the more usually phlegmatic Richie Benaud urges in commentary, 'oh, he's gone I think...' – the ball-watching Tasmanian trudges back to the pavilion, not bothering to hide his disgust. Later, he will openly complain about 'over-use of substitutes'... of tactics contrary to the spirit of the game.

Meanwhile swamped by jubilant teammates – Vaughan, Kevin Pietersen and man of the match Flintoff among them – Durham's Gary Pratt cares not one jot about any of that. And why should he, having just produced one of cricket's most celebrated dismissals?

The Wicket Men

Tony Hannan

CHAPTER ONE
UNLUCKY FOR SOME

Gary Pratt no longer wishes to dwell on Ricky Ponting. Sure, for a 23-year-old county cricketer out to make his mark, running him out was at the time his wildest dream come true. The sudden fame took him to places he might otherwise never have been, fun for a while. But looked back on now, it also turned a promising sportsman with the world at his feet into an answer in a pub quiz.

And anyway, all of that is thirteen years ago. Long enough for a budding first-class career to disintegrate. And long enough too for achievements outside the media glare equally dramatic in their way, which helped him find some sort of acceptance, if not quite inner peace. In 2018, Pratt will captain Cumberland CCC in the Minor Counties Championship, just as he has since released by Durham some twelve months after that Ashes glory. Nor is he keen to rake over the coals of that further little episode right now, but promises to do so when he hasn't got a game to concentrate on.

It's the first Sunday morning in May and he and the team are at Booth Park, home to ECB Premier League side Toft CC. Formed in a neighbouring civil parish of that name in 1928, nowadays the club sits on the outskirts of what road signs call 'Historic Knutsford,' in a leafy part of Cheshire that is home to *Coronation Street* divas and footballers' wives, among other such celebrity residents. This is also where, every ten years since 1980, a penny farthing endurance race has taken place, the last, in 2010, ending in controversy as the celebrations of Czech competitor Josef Zimovčák – 'best penny farthing rider in the world' – were cut short when he learned of his expulsion on only the second lap. Organiser Glynn Stockdale told *Cheshire Life*: 'It's a great tragedy that he had to be disqualified and didn't take kindly to it. He was riding recklessly, took out two other riders and was immediately disqualified by the race marshal, but he doesn't speak English and didn't understand so he got back on...'

With over four hundred members, three senior sides and an over-40s team, Toft's last big success was in 1989, when they won the National Village Championship Trophy at Lord's. On a weekend set to be the hottest since the early May bank holiday was introduced in 1978, the scene at a ground tucked beside a country road in a part of town marked by white-walled cottages and the whiff of money and fresh-mown lawns, is one of sunshine and cherry blossom; the sort of spot where the driver of a vintage Triumph 2000 can wave at a touring caravan through her sun roof while motoring cheerfully on by. The ideal setting then to play game one – in Group 1 – of a fresh Minor Counties initiative this season: Twenty20 cricket.

Today, therefore, Toft are mere landlords and it is Cheshire who are to meet Cumberland in the first of two fixtures against the same opposition in one day, with a 45-minute break for tea and cakes in between. This group also features Staffordshire, Lincolnshire and Northumberland, the latter pair about to snare one win each in Jesmond. Staffs begin tomorrow, Cheshire doubling up as visitors on Bank Holiday Monday with one victory and a defeat.

Pratt may be the most famous member of the Cumberland troupe, but only marginally less illustrious in the Minor Counties is Toby Bulcock, for whom conversation is seldom a chore. 'Where's mine?' the spin bowler demands, hefty of frame and personality, as he barges into a cramped changing room, hauls a huge bag off his shoulder and throws it to the floor, narrowly missing player-coach Chris Hodgson and veteran quickie Adam 'Syds' Syddall, a Cheshire player formerly himself.

'There,' Syds says, tossing his teammate a polythene bag, 'XL.' Inside are a pair of black and bottle green pyjamas, courtesy of club sponsors Lorimers, a sportswear store in Bishop Auckland of which Pratt, warming up outside, is nowadays manager. Chris and Syds both greet their old friend with amused affection.

'Stick another X on and it'll be fine,' says Toby, whose partner Gemma gave birth to the couple's first child on Friday night, an as yet unnamed daughter. He pats his own belly: 'I have wintered well.'

Delving into his kit – the bag éclair-shaped and thus known as a 'coffin' – the comedian dresses quickly and, being the last to arrive, trots back outdoors where the rest of the side kick a football around. Cheshire prepare with a few looseners in the nets.

'Some clubs have cones out and do catching practice,' Toby says, of the difference in approach. 'All you need is to be stretched, get the reflexes going – if you can't catch a ball now you never will.' No, he isn't exhausted and pooh-poohs the very idea of sleepless nights, new baby or not. 'I don't sleep anyway. Three hours, if I'm lucky. Just lie there, staring at the ceiling.'

Despite the billing, this isn't quite the Minor Counties' first go at short form cricket, or 'the era of coloured clothing' amid 'the T20 revolution', as this year's *MCCA Annual* puts it. A previous 'brief encounter in whites with a red ball' in July 2015 was 'a rather lukewarm effort,' its publishers admit. Well, not in Cheshire it wasn't. They won the thing, overcoming Oxfordshire in a final at Banbury, after a contretemps with Cumberland en route so disagreeable it made the papers. The Cumbrians' long-time treasurer, Eric Carter, let's slip a few clues and an online search engine reveals the rest.

The fixture in question was at Boughton Hall, Chester, in June of that year. The day was reported 'blustery' and, after Cheshire and Cumberland saw off Northumberland and Staffordshire respectively in early games, the major squall erupted when Cheshire players, on a balcony, were accused of tipping beer over the Cumberland boys. Nor did a 36-run defeat for the visitors dispel the unpleasantness. 'It was terrible,' says Eric. 'I wrote a letter of complaint. All friendly now, though. Everyone's on their best behaviour.' Indeed they are. 'Privilege to see you, as ever,' he says suddenly, breaking off to greet a more familiar face. 'Are you well?'

There is calamity aplenty, mind, in the latest *Stoke Sentinel* where it is reported that Cheshire will begin the season without their captain, just jailed for 'inappropriate activities' at the school in which he worked and thereafter perverting the course of justice. However elsewhere in its pages is a more uplifting tale of how Cheshire hope to 'set the early pace', intending to take the T20 very seriously indeed.

The same cannot be said for Cumberland, who lose both coin-tosses and are asked to field first in the hot sun. Twice.

Pratt walks back to the changing room and busies about a bit, contributing an occasional comment in his soft semi-Geordie burr, otherwise relaxed. There is no talk of tactics or any rousing speeches. No obvious gameplan, or anything inspirational in the way of goal-setting or motivation. No blast of *O Fortuna*. Ahead of the opening encounter in what could be a crucial campaign – perhaps the very last Minor Counties season of all – a competitive buzz is strikingly absent. And for that matter, a collective sense of purpose.

*****

In a little car park behind a wood-panelled clubhouse hung with the last of the spring bedding plants – snapdragon, pansies, varieties of primrose – an ice cream freezer arrives in anticipation of a turn-out that, throughout the day, will number a couple of hundred. Gates on a farmer's field next door are open for the overflow. Above a door leading to a white picket-fenced viewing area is the club crest, bearing an image of what is know locally as 'the red-arsed roebuck', though its horns suggest otherwise. Toft CC's nickname is 'the Stags'.

Eric, who stayed over with the team last night, says that as it is quite a small ground he expects there will be plenty of boundaries. That is not how it turns out, for Cumberland anyway.

On paper, Cheshire look strong, 32-year-old former Derbyshire all-rounder Wayne White considered key to their success given his sixty-one T20 matches in the first-class county game. Yet he troubles Cumberland little in game one – out for a duck and no wickets taken – before coolly collecting a half-century from thirty-two deliveries and a couple of victims in the second encounter.

If Cumberland don't appear to be taking matters seriously, the same cannot be said for the MCCA, whose umpires are kitted out in smart green, blue and red tops with an ECB logo, belted navy trousers and bum-bags, sunglasses perched on wide-brimmed hats. A box of white balls is scrutinised and the usual sightscreens hung with black netting, the better to follow the flight. A chap in a deck chair tests a microphone next to an electronic scoreboard. Banners point to kids' cricket website *allstarscricket.com,* alongside a canvas awning on which food is advertised … 'Burgers – £4' … 'Hot Dogs – £2.50' … the bar in the clubhouse already doing good business.

It feels like what it is. A day at the cricket in glorious weather, small in scale but with ambitions otherwise, albeit accompanied by none of the hyperbole associated with professional T20. There is no carnival atmosphere. No fancy dress. No foam hands pointing the way back to the sheds at the fall of every wicket.

There is, however, music. Or will be once the fellow in charge can work out the speaker. Meanwhile, people mill around discussing the outcomes of games they saw or played in yesterday. Eric, along with being club treasurer, is also a long-serving umpire in the North Lancashire and Cumbria League. He took charge of Keswick v Cockermouth. 'Not a bad match,' he says, as though the contrary had been expected. He too is under a wide-brimmed hat and wears a light blue shirt and tie in traditional club colours – bottle green, red and gold – as sported by all the Cumberland officers.

Little Sam Dutton of Furness was a late cry-off, so the visitors have a twelve rather than thirteen-man squad and Chris Hodgson takes a watching brief, game one to begin at 11.30am. The mercury continues to rise. 'Too hot,' says one player, spikes crackling on concrete. 'Beer garden weather, is this.'

Steve Sharp, Cumberland's chairman of cricket, arrives wearing shorts and an enormous grin, as the smell of fried onions wafts over from a barbecue and one umpire rings a bell, customary five-minute warning. Steve, dressed for relaxation, looks on as the lads jog on to the outfield past one Toft official, tending the boundary with a leaf-blower. After a brief huddle ('They all know what they have to do,' Pratt posited beforehand), the group offers a smattering of applause to Cheshire's openers as they go by, en route to the middle.

There are rumours that the MCCA is about to implement the wishes of its ECB paymasters and raise the requirement for locally-sourced players among its clubs. Cockermouth's Matty 'Sempy' Sempill is the single homegrown Cumbrian in this particular line-up. In fact, their hosts have as many – opener Jack White hails from Kendal. The hosts also have four Cheshire-born lads in their side.

Given how the ball is white, dark colours are the order of the day, so Cumberland 'keeper Ben Howarth, of Northern Premier League club Blackpool, wears his pads under his trousers. Cheshire's batsmen have pads as black as their kit, helmets too, with a flourish of purple epaulettes. In fact, the whitest things on display other than the ball may be Steve Sharp's legs. Having checked the requisite number of fielders and wakefulness of the scorers, the umpires get things underway and following a four from the very first ball off ex-Lancashire under-19s captain Liam Grey, Cheshire end the over 12 without loss. 'Told you,' one observer says. 'Game of rounders, lads.'

Adam Syddall joins battle and soon that reads 23 for 0, Eric's boundaries theory apparently accurate. It is then that club secretary Rob Cairns arrives with his wife, Lesley, imparting warm greetings, their dispositions sunny as the sky. With a headful of silver hair and clipped beard, Rob, an Everton fan since youth, nowadays resident on Walney Island, has no need of headwear, unlike his follicly-challenged colleagues. Inveterate holidaymakers, the Cairns are as happy as a couple of camels and blessed with the thirst to prove it.

Already in a ground encircled by horse chestnut trees, beeches and the occasional elm, around one hundred spectators recline on fold-up chairs, or sit at park-style benched tables in front of the clubhouse. As the game proceeds, some take a gentle stroll – known as 'a lap' – around the perimeter of a pitch mown in various shades of green. In over three, Toby takes his side's first wicket of the year, Rick Moore's lob to midwicket being caught by Chris Brownlow of Bolton, another former Lancashire under-19s captain. Two overs later, however, Cheshire have motored past the half-century and Will Evans reaches his individual 50 soon afterwards.

Among those walking is pensioner Gilbert Johnstone, stalwart supporter and former club official of many years' standing, tanned and smartly attired in Cumberland shirt, tie and jaunty bottle green baseball cap. Among many positions filled, Gilbert stepped down as club secretary in 2013 when Mike Latham, who isn't here today and no longer fills the role, came in as chairman of cricket. Thereafter the club went on to enjoy great success, though Mike has this year made way for Steve while retaining a place on the committee. 'You've got to stand aside for the younger generation, haven't you?' says Gilbert, with regard to his own decision to take life a little easier. Even so, he can seldom move along an inch before some or other fellow spectator lures him into another trip down memory lane.

When Sempy drops a catch in the deep, Cheshire are 71 for 1, although his blushes are saved a couple of runs later when Jacques du Toit claims his first wicket for Cumberland. The bowler is an England-qualified South African signed from Northumberland over the winter, the batsman Rob Jones, caught in the deep by Sam Wood, Pratt's teammate in his club side Richmondshire of the North Yorkshire and South Durham League. 'Fuck,' says a disgruntled Jones, who also plays for Lancashire. The shot was wild, but that's T20. Jacques then adds Wayne White to his tally, lbw, golden duck, only to be denied a hat-trick by two runs from incomer Luke Robinson. Opener Evans is going well until Toby strikes again, the latter's left-arm spin curtailing an impressive innings. And when Robinson falls in the 12th over – Brownlow this time taking a superb over-the-shoulder catch despite looking directly into the sun – suddenly the game is there to be grabbed.

Mattie McKiernan, another colleague of Pratt's in Richmond, takes wicket number six, lbw, Cheshire still to reach the century. The heat is intense and it is not yet noon, more than a few observers already sipping beer through slices of lemon jammed in lager bottles. Chris dashes on and off with water during breaks in play.

With six overs to go and Toby and Jacques no longer in tandem, the run rate, however, again climbs upwards of ten an over. When Sempy provides the seventh wicket, Cheshire have hit 123 before a brief search for the ball is required in the parkland of adjoining Booths Hall, a late 13th century manor house rebuilt in the 18th century. Historically, the hall also has associations with the nuclear power industry. Laboratories at its rear were a crucible in the 1980s for the type of reactor recognisable to anyone who worked at, say, Sellafield in Cumbria, Eric and Steve among them.

With the ball returned, thoughts return to cricketing matters. Only one more wicket falls – Oliver Griffiths caught McKiernan, bowled Grey – but Cheshire continue to let rip. A further 61 runs are added before their innings closes on 184 for 8, Wythenshawe's Edward Fluck an unbeaten 58. Mercifully, by the time his name is read out, the loudspeakers are in full working order.

Fifteen minutes later, Gary and Ross Zelem begin the reply, amid grumbles from those who are set to follow: 'Stupid, playing the same team twice.' And the lack of enthusiasm is confirmed by an opening over in which no boundaries feature. When a four does arrive in over two they are leg-byes and Zelem is soon gone, caught behind, clipping an attempted pull. Pratt looks secure if hardly full of shots and after Brownlow – yet to score – is caught slogging, the visitors are a quarter of the way through the innings before Mattie McKiernan hits their second boundary. As a spectator, it's hard to imagine a more pleasant setting in which to idle away a Sunday, but the soporific mood extends to the crease. Few chances are taken and every shot, however well struck, finds a fielder. At least partial credit must go to Cheshire for that, their fast bowling is merciless, controlled and precise. Cumberland, though, show no inclination to ride their luck a little and try to disrupt it. 'We've got to do this all again,' says one batsman-in-waiting, wiping sweat from his forehead.

Cumberland only pass the half-century midway through their twenty-over allocation. With three overs remaining – and three men down, Mattie clean-bowled – that has risen to just 107. It is clear they do not have the appetite for a run chase and as unbeaten Gary Pratt collects his 50 in the final over, Jacques having belatedly rattled the tins with a quickfire 30, a closing total of 134 for 3 sees the visitors well beaten. Never mind. It's time for lunch.

*****

Inside, players and club officials sit at tables stocked with flans, pies and pasta, in the first instance pouring jugged orange juice or water and in the latter a drop or two of red.

Outside, every third person seems to have his or her head in a book, or takes a lap around the outfield, catching up with old friends. Others chat idly: 'You shouldn't overthink what people think of you darling, you've got lots of friends…' Rather incongruously, one chap pumps an arm Andy Murray-style, tuned in to racing at Newmarket on his radio, before Cumberland amble back on.

'Have you got your sunscreen on, Gary?' quips Toby. 'You're looking red.' Cheshire smash a six off the very first ball.

In this innings, though, the opening bowlers thereafter tighten up, ensuring Cheshire chew up fifteen overs before reaching their century at a cost of five wickets. Star of their show is Wayne White, whose 53 off 32 deliveries is curtailed only by a fine catch from Gary in the deep off Syds, a shot that had almost entered the flight path of nearby Manchester Airport. 'Oh, dear,' says a well-spoken elderly lady in a Panama hat.

Beneath a beech tree in the shade, stands a celebrity. Resident in these parts, former Lancashire and England left-hander, coach, umpire and now Sky Sports pundit David 'Bumble' Lloyd is a former Cumberland cricketer himself. He largely passes unnoticed, though seems happy to chat with anyone who spots him. He even poses for a snapshot to go in next year's *Cumberland CCC Yearbook*. His son Graham played for the county too once upon a time, as many a tale in the months ahead will confirm.

David Lloyd stories abound, such as the one related by *Wisden* in their Hall of Fame profile of Birmingham League 'run machine' Steve Dean, a Staffordshire Minor Counties veteran. During the MCCA's knockout final in 1991, Dean was out for 99 just before lunch against Wiltshire, his straight drive hitting the non-striker's boot and caught at mid-off: 'Surely the only Minor Counties incident to feature on *A Question of Sport*,' mused writer Scott Oliver. As for Bumble: '...at Cumberland, he was overheard in the bar dissecting the day's play: "We had 'em 50-4 then this little fat bastard smashed a hundred."' Dean proudly monogrammed his pads – 'LFB'.

Bumble holds other opinions too, as per this one in his Sky online blog: 'There are 14 four-day County Championship matches! Be like everybody else in the world and play ten. Make the 50-over competition a straight FA Cup-style knockout and get the Minor Counties back involved. When I was a player, and a coach, we used to shudder if we got drawn against a minor county.'

Cheshire aren't exactly shuddering, but at least they are being tested. Further wickets include a quick-witted stumping by 'keeper Ben, to the delight of his watching parents. Zelem too takes a catch in the deep, this one ricocheting down his throat via a soon-to-be blackened fingernail, which sees the Oldham-born Leigh CC opener replaced for the rest of the innings by Chris Hodgson.

A Cheshire collapse would be handy, but it never materialises. The century is passed when Jacques's right-arm off-spin is hammered for six into a sightscreen as the hosts again accumulate runs. Rob Cairns, on a lap, yells: 'Any chance of winning this one?', a grin seldom off his face. He had been dispatched to get Lesley some pop, but has stopped so often the contents are sizzling in the can.

Cheshire motor to 158 for 8 by the close of an innings that ends with a flurry of run-outs, 34 fewer than they managed in game one, still a decent target. Could Cumberland match it?

To begin with, it looks as if they might. In recognition that they may have been a bit stately in game one, perhaps, with Ross nursing his finger Gary's new opening partner is Toby, more often among the middle order. And after five overs the pair are 33 without loss, a much better scoring rate though they will still need to step it up.

'Is Bumble still around?' one Cheshire spectator enquires.

'No, he's gone. Here to see a lad called Mattie McKiernan...'

At one point, Gary steps into the path of a fielder reaching for a Toby lob, which may be an accident although the bowler isn't best pleased. 'He gets away with stuff like that all the time,' chuckles one member of the Cumberland contingent. 'Umpires love him.' When Toby is then caught on the boundary, hitting across the line of a ball that, in his head, is destined for Knutsford high street, he slopes off, hair plastered to his brow. 'I hit it with a biscuit,' he reflects, before throwing down his bottle green pads and heading for the shower.

Gary, though, suddenly gets a spurt on and the team passes 50 in the eighth over before their skipper too is caught out, this time via a top-edge to gulley for 47. One hundred or so runs are there for the taking if they crack on a bit in the overs left. The skipper's shower can wait – apart from the water he squirts over his head. He takes a seat on a wooden step, from which to contemplate proceedings.

With Mattie again bowled by Robinson – for 16 this time – Jacques du Toit stubs out his cigarette and strides to the crease before belting an immediate six into the trunk of a tree. It is precisely the sort of buccaneering approach the visitors need and, at 104 for 3 with six overs remaining, potentially a game-changer. Toby, refreshed, settles down in '...proper whites. You sit there in your black outfits if you want, this dispels the rays...'

At last there is interest in the outcome and although the alcohol now flows among the spectators, the atmosphere remains civilised and good-natured, not remotely rowdy. This may be T20, but there are no gangs of nuns or Mutant Ninja Turtles. No beer snakes strung out in plastic cups. This isn't Headingley or Old Trafford.

Disappointingly for the visiting party, with three-quarters of their innings complete, Jacques offers a soft catch and, on 108 for 4, the run chase is back to ten an over. In T20, with five overs to play with, that ought not to be impossible, but it is simply not going to happen here. 'I'm not a cakey person, I'm a pie man,' Toby says, apropos of nothing, as Sempy is stumped.

Three overs to play and 32 runs are needed, yet the sense of urgency introduced by Jacques has all but evaporated. The hunger just isn't there until, without warning, Chris Brownlow starts to find the rope and, come the final over, somehow 'only' 14 runs are needed for an unlikely victory. A dash of late drama.

The first ball brings a single, but then Sam 'Spud' Wood is bowled and Liam Grey goes in. 'Get him on strike, Greysey,' says Gary, as the lad gets to his feet. With only four balls left he does that, nudging a single. That means 12 runs are required off three balls.

Alas, Brownlow, back on strike, sees this as a good time for an unlikely scoop around the corner and instead plants the ball straight into the 'keeper's gloves. 'Fuck's sake,' he says, loping up the steps after a 30-run contribution while Jacques du Toit looks on. Literally laid back, he lights another cigarette. Keeps his thoughts to himself. Cumberland 149 for 7, nine runs short, and the game is gone.

For the rest, it's handshakes all round, a drink for each player on the bar, far from being the end of the world.

'T20 is not our priority,' Toby states, plainly. 'We don't want to have to travel further afield. It's a waste of time; no one is interested. That's why you are not seeing hearts on sleeves.' The first innings had its uses, he says. Cumberland only lost three wickets, thereby giving their top order useful batting practice against some very good bowling. 'It's all right us playing Cheshire or Staffordshire, they are just down the road. But why would we want to get through to the final and have to take a day off to travel all the way to Cornwall or Devon or Norfolk for a 20-over match? It's crazy.'

*****

Cumberland CCC has no permanent base to speak of, no physical hub, pub or clubhouse in which to gather. At various locations in any given summer they are a collective in the Pickwickian fashion. And in the spirit of Dickens, a faithful record of the 'Perambulations, Perils, Travels, Adventures and Sporting Transactions' of this particular bunch of pleasure seekers ought not, for a while at least, to be entirely posthumous.

Just five weeks before the season's opening fixtures at Toft CC, much of England had been blanketed in snow. A week later on March 26, as Easter approached, the club staged its Annual General Meeting at the Crooklands Hotel, Kendal. Beforehand, minutes from a management meeting the previous September and last AGM were circulated, along with an agenda for the committee meeting that would follow this one. A round robin email by Steve Sharp proposed his own replacement as chairman by Penrith insurance broker Neil Atkinson, and suggested long-serving scorer Geoff Minshaw as vice-chairman. Steve himself would take the chairman of cricket role relinquished by Mike Latham, who was praised for his 'hard work and dedication' and a professional approach 'second to none.'

Crooklands, the village, is in fact four miles out of Kendal, near the M6 turn-off for the market town. The hotel is by the side of a road adjacent to the nowadays largely disused Lancaster Canal, an ideal spot from which to explore the southern Lakes and nearby Yorkshire Dales. Historically, it is in Westmorland, with whom Cumberland CCC shared a moniker before the boundary changes of 1974, when under the now infamous Local Government Act both were subsumed into a new administrative county: Cumbria.

The room was rabbit hole-like, buried within a subterranean warren of corridors and doors, a rumble of traffic beyond its white emulsioned walls on the road above, outside. Secretary Rob, first to arrive, shuffled papers at the corner of the top table, before which were twenty-five chairs in five rows, around half of them to be filled. One was soon taken by Ian Sharp, brother of Steve and so another product of Millom, six miles north of Barrow on the River Duddon estuary. A somewhat gloomy figure, he seemed ill at ease, admitting to having been involved with Cumberland before, three years ago in fact, but his shift patterns were changing and, well: '...it's good to put something back into the game, isn't it?'

Next in was Mark Davidson, the amiable and bespectacled secretary of historic Carlisle CC. 'I hear you've come into money,' Ian said, referring to recent developments at their ground, Edenside. A Roman bathhouse had been unearthed on the very spot where a new clubhouse was to be erected, the old one having been flooded by Storm Desmond. It would hopefully still be built, although there were various archaeological hoops to leap through first. There was a suggestion that a glass walkway or similar might be incorporated, by way of turning Edenside into a tourist attraction. A Cumberland committeeman too, Mark's chief interest lay in junior development.

The top table was actually two tables pushed together with place-names marked for four lead officials – left to right, president Alan Wilson, chairman Steve, treasurer Eric and secretary Rob. Other members to drift in included Chris Hodgson and Toby Bulcock, before Sharp called for a minute's silence for Bob Bowman OBE, the club's long-serving and much-loved patron who passed away in early February. There were ten apologies for absence, Gary Pratt's among them, followed by Eric's statement of accounts. He was pleased to report a profit of £2,584, after a deficit the previous year of £792. 'I did predict a further loss in 2017,' he said, 'however in December we received £2,000 from our late patron and the NatWest switched us from a business to treasurer's account, refunding us £1,061 in bank charges. We didn't do bad, especially with all the long journeys and expensive hotels and so on.' Eric received hearty praise for this welcome upturn in fortunes at the instigation of Toby.

Election of officers. As proposed by Steve in his email, another seat was squeezed in alongside Alan for Neil Atkinson, who then took over the chairmanship. Neil's replacement, Geoff Minshaw, stayed where he was in the cheap seats. The president put in a word for Rob's secretarial skills: 'He has taken to the job extremely well and is well thought of at Lord's now, I'm led to believe.'

'Oh, dear,' said Eric.

'Steven is a cricket man,' Alan ploughed on. 'Going back to being chairman of cricket, he will do the county proud, I'm sure.'

Neil noted a continued vacancy for a sponsorship chairman and asked for nominations. 'Okay. We'll leave that role empty for the time being.' Due to Bob Bowman's death, a patron was needed too.

The committee was proposed and seconded *en bloc*, namely Gary Pratt's partner Leanne Bell, Toby Bulcock, Mark Davidson, Chris Hodgson and his father Trevor, Mike Latham, Professor JM Richardson and Lee Conroy, performance director of a company called Cumbria Cricket Ltd. No further nominations or any other business raised, a meeting that began at 7.15 was declared closed at

7.31pm, at which point Toby went hunting for the bar. Fifteen minutes later, the committee meeting got underway and Professor Richardson, originally thought absent like Leanne, Mike and Lee, revealed himself to be there after all. 'I came in just before the end, Mr. Secretary,' he said.

'Did you?' said Rob.

'Yes. I stay in the background, but see all.'

Ian Sharp had performed the opposite trick and vanished.

Neil asked for comments re the 2017 minutes, of which there were none. Next on the agenda, matters arising, such as the colour of balls in the new T20. Would they be pink? No they would not, but that set the tone for a livelier fifty minutes than the perfunctory quarter-of-an-hour before. When Steve, presenting his chairman of cricket report, mentioned recent meetings with representatives of the ECB and Cumbria Cricket Ltd, there was the first hint of unrest.

*****

The Minor Counties Cricket Championship, for county sides in England and Wales lacking first-class status, was first staged in 1895. And over the next century or so, pausing only for two World Wars, it carved its own niche, fuelled by camaraderie, class and claret while unmolested by anything so vulgar as public attention, within its very own social vacuum. At least that was the wider impression.

Until, on New Year's Day 1997, the case for independence became trickier to make. It was then that the England and Wales Cricket Board (ECB) was formed, harbinger of an age when cold hard cash would trump the old club tie, though that entitled reputation would be trickier to erase. In came such novel concepts as central funding and accountability. The Minor Counties Cricket Association (MCCA) was urged to get on message and adopt assorted mutations intended to reflect changes in modern cricket and society as a whole.

Perhaps the biggest body blow came with a restructuring of elite competitions that led to the ending of one-day games for Minor Counties sides against first-class opposition. These had begun in 1964 in the Gillette Cup – later renamed the NatWest Trophy – a treasured aspect of every season, in 60 and then 50-over fixtures. In

1984, for example, Cumberland faced Derbyshire at Netherfield, in Kendal, and attracted a crowd of around three thousand at a time when old money laissez-faire was falling victim to late-20th century commercial reality. Receipts from that game alone kept the county going a long time.

Throughout the 1980s and '90s, Cumberland and counties like them had been able to build enough reserves to have as many as four or five professionals in the side. With that avenue closed, however, they could not just take their bat and ball home. Money was still required to sustain their activities and so, in 2001, two-day Minor Counties Championship games began to be played over three days. Regulations were self-imposed by the MCCA as a way of proving itself worthy of those central funds, one being that each county must field an England-qualified side, when previously one overseas professional had been allowed. A team's average age must be under 26, an attempt to stress the competition's position as a vital link between recreational and first-class cricket. The Minor Counties needed to be viewed as relevant, not some relic of empire.

However, a fly soon hit the ointment. Namely, regional Premier Leagues, part of another ECB restructuring exercise, this time in the recreational game the MCCA claimed to outrank. Nowadays, most minor counties have one in their territory, pyramid-structured with promotion and relegation. Cumberland is among the exceptions.

Following the boundary changes of 1974 an already sprawling county got bigger yet, over a far wider geographical area. On the south coast, towns like Barrow and Ulverston had been in Lancashire. Kendal, as we've seen, was in Westmorland. Nowadays, the region's oldest league, the North Lancashire and Cumbria League (formerly North Lancashire League) dated to 1892, provides non-Premier League cricket for 'red rose' teams and Cumbrian sides Workington, Furness, Cockermouth and Whitehaven. Meanwhile four of the biggest clubs in modern-day Cumbria – Netherfield, Barrow, Kendal, Penrith – compete in the Lancashire-based Northern Premier League. And as anyone immersed in Cumbria's local club scene will attest, what with all the ebbing and flowing between those competitions and others like the Eden Valley League, Palace Shield and Westmorland League, that really isn't the half of it.

Not that the Premier League revolution went straightforwardly elsewhere. Yorkshire ended up needing four – Yorkshire Premier League North, Yorkshire Premier League South, Bradford League and the North Yorkshire and South Durham League – though they do lead to semi-finals and a 'grand final' to determine the white rose champions. Even then, a traditionally strong Huddersfield League goes its own way, as do several other leagues across the county.

Lancashire has two Premier Leagues – the Northern Premier Cricket League, in which a handful of Cumbrian sides operate as outlined above, plus a Liverpool and District Competition, both having provided players for Cumberland.

The ECB's aim is that the best recreational cricketers should play at the highest level possible on good pitches with appropriate facilities, long boundaries and so on. Nothing wrong with that you may think and, where possible, most minor counties are willing to embrace the concept as long as they are considered the next logical stepping stone into the first-class arena. They wish it to be known – and are keen to educate the uninitiated – that more top-flight and even Test match cricketers have taken the Minor Counties route over the past fifteen years than ever before. Their competition challenges players at the next representative level. Coaches can see how they cope out of their comfort zone across long-form three-day games, rather than the lower-pressure Saturday afternoon stuff.

Most residual distrust however surrounds the ECB's County Cricket Boards, which administrate age-group sides from under-11 to under-17, put development officers in schools and local clubs, grade facilities for compliance with Clubmark standards around racial and gender equality and handle grant applications. Despite sharing regions, individual boards and Minor Counties clubs operate as separate organisations with different constitutions, committee members and so on, and often have a history of failing to rub along. As in any walk of life, a group will have its own agenda, self-serving or otherwise, as will the individuals within, quite possibly outwith the interests of the wider population.

Although matters have lately improved in certain areas of the country, it remains common among the Minor Counties faithful to visualise all of this as part of an ECB plot to render a proud and historic competition obsolete and irrelevant. Such folk, often elderly, can easily be caricatured as yearning for far-off days of oak-dappled boundaries, polite applause and gentlemanly snifters – stuck in a halcyon age when fancy dress meant striped blazers, dash it, not bladdered hordes in laddered fishnet stockings. Yet they might also be heard as a last plea for sanity in a rising sea of change for change's sake; a wall of resistance, futile no doubt, to the commercial tsunami that is set to drain the very ocean to which it owes its existence.

For its part, the embattled ECB, otherwise engaged with plans for yoof-friendly 100-ball inter-city Instagrammable Big-Biff-Boff-Bashathons would, for the moment at least, rather its boards and the Minor Counties cosied up and collaborated more closely.

Which is very much not how it is in Cumbria.

*****

At the Crooklands AGM, minds were thus focussed, albeit some with a more vice-like grip than others. To a large extent, the fate of these clubs is out of their hands, decided upon ultimately from afar.

The Minor Counties Cricket Association pockets around £800,000 a year from the ECB. That amount is then split between its twenty clubs. But there are also MCCA admin costs to consider, treasurers, secretaries and so on to pay, so on average each club gets between £30,000 and £35,000 a year with which to run its affairs.

These share-outs are delivered on a three-year rolling basis, with a decision on the value of the next tranche – or indeed whether there will be any central income at all – due at season's end. Consequently, a working party has been formed to assess the Minor Counties' overall worth, with representatives from both the ECB and MCCA boards. The need for the latter organisation to impress the former with its drive, ambition and willingness to adopt a 'modern outlook' could hardly be more urgent.

The MCCA holds three meetings with members over the course of a year and its officials then have separate meetings with the ECB at Lord's, conveying outcomes back to the clubs with regard to how the wind is blowing politically and policy-wise. As with most team sports in an age of *Fortnite* and *Call of Duty*, cricket faces challenges galore. Kids no longer play hopscotch or climb trees and, as outdoor activity dwindles, so participation rates fall. Adults too are harder to shift from their HD TVs unless enticed by an exciting cultural event, complete with selfie opportunities for 'likes' on social media. Old-style long-form cricket seems far too dull for that, Ashes series such as the one that starred Gary Pratt notwithstanding. What's more, the suits paid to run the sport seem to agree, or at any rate are keen 'to be down with' the commercial prospects. Hence all the talk of a city-based '100', a short-form innovation, currently embryonic, on its way in 2020. Or the children's All Stars project, as advertised at Toft, a campaign imported from Australia in 2017 for five-to-eight-year-old boys and girls which puts the emphasis on fun and is consequently boosting participation numbers to the delight of both the ECB and Sport England, while handily disguising an adult scene in steep decline. Clubs who used to field three or even four teams on a Saturday afternoon now find it a struggle to raise one. Women's Soft Ball Cricket too is spreading, via festivals up and down the land. As the promotional literature has it: 'Whack some balls, bowl some balls, catch some balls. Run about a bit, laugh more than is good for you. Repeat.' Along with a free T-shirt, music and 'all the good things about a festival with none of the grunge', also promised is: '…maximum fun, minimum fuss. No pads, no hard ball, no heavy bat, no head-scratching rules. It's a game for absolutely everybody, no matter your skill level, fitness, or age. Playing time at Festivals is usually about two to four hours, so it never gets boring!'

Meanwhile, participation rates get another lift and the identity crisis in a sport that once knew exactly what it stood for worsens.

By the end of 2018, Cumberland and comrades should at least know more about where they are – or are not – heading, once the funding cycle for the coming six years is nailed down. Thus this year's T20 initiative, a preemptive move to introduce a form of the game that might have been forced upon them anyway, a display of flexibility. To accommodate it, the 50-over Unicorns Trophy has lost its pool stage and is reduced to a straightforward knockout, while three-day Championship fixtures have been pushed back to the end of June, to help with player availability. Games during May and early June often clash with work commitments and university examinations, so that's another way for the MCCA to flag up its willingness to move with the times.

This summer's campaign then is pivotal. Afterwards, for better or worse, things will never be quite the same. And if despite the association's best efforts the green light isn't forthcoming, it may even herald the demise of a level of cricket that has been a part of British sport since Victorian times.

For now, all Cumberland can do is present themselves to the decision makers in as positive a light as possible and, for its part, the MCCA has come up with detailed analysis, including exact totals of players in the competition's ranks who progressed to the first-class county and international scene. There has also been a players' survey in which the vast majority wished to retain three-day games as that is a form of cricket they wouldn't usually get to play, therefore central to the appeal of the Minor Counties. Unlike the one-day and T20 cricket available with their clubs, long-form games are a way to test yourself over a longer period. You go on the road, see different parts of the country and take pride in gaining representative honours.

Cumberland's biggest problem, though, is that the ECB and some fellow clubs want Minor Counties sides predominantly to feature locals. In the far north west, it's claimed there simply aren't enough cricketers of ability to make such a team competitive, and a fair proportion of those who are talented enough tend to quit after one or two games, unwilling to commit. That's a view challenged not only in London but also by the Cumbrian cricketing fraternity at large, who seem to treat the county club with suspicion, accusing it of favouring outsiders from the likes of Blackpool, Leigh and County Durham. There seems also to be a feeling that Cumbria Cricket Ltd, an ECB-backed administrative board incorporated in 2011, wishes to see a natural progression from its own junior development teams, although at Crooklands that could only be surmised because its representative on the Cumberland committee, the aforementioned Lee Conroy, had 'as usual' found more pressing things to do.

Neil Atkinson invited his new chairman of cricket, Steve Sharp, to update the room on a 'County Partnership Agreement' meeting with the ECB chaired by Yorkshire CCC CEO Mark Arthur last November, attended by Sharp and his predecessor Mike Latham and Cumbria Cricket Ltd too. ECB recreational director Jim Wood and MCCA chairman Nick Archer represented the 'steering committee', director Bob Simpson and Conroy there on behalf of the board.

This steering or working group had been going around the minor counties, Sharp said, 'assessing how clubs and boards work together. Some counties, like Northumberland, have big differences of opinion. The chairman of the board up there is very vocal and a bit of a pain. Other counties seem better aligned. That was the first thing they were seeking to do – see how well we got on in Cumbria.'

'Can I include expletives in the minutes?' joked secretary Rob.

'I think we get on reasonably okay,' Steve continued, 'but they do have gripes, mainly around selection and unavailability of players. Whenever there's a meeting, they always seem to get right in there about that. That came out this time too, which I didn't think was very professional and Mike was of the same opinion. It really ragged me off and I'm struggling at the moment to be neutral with them. I knew [performance director] Conroy wasn't coming tonight but I'd have expected Bob Simpson to be here. That's disappointing. So at the moment my relationship with Cumbria Cricket Ltd isn't particularly great." So much so that a planned joint-development team is on the back-burner, a pair of Cumberland two-day games v the Preston and Old Trafford branches of Myerscough College at the end of May organised instead. 'We have a different understanding of how such fixtures should be run and paid for. We believe players should get expenses for overnight stays, they think players and their parents should pay for everything. Anyway, we'll take them out of the equation and get an opportunity to have a look at lads who are on the verge of playing Minor Counties cricket.'

The ECB had also reopened talks about promoting a Premier League in the county, by way of raising standards. 'Obviously, it would take a lot of work before that became reality,' Steve continued. 'There are club teams who aren't convinced a Premier League is the right thing to be doing here, although from our point of view we would prefer there to be a Premier League out there.'

It was also suggested that a name change – Cumberland to Cumbria – might attract more sponsorship: '...that's a constitutional matter that would have to be ratified by the committee. But these are the things other people are thinking about. There's nothing in tablets of stone yet, but this was a precursor to the meeting that Rob here went to in February and gives you a flavour as to what was also discussed there.' There was talk of 'brandishing' a lump sum of the TV monies that are expected to be 'flying around with the big city T20' in 2020, a pot from which an actual county ground might be developed, say. 'These are the sorts of suggestions put forward,' Steve said, before summing up the November discussion as: '...quite a diverse attack. Change is coming. Whatever its speed or whether we like it or not we need to be braced for it. There is an expectation that we will work more closely with Cumbria Cricket Ltd.'

Chairman Neil enquired as to how closely other minor counties operate with their respective boards and, after Steve pointed out that some are joint-entities already, the conversation opened out.

'There are county clubs that had come together and have now broken away again,' said president Alan Wilson. 'It's a mess. Can I just, through the chair, ask Chris Hodgson, since he's here, how many development matches we played last year?'

One seven-run win for Cumberland over Myerscough College at Ashton on Mersey in June was his answer. It was a good game, said the player coach, who as a development officer close to Cumbria Cricket Ltd in his day job was engaged in a diplomatic balancing act. 'There would have been two more games had Cumberland been able to raise a team on the first occasion and Northumberland not had the same problem in the other. In 2016, we played three.'

'How much involvement did Simpson and Conroy have?'

'None.'

'I rest my case,' said Alan. 'They go on about tit for tat, but show no interest. Why raise player selection with the ECB? I asked Bob, have you got six players we could select because, if so, tell me now. "Well there's four in Workington," he said, but two didn't want to play, one couldn't get off work or whatever ... they just talk rubbish.'

Hodgson, in his capacity as a schools coach, pointed out that Conroy did 'do something at Sedbergh' with them.

'Well, that's good. They should show a bit of interest is all I'm saying. They've got eight paid staff in Kendal, so why isn't anyone here tonight? Their only interest is in firing bullets, as Steve says.'

'Proxy bullets as well, via social media,' Toby Bulcock chimed in. 'A lot of mud thrown within closed circles about how bad we are, how Cumberland is an inside clique that players can't get in...'

Alan didn't know much about Twitter but: '...as I've told Mike, and Chris knows this, every time we pick somebody we should have a record. Then if they can't get off work or their wife's ill or whatever and they can't play, then it's down in black and white.'

'There are players with genuine reasons and players with not so genuine reasons,' said Chris. 'A great deal of the time it's about commitment. Finding people who'll give up twelve days a season for the Championship ... six Mondays, six Tuesdays ... it's tough.'

'Well, even committing to three matches out of the six, or four matches or whatever, that would be better than nothing...'

Neil stepped back in: 'Anyway, no doubt we are going to have to work more closely with them as time moves on.'

'Have we got a representative on their committee?' Alan asked. 'Well, we should have. We should be seen to show an interest, with a member of our committee sitting on their committee, just as they should be sitting on ours ... that would start the ball rolling.'

'It needs to be a two-way street though, doesn't it?' came a voice from the floor. 'They've got a chip on their shoulder.'

With that line of discussion exhausted, attention turned to the Premier League debate: 'We've been talking about getting one going in Cumbria for at least five years, but there's just no interest,' said another voice in the seats, to which Alan replied that persuading clubs otherwise is surely CCL's job, as they get paid for it.

And as for a change of name, no material sponsorship had been promised. 'It was just felt by them that Cumbria is more promotable as the modern name of the county,' Steve said. 'Cumberland is seen as archaic now, especially among youngsters.' Alan reminded everyone that it had been changed once already, back in 1984, when Cumberland and Westmorland became Cumberland alone. 'They just see it as more sellable,' Steve went on. 'They reckon a lot of kids here have never even heard of Cumberland Minor Counties.'

'I don't believe that,' Alan scoffed, and nor was it Chris Hodgson's experience. Whenever he goes into a school while wearing the kit, the children often ask him about it.

Neil: 'So when is the next meeting with the board?'

Steve: 'Nothing's been set up yet. There was supposed to be some feedback from meetings with counties in January, but I believe that's been put back to November. So that's the ECB reporting back which shows how highly thought of we are. I think they are trying to put the noose around Minor Counties cricket, yet last week gave Glamorgan £2.5million for *not* staging a Test. It's nonsense.'

That comment drew another from the floor, as the all-round

defence of Minor Counties cricket hit its stride: 'Look how many first-class cricketers we produce...' Nods all round.

One such is Northamptonshire's Richard Gleeson, only recently of Blackpool and Cumberland. He had just done well as a fast bowler in the Caribbean with England Lions against West Indies 'A'. Steve said he was a '...fantastic example of why the Minor Counties are needed. Without us, late developers like him just couldn't happen.' Talent-spotted three years ago at the age of 27, Gleeson hadn't played a single first-class county game at the time, yet was set to begin 2018 with a hat-trick for the MCC against county champions Essex.

More voices. 'The ECB isn't just responsible for professional cricket, they should also be promoting the pinnacle of amateur cricket, which is the Minor Counties.'

'The ECB see second team cricket as more valuable...'

'...except when you ask a cricketer who has played both,' said Alan. 'They always say Minor Counties is harder, don't they?'

Steve and Neil agreed to chat further with a view to taking up Alan's suggestion to get a Cumberland man on the Cumbria Cricket committee. At which point it was suggested that they should also be asked for a hard and fast list of changes they'd like to see made, so the county club might knows where it stands and deal in facts. 'At the moment we are at loggerheads for what appears to be no reason.'

'Well,' Alan said, 'I didn't think we were at loggerheads before Steve mentioned this meeting and them throwing us under the bus...'

At which the new chairman of cricket adopted a conciliatory tone. 'People have different opinions and they are obviously looking after their jobs as well, but it's possible I might have my head stuck in the sand here, which is why I might need to back off a little bit.'

'Yes,' Neil agreed. 'It may well be that I have to take more of a lead on that ... although by the look of it we are not going to get any feedback until November anyway.'

*****

At Cumberland CCC, a feeling persists that Cumbria Cricket Ltd are mere pen pushers with salaries, while they are hardy volunteers.

The players too are only recompensed for travel. An income of around £40,000 per year, from the ECB's £30,000 and £10,000 in sponsorship and membership monies, won't stretch far. Typically, therefore, captain Gary Pratt devotes over twenty days a year without pay; the job in the sports shop his main income. Around half the minor counties do pay wages – Staffordshire have three or four semi-pros – but among those who don't, personal sacrifice is prevalent.

Toby is a professional currently at Leigh, but has it written into his contract that if Cumberland have a game he must play for them first and appoint another pro to deputise for him at his club in the Liverpool and District Comp. Whenever a clash occurs, it costs him £350. In 2017, in the Ribblesdale League with Whalley CC, that happened seven times, so he actually ended up paying around £2,500 to play, leaving aside other out-of-pocket expenses.

The meeting at Kendal moved to on-field matters, Steve Sharp announcing that, along with no players flying the roost, the club had also made a signing. Thus was the name of former Leicestershire all-rounder Jacques du Toit officially revealed, the South African having been 1st XI captain of Newcastle CC in the North East Premier League last year, and also part of Northumberland's Minor Counties squad. On swapping one end of Hadrian's Wall for the other, he too would participate on amateur terms.

Headlines from Eric's audit of Cumberland's two bank accounts were a combined balance of £39,526 and the usual need for more cash. 'Everybody's got the same problems at this level, cricket, football. We need a few more £20 members and £40 vice-presidents.'

One reason for a lack of those may be the empty sponsorship position referred to earlier, but the chairman now pointed out that someone had in fact volunteered to fill the role – Steve's now absent brother, Ian. The air turned frosty. 'He would have to be co-opted by both a proposer and a seconder,' said Neil. 'Does anyone have any views before we reach the stage of a vote, in terms of Ian coming in?'

Toby was first to speak up. 'It's three years now, isn't it, since Ian left the committee? It's time to let water pass under the bridge. Things were said and taken out of context as well. Diplomatically, for the greater good, we should allow Ian back into the fold.'

Eric bristled. 'I'd just like to say, if that did happen I'd find it very difficult to work with him, as treasurer,' he twitched, adjusting his collar. 'You are going to get a resignation off the committee straight away.' Awkward silence.

Neil, regarding the room with a nervous grin, made a tentative suggestion that, as things stood, there weren't any vacancies for a committee member anyway, before being informed that, actually, a place was available for someone in a sponsorship position. 'Well, it would come down to being proposed and seconded based on that criteria,' he backtracked.

All eyes on the top table, Steve felt obliged to comment. '*I'd* just like to say I'm going to keep neutral. I don't want to get involved, but I can see both sides.'

Neil tried to sum the matter up lightly, the swifter to consign it to the minute book. 'It would clearly be an issue for you, Eric. It would be an issue for Mike [Latham] as well.' A voice from the floor suggested it would also be a problem for Gary, the club captain. 'Right, well, on that basis we'll leave the role vacant and not go to a vote. I'll go back to Ian.' It's all very mysterious. What foul antics, a stranger can only wonder, must have stirred such animosity?

Talk drifted back to Cumbria Cricket Ltd, Chris confirming his paid employment with them for day-to-day development work. Alan suggested it would therefore make sense for him to be Cumberland's representative at their board meetings, in the spirit of building a closer relationship, not spying, it was to be understood: '...although the opportunity would be there to spot any mud before it was flung over the turrets.'

And finally, any other business. A letter ought to be sent to ex-Cumberland player Liam Livingstone, congratulating him on his recent captaincy of Lancashire and possible England start, suggested Professor Richardson. The meeting then concluded with the date of the next big get-together on September 26, around one week after this year's Minor Counties Championship final.

President Alan said he would be unable to make it on that date as he will be on holiday then, but backed the proposal anyway.

'You can't please everyone, can you?'

CHAPTER TWO
THE SCUNTHORPE PROBLEM

Some seven weeks after the Crooklands AGM and with that brace of T20 defeats already behind them, it is back to Cheshire for the first shot at a competition Cumberland apparently *do* want to win: the Unicorns Knockout Trophy. The club last won it as recently as 2012, having been runners-up in 1999 and first time victors in 1989.

The venue on Sunday 20 May is Oxton CC, near Birkenhead, on the Wirral. It's a ground with which the host county is more than familiar, having used it forty-nine times for Championship games down the years. This, however, would be only the second Knockout Trophy fixture to be staged at the Townfield Lane ground.

Wider cricketing controversies being not infrequent just now, there were a couple more in the lead-up. First was a report that the International Cricket Council (ICC) aims to ditch coin tosses in Test matches, so as to 'overcome the growing problem of home advantage.' Instead, they would ape county cricket where, since 2016, away teams have chosen whether to bat or bowl first. Traditionalists were duly horrified. Former ECB director Andy Nash, meanwhile, who resigned in March upon the awarding of £2.5million to Glamorgan referred to at Cumberland's AGM, called on the ECB either to 'unify the game' or risk a breakaway, because trust had been adversely affected. 'The game needs to be extremely careful that we don't polarise towards a soccer-style Darwinian structure, where the largest clubs are the wealthiest,' Nash told the BBC, with no hint of irony. 'You could see the ECB operating much as the FA [Football Association] or the RFU [Rugby Football Union] does.' By 'split', of course, he meant the eighteen first-class counties and maybe MCC.

There was however one satisfying note of triumph for the Minor Counties. Somerset off-spinner Dominic Bess – who, when with Devon, contributed two Knockout Trophy quarter-final wickets to a defeat of Cumberland at Furness Park in 2016 – is to replace broken-thumb victim Jack Leach in the First Test with Pakistan at Lord's, the latest MCCA product to ascend the highest level. When the call came, Bess told the papers, he'd been having a row in Ikea. For all their hopes of victory, today's Cumberland side has the look of a box of flat-pack furniture lacking some vital components. Toby Bulcock, who played through all the age groups with Bess, is here, just about, but Gary Pratt is not; the first game he has missed in ages. Ross Zelem's finger still rules him out, while Liam Grey, Chris Brownlow, Sam Wood and Mattie McKiernan are also elsewhere, the latter pair, like Gary, on club duty with Richmondshire CC.

It is situations like this that make a Minor Counties chairman of cricket's job so vexing. Never mind the vagaries of injury and form, the sheer volume of other league and cup fixtures with the potential to impact on Cumberland's own season can make selection a lottery, particularly as the season progresses when the best players tend to be busy doing well elsewhere. Not every pro is prepared to or can afford to put a minor county first, unpaid, as Toby and Gary traditionally have. The chairman of cricket therefore needs the vision of a three-eyed Lakeland crow, aware of the progress of players in and out of the team along with a plethora of results and possibilities, in order to head off any issues at the pass. It is not enough merely to wake early on a Thursday morning and think, 'right, who do we have available this week?' The ability to plan, juggle and fire-fight is vital.

Richmondshire are in a rearranged round of North Yorkshire and South Durham League games washed-out in April. They will win theirs, against Stokesley, with Pratt and McKiernan top scoring on 32 and 58 respectively, the latter also claiming five wickets to help hoist his side above Barnard Castle at the top of a twelve-team table. In Group 1 of the National Club Championship, Richmondshire beat South Northumberland in the second round last Sunday. Were they to get past Chester-le-Street in the semis in early June, they will be in the group final on June 24, a date that would clash with Cumberland's opening Minor Counties Championship match away to Cambridgeshire, at Wisbech. The ECB's National Club Championship would then further pan out to feature other group winners en route to a national final – more potential disruption. If Leigh advance against Wallasey in Group 6 in a fortnight, Toby and Ross, if fit, will be similarly conflicted. With occasional weekday evening games and local T20 tournaments tossed into the mix, the breeding ground for chaos is complete.

Since 2013 and notwithstanding complaints about the lack of Cumbrians in his side, previous chairman of cricket Mike Latham had navigated such scenarios with aplomb while simultaneously promoting a close-knit team spirit. The question now is can Steve Sharp – as knowledgeable as anyone about the Cumbrian club scene and with an impressive playing record to match – do likewise? And why, given his prior tendency to put county before club, has Gary now taken the opposite tack? That query must as yet go unanswered, for among the rest of the absentees is Steve himself, unable to make the trip due to work commitments.

*****

There is talk of Michael Slack, 23-year-old professional with Wigton, being groomed to replace Gary one day. Since his Minor Counties Championship debut in 2015, the former Cumbria under-17 and Durham Academy right-arm batsman and medium pace bowler Slacky has bloomed into an impressive presence at the crease, capable of building scores. A born sportsman, having come through Carlisle United's youth teams, in the winter months he is also a footballer with hometown Carlisle City in the North West Counties.

Absent a fortnight ago but having overcome an 'injured side', he is set for his seasonal start, along with Sam Dutton, son of the former Cumberland skipper Simon Dutton, a fixture and fitting from 1984-2001. Also brought in are Bolton duo Liam Watkinson and Josh Fallows, Greg Hall of Penrith and Barrow's Toby Mowat.

Having begun at Toft with only one Cumbrian, Matty Sempill (before Cockermouth teammate Chris Hodgson made it two when replacing Ross), the visiting team now contains six. They are in the majority. Few can recall the last time that occurred and certainly when the opening trio – today Slacky, Sempy and Dutts – were all homegrown. Of the incomers, 26-year-old Watkinson has been around longest, debuting for the county in 2011, but since having little involvement. He too treads in illustrious footsteps. His father is ex-Lancashire all-rounder Mike Watkinson, who had four Tests for England in the mid-1990s. His son's initial Cumberland selection was the result of a county development link-up. He has been drafted in now due to being – like 12th man Fallows – a teammate of Adam Syddall's at Edgworth, a club that switched to the newly-formed Greater Manchester Cricket League in 2016 after 127 years as a founder member of the Bolton and District Cricket Association.

Greg Hall's dad, Andrew, also represented Cumberland, though is nowadays chairman of Penrith CC. Greg's only involvement with the county so far has been in two Championship games a couple of years ago, which was still long enough to snap a bat in half against Lincolnshire. Paul Nixon, another ex-Cumberland man, now coach at Leicestershire, had lately arranged trials for Hall junior. Yesterday, in club cricket, he collected career best bowling figures of six for 48, ruined only by Penrith's batting collapse at Fulwood and Broughton in the Northern Premier Cricket League. And to complete the hat-trick, Toby Mowat, captain of Barrow this year, is also of former Cumberland stock. His dad, Raymond, played twice sixteen years apart – in the Championship in 1983 and then the Trophy in 1996.

Despite being Cumberland's first Trophy outing this season, this is in fact the second round of the competition. Like Cheshire, they had received a preliminary bye at the end of April, along with ten other counties; the only first round ties played seeing victories for Cornwall, Wiltshire, Buckinghamshire and Shropshire, against Dorset, Wales, Cambridgeshire and Herefordshire respectively.

It's another beautiful Sunday – blue morning skies, clouds of cotton, the hint of a cooling breeze drifting in off the Mersey. On the radio driving in, BBC Radio 6 Music presenter Cerys Matthews played Stax classic 'Soul Limbo', by Booker T. & the MG's. Great tune, annoying apostrophe, long the accompaniment to BBC Test match coverage. As the dilapidated docklands of Bootle gave way to the Kingsway tunnel, calypso rhythms faded with the signal en route to the Wirral peninsula. Coming to Oxton from the east wasn't the swiftest approach. It did though offer stark contrast between the type of inner-city area which cricket claims to hope to reach ... age-worn terraced houses strewn like gobfuls of broken teeth, every other bedroom window festooned with blue or red flags ... and the well-to-do semi-rural suburbs where it remains, in reality, most popular.

Oxton isn't Knutsford, but it's a leafy enough spot, the road in taking a visitor past Flaybrick memorial gardens, with their ruined Catholic chapel, and the imposing St Saviour's Anglican church, red sandstone walls topped by a roof of Welsh slate, huge stained glass window butting on to a crossroads from where one descends to the cricket ground. The flag flying here is that of St George, in honour of Prince Harry's marriage to Meghan Markle in Windsor yesterday.

During Liverpool's economic glory days, Oxton was awash with affluent nineteenth century merchants and tradesmen eager to reside near – but not in – that busy cosmopolitan port. Since 1979, it has been part of a conservation area that nowadays boasts, online, of having 'Merseyside's only Michelin-starred restaurant'.

Having dipped right, a tucked-away venue is betrayed only by cars parked either side of a country lane. 'Oxton Cricket and Sports Club', reads a sign that also offers tennis, bowls and lacrosse facilities, plus sponsors as varied as property consultants, architects, a golf and country club and Simply Debonair Dogs. Boguns Carpets could be quite inner-city, but only if it were in Sydney's western suburbs.

The hill extends to a field with a south-westerly slope. The first recorded game here was in 1882, but Cheshire first played on it three years later, the visitors Worcestershire in the Minor Counties Championship. Oxton play in the Cheshire County Cricket League. Seated in front of the pavilion, a dapper Eric Carter reveals that Cumberland have lost the toss. Everton fan Rob, glass of red already by his feet, is with a man introduced as the landlord of his local when he grew up near here: 'He probably threw me out.'

It would have been a good, if not crucial, toss to win. Batting first, Cheshire build a healthy total on a dry track that looks full of runs, sloping pitch notwithstanding. Liam W concedes the game's first boundary, a four, and Syds its first six in the third over. It's a shot that narrowly misses an elderly chap and his little white terrier, who watch from a raised gazebo belonging to retirement properties behind, ideal for conducting an orchestra or addressing Red Square.

After a pantomime 'phew!' and wipe of his brow, he asks a group below: 'Whom are they playing?' Cumbria, comes the reply, at which he raises an eyebrow, tuts, puts the hound under one arm and totters off, presumably to a safer position. In doing so he misses the first wicket, Cheshire opener Will Evans caught behind by Ben Howarth off Syds for 11, the hosts 16 for 1.

The group in question includes Rob, Lesley – as sports-mad as her husband if not more so – and Eric, who have opted for a better view. With them is Eric's friend, John Patterson, also wearing the club shirt and tie combo. A portly figure with a beaming smile and bushy moustache, John is influential in Cumbrian rugby union circles having been a county selector and prop at Workington RUFC. Rugby season over, he likes to watch Cumberland play cricket, no interest at all in joining the committee. Not that the others don't twist his arm. 'If you are going to do something you have to commit to it wholeheartedly,' he says. 'You can't just dabble. That's no good to anyone, is it?' A likeable and knowledgeable fellow, fun to be around, he has clearly enjoyed many a rugby and cricket club dinner.

Joining Steve on the absentee list are president Alan Wilson and chairman Neil, on a golfing weekend with his insurance firm. Coincidentally, it's in Cheshire so he hopes to pop along later, which in fact he will, gazing paternally from the players' balcony when they troop off at the end. Eric and John arrived last night, in a party of nine all told that included a handful of players like Jacques du Toit, travelling from Newcastle, and Slacky, who'd played in Millom, one hundred and twenty miles or so up the north west coast on the other side of Morecambe Bay. Overnight stays avoid an early rush to make the 11.00am start. Eric tends not to umpire before a Cumberland game, taking time to ensure every arrangement is in place, hotels a priority. 'It's very important to check the right number of rooms and beds,' he says, meticulous attention to detail his philosophy. 'If you just turn up and hope for the best, all hell can break loose.'

All agree they are having real luck with the weather just now in a landscape that here too verges on bucolic, even if the wide-open nature of the venue does give it a vaguely municipal feel. Set against that are long-range views of Welsh mountains. Within a mock Tudor pavilion guarding the entrance, replete with black and white-painted timber, a smart function room is laid out with tables awaiting the players, umpires, scorers and committee members who will gather here for tea. Out front is a benched viewing area behind a picket fence. Wrought iron gates are decorated with swirls and a crossed-cricket-bats-and-wickets motif. On a deck above, a Cheshire CCC flag is draped over a protective railing beneath a most attractive multi-coloured slate roof. To one side of all this are cricket nets, and on the other a stall at which two elderly gents sell club merchandise and A4 printed team-sheets for the sum of one pound. Behind lower boundary hedges, well-maintained tennis courts sandwich a bowling green. Beneath its pebble-dashed gable is the BBC Radio Cumbria awning, commentators *in situ*, although there is no sign of Radios Merseyside or Stoke, stations that serve this county in the absence of a BBC Radio Cheshire. A row of conifers hide modern houses at the scoreboard end, the box in question operated electronically from a little table in the pavilion. As the game progresses, it will provide a major bone of contention for players and spectators alike.

If any part of the ground dominates it is the top edge, where grand stone walls – the historic boundary of choice around here – screen Talbot Road, where the Riverhill Hotel can be found. Owned by Tranmere Rovers FC, on a high after their return to the Football League via a 2-1 win over Boreham Wood in a play-off final at Wembley last week, it is here where Cumberland spent the night. Disproving Merseyside comedy clichés, on a table next to an open door the Vanarama Cup remains on public display in an otherwise empty reception area. The very silverware, in fact, that goalkeeper Scott Davies dropped on his son's head while holding it aloft during Wednesday's civic reception in Birkenhead.

The Knockout Trophy, like T20, is white ball cricket, with the same black sightscreens and coloured kits. This time, however, the players of both sides are taking it seriously. Toby B's flying dive in the covers just fails to nab Cheshire's second wicket. It's a fine effort for such a hefty lad, but after six overs the hosts are 30 for 1.

Liam W is bowling well, ball fizzing off a fast wicket. He looks to be in great shape, athletic and physically fit, like most on the field. Only Toby might be described as 'old school'. Even Syds, who will be 38 in June, has a good engine and when he strikes again Cheshire are 54 for 2. Shortly after though, Liam feels a sharp stabbing pain and limps off before sitting with an ice pack over his left knee.

'It's frustrating,' he says. 'I've been going well.' He means with Edgworth. Lithe and wiry with a close-cropped beard, outside of cricket he is a PE teacher at the same school he attended as a pupil. After such a lengthy absence he is pleased to be back. 'The thing with the Minor Counties is that a lot of lads start out aiming to play first-class cricket, but now just want to enjoy themselves.' He will see if he can bat, but there'll be no scurrying for quick singles. He ends up returning sooner than expected, stand-in skipper Syds giving him a spell in the slips when someone takes a toilet break. Thereafter, he patrols the boundary with a plastic water bottle carrier.

Toby B is called upon and swiped for four, first ball. 'Come on, Tobes,' yells Chris Hodgson, a starter this week, from the deep. The next two rap pads to no reward. Chris replaces Syds and is smashed for six. Time for drinks. The pitch is attended to with a brush and wheelbarrow, whipping up dust clouds as ever more spectators join the scene, delightful this weekend, but maybe not so much when conditions are cold, wet and windy.

One bunch talk lunch. 'It's good here, isn't it?' says a bloke in a Cheshire CCC blazer. 'A most excellent cheeseboard.'

Come the 30th over, Cheshire are 120 for 2, third and fourth batsmen chasing half-centuries. Wicket three though, from Jacques, is a beauty, Wayne White caught by Toby Mowat on 49. It's a terrific effort, the fielder running in from the boundary and diving infield to end a partnership worth 78 runs. The away team is energised. 'Ooh, a bouncer,' quips Toby B, as more du Toit spin fails to dislodge Rick Moore on his way to an unbeaten 81.

Cumberland almost strike again, nippy fielding by Sam 'Dutts' Dutton offering the chance of a stumping, but 'keeper Ben is out of position. He makes amends by whipping the bails off Edward Fluck's wickets in the 36th over to make it 158 for 4, one of Sempy's two victims on the day. The second comes soon after. Cheshire are now wobbling and with six overs remaining Jacques completes his own brace, Nick Anderson, caught Dutts. Understrength on an ideal day for batting, some in the Cumberland camp had feared a target of 300 or so, but that threat has long receded. The seventh and final wicket goes Toby Bulcock's way before the innings ends, 219 for 7. With a full contingent the total would be achievable, but without Pratt, McKiernan *et al*, it still seems rather unlikely.

At lunch, Jacques lopes out of the bar and sits next to Greg Hall. Born in Port Elizabeth and 38 years old, behind his tinted shades the South African has an air of confidence and a reflective manner reinforced by how, unusually in modern sport, he is rarely without a cigarette on his lip. In Newcastle, he works for a bloke who supplies '95 per cent of North East meat,' but still has ambitions in his cricket career dependent on which form takes precedence and what the possibilities are therefore likely to be for a player his age. He's also one of the few at Cumberland to be unperturbed by T20: 'The crowd that turned up at Knutsford showed short form is what people want.' He likes the Knockout Trophy too, the balls they use not so much. 'It's not that they're white, that's fine, but they should change them to Kookaburra. This one goes soft and loses its shape. You can't do anything with it and it's actually breaking bats.' He is also a fan of long-form cricket, not minding the travel around what to a lad from the Cape is a small island after all. 'They've got the right balance now with three day games, T20 and the Cup.' He betrays a slight limp upon standing, stiffness in the limbs. 'You start to feel it, don't you,' he smiles, beneath his baggy green cap.

Before resumption of play, there is also time for a chat with Cheshire historian Tony Percival, who says bluntly that: '...the ECB think the Minor Counties are a waste of money. When we stopped playing first-class counties, there was talk of expansion and greater resources. Yet the level of ignorance was astonishing.' He despairs at talk of a failure to bring young talent through. 'Mike Gatting, for example, thought we were still a world of gentlemen and players.'

*****

Cheshire's attack is as controlled as it was a fortnight ago, runs again hard to come by. The afternoon turns hazy, the breeze stiffens, and ten overs pass with only 19 runs on the board. Openers Slacky and Sempy, having dug in with diligence, then pick up the pace and haul their side to 53 without loss come the drinks break.

Toby B wanders by, sleeping newborn in his arms. 'Meet Luna,' he says. 'Luna Tic.' John Patterson can't understand why everyone describes T20 as modern. 'Back in the 1960s we were playing 20-over games and they were no big deal at all.' Adam Syddall wanders by, a smile on his face as ever. A young woman is selling raffle tickets, proceeds to a heart charity. He hands over a quid and says she should go up on the balcony to wring some money from the rest of the lads.

The first Cumberland wicket falls soon after, hugely unlucky at that. Sempy's fierce drive hits the bowler's fingers and then Slacky's stumps, the latter run out on 36. Dutts immediately settles in and midway through the innings there is still only one wicket down, but just 85 runs scored. The old adage 'run the first one hard' isn't on the radar, with singles where a bit of vigour may have brought two.

Sempy's half-century arrives in 71 balls, a team 100 passed in the 28th over. When Sempy is stumped, Jacques comes in. As at Toft, he injects a note of urgency, dropped after driving the ball hard at the bowler. He reacts to the escape with nonchalance, swatting a four that puts his side exactly 100 runs behind. And when Dutts then drives for a boundary it's fist pumps all round. Runs accumulate nicely, even if the scoreboard itself imparts figures applicable four overs before.

Jacques survives a screamed appeal, swiping and missing, one close-fielder certain it was a catch. A moment later he isn't so lucky, firing one down outfielder Jack White's throat. White, from Penrith, is an ex-Cumberland player who will soon sign for Northants in the first-class county game. Up on the balcony, Toby Bulcock practises a few strokes just as the latest all-Cumbrian partnership is replaced by another, Toby Mowat skittled. His replacement, Greg Hall, hopes to better the duck that marred his bowling heroics yesterday. Wiry as a Giacometti bronze, he helps his side past 150, but with only ten overs left they still need 63 for victory and Dutts then attempts a rash sweep and is out for 31.

Cumberland need quick runs, so who better to send in than a one-legged man? Liam Watkinson doesn't so much stride onto the field as hobble. Undeterred, he does indeed manage a single and just about makes it to the bowler's end only for the man he passes, Greg, to then clip one to Cheshire's 'keeper, Will Evans.

Enter Toby B who, to Watkinson's delight no doubt, also takes a single off his first ball, although without his partner's bad leg one may have been two. Toby knows he needs boundaries and rushes so far up the wicket he might end up in Prestatyn. His bat though fails to connect and, with five overs remaining, it's 176 for 6. Cumberland need 44 runs, approximately nine an over. 'It will take something special to win this now,' says John Patterson, with understatement.

A clearly uncomfortable Liam W struggles on, but then thinks 'sod it' and belts a six that lands on top of the nets at the pavilion end. He then whacks an uppish four – a big over here may change the complexion utterly. He does not get away with his next such attempt, although he and Toby cross to leave the big man with the strike on 187 for 7. Ben Howarth comes in and a single is added by the end of the 46th over. They now need 32 runs off 24 balls, not impossible until Toby B slashes an easy catch to gulley. When Syds comes in at number ten, actual tension has built, exacerbated by a couple of handy wides. And it is now that the players on both sides really make their dissatisfaction with the scoreboard known. Every run counts. Every ball counts. And yet the thing still seems to be lagging behind by a good number of overs.

As an enjoyable game moves toward an exciting finale, how many balls remain? What do Cumberland need? Crucial questions that even after several umpire and player requests stay unanswered.

One man who cannot be blamed is official club scorer, Geoff Minshaw. He, like the captain and team manager, is another no-show, having been at Wembley yesterday to watch his beloved Manchester United beaten 1-0 by Chelsea in the FA Cup final. His replacement is Trevor Hodgson, father of Chris. When Ben hits a six in what will be an unbeaten 18, the scorebox snoozes on. Modern technology, eh? Is there an electrical fault? What was wrong with old-fashioned tins? Ben adds a lovely four to his total and the run-chase is down to eight going into the final over. A draw is no use. Cheshire lost seven wickets to Cumberland's eight; the hosts would go through. That likely won't matter when Syds is run out first ball. His replacement, Chris, contributes two dot balls and a single before Ben too digs out a run in return. All of which leaves Cumberland's number 11 effectively needing a six off the very last ball.

Oxton holds its breath. Will Chris manage it?

He will not. Instead he nicks another single, his team finishing on 216 for 9, beaten by three runs.

Followers of sports other than cricket might expect a side to be devastated by such a missed opportunity, particularly with so little having been expected of them, understrength, largely homegrown and all that. The chance of a quarter-final clash with Lincolnshire (who've had an 88-run win over Northumberland) has slipped from their fingers, interest in the Knockout Trophy over for another year. Yet once again they react with scarcely a shrug of the shoulders.

Cheshire, meanwhile, are destined to win the thing outright, beating Devon, captained by Dom Bess's cousin Josh, by two runs in the Chiltern Hills of Buckinghamshire on August 29. Cumberland would rather have progressed in their place, of course they would. But as fold-up chairs are stacked in car boots for another week, a third defeat on the bounce seems hardly a catastrophe. Besides, in a month or so's time the Minor Counties Championship will begin.

Proper cricket.

*****

One week later, Cumberland are on the road again, their third day-trip of the season. Scunthorpe's Heslam Park is to host its first county match – Lincolnshire versus Cumberland – in two more Group 1 games in the Unicorns T20 competition.

At a general meeting of the MCCA at Lord's in December, the association's treasurer, Chris Farmer, had reported a pre-tax profit of £4,000 in the year, adding that its balance sheet now approached £400,000. He also advised that the ECB would roll over the coming season's budgets less the usual incremental rise, at a cost to each county of around £1,000. The £26,000 sent to counties in 2017 was likely to fall to £24,650 in 2018, he said, £7,245 of that on the basis of 'age compliance' in what is highly likely to be the last year of the current distribution scheme.

The notes from that meeting revealed another couple of other talking points. Along with indicating that he had a good contact re black sightscreens should anyone be interested, Phil Oliver, manager of the Unicorns, the Minor Counties' rep side, said they had been asked to replace MCC Universities in the first-class game's 2nd XI competition. This would involve twenty-seven days' extra cricket with no funding to meet a £60,000 cost, so the offer had been turned down. MCCA chairman Nick Archer was also quoted describing two county board members on the 'review group' as anti-Minor Counties, undertaking their own research in one case. He, it was claimed, had contacted three MCCA clubs already. With 'no limit to his mischief-making', he was trying to build a case that 'the Minor Counties doesn't develop players'. Archer stressed that there was no official remit for such activity, MCCA secretary Phil Caley adding that any contacted county should tell him to 'get lost'. The notes transmit a distinct impression of distrust. A vendetta is feared.

At Heslam Park, MCCA treasurer Chris Farmer is in a more relaxed mood, enjoying the sunshine in front of the Scunthorpe Town CC clubhouse. December feels an awful long way away.

A town blasted in the iron and steel industry, Scunthorpe is no-one's idea of a cricketing hotbed, yet the club side here, formed in 1897, actually won the Lincolnshire Premier Division in 2017 and were promoted to the Lincolnshire Premier League. With four senior teams, four junior sides and an All Stars section, it's an impressive community set-up at a venue shared with Scunthorpe RUFC, who are members of National League 2 North, rugby union's fourth tier. North Lincolnshire Council seem happy to host a county game. On the organisation's website, Cllr Rob Waltham gushes: 'We expect to see fans from right across Lincolnshire and Cumbria' at what is 'another opportunity to showcase our area on a national sporting stage.' He goes on: 'Cricket is such a quintessentially British sport and bringing high class cricket to our area will help local people rediscover [it].' During the day, there would be a chance for families to 'try the game out for themselves', the venue having 'beaten off competition from the likes of Grantham, Cleethorpes and Lincoln.' A £3 entry fee has been abandoned. It would now be free.

The best known link to cricket in a town affectionately known as 'Scunny', is legendary England skipper Ian Botham, who lived at nearby Epworth. Although born in Cheshire, he played eleven times at centre-half for Scunthorpe United in the Football League before deciding he'd be better off batting and bowling for a living (when not being hounded by the tabloids or walking the length and breadth of Great Britain). Botham however took a backseat in 1996, when search engines began to filter the place out of results on account of a hidden four-letter word, a strain of unintended online censorship destined thereafter to be known as the 'Scunthorpe problem'.

Today, Cumberland are just happy to have relieved themselves of the 'Oxton problem'. Gary Pratt is back leading the side and it is he who opens alongside Sam Dutton, the captain having won his first toss of the season and asked Lincolnshire to field. Dutts chances his arm from the off, playing with abandon. As, within reason, does Gary, lesson learned from Knutsford perhaps? Geoff Minshaw too is back in a scorebox that here runs like clockwork. President Wilson aside, there is also a full complement of board members, scrubbed up smart in freshly laundered shirts, floppy sun hats and club ties. Neil Atkinson takes a moment to chat about his plans as chairman while the early innings builds, punctuated by ripples of applause.

'It will develop as time goes on,' says the one-time Ormskirk grammar school boy, nowadays an insurance broker who got into Cumbria cricket upon moving up to Penrith through work in 1994. Bespectacled and outwardly benign, he has the air of a kindly legal executor charged with reading a particularly sensitive last Will and Testament. 'Potential changes are on the way that will need to be dealt with, not least how we work with the Cumbria Board.'

The coming months require a leader who is politically astute and able to adapt quickly and this self-confessed ex-club player who 'didn't reach any great heights' – first as captain of Hawksdale, near Carlisle, founder members of the Eden Valley League but now defunct, and then on his own Penrith doorstep – is considered best qualified. A diplomat by instinct, he weighs his words carefully. He's been on the Penrith selection committee for six years and first came to Cumberland CCC to watch his son play, before being co-opted to their committee too. His day-to-day brokering skills may prove invaluable. 'Basically, I'm involved because we've got a good group of lads,' he says. 'It's very enjoyable to be a part of it all.'

Ultimately, the role will come down to being a spokesperson, he reckons, liaising with clubs, hosts and opposition a big part of it. With Mike stepping down, Eric and Steve will doubtless take care of most other nuts and bolts. He is, however, a fervent champion of the Minor Counties as a player pathway. 'It's a stepping-stone to first-class cricket. If lads are good enough, Championship cricket gives them a platform to take it forward. They get to show they can bat or bowl for long spells.' Not that he'd want anyone to think he dislikes T20 and knockout games: '...but I am a bit of a purist when it comes to three-day matches.'

That is about as controversial as the new chairman is likely to get on record, aware perhaps that the more room for manoeuvre he has during coming modernisations the healthier for all concerned. It's easy to see him at the head of any merged club and county board.

As usual, a number of the party came down last night and stayed over, a ten-minute walk away at the Worthy House Hotel. Even though Lincolnshire have arranged the game with the length of the opponents' journey in mind, Cumberland to Scunthorpe would still be a hefty trek for an 11.00am start. On the field, despite more loose shots – or maybe due to them – the boundaries continue to come. This is more in the spirit of T20 cricket, every four and six accompanied by a loud burst on the PA of Eric Clapton's 'Layla', the lyrical relevance of which somewhat of a mystery.

In 2017, Lincolnshire topped the Eastern Division for the second successive year before falling to double-winners Berkshire in both the Championship and Knockout Trophy finals. Why not try to make an impact on the new T20 competition too? That is certainly how president John Van-der-Vord sees it while referencing Bob Dylan in the club yearbook: 'So perhaps times are changing, they always have and they always will. In order to be successful we must try and embrace the changes for the good of cricket as a whole.'

In the same publication, MCCA treasurer and Lincolnshire chief executive Farmer describes 2018 as: '…a watershed year … for all associated with ECB-funded cricket throughout the Minor Counties.' As someone in the know, he goes on: 'One of the key proposals coming from the ECB review is the concept of County Partnership Agreements. In essence, the county's Premier League, board and club would have a shared vision – to align with the One Game principle underpinning the Cricket Unleashed strategy – and at some time within the six-year programme, the possibility of a single funding payment. It is fair to say that our relationships have been less than satisfactory for some time...' He does, however, now sense a mood of rapprochement and co-operation, while stressing the continued importance to the MCCA clubs of three-day cricket, as underlined by the findings of the recent player survey. 'I do hope that the ECB, having commissioned the research, will not now reject the evidence because the results surprised/didn't suit them!'

It's a thoughtful piece that concludes on a warning that the Minor Counties clubs ought not to be stubborn for the sake of it, or 'cherry-pick' the findings themselves. Time commitment is clearly an issue in the modern era, with travelling distances another matter for concern: '...is it really "good practice" to embark on a lengthy journey on Saturday evening after a full day of club cricket? Would the nature of the game suffer if we limited the first innings to 80 overs and started at 2.00pm on Sunday?' Oddly, given Cumberland's attitude, the survey also showed 'strong support amongst players for T20.' Certainly both sides are getting in the swing of it now.

Toby still has his mind on other matters. Namely, which bit of the shipping forecast is the one off the coast here? Dogger? Humber? Nobody is sure or, by the look of it, cares. Undeterred, he tells the story of the Battle of Dogger Bank, the first Dreadnought engagement of World War One, 'the one with General Jellicoe.'

'That sounds a trifle dangerous,' says Dutts, having been clean bowled for 14 with Cumberland 25 for 1. 'It's bloomin' bouncy, I'm telling you that,' he'd said, walking off. 'It's like a tennis ball, fucking outrageous.' A cheeky little chappie with the look of a fox terrier, he has a beard that he concedes has taken twenty-four years to grow.

Mattie McKiernan is next in, raising the possibility of a lengthy and buccaneering Richmondshire partnership, but he's caught at first slip facing only his second ball, even less amused than Dutts. It had clipped his 'fucking shoulder' on the way through, he glowers before throwing his gloves to the floor in disgust and taking a seat.

'Don't get these wickets in Cumberland, marra,' Dutts tells him.

'Coming in next, Jacques du Toit,' says the man on the PA, employed to explain what is going on to newcomers unfamiliar with the game or its rules. Toby wasn't going to miss the sounded 't'.

'Jack the Twat. You can say that again. This MC is second to none.' He then rebukes Greg Hall, who has retained his place, for smoking and offers some advice. 'Smoking is like a dumb dwarf. Not big and not clever.' Mattie, cheering up a little, asks Toby if he fancies a lap. 'Yeah, I'll have a Rory,' he says and off they toddle.

Mattie and Gary may be back in the side, but Liam Watkinson, Slacky, Toby Mowat and Chris are all absent, as is wicketkeeper Ben Howarth, who hurt his thumb yesterday playing for Blackpool. In his place is another Richmondshire man, Matty Cowling, while a fourth, Bob Carr, also comes in. Twelfth man is Jamie Smith from Edgworth. Their captain and Jacques continue to move the side on and midway through their first innings, a base has been established, 47 for 2. Gary though has again gone on the defensive, hitting singles rather than boundaries and grateful for ten priceless leg byes. Shots are struck beautifully but straight at fielders, gaps tough to find.

At last, Jacques clobbers a humongous six over the clubhouse and PA man says: 'The umpire has gone for a new ball because I don't think we'll find that one for some time.' Eric Clapton concurs. It's the first six of the game and, in retrospect, its turning point. Or maybe that is when du Toit is dropped, moments later, attempting another. His second successful six bounces off a flagpole and back into play, while another lands in the car park. 'Might have to move my gear,' the MC says. 'It's a bit dangerous here.'

The hundred is reached when Pratt slashes a four in the 15th over – and is then dropped, next ball, on 30. These two have had one or two lucky breaks, but they are moving the score along nicely now. A couple of runs bring du Toit's 50 up and with five overs to go they break loose, Gary hitting a fierce six of his own and du Toit sending another through an open skylight – pity those inside – which at least ought to be easier to recover. The final over arrives and although Jacques is run out second ball for 73, Gary – joined briefly by Bob Carr – passes his half-century in a total of 153 for 3. The contrast with Knutsford could not be starker.

Lincolnshire's first wicket falls in only their second over, bowled du Toit, caught Syddall, with five runs on the board, the first in what will be a five-wicket haul, or 'five-fer' in the contemporary jargon. Josh Fallows, another from Edgworth via Bolton, opens at the other end with his right-arm medium and both he and Jacques stay tight. The hosts amass ten runs in three overs before their first boundary, a four, that brings a different blast – 'That's The Way I Like It,' by KC & The Sunshine Band, which at least makes some kind of sense.

The run rate continues to improve when Toby comes on from the rugby pavilion end, another four met with 'Papa's Got A Brand New Pigbag'. The next wicket is in over nine, Sempy's magnificent running catch doing the damage: 54 for 2.

As the day has progressed, so the crowd has gradually grown, smiles all around from people taking delight in the weather as well as the game. 'You enjoying it?' an elderly bloke in a white beanie hat asks a boy who may well be his grandson. 'Good stuff.'

Cowling takes a fine catch behind the stumps and Lincs are 65 for 3, the incoming batsman Harry Warwick, from Grimsby Town. 'If I sit here, will I get hit by the ball?' one woman asks. Maybe. Warwick is soon caught by Greg Hall on the boundary for a duck.

A fifth man goes, lbw, but then Lincs smash a few sixes and look ominous before Mattie dives low to take a brilliant caught and bowled off dangerman Louis Kimber, out for 65. With five overs left, Lincs need 46 runs and whether their tail can wag to the tune of ten an over must be in doubt. Six balls later, ten runs *have* been added, but a seventh wicket has fallen too, Gary calm on the rope under the bowling of du Toit. Going into the last, they still chase 26 and deprived of a couple more wickets conclude game one on 131 for 9.

It's Cumberland's first victory of the season and a deserved one at that. The skipper, however, is having a bit of bother with his knee. Physically, cricketers tend towards elasticity, stretching exercises rather than weightlifting the norm. And it's in such body-flexing postures that Gary can soon be found, curled like an escapologist in an imaginary box on the grass.

*****

Lunch beckons and spectators join in with organised children's activities, dig deeper into their books or head for the bar. The day before, day three of the Pakistan Test, Dominic Bess hit a debut 50 in partnership with his fellow west countryman Jos Buttler. Sadly, that merely postponed defeat. Still, it had for a while given the MCCA clubs something to cheer and showed how the fluctuations of the longer game, its demands on commitment and concentration, were all the more rewarding. That was the gist of the conversation anyway, as the Cumberland committee and their guests joined their Lincolnshire counterparts and both teams in the function room.

'The more you put in, the more you get out,' Chris Farmer tells Eric, as he folds a slice of ham and propels it down the hatch.

Scunthorpe Town have made a real effort. Playing 'Jerusalem' on the tannoy before start of play was one clue they meant business they've been rewarded for such imagination and initiative with a decent turnout. And while this is another ground that conforms to county cricket's tendency to deport itself in the most verdant parts of town, why not, if you are going to sit there all day staring at it? The rugby posts beyond the lower boundary are down for the summer, the pitch reseeded going by a fake hawk swirling wickedly as though high on mescaline or alcopops. Local kids are undeterred, running about before a little empty grandstand watched by coaches and a bright yellow star-shaped All Stars mascot.

Outside the cricket clubhouse, meanwhile, a hog is roasting on a spit and the function room window has a great view of a scorebox whose tiled pyramid roof would not look out of place in *The Mikado*. If not for the clutch of cooling towers in the far distance and a couple of works chimneys similarly positioned, an observer would have no clue that this is reputedly the most polluted town in the country.

Along with his Lincolnshire interests, Chris Farmer is also a member at Nottinghamshire CCC and lives in its county town. 'Instead of going abroad, most of my holidays have been spent watching Test Match cricket up and down the country,' he says. Surprisingly, perhaps, he also loves T20. 'I'm not one of these elderly... this form of the game is fun,' he says, recalling a first encounter with it when Notts met Yorkshire a few seasons back. 'All the happy faces... anyone at Lincolnshire's first games this year against Northumberland saw 1,000 runs in a day. What is there not to like about that? Okay, it may not be proper cricket, in the sense that it's off-the-cuff, but it's very entertaining.'

A qualified accountant who 'didn't really like accountancy,' he wound up in local government and retired from full-time work fifteen years ago. 'The day I left, people were chasing after me to do work for them,' he says. 'An accountant is always good to have in a voluntary organisation. The first person through the door at my leaving do was the chairman of Lincolnshire.' Enticed aboard, he agitated for the sort of player academy first-class counties have and sought to 'find a location where we could have our headquarters and become a hub of cricket excellence.' No dinosaur he.

As we have seen, that sort of thing is more usually the province of the ECB county boards but, again, Farmer takes an enlightened view while admitting to 'friction that has caused a lot of grief.' He puts that down to personalities. 'But look, times are changing and we are on the verge of being able to, not integrate into a single unit, but co-operate and co-ordinate. The thing that bothers me most is that we are really struggling to find good quality players coming through the county board coaching system because the county as a whole is very sparsely populated in terms of level three coaches.'

In fact Lincolnshire, he says, has 'the lowest coaching ratio of anywhere in the country. We are three times less well represented by coaches per club as Cheshire, for example. Why that is I don't know and the history is irrelevant. I just want to get to the situation where we have players coming through our junior ranks that desperately want to be better than those coming in from outside the county. At the minute, we are just not getting that and it's due to no enthusiasm for coaching.' It's another issue that comes with being a sparse population area. 'Our small clubs are spread around so, as a coach, are you going to want to travel to a side that has twenty villagers turning up for training rather than twenty cricketers? In substantial populations it is dead easy to base yourself somewhere and have 50-60,000 people on your doorstep. In rural Lincolnshire, I could draw a 100 square mile plot and there'd be about 2,000 in it.'

Of course, every minor county has its very own personality and issues. 'Yes. Even today people have complained that Scunthorpe is a long way to come to watch the county play, but when we play in the south the opposite is true. Stamford, for example, is halfway to London. We are trying to find a new audience while getting people to appreciate that we do consider them a part of what we are doing.'

And has today been a successful enterprise? 'Well, the club has done us proud, that's the most important thing. I'm sure we'll be back. You can say there was only a couple of hundred people, but at other places we've turned up there's only been thirty.'

Having been both secretary and treasurer in his time, he is now Lincolnshire's chief executive – 'it's just a title' – and one stipulation of those roles is that you must attend an annual MCCA meeting, until recently at Lord's, of the type Eric and Rob go to. 'Because I was competent, they first of all asked me to go on the management committee as Eastern Division representative, and then I ended up replacing a chap from Cambridgeshire who wished to retire. It was part of a plan to get the accounting system modernised. Back then it was being book-kept in fountain pen! Nowadays it's computerised. I wasn't keen on the sort of thing where, at the end of every match, the umpires would have to catch the eye of the likes of me and Eric to be paid, one of the most demeaning things anyone could have to do before leaving. Equally, if you'd just given the opposition a bit of a thrashing it wasn't a good look to be giving them brown envelopes.'

Farmer has been MCCA treasurer for five years now, having already overstayed a promise that five years was all he would do. 'Everything I planned to do I managed to get done in that time, but the problem is we've now moved into this major review stage with the ECB. I didn't feel it would be fair to just expect someone else to come in and try to argue the toss about funding when they are not completely up to speed with how everything gets spent.'

Much of the last two years has been devoted to arguing the case for the Minor Counties' worth and maintaining the level of income currently around £720,000 a year, shared amongst all twenty clubs. 'The minimum amount they give to each first-class county is three times the total they give to all of us. They also want us to play white ball cricket, which as I say I don't mind, though not at the expense of red-ball three-day cricket. If you ask any of these lads how they might get picked up by a top county, it won't be by knocking out sixes and fours in a T20 game. Scouts don't watch these. They are all at three-day fixtures because that's where the real talent emerges. T20 is entertaining, but you don't see what a real cricketer is about.'

The ECB are reluctant to accept this rationale. 'They just don't understand and would rather we didn't play them. But that's just to save £300-400,000, which they could quite easily save by just dropping a couple of first-class counties, Leicestershire or Derbyshire say. Let them come into our league, give us their money, and then we'd all improve and it would be a much better investment.'

He's not finished yet. 'Every first-class county spends between £20-30,000 flying a couple of people over from South Africa, West Indies or wherever for two T20 games. Glamorgan get £2million for not playing. Yet they are just not interested in getting into a debate about what does represent good value for money. They are just hell bent on getting rid of three-day cricket. Thou shalt play with white balls. It's seen as the way to attract more people to the game, but no one says how then to interest them in playing it properly.'

And although attendance figures are far from huge in any form of Minor Counties cricket, particularly on Mondays and Tuesdays for three-dayers, the needs of often long-serving spectators surely ought to be considered too. 'We get some pretty good crowds. If you go to Norfolk, in particular, they put on a marvellous annual festival when all three of their home matches are staged over three weeks in the same place. If they didn't have that, getting from, say, Lowestoft to see a first-class match would take at least three hours. With no decent cricket to see live in Lincolnshire – or Cumberland for that matter – people here would completely lose interest in county cricket.'

It must be tough being the treasurer of one club, never mind twenty. How does he manage it? 'I negotiate on behalf of everyone and the beauty of it is that unlike the first-class counties, where they're all divided, as you'll see when they talk about Test grounds or this new 100-ball thing, people fall out because they are not getting a share. The MCCA is one body and we are all in it together. For me, it's easy. They all know that I will do my best for my own club, which means that I will be doing my best for them as well. Every penny that comes in is shared equally. Every time I save £20, I save every Minor Counties club one pound.'

*****

As game two commences outside, the camaraderie inside is palpable. This group of people have known each other years, after long and regular association in the Eastern Division. There is none of the stiff formality experienced at Cheshire of the Western Division.

Picking over a 1970s-style buffet lunch with a choice of ham, turkey, beef or all three, scotch eggs, quiche Lorraine, cheese and onion flan, salad with chunks of cucumber and red onion, rice, roast potatoes, sausage rolls, coleslaw and a couple of bottles of red and chilled white, talk turns to accommodation. Finding digs in the Lakes in high summer, for instance, can be costly, especially for cup ties arranged at short notice. Not just for the away contingent either. Home players travel in from all over the county and beyond.

While reaching the T20 group stages isn't high on Eric's agenda, he doesn't say as much. And with his MCCA hat on, Chris Farmer has news of a finals week at Sir Paul Getty's 3,000-acre Wormsley Park estate in Buckinghamshire. The place has been booked for five days, the T20 semis and finals kicking it all off on Sunday 26 August, with Monday put aside as a reserve day. On Tuesday, the Unicorns rep side will meet the MCC in an annual fixture that, every eight years, is staged at Lord's, though on the widest track possible, the boundary once a ridiculous thirty feet away. On the road, the MCC tends merely to ask members close to the venue if they'd like to play, so the quality of opposition suffers. This year the match will be classed as a 'secretary's game' with ex-Test stars and such invited to appear. Wednesday is the day Cheshire are destined to win the Knockout Trophy, Thursday another a reserve day. The MCCA is clearly taking seriously its need for higher-profile occasions.

All of which makes Cumberland's lukewarm attitude towards reaching one of the two remaining winnable competitions this year so much harder to comprehend. Still, they took game three, didn't they, and Gary winning his second toss in a row and electing to bat is maybe a sign that this could be the Cumbrians' day. The skipper's knee is bothering him, but he and Dutts again open the innings and although the latter is out early for 9, Mattie this time plays himself in and the visitors have advanced to 34 for 1 after six overs. Not that many in the function room see it. The hospitality has continued with dessert, topping the menu crème brûlée. 'The game's not the same,' as someone once said elsewhere.

Before long, Pratt is out for 16, having driven a shot straight to mid-off. 'Dickhead,' he utters, striding off in self-disgust and clearing a way for Jacques, who then builds a classy 48-run partnership with Mattie until, after hitting two sixes, a four and chancing his arm once too often, he is bowled. Cumberland are 83 for 3 in the 11th over, to the tune of Europe's 'The Final Countdown'.

Beyond the boundary, Rob's novelty smartphone case attracts admiration – backed by a flat plastic wine glass containing a blob of claret. Toby Bulcock asks how many actual bottles of plonk the Cairnses have at home and Lesley hazards a guess at one hundred and thirty, before revising that upwards to one hundred and fifty. There are racks in the kitchen, cellar and walk-in wardrobe. 'Daft thing is,' Rob interjects, 'I don't drink at home.'

Since he is seldom seen without a glass of something in hand, this causes much laughter. 'Get away...' someone says.

'No, it's true,' says Toby. 'Just a small vineyard now and then.'

'Really, I don't drink at home,' says Rob.

Because he likes a drop in company, Rob insists, it acts like an advertisement. People always buy him wine for special occasions and they just add up. He isn't a collector or anything. Last Thursday, Lesley had a retirement do and received thirteen bottles. Well, twelve and a bottle of gin. 'The house is full of the stuff,' she admits.

With only three more runs on the board, Mattie falls on 17, before Carr, Sempy and Cowling stiffen their side's resolve, positing another 35 between them before 139 for 7 is eventually reached, Toby and Syds unused and Greg and Josh Fallows not out.

Gary watches Lincolnshire go in from the boundary, the better to rest his wounded knee, replaced in the field by young Jamie Smith. Mattie McKiernan assumes the captaincy. Once again, Cumberland begin well, Lincs opener Conrad Louth caught by Mattie off Josh on ball three with his side yet to score. And in the fourth over, there is a reminder of Scunthorpe's industrial roots when, from nowhere, a rank-smelling sulphurous cloud wafts in overhead just as Cowling takes a stumping off Toby to leave the hosts 15 for 2. Apparently, in the UK, only Port Talbot gets stinkier.

Lincolnshire begin to smack a few fours around to 'Rockin' All Over the World', yet at the halfway mark comes another wicket and they are 40 for 3, thanks to Cowling again, this time off Mattie. It's too soon to say that victory is in the bag, though it does seem likely. Toby, meanwhile, looks knackered, as well he might. Having played in Liverpool yesterday, he was invited to stay in town and watch the Reds in the Champions League final: 'File it under seemed like a good idea at the time,' he says. He hadn't left the pub until half-three this morning, giving himself just enough time on arrival for half an hour's kip before rising for breakfast.

Steve Sharp, alone at the scoreboard end for much of the day with his wife, wanders over as the innings progresses and asks Jamie, fielding on the boundary, whether he's available for the development side on Thursday in Ashton upon Mersey. He says he will be there.

As the innings progresses Toby gets wayward for some reason and is spanked for 37 runs in four overs. Suddenly the game has opened up again. Needing ten an over, Lincs are 83 for 3 going into their final five, and 93 for 3 six balls later. Toby does get the wicket that makes it 99 for 4, but Bilal Shafayat's 50 ends an unhappy spell and, before long, Lincs need roughly two a ball, certainly achievable until Jacques runs out Alex Willerton. With the bat being thrown around, Cumberland need a miserly over to stem the flow and that is exactly what Josh Fallows delivers at a cost of only three runs. With Jacques now turning his arm, Lincolnshire need 24 to win, too much of a stretch. Restricting their opponents to 121 for 5, the Cumbrians can even afford a dropped Greg Hall catch – Shafayat the lucky man during a now unbeaten 60 – on the very last ball.

Defeat to Cheshire last time around left Cumberland propping up the Group 1 table. These couple of victories have lifted them to second. Having missed out on a Knockout Trophy quarter-final, they now face a three-week wait before T20 games five and six on June 17. And those games, against Staffordshire, will be staged at Penrith.

All roads lead to Cumbria.

CHAPTER THREE
COMETH THE FLOOD...

Cockermouth is renowned – or notorious – for a number of reasons. The semi-ruined Norman castle, whose tower tilts precariously over the local brewery. This is the place where William Wordsworth was born; his childhood home draws tourists galore. And then there are the semi-regular floods that wreak havoc here and across much else of Cumbria, most recently in 2005, 2009 and 2015.

Cockermouth isn't so well known for cricket, or at least wasn't until livewire England all-rounder and future World Cup hero Ben Stokes revealed it as his breeding ground. Sandair, down an alley off Gote Road and at the very heart of the Cumberland County Cricket Club story, suffers every bit as terribly from flooding as any other venue hereabouts. Yet having captured international news media attention, 'Cockermouth' was as likely to spark mirth as sympathy, the ideal location for 'Carry On Cricket', had such a movie existed. For the victims it was no laughing matter and anyway the etymology is more prosaic. It is named for its position at the confluence of rivers Cocker and Derwent, bearing the waters of Buttermere, Loweswater and Crummock in the first instance and Derwent and Bassenthwaite in the latter beyond the north west edge of the English Lake District.

The river of cricketing history meanwhile has its source in a still recognisably medieval marketplace, lately regenerated. It is to that evocative part of town that Cumberland CCC's origins – and indeed those of Cumbrian cricket as a whole – can be directly traced.

Cumberland weren't quite born in Cockermouth's Globe Hotel, but the club was certainly conceived there. An imposing three-storey building listed in 2010, English Heritage describes it as: 'Roughcast, with quoins, and eaves cornice on iron brackets. Centre doorway with stumpy columns, round arch etc. in heavy Victorian doorpiece. Three sash windows on each side and seven on each upper floor ... [Scottish novelist Robert Louis] Stevenson stayed here in 1871. John Dalton [atomic theory pioneer] stayed here frequently.' Confirming the Globe's significance for local cricket is a letter bearing seven signatories, sent to clubs on December 15 1883. Reproduced in *Cumberland County Cricket Club – A History*, a book self-published almost exactly a century later by *Cumberland and Westmorland Herald* editor John Hurst, in 1982, it requested 'one or two delegates' from each be sent to a meeting there on Thursday 27 December: '...to consider and arrange how the club should be formed.' After which, a public meeting was planned in Carlisle, on January 2. 'We may add we have received many promises of support from gentlemen in the County, who will, if the Club be formed, become honorary members.' The second day of 1884 would also be 'the first day of the County Quarter Sessions' and a list of honorary members in the minute book of the subsequent get-together, at Carlisle's County Hotel, reveals why that would have been important. At least thirty were JPs, several making their way across Court Square after doling out that year's initial allocation of gaol sentences and hard labour to the region's eloping couples and horsehair thieves.

Alas, this original go at launching Cumberland CCC, eleven years before the Minor Counties Cricket Championship was formed in 1895, proved short-lived, the first of three incarnations. Presided over by Lord Muncaster, it lasted six years. Two decades later, in 1910, the now Baron Muncaster took presidency of a second go, before himself expiring in 1917. This club outlived him, limping on for twenty years before drawing stumps in 1930. Version three, to which the current Cumberland club can most realistically be linked, has been more enduring. It was launched in 1948 and, after a few anxious times of its own, will mark its eightieth year this season.

As Hurst points out in his preface, however, all three clubs are 'firmly interlocked by family ties and relationships,' the root cause perhaps of the perception discussed at the Crooklands AGM of the county side as a clique. 'Edward Burnett, who instigated the revival of 1948,' writes Hurst, 'had one uncle who played for the earliest club and another who captained the side in 1912; Norman Wise, secretary for over thirty years [of the modern club], was originally linked as a player in the 1920s...' By 1982, three generations of the Gill family of Millom had produced Cumberland CCC cricketers.

However, some sort of cricket appears to have been present in this part of the world since the 1820s, if not earlier. In his 1798 book, *A Sentimental Tour*, Northumbrian author and scholar George Thompson writes of seeing students 'laying aside flowing gowns' at Charterhouse School in Surrey. 'A ball is thrown – they strike – they run.' Some twenty years later, similar antics had travelled north west, where 'feasting and drinking' attracted as much attention as the play. Hurst quotes the *Carlisle Journal*, wherein an Edenside (Carlisle) versus Derwentside (Cockermouth) game is described in a report of what Hurst is willing to call 'the first major match' in the county:

> The proceedings were appropriately commenced with a splendid breakfast, given by the Carlisle club to the Derwentside gentlemen. We have seldom seen a more lively or interesting scene. Handsome and spacious marquees were erected for the accommodation of the company. The Edenside club's tasteful flag surmounted the principal tent. Here a dinner was served in between two and three o'clock, and was partaken of by a great number of ladies, as well as gentlemen.

Back then, batsmen collected 'notches' not runs and in an eleven-a-side game of two innings each the hosts scraped home by four – 114 to 110. A low-scoring encounter then, but about which the *Journal*'s reporter was nevertheless ecstatic: 'Four in favour of Carlisle! The ball goes three times into the air! Victory! Huzza! Huzza! Our town forever – right or wrong!' The away team then sent word to Cockermouth by carrier pigeon before 'an orgy of drinking and guzzling' at the Bush Hotel ensued at which the host of the 'champagne supper', one Mr. Blow, 'drank and spoke and spoke and drank, until he fell under the table like a hero of the first water.' Chandeliers were smashed. Our reporter stuck at it until daybreak, when a call went out for 'prime Turkey coffee.'

For the return, Edenside headed south '...in a light post coach,

with four handsome bays and a phaeton.' The *Journal* report of that
trip reads: 'On the road the party was joined by a gig and three or
four equestrians and so drove on to Wigton, some amusing
themselves with segar-smoking [sic], others with making faces at
the rum 'ens they met on their way.' Derwentside won that time by
seven wickets and, according to *Bell's Life*, the new sporting weekly,
there were now 'eight strong clubs in Cumberland, where just two
or three years ago there had been none.' Half a century would go by
before the first Cumberland club in 1884, although given that *ad hoc*
county names elsewhere are recorded from the mid-1700s, it's no
surprise to learn that was as much the case here as anywhere before
an actual County Championship was instituted in 1890. In 1835, for
instance, the Officers of Carlisle Garrison beat a Cumberland side
containing Henry Howard of Greystoke Castle, near Penrith.

These early teams also played inter-county games, Hurst listing
matches at Northumberland in 1873 and, in 1880, at home to
neighbouring Westmorland. The *Cumberland and Westmorland
Advertiser* called the latter attendance exceedingly small: '...whether
from inadequate publicity, attractions elsewhere or the admission
price of a shilling, we cannot say.' Social reputation continued to be
paramount, as exemplified by Col. The Hon. Henry C. Lowther, who
famously went fifty years in the House of Commons without making
a speech. He did find time to appear for Gentlemen v Players. He
was clearly an influential figure in Cumberland, helping to form his
hometown club Whitehaven in 1837. None of which meant he was
any good as a cricketer. According to an 1833 edition of *Gentleman's
Magazine*: 'Colonel Lowther and Lords Strathavon and Clonbrook
ought to play in private, especially the colonel, who was designed
rather to stand for the stumps than to hold a bat.'

Maryport and Workington clubs followed and the game spread
throughout the Eden Valley too, its 'easy-going flavour' maintained.
Games that couldn't be finished on Saturday were allotted a day in
midweek upon which to conclude, a further clue as to whom this
pastime belonged. Public school rules were enforced. After dining,
chairmen must be given a formal vote of thanks. At Kendal, fielders
smoking or lying down were fined sixpence, yet alcoholic 'revivers'
were common. In 1864, the *Cumberland and Westmorland
Advertiser* reported: '...one of the umpires was so incapable through

drink that his place had to be supplied by another. I saw several glasses taken to players who were having their innings...'

There were indications, though, that this might become a more professional and indeed commercial enterprise. Nottinghamshire entrepreneur William Clarke took an All-England XI to Carlisle in 1850 and followed that up with two more 'missionary' trips in 1865 and 1871. The motive was partly philanthropic, to bring star names to remote areas, but in an era when under-arm was superseded first by round-arm and then over-arm bowling, the power of money to drive change betrayed the first cracks in cricket's identity.

That said, in 1871, the All-England XI had severely weakened their team by dropping fast bowler John Jackson in order that his place 'might be taken by a gentleman'. The traditionalist 'elite' were not about to let loose of the reins, even as wider social developments threatened to transform utterly the character of cricket. Having been an almost total preserve of the stinking rich, come the 1850 Factories Act, workers of the Industrial Revolution were free to play sport on Saturday afternoons, leading to a surge of interest in cricket and the various codes of football. With the proletariat involved, an urge for control became inevitable, but so too did greater competitiveness, twin-powered by the profit motive and declining Corinthian values.

Which is not to suggest that dilettantism didn't still hold sway in certain quarters, chiefly though not exclusively in rural parts.

In September 2018, a BBC documentary, *Ian Hislop's Olden Days,* will sum up the 'town and country' nature of the period. Digging through the vaults, Hislop ponders the most important date in British history. Is it 1066: Battle of Hastings? Or 1666: Great Fire of London? Maybe 1966, when England last won the World Cup: 'Or how about 1851?' He inspects a summary of that year's census: '...one of those great Victorian state of the nation surveys,' whose numbers reflect the number of people in towns and cities 'as against those living in what it calls the country parts.' Country: 8,936,800. Towns and cities: 8,990,809. For the first time, England and Wales have more urban than rural dwellers by the relatively small margin of 54,009.

Hislop describes the year as a tipping point and, even allowing for a predominantly middle class interpretation, is on to something. For it was under such conditions that a folk nostalgia for the pastoral took root, in reaction to changes in '...not just where we lived but how,' impacting jobs, self-image and 'most significantly, what we thought about the home that most of us had just left and to which we would not return.' Cut to bucolic images of green hills, blue skies and, somewhat inevitably, a village cricket field.

'The countryside,' he says, 'increasingly became a refuge from troubling realities like national decline, world war and even our own mortality. What we looked for ... was often fanciful, even downright eccentric. But this rural reimagining acted as a creative catalyst, inspiring some of our most powerful art and best loved literature.' And, he might have added, the mythology of one sport in particular.

Owzat!?

None of which precludes the simple joy of playing the game, be it in countryside, big city or the sort of defiantly semi-rural towns dotted around a county where it might be expected a sport with a split-personality would indeed feel most at home. In *Cumberland County Cricket Club – A History*, John Hurst shares a report from the *Penrith Herald* in 1881:

> A curious incident, probably without parallel in cricketing annals, marked Platt's innings in a recent match ... between the United Eleven and Eighteen of Whitehaven. He hit a ball which lodged in his shirt and thence into his trousers, putting him in an awkward fix. If he took the ball out he was out for touching the ball while in play; if he stood where he was till [sic] a fielder removed it before it touched the ground, he was caught out. After a moment's pause he ran for it, attempting to get out of the boundary and then take the ball out. Pursued by the eleven, he made a circuit of half the ground and was eventually pulled down inside the flags, and in the melee which ensued the ball was shaken clear, and the umpires decided Platt was not out.

No innovation was too bizarre to be given a go, another cricketing tradition thereby established. In late-January 1879, a match between Keswick teams took place on frozen Derwentwater, the ice so thick the teams wore skates. In Penrith, there was a cross-code clash between cricket and bowls while, in Kendal, Alderman Willison's XI '...were handicapped by having to use broomsticks as bats.'

The explosion in clubs, meanwhile, meant another outlet for

the continuation of local rivalries, town against town, village against village, street against street sometimes. In Cumberland, as elsewhere, this turned cricketing attention inwards and outwards at one and the same time. Whitehaven must beat Workington, of course, but their county must also get one over on Westmorland, a 'derby' that dominated interest throughout Cumberland's first two manifestations.

Upon the arrival of the third county club in 1948, the counties effectively merged to form Cumberland and Westmorland. However the latter was then sacrificed as a condition of gaining entry to the Minor Counties Championship in 1954, before disappearing forever upon being subsumed into the new county of Cumbria in the 1970s.

*****

On the title page of *Cumberland County Cricket Club – A History* is a perfect summary of what running a Minor Counties team 'in this far-flung, North Western outpost of civilisation' is all about. The contributor is Norman Wise, then club secretary since 1948. Calling it 'a prospect to daunt the stoutest hearted', he writes: 'Our gates are negligible, our population thin and widely scattered amidst Cumbria's hills and dales. However, all connected with the club are fanatics and, though daunted and "bloody-headed," we are unbowed.'

John Hurst's research is underpinned by the statistics of Home Office forensic scientist Keith Barnett, born and educated in Workington but resident in Burbage, Leicestershire. The idea to write Cumberland CCC's first history occurred while watching a Minor Counties match in Penrith in the 1970s. County captain John Moyes is pictured kneeling on the cover, mid-sweep. To readers of a certain age, the year of publication, 1982, may not seem so long ago yet the back page says otherwise. On it is a sketch of a young woman in Victorian dress and a forward defensive stance above the dedication: 'On the arrival of cricket in Cumberland almost 160 years ago, the newspapers invariably reported that the spectators included "a good sprinkling of the fair sex." Over the years they have contributed to the enjoyment of the Summer game as scorers, hostesses for tea (or the sumptuous "cold collations" of days long past) and on the social scene, as well as bringing colour and vivacity to our cricket fields. This book is dedicated to THE LADIES.'

Hurst's preface, meanwhile, gets straight to the heart of the region's sense of itself as being perpetually wronged by whatever arm of the establishment is currently out to get them. 'Cumberland was once described by a former President of the MCC as "not what you might call a cricketing county," he writes, before pointing out that other commentators have been kinder: '...taking into account all the difficulties presented by weather and terrain. Rural de-population is another threat, but cricket survives tenaciously in town and country while at county level you have to wonder at the dedication of men who soldier on ... regardless of the elusiveness of success.'

The social backgrounds of attendees at that original Globe meeting on 27 December 1883 are presented in riveting detail. The club: '...owed its existence to the magistracy, with legal backing from solicitors, barristers and even a Judge.' Initial membership was male, high-minded and enthusiastic, certainly for cricket but also hunting. The Cumberland Foxhounds came under the Masterships of Sir Wilfrid Lawson of Brayton Hall (several of whose hounds were bought from huntsman John Peel) and Henry Howard of Greystoke Castle, neither a stranger to leather and willow. Sir Wilfrid, a liberal reformer, was quite the character, with a penchant for replying to letters – such as the one inviting him to the Globe – in comical verse:

Dear Lamplugh, I'm willing to join
Your club in the orthodox way,
But first have the goodness to state
Who is it you wish me to play?

Recipient Lamplugh Frechville Ballantine-Dykes – a.k.a. the equally eccentric LFB Dykes – was the club's secretary and opening batsman, though: '...no ornamental secretary but the real mainspring of the concern,' according to one newspaperman. Known as the 'Squire of Dovenby' on account of living at Dovenby Hall in Cockermouth, he was flamboyance personified in straw boater, waxed moustache and striped blazer. He was also the first to note that: 'It seems impossible to get gate-money at present for cricket in Cumberland.' Sadly, his death, aged 38, in 1893 was possibly the result of a cricketing injury.

One doubting Thomas at the meeting – Thomas Hartley of Bassenthwaite, future player and administrator – reminded everyone that a similar idea had fallen down three years ago for lack of cricketers. The mood though was that, with so much influence and patronage, that ought not to be an issue this time. Sir Wilfrid agreed. Lots of players were good enough to hold their own against Durham, Northumberland and a few Scottish counties he reckoned, while also injecting a note of realism. The team must be selected on merit and lack 'non-effectives', among which he was humble enough to include himself. The date for an AGM was set and six delegates appointed to the committee from Dalston, Cockermouth, Carlisle, Aspatria, Millom and Workington.

The first match was essentially a trial – 'Eleven of Cumberland v Sixteen of the County'. Then came games with Northumberland and Durham, plus a North Lancashire XI at Barrow. In 1885, the new club took a trip south to face Surrey and MCC sides in London. Though the game was essentially still gentrified, Workington blast furnace worker T. Biltcliffe won a place on the trip, his workmates buying him a blazer, pads, bag and bat so he didn't show them up. Sadly, at Lord's, an MCC bowler claimed the latter was too wide, the umpires agreed, and so Biltcliffe was sent back to the Pavilion for a narrower one, which then earned him the princely scores of 3 and 0. On these and future trips south, each Cumberland player got £3 in expenses, plus rail fare. Otherwise, away-days netted 12 shillings a day, plus fare, or nine shillings and sixpence for home games.

Cumberland mark one, then, had plenty of ambition but no home ground, an absence that brought about its downfall. Two years after formation, members carried a motion that 'endeavours should be taken to secure a county ground' and a four-man committee was set up to that end. The problem might have been solved when a field in Carlisle belonging to the Duke of Devonshire became available on a twenty-one-year lease. Circulars requesting donations from members were posted out before the complaints came flooding in.

'When the decision to form the ground in this city was first made known,' reported the *Carlisle Journal*, 'considerable opposition was expressed by West Cumberland cricketers and a meeting was held at Workington to give vent to this feeling. The main arguments advanced in favour of Workington were that sportsmen there were more enthusiastic cricketers than elsewhere and that there were a considerable number of subscribing clubs in the area.'

The 1887 AGM was consumed by anger and controversy.

Maryport's John Campbell said a large working population there was interested in cricket but would not travel sixty or eighty miles to learn about its 'arts and mysteries'. Someone else suggested that gate receipts from a stadium in Workington would be so vast they would pay for redirecting the railway. The majority of those present were from East Cumberland, however, so favoured Carlisle and very strongly. Secretary LFB Dykes posited one socially dubious reason why that should be so, namely that 'chaff' from the 'gallery' in Workington would put visiting clubs off coming back. Such attitudes towards the 'great unwashed' had moved into sharper focus since the advent of the Factory Act, but it was true that West Cumbria was not 'on the mainline of railway communication' and therefore lacked a suitable volume of accommodation.

Carlisle, then, was set fair to host the county ground until there came a sudden drop in interest. In his book, John Hurst suggests that may have been down to those in the west taking a 'sod you' attitude. Nor was the east amused when visitors began to demand £50 to travel north, with nothing offered to Cumberland going south. A half-hearted suggestion that they should forget county cricket and face big city teams like Manchester and Liverpool came to nothing and, in February 1890, the original Cumberland CCC was dissolved at the Central Hotel, Carlisle. Seventy men had not paid their subs.

Two years later, the £17 17s 5d left in the club's bank account was invested in the Carlisle Cricket and Athletic Company as part-payment for the border city's distinctive Edenside ground, giving Carlisle CC fair claim as the spiritual home of Cumberland cricket. 'Few grounds can rival Carlisle's cricket enclosure alongside the silver border of the river, with the graceful sweep of the bridge arches in the background,' writes Hurst. 'Here the poetry of the flashing blade and the scurry of white-clad figures give the deepest satisfaction to the ardent enthusiast.'

*****

Twenty years later, Cumberland had another try. The interim period had seen inter-county 'scratch' teams formed now and then, but nothing official. In hindsight, the 'proper revival' began when Cumberland and Westmorland went head to head again in 1908.

The man behind that fixture was a rather stern South African, Captain Carleton Salkeld, 'sunken of eye' according to contemporary accounts and a veteran of the Second Boer War. A year later, it was he who dispatched invites to a re-launch at Carlisle's County Hotel. Later he became secretary and was, as late as 1928, club president.

At that 1909 meet, a couple of committeemen from the earlier incarnation warned of various pitfalls. In order to compete with the likes of Yorkshire seconds, Durham and Staffordshire, who each had four professionals on their books, a new Cumberland club must field outsiders. According to the *Cumberland and Westmorland Herald*, ex-treasurer RH Horrocks '...doubted whether there was the same interest in cricket now as there used to be.' Capt. Salkeld though was keen and a committee duly formed in which many a surname from the first go featured, such as the one belonging to Hubert Ballantine-Dykes. To avoid floggings, matches were arranged only with clubs unaffiliated with the MCC to begin with, but they were still thrashed at Dumfriesshire. Having got the hang of it, for years Cumberland were pretty much invincible. In 1911, they beat Durham University by an innings and 170 runs, the county's biggest victory to this day.

Not every observer was happy. Hurst quotes one newspaper in which a correspondent, 'Old Cricketer', shares concerns re standards of sportsmanship. 'If I had presumed to ignore the rules of cricket as advised,' he writes, 'I should at once have been cross-buttocked by our regular umpire, the famous wrestler, William Jameson.'

World War One proved to be as devastating and disruptive for Cumberland as anywhere, temporarily derailing them to the extent that another revival was needed in 1921, although the original club had not been dissolved. This meeting was in West Cumberland, on September 22, held at the Commercial Hotel, Workington.

During the post-war decade, Cumbrian cricket took on a far more working class hue, affecting the game's character in the county profoundly. The dramatic rural backdrops remained, as did certain of the old attitudes, not least the tendency towards insularity. As ever, though, the major issue was money – or lack of it. John Hurst quotes *Wednesday Early Closing*, a memoir by Norman Nicholson who, in 1975, recalls the days of the 'slump' or Great Depression in Millom: '...in the long, workless summers, it was better to practise at the nets than to stand, hour after hour, at the church gates or the street corners. There was always the chance of a collection for fifty runs or even, for the specially talented player, a season's engagement as Saturday afternoon professional with some other club...' Parochial or not, it was then too that Cumberland twice faced Australia and once New Zealand – an international dimension in what, looking back, reads like a magical era for a club inspired by a dominant leader. His name was Roland Saint and he was a real crowd-pleaser in the days when there really were crowds, stylish centuries galore. All the more surprising therefore that at the end of the decade this second incarnation too should go down the pan.

The Australians had won on their first visit in front of an estimated 6-7,000 people at Whitehaven. The date of that game, 21 September 1921, is an indication of why Workington, a short drive up the coast, was the venue for the second Cumberland CCC's post-war return the very next day. Yet when the Aussies came back in 1926, with the sole exception of Saint, the team was representative not of Cumberland but 'the best that English cricket had to offer,' featuring stars like Herbert Sutcliffe and George Gunn of Yorkshire and Nottinghamshire respectively. The Aussies were still too good. Middlesex bowler Patsy Hendren – famed for his wit – got so fed up by his lack of success that he resorted to tossing down a juicy red apple instead of a ball. When, in 1927, New Zealand won by an innings and 18 runs, a loss was made of over £93 on the venture. Letters went to guarantors requesting they come good on pledges. 'Alas,' writes Hurst, 'there is no record of how they responded.'

We can assume not very well. Less than three years later, in 1930, Cumberland CCC was again defunct. The prediction twenty years earlier of original treasurer RH Horrocks had come to pass.

*****

Third time lucky. On Saturday 10 April 1948, launch number three was again at the Commercial Hotel, Workington, where prominent survivors of the previous set-up were once more in attendance and the instigator-in-chief was of legal bent.

Along with captaining Carlisle, solicitor Edward Burnett was a member of a cricketing family in Scotby, back then noted for a strong village side, nowadays set apart from the city by the M6 motorway. Within two seasons, Cumberland and Westmorland CCC, as they now became known, were hosting – and managing to draw with – no less a team than the West Indies, watched by around 8,000 at Edenside. The new club's long-serving secretary Norman Wise called it: '...a sight to gladden the heart of every cricket lover ... I don't think there has been anything like it in Cumberland before.' Other opponents included Sedbergh School, Yorkshire Gents, Aberdeenshire, Perthshire, the North Lancashire League and the Border League. In 1951, Cumberland and Westmorland toured Scotland, beating Aberdeen and North of Scotland. Innovation was in the air and a floodlit game at Carlisle FC's Brunton Park proposed. That at least didn't happen. Workington's Borough Park eventually claimed those bragging rights, though not before September 1981.

Back in 1955, a fourth international side, South Africa, enjoyed a one-sided victory in which, the local paper reported: 'One mighty hit shattered the windscreen of the car of Mr. R Griffiths, captain of Lowther Cricket Club, while another struck Mrs. Stanton of Greystoke who, fortunately, was little the worse.' The visitors sent her a bouquet. It was now clear though that this new organisation meant business, not least because that very same year they had gained admittance to the Minor Counties Championship. Name-wise, that spelled the end of 'and Westmorland', even as that historic county's reach still extended over the land. Cumberland MkIII was destined to win the Championship three times, though the first title wasn't until 1986.

Even so, there is little doubt that the 1950s were Cumberland's halcyon days. The West Indies returned in 1957 (rain stopped play) and, as described by Hurst, it seems like a fine time to have been at a club with: '...a rich social life [and] some uproarious evenings, especially after away matches.' One team member, Whitehaven professional Bill Lawton, was married to Lancashire-born film star Dora Bryan, memorable in such future classics as *A Taste of Honey* and not averse to leading a singsong. The only real problem, apart from rare on-field success, was a continued lack of funds. In 1963, gate monies totalled £39 and nine shillings, shrinking further to £27 by 1965 and £17 in 1967. Thus did outside patronage via interest-free loans and donations grow ever more vital. One boost came from Keswick upon the death of the club's fourth president, Lt. Col. Sir Percy Hope, in 1972. 'He left the club a generous legacy with the thought that the annual income from it could be considered his subscription for all time,' writes Hurst.

Commercial sponsorships too entered the picture and, in 1956, the club advertised for its first professional coach. The sum of £15 plus travelling expenses was on offer for 'the right type of man'. Twenty-four weeks' worth of work would be expected and Yorkshire all-rounder Harry Halliday became the inaugural holder of the role. Yet when John Hurst sent *Cumberland County Cricket Club - A History* off to print in 1982, he was able only to reflect that: 'Few Minor Counties teams have had a more meagre ration of success than Cumberland, with just 17 wins since 1955 in over 200 matches.' He also includes one of Norman Wise's annual reports from the 1960s. These, he writes, put the county's uphill struggle in a nutshell:

> We should ask that the larger picture should not be lost sight of. In organising Minor Counties cricket in Cumberland and Westmorland, and in maintaining a County Club in this part of the "Cricket Empire", we provide an opportunity for local cricketers to play matches in a higher grade, in some cases on Test match and first-class county grounds. For example, all the members of the Yorkshire first eleven, except Messrs. Boycott and Trueman, have at some time or another played against Cumberland.

In fact Boycott had faced Cumberland, in the first ever Minor Counties game at Penrith in 1959. It did though sum up how the county's players: '...soldiered on gamely – and no doubt pondered on how they might have fared if geography had been rather kinder, enabling games with some of the less formidable teams in the Minor Counties competition.' Hurst adds: 'The biggest complaint, however, must be a lack of total commitment in a far-flung area, with few large centres of population and remote from concentrations of league cricket. Full-strength sides are ruled out by players withdrawing to help club sides in cup matches and important Sunday fixtures.' As early as 1955: '...the call went out for less parochialism and more county patriotism. It has echoed repeatedly down the years.'

With a tweak of its title, John Hurst's book was expanded and updated in 2011 as *Cumberland County Cricket Club - History and Comprehensive Record*, by the club's then future chairman of cricket and present-day committee member Mike Latham. By then, all five committeemen whose mug shots had adorned the original had long since left office. The presidency of John C. Wade, in uniform as Lord Lieutenant of Cumbria, ended in 1984. Harold Millican stepped down as chairman in 1992, but then became president until 2003. Secretary Norman Wise had retired in 1981 just before the original book's publication, to be replaced by fellow ex-club captain Malcolm Beatty, who then became president in 2004 and was replaced in that role 2014 by another ex-skipper (and ex-chairman), its present incumbent Alan Wilson. Philip Larkin lookalike Bob Gaskarth performed the treasurer's duties for sixteen years before Charles Mitchinson took over in 1988, today's treasurer Eric Carter picking up the mantle in 2001. Publicity officer Ted Roberts became a vital sponsorship conduit through the 1980s and helped in the creation of the annual yearbook that Mike Latham went on to edit. Hurst had also taken that publication under his wing before his death, aged 80, in 2009, having given permission for an update of his original work. Gilbert Johnstone's statistical revisions were painstaking, literally so given how at one point he underwent major heart surgery.

Joining the Minor Counties Championship in 1955 was a major step forward, Mike now reflected, although the competition back then was: '...run in something of a hotchpotch way.' Rankings were determined by a composite table, some first-class county 2nd XIs included. The two teams with highest averages over a minimum of eight fixtures then played off to determine the title. Cumberland's debut had ended in defeat to Yorkshire 2nd XI by an innings and 35 runs at Carlisle on May 25-26. Their first victory came in the final match of the following season, against then Minor Counties side Durham at Keswick. International players became a feature, South Africans, Aussies, Indians and, most spectacularly, Leonard Baichan, West Indies Test opener of the 1970s, who 'brought some of the charisma of the Caribbean to our cricket fields.' It was now too that BBC Cumbria began live coverage of Cumberland games and Minor Counties reorganisation meant fixtures in the likes of Hertfordshire, Suffolk, Norfolk, Cambridgeshire and Bedfordshire. This in a county where even an away trip within its borders might induce nosebleeds.

'Carlisle have matches as far away as Haverigg and Millom,' Hurst wrote of a round-trip totalling some 200 miles. For Cumbria's county side, that distance would henceforth be as nothing.

*****

Cockermouth's propensity to flood is blamed on a low-lying position with regard to the Irish Sea, combined with the confluence of those aforementioned rivers. Annual rainfall is below the national average.

The cricket ground, down a tight and sudden nook, opens out attractively, shaded by tall firs on three sides of a venue tucked into an S bend stretch of the Derwent. Opposite the gate a tiled pavilion is fronted by a bar extension and seating area, above which are three blind dormers and an art deco clock.

Cockermouth CC has been resident at Sandair since 1823, the club's one and only home in all that time. In its foundation years, it was rented and then purchased from a wealthy local family, the old pavilion closer to the entrance. When a new one was constructed in the early twentieth century, for some reason they placed it closer to the water, doubtless for a picture-postcard effect. It stayed untouched until the 1980s. From the start, this appears to have been a family club, Denhams particularly prominent. Now in his eighties, ex-2nd XI captain, president and current groundsman Raymond Denham continues that hundred year-plus association, working on a well-prepared pitch all year round. In 2017, the venue was renamed the Raymond Denham Oval in his honour.

The 1st XI of a set-up underpinned by a thriving junior section competes in the North Lancashire and Cumbria League Premier Division. Play commences at 1.00pm on a serene Saturday afternoon whose warming sunshine makes light work of gossamer cloud.

Today's visitors are from Haverigg – an hour down the coast – and have a professional in their ranks. Roy Kaia, a Zimbabwean, has a lot of expectation on his shoulders, as might also be said of Cockermouth's Pakistani professional Haseeb Azam. The former will be bowled for four and take three wickets in 15 overs. Azam – a.k.a. 'Hash' – fares better, his unbeaten 16 bolstered by three wickets in 14 overs. It will become clear that paying full-time players at this level is not without criticism, a question mainly of value for money.

The case for is certainly harder to make given the amount of spectators in to see the first few overs. They can be counted on the fingers of two hands and are far fewer in number than the hoverflies that swirl in curtains from the banks of the river beyond. Clubs in the North Lancs and Cumbria are allowed to field one pro' each and similar rules operate elsewhere. In the Northern Premier League, for example, teams are allowed one plus an overseas amateur. That led one side, Carnforth, to join the strictly amateur Westmorland League instead, fearful that a wish to stop paying and 'more fully serve their community' would leave them uncompetitive.

'They cost too much money and wouldn't come here if they were any good, would they?' says one onlooker emphatically, to nods of sage agreement from his equally timeworn friend.

Cockermouth is where Fletcher Christian, chief mutineer on *HMS Bounty*, grew up, so perhaps something of a rebel spirit ought to be expected around here and not just among the older population. The nets that attracted Ben Stokes on his arrival from New Zealand as a youngster remain intact. Before day is out they will be filled with other children, imaginations stirred by bat, ball and traffic cone.

'Couldn't get him out of them,' says Alan Stables, watching from a couple of fold-up chairs alongside his wife, while a friend, Tony, stands nearby. 'You could see he had it, even then. He was hitting it over that tree as a fifteen-year-old.' He indicates a Douglas Fir at the 'Rotary Wall' end that must be at least 130 feet high.

Alan is an ex-teammate of Cumberland treasurer Eric Carter, umpiring today, the two having played at a now defunct Cumbria League club, Heavy Duty Alloys. Son Marcus Stables is a promising batsman who hit a century for the Cumberland development side a couple of years back. While on a two-year scholarship at Sedbergh School, he opened the batting with the current Yorkshire prodigy Harry Brook, but is for the moment a student at Cardiff MCCU.

Haverigg aren't expected to offer much opposition. 'You could have picked a better game to come,' says Cockermouth scorer Geoff Minshaw, who fulfils that function here as well as with Cumberland. As the game progresses, an endearing eccentric who squints through his specs like Mole in *Wind in the Willows* simultaneously organises his building business, one hand holding a mobile phone glued to one ear while the other taps in 'dot balls', 'runs', 'wickets' and 'wides' – face an inch from the laptop screen – as he updates the club's *Play-Cricket.com* website electronically, ball-by-ball. An ECB initiative, it's part of an online service admirable in detail that makes up-to-the-minute scores available for clubs the length and breadth of the country. Admirably so, given how few spectators most lower-level clubs attract. While some local leagues won't participate, or aren't so rigorous in filing, each club is encouraged to maintain and update their personalised site with reports, tables, fixtures and other statistics that are of course accessible worldwide.

Such support is a particular boon for the Minor Counties – indeed it's one of the few means of promoting its activities to a wider audience in a media climate where even the national broadcaster takes zero week-by-week interest. In 2018, the BBC Sport website doesn't even consider MCCA fixtures or results worthy of an online listing. Big bashathons in India, South Africa, the Caribbean, Australia and Pakistan, or New Zealand's Plunket Shield? Fill your boots. Of Lincolnshire, Berkshire, Devon and their like, not a sniff.

Cockermouth versus Haverigg is a 50-over affair in which the visitors start stronger than expected. After a spell in which Kaia hits a solitary boundary and is caught out after facing just eight deliveries they are 52 for 2, Hash with the wickets – an important contribution.

A town centre busy with shoppers begins to deposit more folk through the gate as the sunshine turns hazy, a screech of seagulls in the air. Chris Hodgson, one of a pair of Cumberland players in the home line-up, Matty Sempill the other, takes the third scalp, lbw, before Eric hoists a finger for a run-out, his first real decision of the day. Haverigg are 89-4 and the decision – though clearly correct – is unpopular with the batsman, who throws his bat down in disgust. Eric getting it right ought to be no surprise, since the running joke in these circles is that in forty-two years of umpiring he has never made a single mistake – or at least any he will admit to.

'Backbone of Cumbria cricket,' smiles Alan Stables, fondly. 'Cumberland would likely fall apart without him.' He means it too, so indefatigable is Eric's enthusiasm for the sport and his county.

Play pauses after twenty-five overs, jugs of blackcurrant and orange squash quenching the players' thirsts. It's a moment to revel in a beautiful scene, ancient mountain Skiddaw standing guard over the jagged rooftops of Gote Road, beyond the entrance. Closer to hand, All Saints Church spire appears to be sketched in pastel chalk, a place of worship in one form or another since 1395, site of the font where Wordsworth was baptised. Skiddaw's green slate features on many a rooftop, propped up by rendered stone walls that punctuate cobbled lanes and alleys of a type down which Sandair first appears, the walker having crossed the Derwent bridge. As for poetry, cricket has long lent itself to verse and while his fellow romantics Coleridge and Southey seem only to have taken interest in the chirping variety, Wordsworth did pen a few lines on the subject:

> Dear fellow-Traveller! here we are once more.
> The Cock that crows, the Smoke that curls, that sound
> Of Bells, those Boys in yon meadow-ground
> In white-sleev'd shirts are playing by the score,
> And even this little River's gentle roar,
> All, all are English...

Okay, so it was 'Kent's green vales' that awakened his imagination here, but the game's pastoral appeal to the poet is clear. It is anyway unlikely that Wordsworth would have seen cricket in Cockermouth. By 1823, he was thirty miles south at Dove Cottage in Grasmere.

An artist of another sort, Ben Stokes, did spend his formative years here, as we know. And in August 2017, he returned to support a fund-raiser in the wake of floods that had, as in 2009, submerged the club's amenities if not its spirit. A Thursday evening 20-over game between an England PCA Masters side – captained by Mark Ramprakash – and Cockermouth was Stokes's own idea and made good on a promise he made to chairman George Todhunter, for whom the pavilion was named. For once, the weather gods were kind; especially given how on the very next day it poured down and no play at all would have been possible. Due to England duties, the man himself couldn't take part but was as high-profile a presence as might be expected. He drew the media, an excited crowd of 2,000 and substantial five-figure profit from a match in which Cockermouth beat Ramprakash and company by five wickets with just two balls to spare. It was Stokes, however, who everyone wanted both to talk about and with; each autograph and selfie request agreed to with a smile. 'We'd a junior tournament in the morning and Ben was here for that too,' says Geoff Minshaw. 'All the kids got to meet their hero. Ben's generosity helped ensure the day left a lasting legacy in Cockermouth and West Cumbria.'

Note: *West* Cumbria. This is clannish country, where people identify strongest with their most immediate patch – town, village or hamlet first, county second, country third, the rest of the planet a distant last. It's easy to be sniffy, but such stunning natural beauty cannot surely help but stamp a mark on the soul. How could anyone raised among these mountains, fells and screes, lakes and waterfalls, not be moulded by the experience? There is a fine line, however, between pride and myopia. When familiar with a landscape formed over millennia, the idea of permanence may well be inescapable, but it is still a conceit. Geological movement, however gradual, finds an echo in the far briefer passage of our own all-too fragile humanity.

But then insularity has its roots in folk memory, of an age when travel was more demanding than in the modern era. To an incomer, for example, the attraction of a semi-professional (and maybe one day fully-professional) Cumbria club underpinned by a Premier League of ambitious set-ups from Carlisle to Kendal and all points east to west, with a spread of community leagues below that, seems obvious. It's certainly the path the ECB is intent on promoting. The very idea however risks alienating those unpaid volunteers who keep cricket going, albeit ageing and dwindling in number. While tribal loyalty and long-time rivalries can make for terrific local drama, personal enmities are capable of bespoiling an otherwise stunning canvas. Is it any wonder that well-meaning newcomers who have dared to unleash big ideas here historically end up stomping off just as swiftly, with an exasperated cry of 'Oh, let them get on with it!'

Haverigg pass 100 before wicket seven and Geoff, prodding his phone, is on a business call: 'They need new windows, and if they need new windows they need to be smaller, marra...' Whatever the visitors manage now, at least Cockermouth will have runs to chase. With six overs remaining, there are 50 more, eight wickets down. The ninth is another lbw for Hodgson, before a Sempy catch on the boundary – one ball after Chris is smashed over the pavilion – gives Cumberland's player-coach his third victim, the visitors 169 all out.

During the interval, an ageing gang of four lean on a railing and rip T20 and the new '100' idea to shreds. 'It's for the low attention-span generation,' one says. 'In ten years' time, it will be an over apiece and back to the pub.' Chris, fed and watered, talks junior set-ups, recalling how, as a kid, he played in the same team as Stokes when not messing around with a bat and ball in the nets. 'We'd all of us spend our summer holidays here. This was our second home.'

Cockermouth won't stage a Cumberland county game in 2018 and haven't since being submerged. 'It takes two or three years for a pitch to dry out properly and bed down again,' Chris says. He points out a ghostly line of banking encompassing the oval, unnoticeable at first, which hints at the venue's past use as a velodrome. Ghostly Victorian bicycles suddenly tear around the boundary.

Geoff wanders over for a sandwich and shares his views on professionals, a number of whom, as a private landlord, he has given residence to in his time. 'Cockermouth joined the North Lancs and Cumbria in 2000,' he says, 'and our first pro' was a homegrown lad who travelled up from Barrow. The next was Gareth White, another Cumbrian, who in fact captains us now. In 2001, a fast bowler from Workington turned nasty, Gareth reacted and the umpire banned him for six games, so I had to find a replacement – Riffat Ullah, a spin bowler from Pakistan. When I picked him up at Kendal he couldn't speak a word of English so, divorced at the time, I put him up with me. He stayed for six seasons and scored six thousand runs.'

That experience made an impression on Geoff who, despite his predilection for tall tales and badinage, is also prone to contemplation. He takes pride in cricket, the clubs he serves and his positions within them. 'At Cockermouth, we are forward thinking,' he says, 'as you can see from the facilities. To progress to the top of the league, as we did, we had to have a professional in the side. I was at Whitehaven ten seasons before I came here and I've always been pro-pro. I like to watch them bat and bowl, see sides fielding against them and they lift the rest of the lads. There's a school of thought that if you had eleven amateurs you'd have a better team, but I tend to think professionals improve teammates, improve coaching and improve the kids, who have a great example to follow.'

Being Geoff, however, a humorous anecdote isn't far away, the story in question featuring David 'Bumble' Lloyd's son Graham, who seems to have shared his dad's gift for dry wit and the *mot juste*. 'Once, during a three-dayer, we needed 430 to win on the last day. I taps him on the shoulder and says: "Graham, What do you reckon?" "Ooh, now then Geoffrey, it's a difficult one," he says, and mulls it over for a bit. Then in his finest Lancastrian twang: "I would say the cards are heavily stacked against us." After a couple of early wickets, he taps me on the back. "I'll rephrase that which I told you, Geoffrey. We're fucked."' At one point, Graham Lloyd and Yorkshire stalwart Ashley Metcalfe shared professional duties, three games apiece. His own battle-grounds being sites of ignominious defeat, Lloyd sighed: 'Lord Ashley of Farsley filches the best three wickets in the country and I get all the shitholes.'

Sempy, a left-hander, is one of Cockermouth's openers, the pair clocking up 20 runs between them before Alex Grainger is caught and bowled. With Greg Platten's introduction the pace quickens, helped by wild bowling and fine shot selection from Sempy in particular. In such company, he does indeed look a class above. The ton arrives in over 21, target well within reach and both batsmen on 49. Platten passes his milestone with a well-run two before Sempy's first half-century of the season follows in an innings brimming with style and confidence. Neither batsman, however, lasts much longer. When Platten is caught on 60, Hash strides out as the side needs 30 to win and Sempy is then bowled on 59. Chris is next in, Sempy and Platten both having fallen to Kaia. Still, no sweat. If Haverigg are to have any serious hope of winning there will need to be a collapse.

Hardly ideal then that Chris should stretch so exaggeratedly into forward defence, get rapped on the pad and be sent immediately back from whence he came, as Kaia's third wicket. At least this time the finger didn't belong to Eric. A previously flagging opposition is energised. Chris, more often all smiles, is a picture of absolute woe. After tossing his gear in the sheds, he lays prone, flushed pink on a bench, head in hands. Cricket can be a cruel mistress.

Out in the middle, the batsmen grow jittery and the runs dry up, although by the time 150 is crawled past the danger has passed. Haverigg claim one Cockermouth run was short and Eric comes in for more verbal stick. They know the contest is as good as gone. Two more runs draw the sides level before Hash smashes the boundary that puts a winning 173 for 4 on Geoff's scoreboard. The ball lands in a patch of woodland undergrowth that, no longer now flooded, resembles a dried-up Louisiana swamp, if such were dotted with ragged conifers. You wouldn't bet against alligators, mind.

As the departing batsmen bask in a smattering of applause, their teammates trot back on to the field, persuaded by their captain to pull on the protective covers. Pints will soon be sunk, the day's deeds dissected and stored for anecdotage. For non-members it is time to leave, the drive home offering a bonus pair of Eden Valley games in their closing stages. To begin with there is early evening sunshine, but further east along the A66, clouds broil ominously over Bassenthwaite and its peaks, as little Braithwaite fall to defeat against Carlisle's 2nd XI. Just up the road, Threlkeld, a tranquil village at the foot of craggy Blencathra, complete a draw with Kirkby Stephen.

Come Penrith, Ragnarök looks imminent, the day transformed. In Cockermouth, shirt-sleeves; just thirty miles away it is cold, wet and windy. Two climates, one dramatic county, riven yet by echoes of clanship such as that which once littered these entire British Isles with tribes and chieftains lost, before a kingdom arose, united. And an awe-inspiring landscape inspires imaginative wanderings further back still, when the earth was roamed by diplodocus, tyrannosaurus rex and velociraptor. Only recently it emerged that some scientists now reckon dinosaurs were around fifteen million years earlier than previously believed, and here in the northern land mass Laurasia rather than two hundred and thirty million years ago in southern Gondwana. Suddenly, getting in a lather about 'Cumbria' replacing 'Cumberland' seems a little trivial and, well, prehistoric.

Those dinosaurs are long departed now, of course, but for the odd buried bone and skeleton, perhaps, scattered and coiled beneath geological eons' worth of weight in story, rock and soil.

CHAPTER FOUR
YOU'RE AS YOUNG AS YOU FIELD

June is upon us and the heavens over Tynefield Park are the colour of Kendal Mint Cake as Cumberland CCC welcome Staffordshire to Penrith for games five and six of the Minor Counties T20.

One umpire strides back from a pitch that didn't see much Northern Premier League action yesterday, due to rain. 'Have we got any stumps?' he asks the host county's chairman, Neil Atkinson. There has also been a mix-up over the starting time. The pitch isn't quite ready because organisers were under the impression play was scheduled to commence at 11.30am. The quid-a-pop scoresheet states as much. Umpires and visitors view it differently, however, so 11.00am it is. Ah well, it will get them home for *Antiques Roadshow*.

BBC Radio Cumbria is here, broadcasting live, commentator Mark Mcalindon telling listeners of light showers first thing with the possibility of more to follow. The occasional blast of sunshine teases warmth, but otherwise there is a chill in the air. Even on such a morning, the views rolling out towards the Yorkshire Dales and North Pennines offer an imposing backdrop.

Penrith CC have played here since 1907, south of a settlement that staged its first game of cricket circa 1830, various short-lived 'town teams' rising and falling thereafter. It was not until 1866, however, that 18-year-old solicitors' clerk George Dennison sparked the modern-day club into being, named Penrith United Beacon to begin with on account of playing at Foundry Field, a.k.a. 'Soldiers'

Field', beneath the squat, stone hill-monument Beacon Pike, built in 1719, from where messages were sent by fire and smoke across the Eden Valley and out towards Lakeland and beyond.

At first, Tynefield' would indeed have been parklike, set in acres of lush green woodland and the sort of pastures seen in a watercolour painting donated to Rev. James Fell, the vicar behind the move, on his retirement. Post-World War Two, however, a pair of schools and a housing estate were built around it, giving the venue a hemmed-in feel, those long-range views notwithstanding. And even allowing for that original beauty, Penrith's first year here saw eight games rained off.

Today, for their first game of the season in their home county, Cumberland are unchanged from the side that took the field at Scunthorpe three weeks ago. Having lost the toss, skipper Gary Pratt opens the batting with Sam Dutton, the pair building steadily when Toby Bulcock arrives with his partner, Gemma, and the couple's baby daughter. It's Father's Day and Adam Syddall's wife Ruth and their baby son are here too. In front of the pavilion, Ruth spots secretary Rob Cairns and his wife, Lesley.

'Ooh, you look brown. Where've you been?'

'Tossa.'

'I was only asking.'

Michael Slack is again absent and will be missed. Since opening in the Knockout Trophy defeat to Cheshire, he has been in fine form with club side Wigton. Against Cleator last weekend, he hit an unbeaten 151 in the Cumbria Cricket Board-run County Cup, an innings numbered by many observers among the best they had ever seen. Gary is in jaunty mood, having been in the runs with 89 not out for Richmondshire yesterday, against Barnard Castle. Mattie McKiernan, batting three here, took four wickets in that game, while Bob Carr, Matty Cowling and Sam Wood played too. Of that Richmond quintet only the latter does not start the day in Penrith, but he will turn up later to watch the second fixture.

'Good job it's an 11.30 start,' quips Toby, himself contributing one wicket and four runs in a narrow win at Wallasey, before another late night with Leigh in the Liverpool Comp. Meanwhile, Gary and Dutts motor on, their run rate almost 12-an-over from the off. One slashed shot bounces up the pavilion steps and whistles past Rob's nose as he chats to treasurer Eric, chairman Neil (Penrith being his club) and faithful follower John Patterson. In competition terms, given other results, two wins today and a trip to Wormsley as part of the four-team finals day remains very much a possibility, so there is a lot to play for – has that now sunk in?

Gilbert patrols the boundary, stopping here and there to chat, as is his wont. Due to 'having had a turn' recently his driving licence has been revoked. Temporarily, he hopes. He'd planned to visit Scarborough next week, to watch Yorkshire in their annual cricket festival, but can no longer get there. Also off the radar is next weekend's Championship opener at Wisbech. Nor will Eric be going to Cambridgeshire, the first three-day game he has missed in a decade, due to a hospital appointment. He admits to having made a first umpiring mistake in 43 years at Cockermouth yesterday. This time Carlisle were the visitors and their South African professional edged a catch behind. Eric's finger stayed down and Sempy, Hodgson (12th man today) *et al* went ballistic. He could have reported them to the league if he'd been of a mind to do so, but decided against it.

Out in the middle, the openers are playing shots and finding boundaries on a fast outfield. It's all very T20 and entertaining.

Staffordshire's captain is Kadeer Ali, Birmingham-born older brother of England's left-handed batsman and right-arm off-spinner, Moeen. He is destined to bowl Dutts, but not for a while yet. The boundaries keep on coming, Cumberland reaching the half-century by over five. When the previously expected 11.30 start time arrives, they are already set fair, 83 without loss.

Another four jumps the rope, narrowly missing Rob's knee this time – glass of red held protectively to his chest. Are they aiming for him deliberately? Soon after, Gary mistimes a hook and is caught for 36, before Dutts completes his 50 with a thin edge the 'keeper can't stop, to earn a ripple of applause. His innings is impressive, but this early there aren't many in to appreciate it. Those who are here see McKiernan time another lovely four with his first contribution.

'You don't get scoring like this in the BBL,' says Lesley.

'Barrow Bash League?' quips Rob.

The scorer, Geoff Minshaw, is getting a Big Bash workout too. Mid-way through, Cumberland are 119 for 1, Dutts on 66 and going faster than Donald Campbell. Among a panoply of tricks, he scoops two outrageous sixes over his own head – Harlem Globetrotters-style. The first of those moves him on to 93, the second coming after his only ton so far this season for club or county. It's his second ever for Cumberland CCC, though, the first achieved against Norfolk at Sedbergh (pronounced 'sed-ber' in Cumbria) back in 2016.

A display brimming with confidence ends, bowled Ali, for 112, Cumberland now 180 for 2 with four overs left. BBC Cumbria's co-commentator nips away from the desk to ask Dutts if he'll chat about his impressive stint on air, but slopes back empty-handed: 'He's not scared of fast bowling, but he is frightened of microphones.'

'Disappointing,' mutters Neil, mindful of lost publicity.

The runs though keep coming and as another six flies into the fenced-off school next door, the question arises of spare balls, since they are tricky to retrieve. Eric says they were given eighteen white ones and these must last the season, although Gary had taken one away for practice. 'He's very thorough,' nods Neil. Anyway, with this ball now lost, there are sixteen left, more than enough presumably.

Jacques du Toit enters the fray and looks set to belt it about too, before he is pouched on the boundary for seven. Soon after, Mattie punishes a long hop for his 50. One run later, however, he too is caught in the deep and Matty Sempill is padded up. Gary says 'fours and sixes' as he goes by. Sempy may just be in the mood to celebrate having, on Friday, landed a student work placement with Cumbria Cricket Ltd in Kendal. Among other things, he will help to organise women's softball festivals and an under-19s T20. With Bob Carr out for 1, Sempy and Cowling finish on six and four not out respectively in a total of 221 for 5, before they all limber up again in the outfield.

Staffordshire too start powerfully, with a four and an enormous six in the first three balls. But before the over is out, opener Peter Wilshaw is bowled by Josh Fallows. In the third over, Toby takes Kadeer Ali's wicket, lbw for 8, as skies brighten and a crowd builds. The bar area has a social club feel, its adjoining 'function room' filled with pensioners queuing for Sunday lunch. The woman doing the catering was once a pub landlady and, on packing that in, moved on to the cricket club. Her locals followed, for the food if not the sport. Strung out in a line of seats and wheelchairs, feed finished however, some do take an interest in events through the pavilion windows.

From the bar comes the sound of shuffling dominos as Staffs

reach 64 for 2 after six overs, numbers three and four in their order assuming control. When the latter smashes Jacques for six it looks like both sides will score highly, until the South African then bowls his assailant. When Syds grabs another, caught Fallows, Staffs are suddenly floundering on 79 for 4. Their run-rate is comparable with Cumberland's, but wickets tumble. A couple of balls later, Gary, at gully, contributes the first of three catches for Syds's second victim in an eventual four. The hosts are in good spirits, their enthusiasm matched by noisy banter. 'Arm like a leg, Bob,' Dutts tells Carr after a shy at the stumps, while Syds twice outpaces the younger man to prevent a second run off his own bowling.

One man with a hell of a throw is Mattie McKiernan, fast, hard and direct with pinpoint accuracy. His bowling style, however, verges on eccentric. He licks his fingers, tosses the ball from one crooked arm to the other, makes to set off and takes a little skip, slowing to walking pace for three strides before exploding into life as if cattle-pronged and releasing, with a clockwork whirl of his right arm. Normally, it brings rewards, though not in this match – no wickets at a cost of 22 runs in three overs.

When Gary takes a diving catch off Syds it draws a wolf whistle from Toby, who rarely shuts up in the field whatever the scenario. Staffs move on to 101 for 7 although defeat is just a matter of time, number eight Daniel Richardson a mere nuisance. 'Keeper Cowling stumps him as he wanders down the wicket hunting runs. The game is up when Penrith's own Greg Hall is given chance to turn his arm and duly takes the last two wickets, the first with the help of another Gary Pratt catch, the latter a perfect yorker. Bob Carr feigns disgust, having been promised the next over. Greg's parents then sweep the wicket, foregoing lunch ahead of game two. Three overs left unused, Staffordshire finish 141 all out. And for Cumberland, that means two more T20 points are in the bag.

'They are reading the wrong script,' sighs Eric.

*****

Greg, like Sempy, was active in a couple of other county fixtures late last month – those development games against Myerscough College promised at the Crooklands meeting. Both were one-dayers, played midweek and on the road, in which a squad of supposedly up-and-coming county talent faced two teams of students from that seat of learning's Preston and Old Trafford campuses. The first was staged on Wednesday 30 May at Fleetwood CC on the Lancashire coast, its follow-up a day later at Ashton on Mersey CC. In both fixtures, the 22-year-old Hall was team captain.

As will later become apparent, Cumbria Cricket Ltd, primary providers of development in the county, take a structured approach to nurturing talent, with seasons organised across several age groups and both genders. By comparison, Cumberland's activities are more of an afterthought and not just in terms of the calendar. In reality open age, club players from beyond the county borders are invited to participate, with a view to exposing them to cricket at a higher level. Indeed that's the route into the Minor Counties several current squad members have taken. Wednesday's development side featured three lads from Cockermouth, two each from Carlisle and Blackpool, and one apiece from Penrith, Egremont, Workington and Newcastle. At Ashton on Mersey, Blackpool's duo were to be swapped with a pair from Rainhill and Edgworth.

Ahead of a 50-over game in which no bowler was allowed more than ten overs, Eric and Steve Sharp were busily re-arranging their accommodation plans. The squad was booked in for an overnight stay at Bloomfield Road, home of Blackpool FC, eight miles south down the Fylde coast. Scorer Geoff was also in situ, along with coach Chris Hodgson, who has been known both to play for and captain the development side but did neither this summer.

Newspaper back pages revealed that among the players called into the ICC's World XI for a T20 international fund-raiser against the West Indies at Lord's was fast bowler Tymal Mills, who'd turned out for Suffolk in T20 clashes with Bedfordshire the Sunday before. Set against that was an article in *The Cricketer* – '10 Premier League players for counties to watch' – based on data from the analyst Dan Weston, in which their vision of the dominant stepping-stone to the first-class game was laid bare. Among names plucked from East Anglia, Yorkshire, Nottinghamshire, Birmingham, Bradford, North Staffordshire and Cheshire was 21-year-old Alex Willerton, who had just faced Cumberland in Scunthorpe but was listed here with club Bracebridge Heath of the Lincolnshire Premier League. Others had

Minor Counties experience too, yet nowhere did that historic competition merit so much as a passing mention.

Fleetwood, in the Northern Premier League since 1952, have played at Broadwater since May 1924, having in 1902 been founder members of the Palace Shield. On the outskirts of town, their ground is reached by negotiating tram-tracks and an eccentric roundabout, complete with a statue of Eros and sponsored by throat sweet manufacturer Fisherman's Friend, whose factory is just up the road. Its product, developed by local pharmacist James Lofthouse in 1865, originally came in menthol and eucalyptus liquid form rather than the now familiar lozenges, according to the website. But glass bottles weren't exactly compatible with trawlers ravaged by icy waves in the storm-tossed North Atlantic, hence the need for reinvention.

There was another reminder of Fleetwood's prior position as an important fishing port in the colonies of seagulls that nowadays target chips rather than ships. On every second streetlight they perched, impassive, as morning haze turned to afternoon sunshine. Myerscough's coach, Brett Pelser, a South African, had the air of a PE teacher. 'Did we win the toss?' he asked his young skipper.

'No,' the lad replied in all innocence. 'They lost it.'

Scorebox out of order, Geoff was seated behind glass at a trestle table in the pavilion, occasionally wafting a white card to acknowledge the signals of umpires unable to recognise his hand signals. Later, he'd complain of 'about fifty flea and midge bites' at a ground built on a traditional Victorian footprint – cricket field adjacent to football pitch, bowling green attached. As the game began, Cumberland's 15-year-old fast bowler, Sam Thompson, fired them down with pace and accuracy, having got three wickets for Workington's open-age side lately. He failed to take wickets, however, which was not the case for Blackpool spinner, Josh Boyne, who bagged two. He would also contribute an unbeaten eight runs, one more than batting partner Marcus Stables, son of Alan, last seen spectating at Cockermouth. Home from uni, Marcus had just played in his first North Lancs and Cumbria games of the season, against Workington and then Carlisle on Bank Holiday Monday. Quickie Coady Scott, meanwhile, had taken all ten wickets for Egremont the other week, in Division One of the same competition. Not yet 20 and inexperienced, Steve and Chris suggested he might need to move clubs to develop fully, not just mess around in his comfort zone with mates on a Saturday. And this was his chance to impress. 'He'll be nervous,' Steve predicted, but the object of discussion took his and Cumberland's first wicket in his debut over, before going on to collect an eventual 'four-fer'.

Before a red-brick clubhouse with a whitewashed frontage and bolted-on squash courts, opened by West Indies and Lancashire captain Clive Lloyd in 1977, Chris rocked back on a bench, took a swig of what looked like cappuccino and spoke of his ambition to foster a club mentality in a group of – largely – strangers. 'Hopefully young club players can see this as the next step up,' he said, 'get a taste of how it would be in the Minor Counties. They are put up in hotels, have their expenses paid and so on.' Before the formation of this set-up six years ago, there was no such bridge. Yet only the other week at Cheshire, the county had been able to boast six Cumbrians in the side, each of them having moved up via this very 'system'.

Chris, born in Whitehaven, has played cricket since the age of five, when his parents were sent a letter from school inviting their son to try the game at Cockermouth. That he did and it was nothing less than the start of a love affair. Aged 12, a left-hand bat and right-arm off-spinner, he won selection to his first county representative team, thereafter having his ups and downs, dropped by the under-14s before being recalled a year later. 'From under-15s there is a big jump to under-17s, who play two-dayers,' he said, and that helped him towards Cumberland, for whom he debuted with 'a nice little trip to Norfolk' in 2011. 'It pushed me to another level.' So much so, he spent three years as a professional at Wigton, until Cockermouth asked him to return. Having played in their second team as a 13-year-old he was pleased to do so and acted as their professional too for a year. As was seen against Haverigg, he is at Sandair still.

Cockermouth is also where he met Ben Stokes, one of a bunch of childhood friends who would: '...play down this lane, five to ten of us, with a tennis ball.' In summer holidays, they went to the club to play cricket. 'We had a very good team through the age groups, all mates together. I captained the under-15s when we won the league and cup. The under-13s and under-11s did likewise, happy days. Youth cricket in general seems a bit dire now in Cumbria, but at Cockermouth we are in schools and still attract a lot of kids.'

Time moves on as Hodgson, now 29, is only too aware. 'We

had no iPads or Xbox or anything like that,' he said. 'You still played outside back then, plus cricket was on terrestrial telly, so more people could watch it.' In evidence, he cited the 2005 Ashes. 'I used to work over the road from home and my dad would come and get me whenever there was a wicket. He knew the owners. I remember Gary's run-out, of course, like everyone else. Who could have guessed that one day we'd be in the same team?'

And it turned Chris has been coaching almost as long as he's played. 'I was asked if I'd help with the younger ones at the club and loved it. I thought this is what I'd like to do. In Year 11, you did work experience, so I went around the schools with my under-13s coach, John Gibson, who used to do this job, and helped him for a year. Then I went to university and did a coaching degree. Finishing there, I had a word with him about how to set up my own business, which he also helped me with. At first, I was doing after-school clubs and associating with schools that already knew me, built a reputation. When John had too much on he gave it to me and luckily I got quite a big contract off the School Sports Partnership. John retired and all his contracts came my way. That was eight years ago now.'

Is there a decent living to be made as a professional cricket coach? 'Yeah, I can live on it, for sure, and I enjoy what I do. Some schools get me in privately, out of term, so I'm active all year round.'

Then there's the relationship with Cumbria Cricket Ltd, the county board with which Cumberland CCC has its issues, and vice versa no doubt. Hodgson helps coach their district team in his area, age group sides from under-11s to under-15s: '...and this year I've been doing a lot with the women's and girls teams, which is kicking on and being pushed more.' Is there any conflict with Cumberland and its development team? 'It has its moments but, overall, it's nice for me to see what's coming through for both organisations. I can push players on to Cumberland, which has happened over the past few years and, with kids like Sam Thompson, is happening today.'

The one thing being player-coach of Cumberland CCC does not involve is any actual coaching of the senior county side: 'Maybe a tinker in the nets to sort someone's action or whatever. In the past we've had a get-together before the season, but that's just about checking on fitness and catching up. There are no sessions for the first team because it's hard to get everybody together with the distances between everyone. Anyway, they play regularly with their clubs, scattered around the country, and know their game by now.'

For Chris Hodgson, cricket is seven days a week commitment. 'It's my life, isn't it?' He might get Monday night off, if there's no three-day Minor Counties Championship fixture, otherwise he nets every night or is at some form of training, works through the week and plays on Saturday and Sunday.

As Myerscough's innings drew to a close, 195 all out from 44 of their allotted 50 overs, Chris and Steve weighed up the batting order. The latter scribbled numbers on the teamsheet and passed it to the former, who nodded as Fleetwood's groundsman rode by on a motorised roller, his pet collie flirting with being flattened while trotting loyally alongside.

*****

Eric Carter has several more miles on the clock. A committeeman since 1986, he has been Cumberland's treasurer since 2001. Well before then, in 1979, he acted as treasurer of the Cumberland Senior League that, a year later, amalgamated with the Eden Valley League to form the Cumbria Cricket League, the name of that comp lasting until 2005 when Eric stood down.

In 2006, the CCL merged with the North Lancashire League, Eric by then just as well known locally for an umpiring career that began in the Cumberland Senior League in 1970 and lasted there a decade. Around halfway through, in 1976, he also began umpiring in the North Lancs and continued to do so when the competitions merged, granting him status as the North Lancashire and Cumbria League's longest-serving active umpire. The chronology encapsulates a long, winding and very often confusing road for league cricket in a county that seems never quite to have known how to organise itself for the last half a century at least. Eric though has been a constant, carrying out his every duty with trademark attention to detail, every thrust and parry of fortune – and misfortune – met with the trusty swordsmanship of his heroic lookalike, Touché Turtle.

Born in Workington on 27 August 1946, just as the dust clouds settled on World War Two, he came to the game while an apprentice toolmaker at Heavy Duty Alloys who played in the Cumbria Senior

League, cricket being a working class sport in the town. Unlike his old teammate, Alan Stables, he wasn't very good: 'But in the second team you'd to provide your own umpires, so that's how I got involved in that.' Soon he was playing only in midweek and, by the age of 22, spending his weekends counting to six and helpfully holding hats. A workmate, Joe Lister, introduced him to other leagues too.

Like most work teams High Duty Alloys are no more, their closure having nothing to do with Eric's exit after thirteen years. He then spent the same amount of time at British Steel before becoming technical publications manager at BNFL for eighteen years. Seventy-two in August, he hasn't missed a season subsequently, with pocket yearbooks to prove it. 'The minimum number of games I've done is ten. When I was doing it "full-time", I was umpiring weeknights and twice at weekends.'

Being the longest-serving umpire bookends nicely with how, at the start of his journey, he was the youngest ever to take charge of a Higson Cup final, culmination of the North Lancs and Cumbria League's knockout competition. As pals hit fours and sixes and got worked up about their rightful place in batting orders, Eric revelled in being a facilitator. 'I like to organise,' he admitted, gazing glassy-eyed at Fleetwood's clubhouse opposite, from where Cumberland's batsmen were soon to emerge. 'I like to manage what's going on, like today. I'm happy when I'm in control.' Control freak then? 'I wouldn't say so, but I don't like for people to be asking what we are doing and where we are going and so on. It's good for the club, knowing someone has it sorted and that it all fits together like a jigsaw.'

At the start, he wasn't interested in joining Cumberland and continually rebuffed the approaches of Ted Roberts, the club's long-serving publicity officer. Engaged in a fifteen-year spell as treasurer at Workington he had enough to do, until persuaded otherwise by his hometown club's persistent former county player Barry Parker, then on the committee and later Cumberland's chairman of cricket. Even so, by his own admission, Eric didn't get involved much in those early years. It was only upon becoming treasurer that it began to consume his life. And since retiring from work ten years ago, his contribution to the overall running of the club has widened, more so with the arrival of Mike Latham as chairman of cricket in 2013.

'You sort of progress into things without meaning to – jobs

need doing, so you do them. Especially when you can't trust others to do them right.' Indeed, the go-to catchphrase around here is very much: 'See Eric...'

Generally, he takes such responsibility in his stride, although there are irritations. 'What I don't like, I'll be quite honest, is when people phone up on a Saturday morning asking if their girlfriend or wife can come. I don't mind organising the hotels, but that annoys me. "I'm not going to be there tonight, I'll be there in the morning..." It's just a nightmare. What you are trying to do really is save money for Cumberland County Cricket Club and it's very difficult.' Other problems are less common. Being 15-years-old, young Sam couldn't room on his own or with older lads so would have to share with his dad, who was handily there as a spectator. How many hours a week does Eric put in? 'I wouldn't like to say – if you asked the wife she'd say "too many".' Fortunately, Margaret enjoys cricket. 'When we got together she would come around all the grounds but sit in the back of the car, reading or knitting.' She had come on this trip too, but wasn't about today, opting to go shopping in Blackpool instead. 'She's looking for a jacket for a wedding. No,' he corrected himself. "Actually, she's on to accessories now, I think she's after a fascinator...'

Never a day goes by when Eric isn't up to something cricket related, Christmas and New Year's Day included. 'Once the season finishes, Mike starts the yearbook and is asking questions about this, that and the other. And then when it's put to page, he'll send it to me and I'll proof read it.' It's then that his BNFL experience comes in handy. 'I don't mind helping Mike out. During the years John Hurst was editing it I kept that quiet – I didn't want another job!'

Having been around the club so long, Eric is in prime position to judge how the spirit of Cumberland CCC has changed over the years. 'In the early days it was very cliquey, but it's not anymore. We have tried to develop into a club rather than a representative side. When we go out, as you'll see in the three-day games, we all go out together. Not two going here and two going there. It seems to have filtered down to such as today, when they all seem to be getting on. The atmosphere on the field has been pretty good, hasn't it?'

With the county side, he credits Gary Pratt's tenure as captain for having a lot to do with that, the skipper and his partner, Leanne, having become firm friends with the older couple. 'They call us their adopted parents – and now Leanne is expecting their first baby they want us to live over there, near them! It's the Championship games that help to build such relationships. We had a weekend away once at Bolton Wanderers' hotel and, after walking around for a while, stopped for a drink. There was Richard Gleeson and Toby Bulcock sitting with their arms around each other in the beer garden. Richard was about to become a pro at Blackpool, while Toby was off to be pro at St Annes – local rivals. In another two weeks they'd be at each other's throats on the field. It's a small world this. We get players recommended to us, such as this lad Mike told us about, Josh Boyne, who is doing okay today.'

But what of the bigger picture? Summertime and the living is easy – unless you are a Minor Counties treasurer. According to Chris Farmer at Scunthorpe last Sunday, the cotton ain't so high.

'The Minor Counties is going in the wrong direction with T20 cricket. You've got to play it, but no one wants to travel all over the place. We've got to do it to get the ECB funding; we'll see just have to see how it goes. Ask anyone on the MCCA committee, we really don't know what will happen in the next two or three years. They are trying to push the Cumbria Cricket board and us closer together. Well, as I stand talking here, we aren't.'

The ECB would certainly prefer to see development games like this as a joint-effort. 'We've told [Cumbria Cricket] not to bother giving us any funding for this, this year, because what they've provided for a full season in the past doesn't even cover the cost of money for petrol or feeding the lads tonight. They expect them to pay for all that themselves.'

Eric confirms Chris Hodgson's explanation of Cumbria Cricket Ltd as looking after everything up to under-17s, but with nothing representative above that – 'which is where we slot in'. Nor, despite its youthful purpose, does he see any sense in reframing the side as a Cumbria, rather than Cumberland, Development XI.

'Anything they run always goes under Cumbria. Anything we run is under Cumberland. This Cumbria-Cumberland business ... years ago rugby union were like us, Cumberland and Westmorland. When they merged they switched their name to Cumbria to be more modern, but now wish they hadn't because they lost their identity. We, on the other hand, retained Cumberland and have still got ours.'

*****

The sun went into hiding, afternoon turned grey. Rain looked ever more likely, so a strong start was needed if the batting side was to find enough time to turn overwhelming dominance into victory, although development games are less about result than performance.

As openers Ben Davidson and Matthew Houston, of Carlisle and Blackpool, prepared to enter the field, Marcus Stables, at three, was ticked-off by the umpires. Towards the end of Myerscough's innings, he'd dropped a catch and kicked a plastic boundary flag in his frustration. The thing ended up on the pavilion roof. 'What happened?' one umpire asked, pulling the offender to one side for a mini-lecture. 'If this was a county match, that would be reported and there would be a two-match suspension at least.'

'Have you banned him?' asked his skipper, Greg Hall.

'Yes,' said the umpire, en route to the middle. 'Four matches.'

'Can you make it five?'

The first over was torrid. Davidson and Houston did well to withstand a dose of very quick bowling and earfuls of racket from opponents up close and out to intimidate. The tactic failed. The duo hung in for 61 runs in 15 overs and the fielding side dispersed.

Ben Howarth, another Blackpool player, came around on a lap, here in support of his Saturday clubmates. The 'keeper had missed the T20 games in Lincolnshire having been hit on a finger-end, an X-ray revealing no break. Eric told him Matty Cowling would keep again at Penrith, so he could rest the digit and be back in the side for the first three-dayer at Wisbech. His replacement couldn't play then, anyhow. Cowling works in Gary's shop in Bishop Auckland and would have to mind it while he was away.

More best laid plans...

Ben, 20, a former Lancashire under-19s player, is quick-witted and acrobatic behind the stumps, belying his diminutive frame. Off the field, he's as relaxed as they come, though with the countenance of someone troubled by an overdue library book. Born and bred in Britain's best known seaside town, he was immersed in cricket from the start. While other kids were riding donkeys on the sand he was out with a bat and ball, in thrall to the club on his doorstep.

Growing up, he was taken by the same father who watched him the other week in Cheshire – and who would thereafter follow his son all summer – to see Lancashire at Old Trafford, when Freddie Flintoff and Matt Prior were in their pomp, the latter a particular inspiration given that he kept wicket. Still, in the way of these things, he fell into the role. 'When I was 11, a coach asked me to do it, as we didn't have one. I was a bowler until then.' True to his phlegmatic nature he said: 'Yeah, why not.' Cumberland came via a call in 2016 from Mike Latham. 'He'd had a recommendation and asked me to join them. Obviously, I did.' He has appeared in most games since: 'I enjoy playing with really good lads.'

Any ambitions? Like his role model and sometime Blackpool teammate, Richard Gleeson, he'd love to play first-class cricket if the opportunity arose: '...so I will keep trying to be the best I can be. You've got to aspire to play at as high a level as possible, haven't you?'

As the 26th over passed, Cumberland moved on to 103 for 0, team manager Steve Sharp mulling over when to retire his openers and give someone else a chance. For now, both were on the fringe of half-centuries. Left-hander Houston, on 49, flicked two runs off his legs to pass that landmark and was called in from the crease just as the paving stones began to speckle green with water. That was the signal for Davidson, on 48, to get a shift on. First, he tried to sweep a ball that just cleared his stumps. Then having been almost run out by the incoming Stables, he notched a single before being caught on the boundary for 49 – no retirement needed.

As Ben Howarth's pal Boyney called for his mark, spots turned to drops. Geoff's scoreboard showed a target of 83 in 21 overs that, it was clear, would only be completed in some parallel universe. The pair faced fewer than 20 balls each, the plug pulled with Cumberland on 143 without further cost, match drawn.

*****

Pub quiz question: name the professional football club closest to the Mersey? Liverpool? Everton? Tranmere? No. It's Stockport, where the river begins, south-east of Manchester, at the merging of Goyt and Tame. Were the riddle about cricket, it's hard to imagine a club nearer to it than Ashton on Mersey CC, tucked down an old mud track on a smelly stretch of water, some twenty miles west of its source.

'Tucked' doesn't really do the club justice. Few can be so well hidden from view, which has been both a plus and disadvantage. On the one hand it gives a ground about a Ben Stokes six from the M60 an otherwise parallel, otherworldly feel, Manchester's busy outer ring road little more than a distant murmur. On the other, being surrounded by semi-rural farmland and conifers disguising a golf course behind one boundary, the pitch laid beneath winding banks of the emergent Mersey on two more, no-one can hear you scream.

While it's hardly rare for cricket grounds to fall prey to fire, the club at the end of Little Ees Lane – only tarmacked since 1991 – has felt the heat not once but thrice since coming here in 1919, having been founded in 1897. According to a wall plaque in a pavilion that has also staged pantomimes in its day, the first blaze ravaged a then wooden facility in 1960. The second, in 1985, led to construction of the current brick building, and as recently as 2013 an outbuilding and part of the scorebox was lost to flames. If that wasn't enough, in 1958 a whirlwind blew off the roof.

To give the set-up its full title, the Ashton on Mersey Cricket and Tennis Club has enjoyed more welcome moments of fame. West Indies star Clairmonte Depeiaza – whose seventh wicket partnership of 347 with Dennis Atkinson in May 1955 set a new world Test record – played here. The Sale-based comedy writer and cricket lover, Peter Tinniswood, best known for his sitcom *I Didn't Know You Cared* and Uncle Mort, personification of northern gloom, was a member in the 1960s and '70s. He went so far as to have an episode of his 1986 BBC TV series *Tinniswood Country* filmed on the site.

Mort's view of life as a 'rich pageant of woe and calamity' may have found favour with a Cumberland Development XI who, when invited to bat first in their second and last game of the season a day later, lost five wickets for 65 runs. They'd amassed 20 of those before the fall of the first, Ben Davidson the victim on seven. Fellow opener Tyler McGladdery, in the side having been with Lancashire Seconds yesterday, enjoyed four balls more, out for 20, Marcus Stables adding three. Batsman number four, the other newbie Jamie Smith, last seen at Scunthorpe as the Cumberland senior team's 12th man, tumbled fifth with 14 after Sempy was caught for 5. At least Smith received a round of applause from another noisy Myerscough outfit when hitting his first run, being a former student at Old Trafford himself.

It all left Greg Hall and wicketkeeper Kieran Trevaskis, brother of Durham all-rounder Liam, with a job on their hands. Happily, they were up to it. Trevaskis forged an impressive 78, aided by a skipper who contributed 31 to an 80-run sixth-wicket partnership. Nor did the lower order do badly. Coady Scott made 25 and Henry Walker a useful 32 in a 50-over wash-up of 249 for 9.

Watching it all unfold was Steve Sharp, as ever a softly-spoken and unassuming presence whose humility belies a personal playing record that puts him among the county's greatest all-time batsmen. He is, however, Lancastrian by birth, not Cumbrian, born through necessity in Barrow-on-Furness in the days when that was foreign land. Not that he sees himself as anything other than Cumbrian now. 'There's no hospital in Millom, my hometown, so when you need one it's either Whitehaven or Barrow ... Barrow was closest.'

His love affair with cricket – and love affair it is – began as a kid in the 1960s, when he, brother Ian and the rest of the Sharps went to live 150 yards away from Millom CC. 'My father was quite sporty. Rugby league was his main game. He became secretary and then president of the local amateur club, but he also played a bit of cricket for Millom's 'B' team.' Uncle Ray, though, was a cricketer and a good one at that. 'He moved away to play for Northwich for a number of years in the Cheshire League. Sport ran in the family.'

From around five-years-old, the lads he played with in Millom's back streets were older on the whole. 'That brought me on a bit, I suppose. At 11, I was opening the batting and bowling for the club's under-15s. At 12, I was in the county under-15s side. So at a reasonably young age I knew I was half-decent, shall we say.'

Not that he was – or is – likely to shout about that. It is just a bare statement of fact borne out by future achievements. Many of his Millom teammates weren't bad either. 'The club always had three or four lads who played Minor Counties. The standard was good.'

Sharp – in his pomp a jackrabbit with floppy hair – has a look of Ward Kimball, creator of Jiminy Cricket, about him nowadays. And like that character he opts to look on the bright side with regard to youthful ambitions never to be. 'I played for Lancashire from the age of 15 to 18, but only the odd game here and there, so you never really felt part of it,' he said. 'One of the Cumberland selectors at the time was from Millom and he asked me to play for them, so I did.'

Steve first represented the county in 1982 while turning out for Toft, scene of this year's opening T20 games. 'I didn't drive at the time and it was a fair old way to travel, Cheshire and back.' He played twice for Cumberland that year and twice in 1983 before a far bigger problem than transport threatened to end his burgeoning career. On a tour to South Africa with the Northern Nomads, a team of club cricketers from Cumberland, Cheshire, Lancashire and Scotland, while bowling he got the yips. Suddenly everything went wrong.

'I prided myself on bowling to a certain standard and struggled to cope. It took me three years, first to accept, and then recover from.' His confidence on big stages was shattered. 'It helped that I carried on at Millom, which got me into a better psychological place as I still opened the batting.' Until, in 1986, persuaded by a friend who was playing for the county, Sharp returned to Cumberland.

'In my first year back, we actually won the Championship. I was a middle-order batsman, batting six, and finished up bowling in the final at Worcester. Two seasons before, I would not have been capable of that at all. That was a big mental breakthrough.'

A year later, things really came together. Sharp was appointed professional at Ribblesdale Wanderers, in Clitheroe. Lifted by the extra responsibility he scored a lot more runs for Cumberland. The undoubted highlight of his playing days though was yet to come.

In 1989, after seeing off Durham, Northumberland and Devon, Cumberland made the final of the one day Holts Cup at Lord's. The game ended with a nine-wicket win over Hertfordshire in which Sharp contributed a magnificent century off 114 balls, reaching the milestone with an enormous six over the Tavern boundary off the Herts skipper, David Surridge, and winding up undefeated on 108.

'I'd been having a good year – the ball was massive. I'd already scored five hundreds for Millom and this particular day everything came off. It was hitting the middle of the bat, one of those times.' Even more remarkably, given what had gone before, while turning his arm he bowled eleven overs at the cost of only 17 runs. 'David Halliwell got three early wickets and they tried to consolidate after that, but it was still nerve-wracking as there was a short boundary on one side.' He shook his head at the memory. 'That was tough.'

How does the Cumberland side of this era compare with the Cumberland of the late twentieth century? 'Back then the average age was quite a lot higher. Now, we are under direction to have an average age of under-26. If we achieve it, we get more money. That's good, I think, because it means we have to play younger players and that's right for their development. They go back to their club, raise standards there, and consequently lift the local leagues as a whole.'

Though justifiably proud of his contribution to the history of Cumberland CCC, Sharp isn't one to dwell in the past however. At least one eye is trained on the future, hence his role as Development XI manager and interest in giving the county's brightest talents an opportunity. Like Chris Hodgson, also at Ashton in his wrap-around shades, he sees value in removing lads from familiar environments and asking them to play for themselves – part of a team, but with the onus on personal performance. 'You can then see how they step up.'

Employed like so many at 'a particular nuclear establishment in West Cumbria' – Sellafield – he is also well placed to take a view on matters tangential. 'I've been there 37 years, all my working life just about. The company were really good when I played cricket, giving me an extra five days' paid "special leave". That helped as it took up 12 or 13 days' holiday a year, often more. 'That's a lot when you've only 25 and a half days. It's a drain, especially when family comes along.' Not that he accepts work patterns as a valid reason for some clubs' difficulties in getting sufficient numbers on the field. 'There's a perception people can't play due to work commitments or work patterns and that happens on occasions, but not very often.'

This summer will not be Sharp's first as chairman of cricket. He filled the role previously before standing aside and taking over the chairmanship proper when Mike Latham so successfully took the reins in 2013. He wouldn't say in so many words that he expects this to be a busy year of transition rather achievement, but did infer it.

'I'll be more involved with getting a team on the field, so expect a lot more time and effort to go into that. A chairman of cricket has to be in communication with the captain, to make sure we've got a balanced side while trying as much as possible to get locals involved. In the last couple of years, the lads coming in have started to improve nicely. Six Cumbrians the other week, five of them top of the batting order – with 36 and 62 from Slacky and Sempy, the openers – that was really good to see.' Not so helpful are those absence headaches, due to competing obligations in the various club competitions.

'Early in the season when a lot are involved in cup matches, that's a problem because a lot of these lads get paid by their clubs. We don't pay them. People like Toby Bulcock commit and lose money, like Gary Pratt has in the past. It's only this year that Gary has been under pressure to play for Richmondshire, as for a decade he put the county first, which has been brilliant. But to compete you need your best players and Gary is one of those. For some of our 19 or 20-year-olds, cricket is the only source of income; they don't have a full-time job. Maybe they go to Australia or South Africa in the winter, somewhere abroad, and have no other steady cash. Nor are we talking massive amounts. I'd say in the region of £4-8,000 a year. It's not mega, but for a lad living at home nor is it too bad.'

With cricket there is always the carrot. 'If they do well with the Minor Counties, go away for the winter, improve, then think about playing second team stuff they can maybe get picked up by a first-class county. Several live on that hope. Some will in the end just have to accept that they just weren't quite good enough. Others, like Richard Gleeson, might get the chance later than others and take it.'

Is there an age when people have to accept it's just not going to happen? 'Well, Richard was 28. Jack Simmons didn't start playing at Lancashire until he was 28, did he? Another of our old boys, Graham Monkhouse, was 26 when he went to Surrey in the 1980s. Some first-class counties now look to pick up late-developers, whereas they didn't get much of a look-in before. Particularly among the smaller counties like Northamptonshire, Derbyshire, Leicestershire, I believe there is a greater respect and understanding that the Minor Counties is good and competitive and generating decent cricketers. The lad we saw at Lincolnshire, Louis Kimber, looks good. He scored 162 runs off 55 balls the other week in their first T20 game at Northumberland – 15 sixes and 12 fours. That's something special.'

It is indeed, although for all Sharp's optimism doesn't ECB head office appear to view the Minor Counties as a relic of the past?

'Obviously, we are under the cosh from a financial point of view. First-class counties get money easily; we have to fight for everything we get. It really is tough, so we've to generate funding of our own.' Even so, the club would rather have raffles than entrance fees. 'We tried charging for entry and it didn't work; better to give people the chance to win something. It's easier doing that than asking them to put a couple of quid in a box for seven hours entertainment!'

Steve, paid audience or not, is aiming for a competitive side in the Championship. 'I've always tried to field those, but the difference between winning and losing is marginal really. We'll compete. The strength of the middle order, with Jacques du Toit in it, shows that we ought to be fairly strong. We've a balance of experience and youth – your older heads, three guys past 35, but a couple of lads of 20 to counterbalance that. We've got strength in depth.'

And he insists that more young cricketers than ever are keen to represent Cumberland. 'Once you start winning, the easier it is to get a team out. When we won the Championship in 2015 we had no problem getting players involved. Same in 2012, when we won the one-day competition. Everybody wants to be part of it.'

When Myerscough got underway, an enthralling game soon developed with the college's Scotland 'A' player, Owais Shah, heading for a somewhat jittery century before being toppled one run short on 99, the first lbw decision of the game. That undeniable bad luck perhaps made up for a charmed life in reaching that point. Debutant Tyler McGladdery proved his worth with a sensational catch in the deep – 'His mother was in the Horse of the Year Show,' advised factotum Mike Latham, here with his dog, Toby. Workington's Daniel Robinson topped Cumberland's wicket haul with three. But in a thrilling finish Myerscough passed a testing target for the loss of seven wickets with only five balls remaining.

Steve Sharp looked happy with a useful exercise. 'If a game goes to the final over it's a good one, isn't it?' Matty Sempill, meanwhile, just looked knackered. Having played for Cockermouth on Saturday, the two T20 games in Scunthorpe on Sunday, and then two 50-over games yesterday and today, he needed a rest. Yet come Saturday he'd be standing in a field half the day with Cockermouth again.

*****

One of the few fixtures it seemed Sempy did not play in during the summer of 2018 – Cumberland's only ever-present player – took place a fortnight later, when Cumbria's over-50s met Durham's old-timers at Keswick. Led by skipper Paul McKeown – a.k.a. 'The Chief' – the side is in Group 1 of an ECB 50+ County Championship split into five groups of eight, alongside Lancashire, Nottinghamshire, Yorkshire, Derbyshire, Cheshire and Northumberland. Of their three games thus far, Cumbria had lost two – to Yorkshire and Nottinghamshire – and tied in Derbyshire.

Played primarily for fun and good health – *mens sana in corpore sano* – with limbs that have seen looser days, there is a perhaps surprising edge of competitiveness to cricket at this level, middle-age spread and all. Group 2 is comprised of Suffolk, Huntingdonshire, Leicestershire & Rutland, Lincolnshire, Norfolk, Northamptonshire, Cambridgeshire and Bedfordshire. In Group 3 are Cornwall, Devon, Somerset, Wiltshire, Hampshire, Dorset, the Channel Islands and Isle of Wight. In Group 4: Oxfordshire, Wales, Gloucestershire, Staffordshire, Worcestershire, Warwickshire, Shropshire and Herefordshire. And in Group 5 are Berkshire, Essex, Buckinghamshire, Hertfordshire, Sussex, Middlesex, Kent and Surrey. Come July, it all reverts to knockout games leading to a final, although past form suggested Cumbria had little hope. Rarely have they come close. Taking 2008 as a decade's starting point, Derbyshire led the winners' table with three, last year's champions Yorkshire had won it twice (and would again in 2018), Leicestershire & Rutland, Middlesex and Oxfordshire once. Today's opposition meanwhile, Durham, had twice won the competition in 2013 and 2014.

On a beautiful Wednesday afternoon at the foot of magnificent Skiddaw, Lakeland tourist central, the visitors, batting first, had reached 124 for 2, some 25 overs into their allocation of 40. Cumbria took heart from that. Keep the bowling tight and a catchable total and first victory of the campaign may yet have been on the cards.

Some years ago now, *Wisden* voted Fitz Park the country's most picturesque ground, a verdict with which only a fool would quibble, especially on a day like this. The backdrop is truly glorious, majestic, formidable, though as elsewhere the impression of permanence is an illusion. This is an altogether capricious landscape.

Close to Derwentwater and Bassenthwaite, at the heart of the Lake District National Park, the market town of Keswick, population circa 5,000, is a day-tripper's delight. Some come merely to window shop in its charming square, others to feed their belly before or after the enveloping fells and gorges have nourished the soul. And there's Skiddaw itself, of course, coated in purple heather, and its neighbour Dodd, kingpins in the chain of upland peaks encircling the place, each requiring a lifetime here to know in all their glory. Lonscale ... Carl Side ... Latrigg with its ridge on top. Grisedale Pike ... Helvellyn ... none of whom would be out of place in *Game of Thrones* or on Middle Earth ... the Scafells ... Maiden Moor ... Catbells ... Walla Cragg ... Ullock Pike – Ullock in old Norse meaning the hill or fell where wolves used to play ... the valley of Borrowdale.

That Norse connection remains evident within the dialect, the majority in these parts ascended from Danish and Nordic farming stock that settled in the tenth century, here to work land rather than rape and pillage as per mythological stereotype. Latrigg, pronounced 'Lajdrigg', means 'bridge of the dead', the name originating with the chieftains buried up there, the better to continue looking down upon their homes and presumably nowadays watch the cricket.

That the area is, however, more likely to have been settled since prehistoric times ought to come as no surprise, the scenery demands it. Evidence of more recent history is abundant and not just in the town's 'world famous pencil museum'. The marketplace itself, in use since the reign of Edward I, is seven hundred years old, Keswick and its surrounds more lately reinvented as a bastion of the arts, evangelical preaching and wildlife conservation. Yet the day before football's 2018 World Cup kicked off with a human rights supporter's dream ticket – Russia v Saudi Arabia in Moscow – came a weather warning closer to home, Storm Hector was about to whip across the north. It was a reminder, if one were needed, that what in nature seems benign and dependable can swiftly turn brutal.

Top tip: Parking in Keswick can be tricky, so if driving west along the A66, don't take the first signed turn into the town, follow the second and park in the grounds of the football club just past a cottage hospital. There is an honesty box for payment – £3 a day. The road sign itself comes soon after another that helpfully advises motorists of a public telephone in Threlkeld, a quarter of a mile away.

From the car, a stroll along a placid River Greta in the company of elderly joggers led to a cricket ground whose surrounding fields were filled with hikers, dog-walkers and a couple of games of mixed-sex rounders – or was it baseball? Ducks splashed in the water and a heron stood sentinel on a rock, mid-stream. As the day progressed and turned milky, Skiddaw would come to be viewed as if through gauze. A vision to inspire poetry. In 'The Cricketers at Keswick', a contribution to *A Breathless Hush: The MCC Anthology of Cricket Verse*, (Methuen, 2007), Bob Horne took up the challenge:

> *Light on the wind and eye,*
> *In their mayblossom whiteness they seem like a newsreel*
> *of something their grandfathers did in the Thirties,*
> *talking at tea of Larwood and Bradman, Verity and Voce,*
> *or sitting beneath black drizzling crags waiting for play.*

The poem concludes:

> *The diving catch at deep extra cover,*
> *the desperate second run to short fine-leg which wins the match*
> *is their vindication, perfection in a perfect world,*
> *as nothing else between birth and death can ever be.*

That this was nominally a Cumbria Cricket affair did not deter Cumberland super-fan Gilbert Johnstone from making the trip from Workington. Embarked on his usual lap, a smile on his face and friendly word for all, he stopped before a pavilion that could relate many a tale of its own. Here sat a few locals and ex-Cumberland players with whom he could chew over old times, former county wicketkeeper Dickie Spruce among them. Also in Gilbert's sights was Keswick's 68-year-old groundsman, Keith Richardson.

Keith, lithe, sun-tanned and enthusiastic, is a local author and publisher and cycled off home to get a few self-produced books he felt would put a club and part of the world he adores into its proper context. No surprise then that along with being a former chairman of the club he is also its publicity officer. 'I thought that was enough jobs to be doing,' he quips. For five years, first-team captaincy was an added responsibility. Having hung up his boots last season, there remains much to be done, some times more testing than others.

Keswick's 1st XI play in the North Lancashire and Cumbria Premier Division, but they have three open-age sides, 2nd and 3rd XIs in the Eden Valley first division and Sunday League respectively.

With junior teams at under-11 and under-13, and a women's and girls squad growing fast, the future he said is bright.

'The other good thing is the All Stars, a wonderful ECB initiative, which has worked really well for us. We get loads of kids coming down, aged between seven and nine.' Keith isn't one to dwell on negatives. 'Grassroots cricket is a battle, but we are bouncing. The answer is to be a focus of the community, so people want to bring their family. Play competitively at the top, but make it somewhere to enjoy yourself.' Activities include an annual fund-raiser at the Theatre by the Lake, '...a lovely facility. We have a big show on there with tribute bands, Elvis, the Beatles ... this next one is Dolly Parton and Kenny Rogers. "Islands in the stream, that is what we are..."'

Being a Wednesday, spectator turnout was low, despite a busy town centre being only yards away. 'But on a Saturday when the first team play and all the townsfolk and visitors come down, we get an average of three hundred, especially if the sun's out. The bar is full, people spill out, we have a barbecue going...' A thought occurs. How come Cumberland don't play Championship matches here? In fact, why isn't Fitz Park their county ground? It's an astonishing setting, handily placed for transport, ready-made audience on the doorstep. It turned out they once did so, until the climate intervened.

Keith has been a regular at Keswick since the age of 11, when he first came down to junior nets.

'They are still trying to get me to play this year, but I'm not sure.' Didn't he fancy a dabble in the over-50s? 'They're a bit young for me and I enjoy watching.' According to Keith, Keswick born and bred and the town's chronicler-in-chief, cricket has been played here since the 1860s, though no record of it then exists. The pavilion – or latest version of it – was built in 1995, retaining an old wooden structure at its centre that is a remnant of the original Victorian one built around 1880, when the club was constituted. That was also the year when the park itself was created. 'Somebody had a bit of vision. A suggestion that it be sold off as building plots worried a fellow called Jenkinson, who campaigned to raise funds and buy it on behalf of the town as a leisure space.'

A one-time features editor of the *Cumberland News* who then went to the *Cumbrian Gazette*, Keith officially retired in 2007, though the tap of work was never fully turned off. What with a club to run and all those books to write and publish – the first of many being *Ivver Sen* – '...which in the old Norse dialect means "ever since" – the days are just not long enough. He points to the trees that hide Great Hall, home once to Samuel Taylor Coleridge and Robert Southey. 'I've been asked to do a talk to raise money for providing accommodation on Skiddaw, a fund-raiser,' he went on. 'I'll tell them about 1815, when the Duke of Wellington beat Napoleon at Waterloo and people from the Hall climbed Skiddaw, lit a bonfire, got drunk on rum and rolled barrels of blazing tar down the mountainside. Imagine that!'

As elsewhere in Cumbria, a real and present danger came via the floodwaters of December 2015, in Keswick's case with deposits carried by the normally benign Greta flowing past the lower outfield. 'Storm Desmond was the worst thing that's ever happened to this club,' Keith said, of what became a horror show. 'Water came under that gap by the bridge and submerged this entire area, including the cricket ground and pavilion. If we were standing then where we are now, we'd be under water. Inside the pavilion, it was three feet deep, but the real trouble was everything else it brought with it.' Namely, hundreds of tonnes of silt from landslips upriver. When the water receded, Fitz Park was covered in the stuff. 'The whole square ... we had boulders on ... entire trees. A caravan site washed down! The tangled wreckage all ended up on here.'

At which point, you have two choices. Either throw in the towel or set about clearing things up. No prizes for guessing the route taken by Keith Richardson.

'First of all we decided to get what we could off the square – using chainsaws if we had to. Then a light JCB removed all the silt, which took a fair while.' Upon closer inspection just under three years later, scars on the pitch made by the wheels of lorries removing those mini-mountains were still clearly visible. 'The drivers kept to the same tracks or they would have done a lot more damage; the furrows were about three-foot deep by the end.' The transferred debris was then piled high behind the ruined clubhouse.

Fortunately, along with being a natural optimist, Keith has his pragmatic side. 'We didn't bother to contact the environment agency. They would have said: "Don't touch it. It will be contaminated." We just got on with it. Having never been flooded before, it took us two days to come around, but then we rolled up our sleeves and got stuck in. We had to scrape it off the surface with buckets, couldn't use big JCBs as they'd chew it all up. The silt was over four-foot deep.'

Nor was just the cricket field affected. 'Water filled the entire park, football club included. We got the silt off here as quick as we could, because if we hadn't the grass would have rotted underneath. Everything would be ruined and we'd have been off here for at least two years. It could have finished us. If you haven't got home games it's very difficult.' In fact Appleby, a club in a similar predicament, had been struggling without a home ground for two years. 'They hope to get back next summer; that's how long it has taken.'

Through it all, Keith stayed committed to the cause. 'In January 2016, a lass came to interview me from Border TV, with the river in the background and mountains of silt over there. I told her: "We'll be back on here in May" – and we were!' The square was rough and ready, ravaged by the digger, but just about playable.

As for the Minor Counties, Keith confirmed that period when Keswick did host games. 'It's like everything else, you might have a good groundsman, but then go through a period when there is a bit of a lapse. [Asked later, Cumberland chairman Neil Atkinson will mention leaking covers on one particular pitch.] But we've got the over-50s here now, which is good, and if you look at that square now... We are volunteers, a lad called Tom Bryson, who is actually older than I am, and myself. I do the senior wickets and square while Tom does the junior wickets and outfield. We share the load.'

Keith has the craggy colouring of a man who spends much of his time outdoors. 'Oh, I do, I do. I like being free to come down here and find cutting grass and preparing pitches rewarding. And I absolutely love cricket. There is something very civilised about it, yet it's also complicated. It can be demanding, but rewards the input of players, spectators and everyone involved.' Bursting with civic pride – and why not? – Keith indicated an eye-catching building that is home to Keswick Museum & Art Gallery: '...a fantastic facility that has just been renovated. Beneath it is Café West, where they employ people who need help to get by. The people there are just lovely.'

The Keswick football club chairman, Ben Challis, wandered by, on duty today taking photographs of the cricket, presumably for the local paper. Saying hello, he drew Keith's attention to the workers currently tiling the pavilion roof, the tiles in question having come from the Honister Slate Mine up the road, the last such working site in England and a tourist attraction in its own right. In fact, Keith's dad worked there. 'They are jiggered,' he said, as the builders, by the look of it undistracted by cricket, continued to defy the heat. Keith and Ben then talked T20, the former saying that Keswick proposed just such a competition to the North Lancashire and Cumbria League, but had been knocked back. All clubs are finding it difficult to attract players, he said, 50-over games taking up an entire day or even weekend being the prime culprit. This season, though, was going well, not least due to a couple of dry months and certainly in comparison with 2017 when, after incessant rain, they only played four home games, another reason for Cumberland's reluctance.

Keswick may be the wettest town in Britain – the topography having much to do with that. Before fast roads and trains, travelling here must have been like venturing into *The Lost World*. Yet people did and still do so, in numbers. One such is Keswick's full-time professional, Geeth Kumara, a Sri Lankan who conducted an *ad hoc* coaching session in the nets for a group of young children on the boundary – 'arm higher, straighter... yes, much better.'

'He's a smashing lad,' said Keith. 'This is his seventh season. He coaches all the juniors, gets involved in everything. Just a good man.'

Geeth arrived in 2012. 'I was very excited because I'd never been to England before,' he said. 'But the people were very welcoming and now, although I'm here to play cricket, I think of it as my second home. Cumbria is a wonderful place.' Hailing from Colombo, he plays first-class cricket for that city's Lankans club and through the close season, from April to September, comes here. 'I'm an all-rounder, a batsman who can bowl leg-spin, which is quite useful in these conditions.' He was, he said, made welcome from the start, debate about the value or otherwise of professionals at local league level notwithstanding. You would expect him to be in favour and he is. 'Having a professional can be helpful for the youngsters. And whether I am on or off the field, I try to be a role model, someone they can look to and try to imitate. They listen to me too. Without professionals it would be like village cricket. It's really hard to learn without being around people who are good at it, and have been coached themselves by people at the top level.'

Although the day stayed warm, cloud cover had increased by the time Durham concluded their innings on 218 for 5, a total that ought not to strike terror. The quality of play had been leisurely but otherwise good, creaking bodies running quickish singles should the opportunity arise. Several fielders weren't so bendy nowadays, although just about everyone could see their toes, if not quite touch them. One Durham opener looked distinctly bow-legged, a social phenomenon that, like egg and water cress sandwiches, you don't seem to see much anymore. At tea, the time tunnel feeling persisted courtesy of a TV tuned to a Ceefax-type service and not the actual live match at the Kia Oval, where England's one-dayers were beating Australia in a first meeting between the old rivals since an infamous ball-tampering scandal in March. While the Cumbria and Durham players got stuck into their Battenberg, now seemed like a good time to cross the new bridge and explore the town centre.

The walk-in revealed more Westmorland slate, lots of it, atop rows of guest houses with immaculately ironed table cloths, up-turned teacups and signs reading 'No Vacancies' in the window. To the right, the aforementioned pencil museum, 'Home to the World's Biggest Pencil' no less. To the left, the market square, where jostling with ubiquitous pasty and coffee chains are outlets like Keswick Woollen and Tweed Mill, 'traditional' tea rooms, 'craft' bakeries and traffickers of boots and rucksacks. Pitched beneath a tree, a female soprano busked arias to the approval of ice cream-licking pensioners in a row of wheelchairs before the Skiddaw Hotel. Passers-by dropped coins in her hat, both in tribute to her courage in performing alone – *a cappella* – and out of heartfelt gratitude and admiration, many a shopper hypnotised by a truly enchanting voice.

Back at the ground, Keith swept the wicket, trailed by dust. The wind got up, a hint of rain in the air, Skiddaw's horn threatened to puncture a menacing cloud. Gilbert sat in conversation with skipper Paul McKeown, two popular figures together, in front of a pavilion opened by the latter's brother-in-law, Paul Nixon, Leicestershire coach and columnist in *The Cricket Paper* – 'out EVERY Friday from Test match to village green' – both having married sisters. Chief has been 'a cricketer for ages', still turning out for Workington's 2nd XI. He never played for the Cumberland county side but, around four years ago, became involved with the over-50s and is credited with having re-energised it, communally at least. In fact, he admitted to being critical of Cumberland CCC's selection process, until coming to realise just how tough that job can be.

'It's fair to say we were struggling; the player pool was pretty limited,' he said, as Cumbria's openers, Jonathon Draper and Chris Baldwin, made a solid and controlled start to their chase. 'We had too many players nearer sixty than fifty, so I went around lads I'd played with in the North Lancashire and Eden Valley Leagues, spreading the word.' Matters improved to the point where fixtures were no longer conceded. 'We used to do that a lot. Taking eleven to Nottinghamshire and Derbyshire, which we've done this last three weeks back to back, would have been unlikely.' Nor are Cumbria the walkovers they once were. 'We've got a great team spirit – everybody is proud to wear the red, green and gold. It's a huge honour.'

At the wicket, a steady start improved. Both batsmen looked comfortable, played shots and kept the scorers busy. Such have the Chief's views of Cumberland changed, he contributes an amusing and somewhat eccentric annual review of the over-50s scene to their yearbook, self-deprecation to the fore. It's written in fun, but these were not the well-meaning has-beens his comical pieces might have led one to anticipate. In a record opening stand of 118 by drinks, Baldwin made his half-century, Draper adding 48: '...but hold the mountain goat,' their captain would later write, 'it wouldn't be an over-50s game without a bump in the road...'

In Keswick, Chief had said: 'This is ECB affiliated, not Mickey Mouse. Last year went okay – the side hadn't won for five years but we got two wins in 2017, over Derbyshire and Cheshire.' The recent draw had also put an all-rounder who will 'always try to play with a smile on my face' in good heart. Another big reason for Cumbria's failure to get close to the play-offs was the strength of the pool in which they played. 'The champions for the last six years have come from it – Derbyshire, Durham and Yorkshire dominate – so this is the hardest division to get out of.' There is also an over-50s England side; three or four of the Durham lads at Keswick are part of it. Cumbria had never had anyone selected. 'The criteria normally starts to kick in once you get to the knockout stages.'

At one point, 61-year-old Tony Barrow, from Carnforth, leapt from his seat and tore off after the ball, as another boundary was struck. Well, 'tore' may be exaggeration. Lumbered, perhaps. In any case, it put a target on his head.

'What did you do that for?' his teammates asked, incredulous.

'We've only got two balls and I thought it might go in the river.'

A competitive streak also showed when, in attempting to save a four, one fielder's trailing leg hit the rope. 'Four! Four!' yelled the Cumbrians before groaning in unison as, arms wide, he indicated he hadn't known whether he'd touched the boundary or not.

'Listen, bonny lad,' he told one critic, interpreting the reaction as a rebuke. 'If I'd felt my foot touch the rope I'd have said something.'

'What did you think it touched? A dandelion?'

Another fielder confirmed four runs to the umpire.

Chief was revealed to be a moderniser at heart, albeit less than keen on recreational sides fielding professionals. 'I've been to clubs that pay £8,000 yet haven't had a working shower,' he said. 'On balance I'd have one, but a bad choice can have dire consequences.'

His ideal structure would see recreational clubs playing 40-over games or T20, or whatever, below a Premier League made up of the county's largest and most ambitious clubs. These would feed into the Cumberland (or Cumbria) Minor Counties and his own over-50s set-ups, under-17s etc. A unified connected pathway in other words. Chief accepted though that the present relationship between board and county almost certainly puts such ambitions out of reach. 'It does seem fractured. Maybe that's where differences of opinion and confusion set in. Lines of communication break down and they maybe have different goals. I am certainly in a favour of an affiliated Cumbria Cricket Association. You are stronger together.'

And what of the accusation levelled at the county side that it features too few Cumbrians? 'I don't know the rationale behind that, I don't pick it, but know for a fact that there are good players in the Northern Premier and North Lancashire and Cumbria leagues who would like a chance. The argument is that when they are selected they haven't always made themselves available to travel, and I'm sure there are pros and cons. But Cumbrians always want to watch their own, whatever the sport. I do know from running this, though, what a thankless task selection is at times. There's always someone with an opinion that's different to your own.'

Critics frequently point out that when Cumberland won the

Championship in 1986 and 1999 it was with a team of local talent, although that turns out to be an urban myth. While the '86 side had seven Cumbrians in its eleven, in '99 only two players could claim Cumbrian heritage. Still, Chief thought more locals would boost spectator interest. 'It'd be nice to see a majority of Cumbrian players,' he said, though added that to attract young players, both the sport and county must embrace contemporary thinking. 'One of the things we notice with Saturday teams is that once kids get to the under-15s or under-17s they are gone. The availability levels just aren't there. I've played in and against sides with as few as eight players on the field. Recreationally, 50-over cricket doesn't work anymore. Games are too long.'

Thoughts returned to Keswick, where Chief saw this year as the Cumbria over-50s' best chance ever of a top-four spot. 'We've played the harder teams and are competitive. I'm expecting, if not to qualify, then to win three of our nine games.' That would turn out to be over-ambitious. By season's end, Cumbria's tally will read: won one, drawn one. Drinks taken, the slump in on-field fortunes could be said to have begun right then. In his yearbook review, Chief wrote of 'a collapse of biblical proportions,' in which the last nine wickets fell for only 81 runs: '... noooooo. Disappointment doesn't do it justice...'

Victory over one of the top teams had been in their hands, but now the wickets tumbled one by one. 'Sprinter' Barrow was run out going for a single a man half his age would've done well to complete. As he traipsed off like Charlie Brown, a Durham fielder in the deep took a seat on the ground and appeared to nod off, before awakened by his captain's call: 'New batter!'

Chief went in at six, played across the line and was bowled with only two runs added, the game rapidly slipping beyond them. That said, Julian Cann, a music teacher from Kirkby Stephen, batting at three, did his best to keep at least one end up. But when he was bowled on 37 to leave his side 174 for 8 with five overs remaining, the match went with him. Still, as Chief also reflected in his annual summing up: '...we have to look to take the positives.' One being the presence of '...representatives from all the Cumbria leagues.'

And then there are those health benefits, all the more vital upon entering the autumn of your life with the realisation that your time on this earth is drip-drip-dripping ever more inevitably away.

'It's a Wednesday afternoon and not everyone is retired,' Chief
said. 'In fact most of the guys work and take holidays to play. You've
got salesmen, builders, a physiotherapist, two are retired ... a real
cross-section.' Chief, for example, is a packaging company salesman
in Wigton. 'It's a real commitment, the over-50s, but its nice to play
representative cricket on grounds like these. It reminds you that
reaching 50 years of age doesn't mean you are finished. It may be a
bit slow motion, but we are all of us still young at heart.'

*****

The following weekend at Tynefield Park, ahead of Cumberland's
sixth T20 clash of the season and second game of the day at Penrith,
Gary Pratt has won the toss, but opts to bat first again anyway. Talk
in the clubhouse is of Staffordshire feeling they bowled too short
while the hosts bowled a good length, harder to hit off the wicket.
Staffs are expected to try and remedy that.

Given how Cumberland's first win has nudged them up the
table, interest is now taken in events elsewhere. Cheshire have won
their opener with Lincolnshire. Should they win their second game
none of this will matter. If they lose and the Cumbrians win, with
Cheshire's T20 schedule already completed, Cumberland will then
meet Northumberland at Workington on July 15 with high hopes of
reaching the Finals Day at Wormsley in August. An astonishing
turnaround considering their lack of interest.

The prime spectator spot is a raised grass bank that runs along
Tynefield's uppermost boundary. It is there where a row of benches
is perched, precariously in some cases, extending further the distant
views of limestone uplands subsiding into sandstone valleys. A
number of seats lean so far forward their inhabitants don't so much
sit on them as prop themselves up, held by the seat of their pants.
Good exercise for the calves. Happily for Minor Counties Cricket
Association chairman Nick Archer, the seat he shares with former
Warwickshire batsman and, since 2010, Unicorns representative side
coach Phil Oliver is set upon more stable ground.

Having served four years on the MCCA management
committee, Archer, tanned and bespectacled, close-cropped silver
hair, is in his second year of leadership, predecessor John Pickup

having held the post for twenty-one years. Given current turbulence, for him to last anywhere near as long would be an achievement. Yet despite that, a man of long involvement with Staffs, as captain and secretary, has thus far proved himself a safe pair of hands. 'I think it was generally felt, and John agreed, it needed a bit of fresh blood.'

Based in Walsall, this former England amateur and schoolboy player has been general manager of Edgbaston Cricket Centre and the Warwickshire Cricket Board too, so understands the workings of the first-class county game. And eleven years playing Minor Counties and Birmingham League cricket mean he can offer insight into how this level of the sport has changed.

'Massively. The biggest difference now is the Championship. We've always regarded it as our jewel in the crown, different from normal club cricket. It's three-day games, whereas in my day it was two, which felt contrived, like two one-day games stitched together. One of the results is that it has become a younger man's sport. Also, there were no restrictions on player ages whereas now, to get your full payments from the ECB, you have to meet certain criteria.'

Having strode confidently to the wicket, Gary and Sam Dutton again make a solid start, albeit in less buccaneering style. Runs prove harder to come by and the skipper again falls first, caught and bowled for 20, the score 47 for 1. A wonderful low catch in the deep sees off Mattie McKiernan for 7, halting progress to the extent that as the halfway point approaches only 70 runs are on the board at the cost of those wickets. When Dutts, doing well again on 37 not out, is dropped on the boundary he belts the next ball for six.

Now seems as good a time as any to get the official line on the value to the Minor Counties or otherwise of T20 cricket.

Archer is candid. 'There is a place for it, simply because that's the direction the ECB wants us to go in,' he says. 'We are beholden to them financially, so we'd be pressing the self-destruct button if we railed against it. It's not everyone's cup of tea, but it's the trade-off we need to make to try and ensure that three-day cricket continues.'

How about the bigger picture? The Minor Counties' misgivings seem to be one more expression of widespread dissatisfaction, often vehemently expressed, towards the revolutionary eight-team city-based T20-style competition scheduled for 2020, for example.

On April Fool's Day 2017, a *Sport500* blogger had insisted this latest abomination threatened the 'beloved County Championship, which has underpinned English cricket for nigh on 150 years,' as well as the domestic 50-over game – 'Oh, for the halcyon days of sold-out one-day finals at Lord's'. The already divisive T20 Blast was also at risk: '...the 18 first-class counties will become obsolete as crowds dwindle,' he or she predicted. 'The "next generation" to which the ECB refers will have little interest in watching low-key, second-rate T20 county fare after witnessing the high-octane excitement of inter-city T20, replete as it will be with the cream of the international and domestic crop.'

Following that online take, a writer of higher profile, Matthew Engel, former editor of *Wisden*, contributed a piece to *The Guardian*. 'Cricket is rotting away ... Everything worthwhile about it is being destroyed,' he wrote, in far from the first or last doomsday feature to appear in the mainstream media. In his stride, he went on:

> This is not the game that enraptured me when I was six years old. Nor the game I have written about happily for much of my adult life. I don't care about the St Lucia Zouks. And I won't care about whatever names the 12-year-olds in marketing invent for the new made-up teams when the existing English Twenty20 is engulfed by yet another new competition in the years ahead. This wretched idea was sold to county chairmen by bribery – an annual £1.3m sweetener per county – with a tacit undercurrent of threat. My only interest – in common with many other cricket lovers – is the hope that the damnable thing is a total flop and that we can somehow save the game I once adored, and still love more than the people who have seized control of it. One can say that athletics is in crisis but at least we can be sure that, as long as humanity survives, kids will still try to run faster than their classmates. Cricket's crisis is an existential one.

By July, this new ECB competition will be revealed as 'The Hundred', fifteen traditional six-ball overs and a final over of ten – twenty balls fewer than a T20 scrap. According to BBC online, Southampton, Birmingham, Leeds, London, Manchester, Cardiff and Nottingham will be selected as venues for the five-week competition, '...which will not overlap with the T20 Blast'. Their cricket correspondent,

Jonathan Agnew, will say interest among existing fans is 'lukewarm at best,' backed by reactions below the line. 'What about jetpacks for fielders?' 'Invisible bats?' 'Why not make the stumps out of jelly?' 'Why pander to those with the attention span of a gnat?'

Engel, otherwise basking in 'the tumult of this extraordinary sporting summer', will then rejoin the fray, this time quoting Marvell – 'But at my back I always hear/time's wingèd chariot hurrying near' – before re-aiming both barrels at '...that hotbed of fuckwittery, the England and Wales Cricket Board offices at Lord's. ... The year 2020 has, appropriately, long been designated as the year English cricket would be transformed by the introduction of a new city-based Twenty20 competition to run alongside the existing county-based Twenty20 (founded 2003) known this year as the Vitality Blast, which sounds like a rival to either cornflakes or Red Bull. All week Lord's has been leaking. Five-ball overs! 15-a-side! No, 12-a-side! Abolish lbw! Hey, let's make it 10 overs! No, a hundred balls! That's it!' He will call the concept disastrous. 'English cricket's fundamental problem ... is that it has lost the plot by having far too many different simultaneous plots, making the whole thing incomprehensible. Creating yet another, with completely different teams, is insane.'

Other views will be expressed with greater reticence, concerns clear nonetheless. Only a day after these T20 fixtures at Penrith, for example, Michael Atherton will interview his fellow Ashes old-stager Steve Waugh between innings during Hampshire's Royal London 50-over semi-final with Yorkshire, on Sky Sports. The pair will discuss the difficulties of maintaining tradition: '...while at the same time adapting to the commercial imperatives of the present,' as the record-breaking former Lancashire and England captain Atherton, nowadays an equally astute pundit and journalist, describes it.

'Yeah, look,' Waugh will reply, no slouch in the record books himself. 'Even as a former cricketer you are often not sure which teams are in what final, and with which cricketers.' But the fact is, he'll admit, youngsters love T20: '...and it's getting people [interested] who otherwise wouldn't watch.' Asked whether Test matches are under threat, Waugh will concede what empty stands in the West Indies, for instance, make plain – more and more players are being tempted by vast remuneration, seeing no need to expose themselves to a poorer paid and more demanding game, although: '...genuine players want to know how good they can be.' Test matches test you 'technically, physically, mentally, socially, emotionally, no other sport does that. Twenty20 is great for spectators and great for players, but I'm not sure where it's going to be in ten or twenty years' time.'

As with Tests, so with the Minor Counties Championship.

'Short-form cricket is the way the game's going, we've got to be realistic about that,' Nick Archer says, as his side continues to blunt Cumberland's attack. 'I wouldn't say first-class County Championship cricket is under threat, but it is marginalised, pushed to the start and end of the season. We must be careful not to ignore those signs.' Some form of restructure though is obviously on its way.

In April 2018, Archer's preferred outcome was, he told *Stoke Sentinel* reporter Chris Travers: '...a Premier Division of six with two regional divisions of seven.' He conceded, however, that were Devon and/or Cornwall to be in the Premier Division with Cumberland and/or Northumberland say, players would need five days off work for a three-day game, including a travelling day either side of the match. 'I don't think ECB funding will cease entirely, because they seem to view 50-over and 20-over cricket as a valuable part of their strategy, but ... I don't think they are convinced about the merits of three-day, red ball cricket, which is a worry.'

So how to go about winning them over? 'There are three things we sell it on really,' he says now, as a third wicket comes in the 11th over, du Toit's skied swipe pouched by the Staffordshire 'keeper. 'There's the player pathway of which Richard Gleeson is a good example, coming through Cumberland and making it at Northants. It's got to be the pinnacle of the recreational game, so the best Premier League or club players get the opportunity to play in something a bit different. There are some very good cricketers who haven't got the inclination for first-class cricket. Maybe they've an academic or commercial career, or aren't quite good enough, but still want to play at a high standard. The third is often missed. Research says that our twenty Minor Counties cover 18 million of the total UK population. Those in remote parts, like Norfolk, Suffolk, Devon and Cornwall are well supported and quite a long way from any first-class cricket, so our level of the sport maintains an interest in the sport there as well.' Which in turn, it can be assumed, boosts viewing potential for broadcast partners.

Adam Syddall, passing by on a lap with Josh Fallows, says: 'Different game, isn't it?' There is a line of thought about the two-game T20 scenario which holds that the intensity of victors in game one drops for game two, while the losers' lifts because they tend to be hungrier for victory, a theory backed up so far. It has also turned colder, the last rays of sunshine departed, though dogged Dutts warms everyone up by reaching his half-century before falling victim to another terrific catch in the deep six runs later.

Then comes the collapse. Gary's Richmondshire colleagues, Bob Carr and Matty Cowling, fall with just twelve runs added, before Greg Hall's random reverse sweep finds a fielder's hands and it's 117 for 7. Toby Bulcock contributes an unbeaten twelve, a couple of comedy runs among them, and escapes censure for obstruction on the very last ball. By then Matty Sempill has also been dispatched and Cumberland finish on 133 for 8. Will it be enough?

Nick Archer fancies it may not be, before offering a prediction, when pressed, as to the future of Minor Counties cricket itself.

'My current belief is 50-over and T20 cricket are assured for the next five years, but I'm more fretful about the three-day game. Whether it's on the same level, same volume, I don't know. My big concern is that even with one less fixture than now, only one game needs to be wiped out by the weather and it starts to lack integrity. At the moment the ECB blanket-funds our counties but, in future, it may be that they go down a bespoke route. I wouldn't rule it out. It might put the onus on clubs to raise money themselves, but the common belief is that while some could exist for two years without central funding, the majority would only manage one year.'

And once they start to disappear, there'll soon be no opponents left to play. 'Realistically, there is a very limited lifespan without central funding, so you have to negotiate things, don't you? That's why at the moment T20 is for us the proper trade-off to make.'

Yet the question must be asked. Don't those ECB working group cynics with whom Archer and secretary Phil Caley apparently bash heads, who see the Minor Counties as a drain on resources or rest home for ex-pros at worst and an anachronism at best, have a point? At this stage of cricket's evolution is the MCCA still relevant?

'Absolutely. I think you go back to two weeks ago, when there was a whole set of Royal London 50-over games played. Across 18 first-class counties were 42 players who have played Minor Counties cricket. Alongside that, nine of the England under-19s squad at the World Cup in New Zealand played in last season's Minor Counties Championship. That's got to have relevance. The Richard Gleesons of this world and Ben Sanderson, who when dropped by Yorkshire was able to resurrect his career at Shropshire, are relevant too. Some people would like us to churn out seven or eight players per county per year, but that's never going to happen, is it?'

In the here and now, Cumberland's body language says it all as they amble back on-field. All wear tracksuit tops but Josh Fallows, who will open the bowling again, and 'keeper Cowling. Gary claps his hands, though maybe only to warm them up: 'C'mon fellas.'

A note of urgency is restored however when Bob Carr dives low to take an astonishing catch off the very first ball – Staffs opener Peter Wilshaw, built like a burly, bearded farmhand, having shaped to be a big hitter before falling in game one. By over five, the visitors are 20 for 2, Worcestershire youngster Zen Malik, on debut, caught McKiernan, bowled Bulcock; the fielder doing superbly well to take a white ball descending from grey cloud. Five overs later though, the scoreboard reads 60 for 2, target back in sight. Cumberland have failed to capitalise. Batsman four belts a huge six and Toby is back to seeing the funny side: 'You only have to clear the rope, Michael.'

'Well,' says Dickie Spruce, here too and chatting with Gilbert. 'It's a day out, but it's not proper cricket, is it?'

Michael Hill has become a thorn in the hosts' side, so when Jacques du Toit bowls him for 36, with Staffs now 86 for 3, it heralds a late flurry of enthusiasm that ratchets up a notch when Toby denies Kadeer Ali his 50 by a single run before backing it up with a golden duck for the incoming batsman. A hat-trick eludes him however and Staffordshire are able to settle the ship.

Even so, with three overs remaining, Staffs still require 19 for victory. Du Toit is whacked for six, but hopes rise again as Cowling claims a skied catch to make it 126 for 6. There are still two overs left in which to find the now eight runs needed. When a six is hit off the last ball of the penultimate over, it winds up one win each.

How have Cheshire gone on? 'Lost by eight wickets,' Eric says. 'It's still on! If we hammer Northumberland in Workington...'

He almost sounds excited.

Lap One

The Furness Peninsula

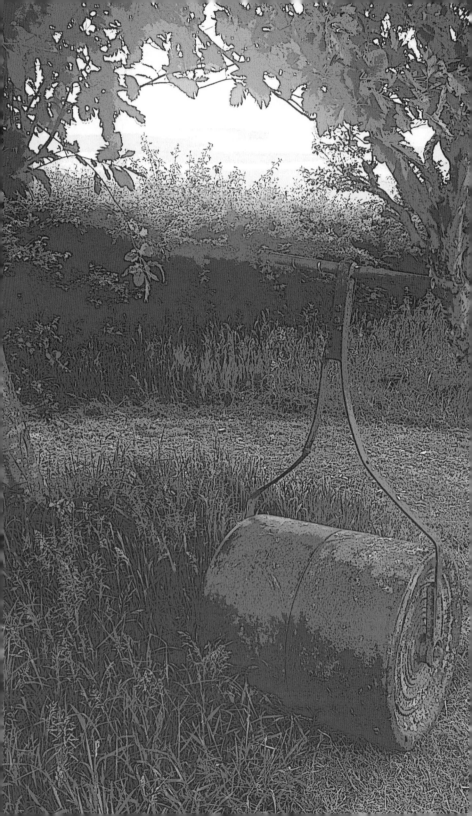

A wet Saturday in June, mist on the hills. We motor along the A590 – 'the longest cul-de-sac in the world' – on course for Walney Island, where Morecambe Bay meets the Irish Sea. Our chauffeur and guide is Cumberland CCC committeeman Mike Latham. In the back sits Toby (the dog), as chilled as a Border Collie can be.

Few have seen more cricket grounds than Mike, as footsore a groundhopper as ever there was. An accountant by trade, he likes a pie and has a finger in several. Player agent, rugby league chairman, historian in several disciplines, he is also blessed with a contact book and inside knowledge anyone out to gain so much as a fraction of a handle on Cumbrian cricket would be a fool to ignore. And already, this is in danger of becoming an unlikely Jeeves and Wooster tribute act, had Jeeves been a sports enthusiast born in Leigh and raised in Bolton rather than a gentleman's valet, and Bertie a distant product of Jer Lane juniors in Bradford.

'Actually, the character of Jeeves was based on a cricketer,' Mike says, taking zero offence to such Machiavellian comparisons as the River Leven estuary, to our left, continues its journey to the sea from the southernmost end of Lake Windermere. 'P.G. Wodehouse was on holiday in Cheltenham. Out walking, he saw an impressive all-rounder at a cricket match, Percy Jeeves, and borrowed his name for the butler.' Furthermore, since I'd mentioned it, the original Jeeves was a Yorkshireman, from Dewsbury. 'He'd been spotted at Hawes, in the Dales, and played for Warwickshire pre-World War One before being killed in the Battle of the Somme, in his twenties, I think. They never found the body. Sad story.'

Dipping in and out of the old county palatine, we pass through Ulverston, over which the Hoad monument stands guard, named for the hill it was built on rather than the eighteenth-century worthy it commemorates, Sir John Barrow. Ulverston is also the birthplace of one half of another celebrated double act, Laurel and Hardy, who have a museum here to their memory. A mental note is made to pay it a visit when Cumberland play Hertfordshire at Furness in July.

'There's an old joke told by a famous barracker on the Hornby Stand at Old Trafford,' says Mike. 'Which two comedians come from Ulverston? Answer: Stan Laurel and Willie Hogg.'

'Willie who?'

'Willie Hogg, sir. Right-arm fast bowler for Lancashire and Warwickshire in the late 'seventies, early 'eighties. Over two hundred wickets in less than a hundred games. Not a bad average, I would venture to suggest. No idea why they picked on him.'

Pure swank.

Norman Gifford, who played fifteen Tests between 1964 and 1985, is another old cricketer to hail from here.

At the tail end of Cumbria we would once have been driving in Lancashire, through Swarthmoor and Dalton, where the A595 coast road heads up to 'proper Cumberland'. We drop into Barrow via Abbey Road, a thoroughfare designed to impress, passing Furness Abbey and a General Hospital in the Hawcoat part of town, complete with a helicopter landing pad handy for rescuing over-zealous ramblers on the fells. Otherwise, Abbey Road's main claim to fame is listing one of TV's *Hairy Bikers* as a former resident. A sign reads: 'Shipbuilders to the world,' a proud boast that rings hollow these days, although the greatly diminished shipyards in question are still visible in the distance. Vickers, now BAE Systems, held godlike status, employing over 30,000 people. Today it's more like 6,000, still a good number, though way less influential.

Eponymous Vickerstown, on Walney Island, will host the first game we're here to see, a top-of-the-table North Lancs and Cumbria Division One clash with Egremont, a town around fifty miles north. The ground is reached by heading through Barrow to the Jubilee

Bridge, which spans the narrow channel that separates island from mainland. It's a route that takes in a couple of sporting statues. Most prominent is Emlyn Hughes, a Barrow boy and the first Liverpool captain to lift football's European Cup, now fronting a modern office block. Less noticeable but also worth a stop is Willie Horne, shielded by trees in a public garden near Craven Park rugby league ground. He led the town team to glory over Workington at Wembley in 1955, in what's still the only all-Cumbria Challenge Cup final. That though is as good as it gets among a mishmash of modern-day retail parks, ornate Victorian institutes, charmless roads and mini-roundabouts. Pubs like the one that was once a Customs House – now promising 'live sport' – and a few giant magnolia hangars add to the 'planning'. Somewhat miraculously, given how everything appears to have been thrown in the air and left it where it landed, a lone row of old terrace houses hangs on by the dockyards. It's a dispiriting spot.

Cross the bridge and you are on the Isle of Walney, largest of the Furness Islands, population 11,000, among whom Cumberland's Rob and Lesley Cairns can be counted. The couple live in an old piggery to the south, part-owners of an independent brewery-stroke-pub of which Lesley is chief executive. Sadly there is no time to call in for a pint – they'll likely be off watching cricket anyway.

Walney also has a pair of nature reserves – no more than a mile wide and eleven miles long, top to tail – plus several sandy beaches. Time to visit those is lacking also. If all this sounds seaside pretty, it isn't really, at least not this bit. The size of the population owes much to the worker-town built here at the turn of the nineteenth century, serviced by the bridge a decade later. Pivotal in Vickers' success was the construction of submarines for World War One. As the twentieth century advanced, that led to housing estates such as the one beside Vickerstown CC, whose ground is named Rainey Park. Grey clouds do seem to be gathering inland, as viewed over the estate rooftops.

'Vickerstown is in *Thomas the Tank Engine*,' says Mike, as he tips the hatchback and releases Toby for a toilet break and stretch of the legs. And later research reveals that this is indeed the real world inspiration for 'Vicarstown', fictional heartbeat of the Rev W. Awdry's Railway Series of children's books, adapted for TV as *Thomas the Tank Engine and Friends*, Walney being the island setting, Sodor.

The boundary rope suggests sea-going vessels. It is huge and draped loosely around an outfield that in other circumstances might be home to grazing sheep. As revealed on entry through a gap in a wall behind the bowler's arm, there are no sightscreens in a venue down at heel. The game is underway and the batting side sits in front of a shed, opposite, with boarded-up windows. Strewn around is broken glass and tell-tale debris of burnt and blackened tin, ripped from fizzy pop cans. The scorebox is derelict. Vickerstown's openers are watched by two men and a dog – namely ourselves – while the fielders and waiting batsmen gape at us in wonderment.

Given how Mike is well known in Cumbrian cricketing circles, it's likely he has piqued their interest. Might he be here on a scouting mission? If so, a good candidate would be Coady Scott, a.k.a. 'Flash', who played for the Cumberland development side the other week, impressing with a wicket and 25 runs at Ashton on Mersey. Today he'll take another couple as Egremont skittle their hosts for 91 runs, before being bowled for 81 in a less than free-scoring encounter.

Given the above – and an esoteric warning scrawled on the wall outside: 'JUNS OFF – NO JUN GAME AT HAVERIGG' – it's a surprise to discover our smartphones still have a 4G signal via which other results can be tracked, though old gadgets can be handy too. One umpire has an umbrella, not necessarily expecting wrath from the weather gods. Having waddled to square leg, he stabs the pointy end in the turf and proceeds to sit upon the handle.

There is an appeal. A finger at the bowler's end rises, as if to divine the direction of a stiffening breeze that ruffles surrounding tufts of rough purple grass. At which the incoming batsman unzips his trousers, jiggles his gonads and thrusts in a protective box, clearly used to the lack of an audience. For us, half an hour is enough.

Over the bridge and driving back up Abbey Road, conversation switches again to Willie Horne, who was also a prominent cricketer here. 'He played for Vickerstown in the North Lancs League and owned a sports shop in Barrow,' Mike says. 'Never made any money because he kept giving boots and playing gear away to poor kids.'

There'll have been plenty of those. A spirit of grandeur remains here and there, but as in most industrial towns and cities the riches made somehow evaded those who worked for them hardest.

We turn left at a crossroads on which stands 'the best-known pub in Barrow,' The Strawberry, and arrive at ground number two in an area where, even today, it's clear the more socially aspirant would have gravitated. And in fact the leafy surrounds of Hawcoat Park once housed Vickers' 'works ground', a philanthropic gesture to the community since sold-off by successors BAE. Nowadays it's a 'sports and social club' and the contrast with Vickerstown could not be starker. Where that ground was virtually deserted, this one is absolutely packed with cars, noise and people.

Hawcoat Park CC share a multi-sports complex with a pair of West Lancashire League football and Cumbria League rugby union clubs. The pitch they play on – above the cricket field – is heaving, as is an adjoining bowling green. A sign reveals that Barrow Carnival is in full swing at a venue where, in the 1950s, cup finals were staged and attracted big crowds. One clue to those past glories is an actual grandstand in which spectators watch Hawcoat's 1st XI play Furness 2nd XI in another North Lancs and Cumbria Division 1 encounter. How they can see much without binoculars is a wonder, the pitch being far away across an entry road that separates the two.

Equipped for multitudes, the ground has an old-fashioned civic feel, a tonic in an age when leisure time is increasingly spent indoors or shopping-until-dropping. Having won the toss, Furness are in the field. One bowler looks barely 14 years old. A young woman stands at midwicket. Here and there, five-a-side football games are going on too, enjoyed by young and old. Groups sit on picnic blankets and in fold-up chairs. On a currently fallow rugby field raised behind, bouncy castles, fairground rides and pop-up food stands evoke comparisons with Sunday promenades in Victorian public parks, albeit with less buttoned-up courtship rituals. As get-togethers go it is uplifting and has one-day cricket at its heart.

Wafted along by the thump thump thump of Lady Gaga and whiff of fried onions on bangers and burgers, our next stop is just around the corner and a less cheery experience – a top-of-the-table Premier Division clash between Furness and their title-rivals Cleator.

As later visits this summer will confirm, Furness CC has its virtues, but a cheery welcome to strangers is not among them when the 1st XI are at home. Had the makers of *An American Werewolf in London* preferred a daytime location for their Slaughtered Lamb scene, when the hikers come in off the moor and are met with cold silence and a pubful of stony-faced Brian Glover-types, Furness Park would have fit the bill. To step inside is to run a gauntlet of glares, be it from an imposing players' balcony, or the scowling unfriendly brotherhood chiselled into a row of benches sunk into the outer wall. And heaven forfend if, while disorientated on entry, that visitor should step into anyone's line of vision.

Cricket has plenty of unwritten dos and don'ts; they help to maintain its self-mythologising as the last bastion of fair play and social rectitude. Such codes are also a good way to detect an outsider, be he of the great-unwashed in the Industrial Revolution or potential waver of foam fingers in the here and now. Some of these rules, like not moving behind a bowler's arm, are important. They can have a direct influence on the outcome. Others, like waiting a second while the bowler runs in, are a matter of simple politeness. At most grounds it is anyway easier to walk behind someone than squeeze by in front. Not so here. From that split-second moment of entry, a visitor must stand stock-still or receive daggers. Then, as play progresses, he or she may take one or two steps further along before being glared at by the next lot of gargoyles. It is only when the over is done that the scoundrel is allowed to proceed again, unmolested.

Such miserablism is contagious. What right-minded person, in the face of such passive aggression, would *not* consider eschewing the convention all together and walk wherever they damn well like … rumba back and forth perhaps, on the spot, like Carmen Miranda in *Nancy Goes To Rio*, singing: 'Can you see all right now, eh? Can you see now? Eh? Eh? Can you?'

Where were we? Oh yes, at the cricket. Furness versus Cleator is (eventually) a class apart competitively from what has been seen on our lap of the Furness Peninsula thus far.

Although early in the season, there is a lot to play for and the home side's new professional arrived today, doubtless feeling the pressure. Well, wouldn't you be if your 'sub pro' (clubs are allowed a stand-in before the actual pro arrives) had just notched the highest individual innings ever seen in the North Lancashire and Cumbria League's 126-year history – 261 not out – from 23 fours and 16 sixes in 152 balls. Not only that, he followed it up with a further 98 runs on Bank Holiday Monday.

In fact, 'Jeeves' Latham had a hand – or microphone – in that too. Twenty-two-year-old ex-India under-19 Shubham Khajuria, from Jammu and Kashmir but summering in Accrington currently, was brought to the attention of Furness when his exploits at church side Oswaldtwistle Immanuel, in the Green Thumb Ribblesdale League, were featured on Mike's midweek cricket show on BBC Radio Lancashire, broadcast from Blackburn.

Premier Division runners-up in 2017, Furness have a great pedigree, founder members of the North Lancashire League in 1892. As the previous tirade suggests, their ground sits in a residential area walled in on all sides, promoting the sort of insularity perhaps that saw the neighbourhood object to their plans for improved training facilities, like nets and a cage, in December 2009; boot on the other foot. Still, life goes on and batting first, Cleator, another coastal club from up the A595, are 50 without loss after nine overs, a promising start. Roared on by support from the pavilion balcony, now blessedly at the other end of the ground, they are soon amassing runs for fun. Sixes ... fours ... none of it healthy for a new ball that keeps smacking sickeningly into the road or those breeze-block surrounds.

Beaten here by Cockermouth the other week, the hosts' title credentials are again being tested. And unlike at Hawcoat Park, the noise from which travels like a distant rumour of jollity, a beautifully manicured pitch prepared by a groundsman who clearly takes the job seriously is the perfect surface for a high-quality contest.

Cumberland's Sam Dutton is fielding, watched by his mum and the family beagle. Sam's dad Simon, a captain of Cumberland for ten years, was a player here too. In fact, the family lives just beyond one of those walls. As he's on the boundary, to be sociable we stop to say hello, between balls of course. The brief exchange however earns Dutts a rebuke from a skipper who, were he captain of England or Australia say, would presumably be rendered apoplectic at the sight of players signing autographs in the deep at Lord's or the SCG. Nor does it impede the fielder's concentration. Almost immediately, it is his catch that brings Furness their first wicket of the innings.

It won't matter in the end. Cleator will reach 238 for 5 before knocking Furness over for 109, via a couple of 'five-fers' from Darren Clark and David Blackwell.

Another Cleator bowler and minor celebrity, the veteran David Rooney, won't be called upon at all. 'He captains England's "Barmy Army", Mike points out, as we extricate ourselves from a bench now revealed as tacky with fresh green paint. Perhaps that's why the old-timers by the gate were so forbidding; they were stuck fast to their seats. 'In 2015, Cleator won the National Village Cup at Lord's, when Rooney and Ian Clark [father of Darren, Graham and Jordan Clark], came in at nine and ten. They needed 60 to win and saw the side home.' The result here, meanwhile, will shunt Cleator to the top of the table, Furness dropping to fourth behind Cockermouth and Carlisle.

Again, we don't have far to travel. The Ernest Pass Memorial Ground, home to Barrow CC, is just up Abbey Road, next to the hospital passed coming in and named for a World War One soldier whose father bequeathed a piece of land previously known as Monk's Croft – because that's what it had been – to Barrow in 1937. In 1984, Cumberland gave the place its Minor Counties debut – visitors Northumberland – amassing twenty-four such fixtures afterwards before the most recent county visit, a low-scoring two-day victory over Buckinghamshire in June 2014. This is also the club that found and developed Minor Counties success story Liam Livingstone, who was recently made captain of Lancashire.

The reason for Cumberland's absence is that, in their blunt judgement, the pitch has gone to pot. 'We had a low-scoring game against Bucks that finished in around 160 overs, rolled them out for 54 and 116 and haven't been back since,' says Mike. 'It's a shame as the facilities are great and the people obliging and pleasant.' Furness, (which to their neighbours' dismay does stage Cumberland games), Hawcoat Park and Barrow are all within a mile of one another.

Barrow however face more pressing issues. Batting first, they are playing Morecambe in Division One of the Northern Premier League, a mid-table outfit from whom they desperately need to take points given how they are already shaping up to be in a relegation scrap. That's a very recent phenomenon in the NPCL, enabled by a link-up last year with the Palace Shield Premier Division into which, in 2017, Kendal and Lancaster fell, to be replaced by Garstang and Fulwood & Broughton. Every 2nd XI too decamped to the Palace Shield competition, leaving the NPCL now with a single division.

Unsurprisingly, then, a drab affair unfolds played to a similar level of enthusiasm as that shown by the club flag, hanging limp by the pavilion behind which the hospital stands. The helipad is to be found alongside the drive leading up to the ground, meaning play may be stopped if a chopper should need to land.

Of most interest today is the chairman's son – and Cumberland squad member – Toby Mowat, who contributes 19 runs with the bat as his side is bowled out for 190. That though is enough for some much needed breathing space, given how his five wickets then help to skittle Morecambe – destined to be relegated themselves at the end of the summer – for a lowly 109. Not that we see much more of the game. With the rain just about holding off, we again hit the road, heading north-east to Dalton-in-Furness this time, where the 2nd XIs of both Dalton and Ulverston are doing battle in Division Two of the North Lancs and Cumbria League.

Well-disguised cricket grounds are far from rare in Cumbria, as has been noted. Railway Meadow must however be among the easiest to miss, tucked down a back street in a town of 8,000 that is best known as the location of the South Lakes Safari Zoo, so toss a few kangaroos, giraffes and penguins into the population count also. Tragically, that is also where 24-year-old Sarah McClay was mauled to death by a tiger in 2013, the most serious in a number of alarming incidents that got the previous owner in bother and only this winter were the subject of a BBC Two documentary, *Trouble at the Zoo*. Under new ownership, nowadays it has regained the approval of the RSPCA, satisfied with its improvements to animal welfare.

As Ulverston's 2nd XI prepare to defend a first innings total of 153 for 6, there are no giraffes in to see the attempt, though were it different even they would struggle to spot the railway line that gives the ground its name, or indeed note any 'meadow'. The train tracks are well-disguised beyond a mass of trees to the rear of the site, while the surrounding fields have in some more recent period been lost to allotments and scrubland. The upshot is that an arena formerly of standing now appears unloved. A pebble-dashed pavilion has a whiteboard out front standing in as a makeshift scoreboard. The actual scorebox has long since gone to grass, always a tragic sight.

Here too an outsider might be stared at, though more out of bafflement than animosity. 'Why would you come here?' the few present seem to say. In the allotments, someone has been gathering firewood, among which is a pile of timber torn from said scorebox, complete with 'Wickets', 'Overs' and 'Last Man' windows, a metaphor if ever there was one. Dalton will take the points today, a five-wicket victory with four overs to spare.

A trip to Lindal Moor, hosting Whitehaven at their pretty little ground, is a more uplifting experience for visitors and ball alike. Both sides are in the North Lancs and Cumbria Premier Division, though jostle in its lower reaches. Come season's end one will go down. Given today's state of play, guessing which ought to have been easy.

On arrival: pandemonium. Whitehaven are 217 for 3 after 34 overs. Their number three batsman, Chase Young, is rattling along on 167, his batting partner a mere spectator with 13. Were overs lost due to some isolated rainstorm that somehow passed us by? No. So many sixes have been dispatched into fields or a neighbouring country lane that the 'contest' has been constantly delayed by fielders searching for the ball. The umpires are sympathetic. There will be no punishment for timewasting and it will remain a 50-over fixture.

Another very obvious explanation is the size of Lindal Moor's field, by far the most picturesque venue today. High on the road to Ulverston, it's a beautiful if tiny setting and Whitehaven's rampaging assassin is a beast. Young, a hefty South African, came to Cumbria, met a local girl and stayed. Almost exactly four years ago, it comes as a surprise to learn he played in Cumberland's development team against Durham Academy, but on that occasion did not hang around, as per the usual complaint. Nowadays, he is a car salesman.

He is not hanging around here either, intent on amassing far more runs than the eight he managed in that 2014 outing. As he belts ball after ball over the wall, it's hard not to feel sorry for the poor saps on the receiving end. Twenty-eight runs are added in the very first over we see and Chase moves to 190 as 300 comes up and Lindal Moor's skipper is left to reflect on the wisdom of – having won the toss – inviting the visitors to bat. That's all hindsight, of course, and to be fair they had taken a wicket with the very first ball. Whitehaven captain Jonathan Stewart was the victim and Keshan Wijerathne the bowler.

Twenty-two-year-old Wijerathne is Lindal Moor's Sri Lankan professional and by now, his early wicket apart, the lad appears to be having a torrid time of it.

As Chase's double-century comes up with a four in the 39th

over, one elderly spectator is distinctly unimpressed. '£7-8,000 for that shite?' he grumbles, his face the picture of incredulity. 'Fucking rubbish. He's no good coaching, neither. Can't speak English.' Another six sails into the middle of next week. 'I don't know where they dug him up from, but he can go back.'

Suddenly, Shubham Khajuria's record innings of 261 not out for Furness against Dalton last week is under serious threat, as Chase reaches 224 via another assault on the Brown's farm shop's forecourt, over the road. 'It's one of those days,' sighs home captain Edward Waind, who vaults a drystone wall and confirms his nemesis has been dropped four times. 'C'mon boys. Let's keep them under 400.'

With three overs remaining, Chase is caught on the boundary, off Wijerathne, going for his latest big hit, and departs on 245 – just 16 runs short of the record. At 388 for 5, the only question now is can Lindal Moor indeed keep Whitehaven under 400? As the last over staggers punch-drunk into view, Wijerathne bowls as tight an over as could be wished in the circumstances only to see Waind drop another catch on 399. With a ball to go, Whitehaven need a single and their tail-enders duly oblige, wrapping up with 400 for 8.

We, however, have a couple more grounds to squeeze in. First up, Ulverston CC, passed en route to Walney Island, whose 1st XI are playing Seascale in the second tier of the North Lancs and Cumbria League. Overlooked by its 100ft tower on that hill to the north-east, theirs is a nondescript ground otherwise, a raised bank parallel to the pitch and a main road the optimum viewing platform. 'We used to play at Tarn Close,' one of a handful of spectators says. 'We've only been here 40 years.'

Ulverston Sports Club, a sign states on the way in, is shared with an amateur rugby league club whose players, having finished their game, watch cricket for a while using a 1970s-style municipal leisure centre as a windbreak. Weeds grow on an outfield looked over by a pair of phantom football dugouts, declining in tall grass. There is little else to see. Ulverston pair Ben Dryden and Milind Metha head comfortably towards a Seascale total of 168 as we depart for another Division One game, Kirkby-in-Furness v Cockermouth 2nd XI, just up the coast towards Askam and Ireleth.

Here is an area that grew prosperous towards the end of the nineteenth century thanks to the discovery of large deposits of red iron ore. A veritable boomtown it was, though alas no longer. A hilly approach still boasts stunning views over the Duddon Estuary, out towards Haverigg and Millom, from where that ore was shipped. 'Askam had a strong rugby team in the late-1890s,' says Jeeves, 'funded by a blast furnace owner. The man was also a cricket buff with links to Ulverston, name of Myles Kennedy.'

Kirkby-in-Furness CC co-shares its home with a community centre and a Furness Premier League football club. It's a compact venue overlooked by mountainous Black Combe and Corney Fell, the former peak shrouded in heather and bracken to lend it an otherworldly, out-of-focus appearance, even on a brighter afternoon. The flashing blue lights of police cars and ambulances, racing to an accident on the A595, reinforce its hazy translucent aspect.

None of which detracts from the match, as Kirkby try to hunt down a Cockermouth total of 142 for 9. Matthew Hodgson, brother of Cumberland's Chris, is about to bowl, having been out caught for 15 while batting. 'Hi Mike,' he says, cheerily, midway through a four-wicket spell that will ensure his side victory with 17 runs to spare.

Also in the side is middle-aged Cockermouth 2nd XI captain Steve Chambers, his first appearance since having a couple of new knees fitted. As set against the charming backdrop of St Cuthbert's Church, whose graveyard butts up to the rear of a working scorebox, hallelujah, it provides an uplifting end to a pleasant, educational and thoroughly exhausting day.

Before heading home, though, there is still time to call in again at Lindal Park. Mike has a feeling the tale there may yet have a final twist and in a way it does, though not in the manner expected.

As the last remnants are removed for 265 (Wijerathne the hosts' top-scorer with 81), Mike spots Whitehaven secretary and chairman of Cumbria Cricket Ltd, Arthur Brown, enjoying a lap with his own pooch. In a spirit of 'What-ho!' our sagacious valet wanders over to say hello, but is roundly and inexplicably blanked.

Days later, an explanation arrives by email.

Arthur had not meant to be rude. It was just that his dog gets excited around other dogs and, what with Mike being there with Toby, he hadn't wanted to put off the batsmen.

CHAPTER FIVE
UMPIRE OF THE SUN

Sunday 24 June, Wisbech, Cambridgeshire. There are no rousing speeches ahead of Cumberland's opening Unicorns Championship match of the season, merely the snap of rubber as Dutts – a bag of nerves – fiddles with his bat handle. 'Got your suncream on, bro..?' Jacques asks, although, having won the toss, Ross Zelem, Matty Sempill and Michael Slack will be sent out first.

Someone passes Dutts a grip-applicator, a.k.a. the 'bat cone'. 'Thanks,' he says, 'this is going to take me ages...' and it does.

Ten minutes before an 11.00am start, the atmosphere in the dressing room is far from intense, light-hearted even, in anticipation of the year's first three-day fixture. A few butterflies perhaps, as manifested in Dutts's cheeky-chappery, otherwise all is calm and congenial. But there has been disruption. Adam Syddall will captain in the absence of Gary Pratt and Mattie McKiernan, Richmondshire having indeed reached the regional final of the ECB National Cup. Today, they are to face – and beat – York. As Geoff Minshaw wanders in to wish everybody luck, Dutts breaks into song: 'One kiss is all it takes, to fall in love with me...'

Another rarity: due to that hospital appointment, treasurer Eric is also missing, as reliable an influence off the field as Gary is on it. Word is, Mattie tried – though obviously failed – to play in this game instead. Currently, he is having trials with Derbyshire, whose 2nd XI he is expected to represent tomorrow.

As outlined earlier, the Minor Counties Championship is split into two ten-team Eastern and Western divisions, with Cumberland (geography notwithstanding) and Cambridgeshire in the former. Nine games a season would be too many, six is more manageable, so each county plays the others in its group twice over a three-year period, by which time eighteen matches will have been staged, an elegant solution mathematically.

It all culminates annually in a four-day final, staged alternatively at venues east and west until recently. The system worked fine before Cumberland won their group in 2015. The final was at Carlisle, the pitch wet, as it usually is up there once autumn nears, the fixture concluded by lunch on the second day in favour of the hosts. Since when, it has been held on neutral ground. All of that though seems a long way off as Ross and Sempy stride to the crease on a scorching hot midsummer's day, in a side handing debuts to a couple of development discoveries, Tyler McGladdery and Josh Boyne.

Elsewhere, a summer of sport is in full swing, the longest day on Thursday attracting hundreds to Stonehenge for the solstice and many more to TV screens to watch England close in on a first one-day international series whitewash over Australia. Football's World Cup too is underway, England's victories over Tunisia and – today – Panama all but ensuring safe passage into the last sixteen. Royal Ascot finished yesterday and next week Wimbledon will roll around.

On smaller stages too, cricketing pastimes continue unabated. On Friday night, the Cumbria board posted an online video of women's softball and All Stars children's initiatives sharing facilities in Kendal, and very busy it looked. Days earlier, the National Club Championship was in the headlines when High Wycombe, coasting on 186 for 3 and needing three runs to win from the last two overs, lost seven wickets in eleven balls to Peterborough Town. 'There was some uneven bounce and a bit of turn,' said skipper Nathan Hawkes, unbeaten on 59, 'but it was a little embarrassing.'

At what is supposedly the next level up, around thirty people are scattered around the boundary at Harecroft Road in the pretty outskirts of a market town that brands itself 'the capital of the Fens'. Wisbech is also an inland port, making use of the tidal River Nene that, having been diverted here in the seventeenth century, brought great wealth at a time when draining the Fens was fiercely resisted.

Among those in fold-up chairs or perched beside parked cars, are three of Cumberland's faithful followers: Tony Hutton, his wife Jennifer and Peter Lingard, their friend. Having settled to the right of a sightscreen, they sit as though in a doctor's surgery, waiting to be called. Although Cumberland members, surprisingly perhaps each hails from Yorkshire; more specifically in Tony and Jennifer's case, Leeds. No, they will not be attending every game, though do intend to go to Furness. 'Aye,' says Jennifer, 'and Netherfield for the next one. A day there and hopefully Carlisle at the end.'

What brought them all the way to Cambridgeshire? 'We watch cricket every day of the summer somewhere,' says Tony, adding that his reasons for supporting Cumberland are 'a long story.'

'Well, you've got time,' says Jennifer.

'I retired in 1995 and have watched cricket non-stop since, all over the north of England and sometimes the south.' He likes Minor Counties best: 'In a ground like this with very few people around, you are not surrounded by idiots, talking and carrying on.' It's for that reason the couple recently gave up on the Scarborough festival, where Yorkshire play every year and will again this week. 'It's so crowded. You can't get peace and quiet.'

'We watch all forms, don't we?' says Jennifer.

Tony nods. 'We were at Sedbergh School watching them play the Durham academy the other day. That was beautiful. Perfect.'

Since moving to Cumbria from Todmorden, near Halifax, Peter meanwhile has lived in Kirkby-in-Furness for fifty-four years and jokes that he and his wife, not here today, are still considered offcumduns. 'I know someone who married a local, lived there forty years and was still referred to as "that woman from Liverpool".' One reason Peter likes Minor Counties cricket is because: 'We can drive onto the ground and stay in the car if it's cold.'

'It's civilised,' says Tony.

'It is, but they play the game as it should be played. You get your money's worth,' says his fellow Yorkshireman, of a game to which entry is free. 'There's a lot of overs in the day. When you look at how the numbers of overs in Championship cricket drop and keep dropping... I mean, in Test cricket it's scandalous...'

That's the current debate, isn't it, long form versus short form. Have they seen much T20 this year?

'No,' says Jennifer. 'Forget T20. Dirty word. I mean, we'll watch Yorkshire seconds occasionally and have seen the odd game, and we've seen the ladies play T20...'

'But all this music and that...' Tony interjects.

'Yes, we came across it by accident, didn't we?'

'We went to York the other week and there was one on...'

'And you looked around at the crowd and they were all our age group... they don't want it.'

Certainly it would be harder to make a case for the appeal of T20 here than it would at, say, the Ageas Bowl or Sophia Gardens, bustling with young people enthusiastically buying into the concept.

'This is the game as we remember it when we were young,' says Tony, who concedes that evening league cricket used only to last around twenty-five overs back in the day. 'But that was in whites and they played proper cricket. No music and fancy dress.'

*****

Driving to Wisbech yesterday, over the River Welland and on into South Holland, 'traditional English strawberries' were on sale by the roadside, the nationalities of those who picked them only to be guessed at. On the radio, Elgar's *The Dream of Gerontius* provided musical accompaniment, an oratorio with words by the poet John Henry Newman, in which the eponymous soul journeys from death-bed through judgement to purgatory, meeting demons and angels after a life lived, you suppose, in a landscape not dissimilar to this: 'But hark! Upon my senses comes a fierce hubbub...'

Saturday 23 June had been the second anniversary of the Brexit referendum, marked in London by a People's March for a fresh vote, although the Anglia flags at various points along the A17 suggested any such about-turn would get short shrift here from a population that presumably would rather pick its own fruit.

Elme Hall Hotel, beside a busy trunk road on the Norfolk and Cambridgeshire border, a mile or so outside Wisbech and a fifteen-minute drive from the ground, is Georgian in character like the town itself, with penny-stamp windows and a pillared entrance. As the pro-EU campaigners thronged in Parliament Square, however, the cricketers of Cumberland, set to be berthed in an adjoining lodge, were still in fields some two hundred and fifty miles to the north. Here it was quiet as the grave. 'Will you all be dining tonight?' asked a lone receptionist. That seemed unlikely given that the majority would not arrive until the early hours. A chink of cutlery on china betrayed an elderly couple in an empty dining room, devoid even of serving staff. In the lounge, meanwhile, Germany played Sweden with the sound off, haunted by a couple leafing silently through a pile of newspapers, *Daily Mail* prominent. 'Oh gosh, someone has scored a goal,' the woman said, as the pair, discomfited by the sudden intrusion, rose a little too nonchalantly and made for the door.

Of Cumberland's party, Rob and Lesley Cairns were first to arrive but went straight out into Wisbech, a town that feels as if it has somehow mislaid the sea. The odd moored yacht brings colour, berthed on the river running under bridges traversing the centre, while out past a canned food factory and housing estate – on Mount Pleasant Road – a clutch of tatty boatyards are stashed. The cross of St George is draped in many a window, most likely with the World Cup in mind, who knows? Maybe always.

Not five years ago, a reported eighteen per cent of a population of some 30,000 were Lithuanian, around half the East European total, Poles and Latvians making up a third of Wisbech's citizenry. And it is now ten years since the *Daily Express* caused controversy with a report headlined 'Death of a country idyll', rebuffed by at least one local newspaper, wherein a rise in gang crime was pinned on a 'Baltic mafia ... terrifying local residents'. Whatever the truth of that, on this particular weekend a once fashionably elegant streetscape had given up the ghost, very few signs of activity – indigenous or otherwise. A town whose museum is proud to exhibit the original manuscript of *Great Expectations* had the feel of a sinking ship.

Back at the Elme Hall Hotel, the first player swung into the car park. With his eight o'clock shadow and cool demeanour, Marlboro Light dangling precariously from his lower lip, Jacques du Toit padded into reception like a gunslinger for hire, though in flip-flops rather than cowboy boots. Had he worn a hat, he'd have tipped it. His club, Newcastle, had bowled Stockton for exactly 100 runs in Durham and chased them down in 20 overs, so he could set off early, not needed to bat. Handy. But the drive had still been long and he was hungry. After collecting a room key and signing in, he explored the feasibility of a club sandwich.

'Is that French?' the receptionist enquired before adding, a little too swiftly, that no, regretfully, she could not provide such an item.

'Oh, okay,' said Jacques, unflappably switching tactics. 'Well, can you do me a chicken and bacon sandwich instead?'

This she agreed to do, whereupon he took it back to his car and ate it in the driver's seat, before lighting up another cheroot.

Two hours later, when the clock struck ten, Dutts and Slacky were next to roll up, companionable and chatty after an even longer journey. They too escaped early. Furness bowled out Whitehaven for a measly 80 runs, a total passed for the loss of two wickets, Dutts contributing an unbeaten 10. Slacky's Wigton, however, were skittled for 84 against Cockermouth, still flying high. The Cumberland man had contributed 46 to that run total on his own.

By now, the football on telly was replaced by rugby league – England v New Zealand in Denver, Colorado, live on BBC2. Rugby league at Mile High Stadium ... what is the sporting world coming to? Belying his diminutive stature, Dutts, an all-rounder, has dabbled with that game too, playing at amateur side Roose Pioneers. Yes, he is unhappy at Furness, he admitted, and would be off to Newcastle or Leigh next year. Preferring a round ball, footballer Slacky opted to watch the World Cup highlights alone in his room.

Geoff Minshaw and Sempy, also at Wigton with Cockermouth, soon followed Rob and Lesley – back from a 'not very good night out' – into the hotel lounge. Dutts observed that the landscape was very flat around here. 'Well, it is Fenland,' said Geoff.

'Finland?' said Dutts. 'Is this the capital of Finland?'

By then, an already scant staff had thinned out further, only a French nightwatchman at the crease. After scanning the room, he switched channels to *Match of the Day*, despite everyone watching the rugby, before shuffling off again with a tip for Mexico or Croatia: 'I don't understand cricket. The further you hit it, the more you get?'

Just before midnight, Greg Hall of Penrith and Blackpool's Josh Boyne arrived – the latter, originally 12th man, replacing another Josh – Fallows – whose bad ankle meant he would now assume that role. And as the wee small hours edged towards dawn, so the rest of the cast completed their own gruelling treks before rising, bright and early, for the commencement of the one hundred and thirteenth Minor Counties Cricket Championship.

*****

The caw of seagulls greets Cumberland's first championship runs of 2018, roused by polite applause for a straight four in the second over from Matty Sempill. As the day advances in baking heat, audience numbers will rise with the mercury. They will include many a dog-walker, such as the couple looking on with a Dalmatian beyond a flood ditch at the town end. Three overs later, Sempy clips a difficult chance past the Cambridgeshire 'keeper, but then settles into a commanding spell with Ross that will not be broken until their partnership is one run short of a century.

At breakfast, all were hale and hearty. Even Toby, here on the back of four wickets and 13 runs in a draw with Rainhill, as keen to greet the morning sunshine as anyone. Stand-in skipper Syds, as usual, had Ruth and son in tow, personalised registration-plate: SYD. John Patterson, dapper in white shirt and club tie, slid a slice or two of toast beneath his bushy moustache.

Sempy and Ross began the day sprawled on the grass, while Ben Howarth, Toby and new boy Tyler made their introductions. Geoff span his latest anecdote. After persuading last night's French nightwatchman to sell him beer despite the bar officially being shut, his appreciation had been vocal: 'Hey, this is good stuff!' In the light of day, the brand had been revealed: Becks Blue. 'Non-alcoholic lager!' he screeched like a Cumbrian macaw. 'I've never had a non-alcoholic drink on a Saturday night in my life.' Soon after 9.00am, a flotilla of cars completed the short trip to Harecroft Road, where one clump of Cambridgeshire players loosened up with a kick-about and Cumberland's squad – wearing black T-shirts and shorts – were soon knocking a football around too. Syds got busy with paperwork, while Jacques, Sempy and Ben took to the nets, the South African having immediately inspected the wicket, fag in hand, in the company of a twitchy Dutts.

Home to Wisbech Town Cricket and Hockey Club, the ground is in a semi-rural setting partially encircled by ash and Scots pine on the road side, oak and poplar masking a cemetery and supermarket opposite. In the middle distance, fronting a skyline of rooftops and spires are adjoining fields studded with rugby and football posts. Bob Burgess, the host club's chairman, said of the land's provenance that the Peckovers, a family of Quakers influential here from the late 18th century, dedicated it to sporting pastimes in perpetuity. More recently, however, it has been in the hands of the National Trust, to whom Wisbech pay a commercial rate as tenants.

Dutts and Boyney joined Jacques, Ben and Sempy in their drills, the former timing his shots well. Jacques suggested the latter should not get so far forward. 'Hitting it later means hitting it straighter,' he encouraged. 'Good shot, good shot. Good shot!' At 10.30am, half an hour before start of play, Syds and his opposite number, Ben Howgego, walked out with the umpires for the coin toss. 'Think Syds has won that,' Jacques drawled from his seat on the patio, in front of a wooden pavilion. 'Yeah, we are batting.'

Cambridgeshire secretary Keith 'Yogi' Coburn, something of a celebrity on the Minor Counties circuit since he is also on the MCCA's six-man cricket committee and an umpire to boot, though not today, was engaged in pre-match administration. Forced to retire through injury at 28, his true calling came when an elderly umpire told him he'd go further in that role than he would playing. Thirty-one years later, he is a Minor Counties mainstay who also spent four years on the first-class reserve list until: '...it became accepted that there weren't no room on the panel for someone who hadn't played the first-class game.' Old pros now got the gig and that was fine as it was their life, but: '...it's a gentleman's club really. Anyone from outside is an interloper.'

There have been compensations. Forced to concentrate on the game at this level, he is now at the heart of an organisation he loves. It may even be an obsession, albeit one flavoured by self-deprecation. After over a decade as under-19s coach, the opportunity arose, in 2003, to become team manager of Cambridgeshire's 1st XI. 'It was a good start,' he recalled. 'We beat Shropshire by three wickets in the one-day final at Lord's and haven't won a thing since.'

Hailing from Cambridge with the East Anglian accent to prove it, Yogi also umpires locally, further ensuring his many and varied views on the state of cricket stand on knowledgeable foundations.

Such as: 'Minor Counties games are more competitive than first-class 2nd XI fixtures.' Why? 'The talent may be better, but they are playing as individuals rather than as a team.'

On the struggle to find new umpires: 'Other sports last an hour and a half. In the Cambridge Premier League, we start at 11 and can be there until seven. It mirrors society, doesn't it? People haven't got time. Sunday cricket is almost dead. They play longer formats on Saturday and find other things to do on Sunday. Got to accept it.'

Did he see short-form cricket as the way ahead? 'Not really, but the ECB does. Look at the County Championship, played in April, then September, with a couple of pink ball games in the middle. To be fair, the counties themselves have no interest in red ball cricket because it doesn't bring in the money. They can fill Bristol with a T20 game and that's what keeps them going.' No surprise, therefore, that Yogi too is an unshakeable fan of the three-day game: 'Of course. The players enjoy it. Half a million pound is spent on Premier League cricket, which would survive without that status. A thousand pound a club! Where does it go? Nowhere. Money we'd like to get into the Minor Counties to protect three-day cricket.'

What are his expectations of how the debate will pan out? 'Due to travel, I think we'll go to four divisions of five, which mirrors the T20, play more locally, with a semi-final and final. That retains three-dayers, though four games instead of six. You'll still get a champion county.' Would he be happy with that? 'If we save three-day cricket, of course. There's got to be a compromise somewhere along the line. I'd rather have four games than none.'

Yogi's responsibilities with the MCCA extend to what is effectively its representative side, the Unicorns, with whom he acts as team manager alongside coach Phil Oliver, last seen at Penrith when Cumberland met Staffordshire in the T20. That means he must keep a weather eye on national talent too. Toby is a regular and Dutts would have played for them last week on the Isle of Wight, before his outdoor maintenance job with South Lakes Services intruded.

'I heard about a wicketkeeper, so did his game yesterday and he dropped four catches. That's a one-off. You can't judge on that. We pick players not only from the Minor Counties but the recreational game as a whole, part of the player pathway. If a first-class county then spots them, that's that. They can offer a paid contract and we can't. That does make it difficult sometimes to get a side out; we've already had four seamers go to Worcester this year. In the last game, against Hampshire, we had to go in with five spinners.'

The Unicorns side then, like much else at this level, feels under threat; best days behind it. Indeed, the name is a call back to the original MCCA symbol, which featured the mythical beast. Having played as the Minor Counties under-25s for some fifteen years, with only MCCA cricketers selected, in 2009 came entry to the NatWest Pro40, a one-day league for first-class counties in which the side became representative of the recreational game in its entirety. 'Those four years were good for us,' Yogi said. 'Our players were on a stage with top cricketers. In some games we competed, in others we didn't, but that's amateur versus professional for you, isn't it? We never paid anybody.' And what's more, again out of step with the current mood, he'd like the recreational ethos of the Unicorns extended to the Minor Counties Championship scene too. 'This is my argument with minor counties, they can be insular when it comes to selection, although you'd have to say Cumberland aren't. We should represent the whole recreational game. In the eighteen first-class counties, some players never get the chance to shine. People want "players from the county playing for the county...", but if locals are good and ambitious enough they'll still be selected. If Unicorns players go on to win a first-class contract, that's a feather in their cap.'

Unlike Cumberland, Cambridgeshire comfortably fall in line with stringent MCCA requirements. 'We've an unwritten rule where we only have two who weren't born, play or educated in our county. But as I say, that isn't always right. If a recreational player in Essex doesn't get the opportunity to play for Essex, why shouldn't he play for a Minor Counties club?' Residency aside, another issue can cause selection headaches. 'We've got three schoolteachers who can't play today, including the captain, as they go back to school tomorrow and Tuesday. At the MCCA, we did put this year's fixtures back to accommodate that. Before, we had two in June, two in July, two in August. We are trying to relieve the pressure a bit, but it's never easy.'

A clatter of cricket studs turned attentions back to the verdant arena onto which the fielding side ambled ahead of the day's play, an idyllic round of birdsong briefly silencing the clubhouse chat.

'Bat long,' Jacques had told Sempy and Ross, as the pair walked by, focussed on doing exactly that. Slacky – padded up – nodded in agreement. If these two hung around long enough, he might yet get to see England versus Panama.

*****

Twenty overs later, when 12th man Josh Fallows limps onto the field with fruit juice, a new pair of gloves and advice for Sempy – 'Keep your shape, hit through the V...' – Cumberland are 56 for 0.

Under the shade of hanging branches, the fortunes of Wisbech Town CC are discussed, one chap apparently dismayed that the club's two overseas professionals have been dropped to the 2nd XI: 'One paid his own way, so if he'd been any good it would have been a bonus. The other, we paid his air fare and everything.'

Josh Boyne meanwhile, on debut, is called by his mum back in Blackpool and tells her he'll bat number seven: 'It's red hot,' he adds. A late starter, 'Boyney', now aged 21, was 13 when Ben Howarth and friends first dragged him to the local club. Even then, he didn't play in an actual match until under-15s. 'There's no cricket in my family – it's all football. Dad's big in football, brother doesn't really play any sport, so I'm the only one.' Opting to become a spin-bowler seems a rather esoteric choice therefore. 'I didn't bowl at all to begin with, just batted a bit and ran around full of energy. Then I tried seam bowling and soon worked out I preferred running in off seven paces.' Since when, although he has played for Lancashire under-19s when they had games in the Northern Premier League, this is pretty much his only exposure to representative cricket.

'One of my mates at Blackpool was in touch with Mike Latham, saying he's doing all right, can we get him a development game?' Thus his appearance at Fleetwood against Myerscough, after which Steve Sharp sent him a text asking him to be 12th man here. 'Then a couple of days later, I got a text saying "you're in." It's been a bit of a whirlwind, much different to league cricket. You don't get any other chance to play three days. I think it will toughen you mentally.' He'd love to play for a first-class county. 'Just got to keep working hard, haven't you, and hopefully the call will come.'

Drinks are taken, play resumes and Cumberland advance to 63 without loss when suddenly, on the horizon at the scoreboard end, a plume of smoke unfurls, charcoal grey, to soil the wide blue yonder. It's a distraction, near the docks by the look of it, that seems not to bother Ross, who reaches his half-century with a pair of lovely cover drives. In the following over, he cracks three more boundaries off Cambridgeshire's off-spinner, while Sempy hangs around steadfastly at the other end, still in his 20s.

Also on the boundary are Ben's parents, Richard and Alison, and grandma Vera. Richard, a cricket buff, was a Lancashire member for 20 years. 'Watched them all over the country.' He's off to Sri Lanka this year, following England. 'I love my cricket. Six months a year, it's fantastic.' And that zeal has clearly rubbed off on his son who, as we've seen, chose the game over football. The Howarths too travelled down last night, arriving at about 1.00am, but are staying in the town centre at the Rose and Crown, rather than the team hotel.

'Giving him his space,' says mum.

They too are champions of the three-day game. 'It's just proper cricket, innit?' Richard says. 'I mean, T20, it's smash, bang, wallop; yes it gets the crowds in, but *this* is me. Most cricket fans love Tests, four-day county games and so on. They demand more of the players and my lad prefers it for that reason. At Netherfield last year, Macca [Mattie McKiernan] at one end, Toby the other, he was on his feet for a hundred overs on a sweltering day. You learn from that. It develops your game.'

Just after noon, chairman Neil Atkinson rocks up in blue shirt and Cumberland tie, perfectly timed to see Ross's wicket fall, caught behind for 72. Slacky comes in and nudges the Cumbrians into three figures to get the most idiosyncratic and charming of scoreboxes – all light bulbs and steampunk gadgetry as if built by Caractacus Potts – moving again. Ditching his boots and pads, Ross pads barefoot over to Ben and Josh at the far end, ostensibly to help man the wheeled sightscreen. If Jacques du Toit is laid-back, Ross Zelem is horizontal, soon literally so. The boys from Blackpool do most of the shoving as their teammate zones out, eyes closed, earphones in.

There will be three sessions daily of two hours and 20 minutes, first innings consisting of 90 overs, with batting and bowling points accrued for hitting certain targets. No bonus points will be available in the second innings, when the number of overs becomes variable within a basic structure of a minimum 110 overs per day.

Slacky is indeed missing the football. Rob and Lesley have the pictures on their smartphone as John Stones scores the first of two goals against Panama. Lunch though is coming as Cumberland, 120 for 1, continue their slow and steady progress with a run rate of just under three an over. As the batsmen walk off, Slacky wants the latest from the Nizhny Novgorod Stadium while, on TV in the bar, Harry Kane hammers another into the roof of the net, England building to a 5-0 half-time lead. It will be a 6-1 victory come the final whistle.

The afternoon session begins under the gaze of Cumberland president Alan Wilson, a man of vast experience and droll humour who has just arrived with his wife, Angela, for a first appearance of the season. The journey to Wisbech had been more demanding than the one he'll undertake for game two at Netherfield in a fortnight. He lives directly opposite the ground. Speaking of scoreboxes, Alan is fed up because his hometown club has changed theirs 'to one of these electronic jobs. I've to go to the bottom of our drive to read it...'

Sempy's 50 comes up with three runs in the 57th over. However it snaps his concentration and not long after he's caught at midwicket and Cumberland are 150 for 2. Cue collapse? Not a bit of it. Dutts is next at the crease and helps to move the score along brilliantly, his partnership with Slacky adding almost as many runs again before the Wigton man's innings is curtailed for 73 – caught behind while attempting an overhead scoop – and it's 246 for 3. Jacques, batsman five, can only contribute six, falling to a great catch off a shot hard and low, but Dutts pushes on to his half-century, ably assisted by young Tyler, the pair guiding Cumberland past 300 with ten overs remaining. McGladdery out lbw, Boyney pitches in with nine runs as the foot goes to the floor. A terrific personal display ends when Dutts is stumped on 84, although a late flurry by Ben, who ends the innings with what is destined to be a seasonal high of 26 not out, and 13 runs shared between Toby Bulcock and Greg Hall, concludes matters, for now, on a highly respectable 372 for 9.

Syds, at number eleven, pats the last ball back. 'He's playing for his average,' quips Alan Wilson, strolling to the pavilion. Sandwiched by all this, was a tea interval whose buffet was something of an effort for those committeemen and guests lucky enough to have earlier enjoyed the hospitality of a splendid three-course Sunday lunch of roast beef with all the trimmings. Rob Cairns, as usual, washed it down with a cheeky glass or two of claret. In this heat, forty leisurely winks wouldn't go amiss, though that will have to wait.

When Cambridgeshire start their innings there is still time for 25 overs before close of play, during which time Ben Howgego, once on the books at Northamptonshire, and 19-year-old Charlie Lewis look utterly at ease, the former in particular clocking up runs. At least one early evening wicket would be useful, but the pitch is flat and dry and even when Cumberland introduce Toby in the 13th over and Jacques an over later that never looks likely, although the duo slow the run rate a little. The levels of concentration are all the more admirable given the endurance test of such a day in the field. In the penultimate over both batsmen are crowded by fielders, but hold on to finish 90 without loss. A breakthrough will have to wait.

Josh Fallows collects orders for each visiting player's first post-match drink, as donated by their generous hosts. 'Put Geoff down for a Beck's Blue,' Dutts tells him.

*****

At breakfast, Alan and Angela Wilson, now at the Elme Hall Hotel, talk Brexit with an expat Brit not of the Cumberland party, visiting from France. Although there is disagreement on the issue – she is worried about the long-term impact of rupture with the European Union, the Wilsons not so much – conversation remains polite.

Donald Trump is also in the news, as usual. The US president's determination to look and sound tough on immigration has seen him use words like 'infesting', his actions leading to shocking images of terrified children being torn from anguished parents. All may be serene in three-day cricket, but beyond these closeted boundaries is a world spinning ever further out of control. 'In some ways, he has the right idea,' says Alan, before his wife Angela swiftly recruits him to her point of view. Trump is essentially a bully.

John Patterson, sat opposite, is no fan of the EU either. 'The common market was a good idea,' he says, nibbling away at another triangle of toast, 'but who wants a vast Euro super-state? We'll be the first out, but we won't be the last,' he predicts.

'It all needs sorting,' says Alan, 'but it won't be us doing it.'

'Yes. It's all a mess,' says the French expat with a sigh.

Entente cordiale retained, everyone is otherwise chipper and raring to go. All had a relatively quiet night of it, club officials and their partners enjoying a curry at the Moghul restaurant in Wisbech, while the team wisely gave a beer festival at the Rose and Crown a swerve and opted for Wetherspoons instead where, in the company of vocal East Europeans, they saw Poland dumped out of the World Cup. Otherwise, the town was deserted, the officials' evening ending with a pint or two in the White Lion, where by chance they bumped into Toby's parents, Steve and Bev, Mrs Bulcock being the owner of a sandwich shop back home in Lancashire – Bev's Baps.

As Alan and Angela leave the breakfast table they are eclipsed by a man of huge frame, who lurches in and orders two boiled eggs. A total stranger, he asks if everyone is here for the Minor Counties. 'We are indeed,' John confirms. 'Yourself?'

The man coughs, pleased to have a fish on the hook. He had been in Bishop's Stortford yesterday, he says, watching Hertfordshire, but came away early 'once the World Cup yobbos' got going. For day two today, he is at Wisbech and tomorrow has Sleaford in his sights, where Lincolnshire are hosting Northumberland.

'You must be a fan of the Minor Counties then?'

'I watch anything the ECB hasn't had its grubby hands on,' he says, as the eggs are placed before him. 'You know what ECB stands for, don't you? Exterminate Cricket Board.' He's from Barnsley, the sort of Yorkshireman who, by birthright, seems duty bound to call a spade a shovel. Ignatius Reet Gradely.

'Twenty20? That's not bloody cricket,' he goes on, erecting little piles of broken shell, and nor, he says, is the '...100 balls thing. Bound to be based in bloody Leeds.' It turns out he nurses a grudge in that direction too. 'Yorkshire only ever play at Headingley, a place no one in South Yorkshire can reach without taking a week off work,' via mule train and after anti-malaria jabs no doubt. As for the county's global superstar Joe Root, don't get him started. 'It's all about money,' he says. 'Will Root be in Scarborough? No, he's playing T20 for England, isn't he? Not interested in Yorkshire, he chooses his country over his county every time.' He pours a hill of sugar into his tea as John, unfailingly pleasant, dabs his 'tache and makes his excuses. After all, there is a game to get to, where the players once again arrive a good hour before hostilities recommence.

The town centre is busier. A working week begins as the cricket contingent prepares for hours under another gorgeous sky.

In the clubhouse, Yogi and 75-year-old Cambridgeshire president Derek Wing – aka 'the Wing Commander' – busy about. Born in Wisbech, Wing's own Minor Counties record is impressive. An all-rounder for Cambridgeshire from 1964 to 1986, he played in ninety-eight Championship matches and several first-class games for the MCC, touring Ireland. Not that you'll hear him boast. He's more likely – with help from great pal Alan – to send himself up, the sort of chap you immediately warm to, a fount of genial conversation.

A poster featuring a cartoon crocodile promotes 'The Crockey Project', a fundraiser targeting £600,000 to 'build a brighter future for Wisbech Town Cricket and Hockey Club'. The money will pay for a pavilion to replace the current one – 'in a sad state of repair' – built in 1961. Better changing rooms, bigger car park and disabled facilities will follow. As will a new scorebox, understandable given the present one's eccentricity, though that does seem rather a shame. The club is a third of the way towards its objective already; perhaps Geoff Minshaw should put in a quote.

Toby gets play going with a maiden. Jacques, next up, is sweaty-palmed, so rubs his hands in dust before the ball is clipped between 'keeper and first slip for four. Signs of movement?

'Oh, lovely Jackie boy, well disguised,' says Toby, king of the mind games. 'Come on, boys, let's work hard.' If Sunday's start was quiet, there are only around twenty spectators here so far today and those mainly of a certain vintage, embowered in shade. Having reached 25 degrees yesterday, the thermometer will rise a further three points today; the joint is roasting by 11.00am.

Adding to the overnight score, Cambridgeshire pass 100 in their 31st over, but their first wicket falls three overs later. Charlie Lewis is the victim, caught down the leg side by Ben off Jacques for 28, but hope of a meaningful breakthrough is short-lived.

Incoming Callum Guest will ultimately contribute 80 runs of his own and he and Ben Howgego move the score along to 199, when the skipper is caught Tyler, bowled Toby, after a magnificent personal 136. By which point, Cumberland have long since begun to wilt in the heat as, out towards the port, the smouldering blaze in what, according to last night's local television news bulletins turned out to be a wood yard, continues to billow diaphanous smoke.

Red-faced fielders may beg to differ, but there can be few more pleasant spots to a spend a summer Monday, especially in the shade of a horse chestnut tree. Howgego's scalp is met with understandable relief by Cumberland, but batsman four, Ben Seabrook, is intent on a good knock too. He sticks around long enough for Guest to pass his 50 and moves Cambridgeshire to 251 before the fall of his own wicket, lbw, to Toby.

That allows chairman Neil to run on with drinks, deputising for 19-year-old Josh Fallows, resting his leg. It must be a frustrating time for the 12th man, product of Eagley CC in the Bolton League, on the southern slopes of the West Pennine Moors, and now at Edgworth. He is here because Gary told Syds that Cumberland needed an all-rounder last year and he was called in for a three-dayer that turned out to be his last game of the season, due to a stress fracture in his lower-back. 'I'd done it before then, but my scan results came after it. That was in the middle of June – I'd three months out.' After his T20 games this time, he was selected for Wisbech but rolled an ankle in club cricket, straining an achilles.

When lunch arrives the host county is 285 for 3 after 71 overs, Cumberland's gate of opportunity slammed shut. Lee Thomason, supporting Guest, is the latest batsman to frustrate. In the pavilion there is another splendid feed, during which Alan presents the Wing Commander with a bottle of Rioja of a type he particularly enjoyed on a recent trip to Spain. The label says 'Chitón' which, given Alan's pronunciation, is the real reason it's here. As for the venue itself, the National Trust charges £3,000 annually in rent, a not insubstantial outlay for a small set-up. The NT does have its uses, however. When travellers set up camp recently in the overgrown field next door, the football club no longer being able to afford to play there, the Trust – 'looking after the places you love' – moved them on, quick smart.

When play resumes, Syds takes the ball and Rob Cairns decides it's high time for a lap of the boundary. The rule, he says, is clockwise if you hope to inspire wickets, anti-clockwise for runs. Naturally he turns left. 'That's why the players always go right,' he says, 'because when they are chasing wickets they are always on the field.' Neil does not subscribe to the superstition, but Rob guides him left anyway.

A former chief executive at Furness Building Society, Rob has always been a cricket fan, getting involved with Cumberland when approached for sponsorship. 'We did it for several years. I went to as many home games as I could, not many away games, because on Monday and Tuesday I'd be working.' Asked to join the committee ten years ago he did so, but at one point decided to resign: 'I thought I wasn't doing enough.' Eric and Mike persuaded him otherwise, pointing out that he is the sort of sociable presence every club needs. 'Just after that, the secretary left. I said I'd do it until the end of the season and have been at it ever since.' Besides conviviality, what else does the job entail? 'Secretarial functions like arranging committee meetings, AGMs, taking minutes and so on, but I tend to do more and more. We do the teamsheets, a good little earner, and arrange catering with the home club. I make sure the returns [reports] are sent off at the end of the game – but good news on that. There used to be three – team captains, umpires and scorers. Now the captains and scorers do theirs on the computer. The only one I have to be bothered with is the umpires', but that's always the latest to come, so I tend to be the last one out at the end of home matches.'

Framed by snowy white hair and a neatly-trimmed beard, Rob has the sort of beaming face that is guaranteed to cheer anyone up, not all of it due to his fermented grape intake. Naturally bubbly with a soft Scouse brogue, he is the type of person you notice most when they're not there. Fortunately, he always is. 'I also stand in for Eric at Lord's, although the majority of meetings now are at Edgbaston. It's more central for travelling and the facilities are cheaper. We still have the AGM at Lord's, a great occasion to go to.'

Resident on Walney Island since 1997, he was brought up in Birkenhead, an Everton fan: 'Delighted Sam Allardyce has gone, we might play football next season.' Cricket, though, has always been an interest. 'Watched all the Test matches as a kid, in black and white on a little telly.' He wasn't much of a player however. 'I joined the building societies in about 1974, when there were loads.' A league was formed in which they played banks, estate agents, insurance companies, solicitors' firms and accountants. 'I turned out for the building society team and sometimes captained them. What was great about that is it gave me the opportunity to play at grounds I never would have played on otherwise.'

He illustrates the standard by recalling a Building Societies versus Bankers fixture at Edenside. While waiting to go in alongside Penrith spinner Richard Ellwood, who did actually go on to play for Cumberland from 1984-2000, he heard one Carlisle committeeman say: 'Why on earth is Ellwood playing with this rubbish?' His team never won anything – '...less males to draw on than accountants and solicitors...' – but had fun, enjoyment a big factor in Rob's book. But back to the plonk...

'The wine I love most is old world – French, Italian, Spanish. I used to drink a lot of bitter, because I like that as well, but got a hiatus hernia and switched over.' He has more information too on that pub on Walney, the Queen's Hotel, in a place called Biggar Village. 'Tell everyone to come and see us, it's wonderful. There are thirty houses and the pub. Every year, on the first Sunday in July, we have a noon-to-midnight music festival, twenty-four acts doing half an hour each. Drink flows ... burger bars, brilliant. You don't get up the next day, unless Cumberland are playing, obviously. The pub actually shut a few years ago for eighteen months and we couldn't be having that. It's our village hall, the only place we can all meet, so we are determined not to let it close again.' A few villagers set up a micro-brewery [chaired by Lesley] in an outbuilding. 'We get it rent free for supplying the pub with cheaper ale. Touch wood, the beer is very good and one day it might even make a small profit.' Given such a cheery demeanour, perhaps the biggest surprise is that, having once lived in Barrow, he is also a member of Furness CC.

With ten overs of their first innings remaining, Cambridgeshire advance to 324 for 5 – Guest having reached his 80 and fallen, caught Zelem, bowled Syds, Thomason caught and bowled by Toby for 39 soon after. The wicket is utterly lifeless, a larger crowd as the day has gone on already judging a draw the likely outcome. Without doubt, though, there is quality talent on display, batsmen who would open for a Premier League club going in three, four or well into the middle order. Even the tail-enders know how to bat. Lads who might normally field in the slips are at third man or elsewhere in the deep. Leaving your comfort zone is what Minor Counties cricket is about.

Mike Latham has driven down with Toby (the dog) and chats with Alan. As ever, the president is in story-telling mood, sharing an uproarious tale of some incident with the Archbishop of Canterbury at Wormsley Park, venue of this year's T20 finals. In the background, Cambridgeshire's lower order post useful runs as Cumberland's total is passed for the fall of one more wicket, the home side finishing on 392 for 6, exactly 20 ahead.

*****

Having already earned bonus points, an away draw without Gary Pratt's Richmondshire posse wouldn't be a terrible way to kick-off and that's just as well. Setting Cambridgeshire a target and declaring on this wicket appears unlikely in the extreme. Ross Zelem, opening again with Sempy, gets the second innings going with a four off his hips. Sadly, he then nicks one to the 'keeper and it's 5 for 1. Slacky is in next again and, for a while, Cumberland recalibrate at snail's pace.

A hot afternoon develops a cooling breeze. Ross, contribution over for the day, lies back on a carpet of daisies and arboreal debris, under surfer-boy ringlets of gingery hair and the branches of an oak. Arms behind his head, eyes shut, wired for sound, he chills to some Lebanese soul fusion, betrayed by tapping feet and the distant tinny rattle of jazz trumpet. Son of footballer Peter Zelem (defender with Chester City, Wolves, Preston North End and Burnley, plus the first post-war Football League player to have a surname beginning with 'Z', don'tcha know), nephew of Alan, a goalkeeper with Macclesfield among others, and cousin to former England youth international Katie Zelem, who will this year play for Manchester United in their inaugural Women's Super League campaign, he might have been expected to pursue a career in soccer.

But no. Cricket it is and always has been.

'I started when I was about nine,' he drawls, unplugged, 'at the village club. Woodhouses, in Failsworth, north-east Manchester. Just with mates, ten minutes from our house.' But while he really enjoys playing – well, batting – he does not much care for watching the game, 'top-end stuff now and then,' taking part is everything. Nor is he likely to give the game head-room. 'It's just something I've done for so long it kind of becomes engrained. I like the feel of a solid shot off a bowler and love the craic with the lads, the social aspect.'

A natural talent, he is 23 now, having gone from Woodhouses to Heywood in the Central Lancs League, where he first played age group cricket with Lancashire. 'Toby was a bit older than me, but I knew him through that – his dad, Steve, was the manager of the under-13s side I was in. I played with most of the lads who are at Lancashire now. We are all similar ages, so you grow up playing with them, don't you?' Did he have ambitions to make the first-class county game himself? 'Yeah, when I was younger.' And now? 'No, I think I'm a little past it. These last few years I've played for enjoyment, love of the game, and probably done better because of it. When you are with a good set of lads you relax.'

Early press photos show him once to have had short hair. It seems that as he relaxed, so it grew longer and curly. 'After leaving school, just turned 18, I spent a season out in Melbourne, a great experience. Anyone who has the opportunity should go. I felt I grew up a lot, not just as a cricketer but as a person.' How did that come about? 'Through being around other people who'd done it, meeting overseas players. They give you contacts. It seemed like a good idea.'

In his fourth or fifth season at Leigh in the Liverpool Comp, where Toby too plays this year, this is only his second campaign on Cumberland's radar. 'I was just enjoying my cricket, not trying to play for a county anymore, knew a few of the lads and they said I should give it a go. I'll be honest, the amount of fun I had, it probably changed my season because we struggled a bit at Leigh. The year before, we'd won the title and were hoping to build on it, but didn't. It was great to play in a good standard with good cricketers.'

Along with Australia, he has been to India too, and his eyes really light up talking about that. 'Every off-season these last few years, I've worked and saved as much as I can to go travelling, see a few places. The winter just gone I went there. Within 20 metres of crossing the border there were games of cricket all around. I'd never seen anything like it. I thought: "Do you know what, I really fancy a game of cricket, I've not batted in ages." So I went to the park, sat down and tried to work out what was going on, the nuance ... hit the ball in one area and it's a six, in another you're out ... but they take it really seriously. Anyway, I'm sat there and someone said: "Do you want to play?" I feigned ignorance, picked the bat up and said: "How do I hold it?" Having a bit of a laugh and that. They batted me down the order – probably thought I was going to be absolutely hopeless. Anyway, they lost a couple of early wickets, playing on a dust bowl with a hard tennis ball, really bouncy, doing all sorts, in a six-over game. We ended up with 30 runs and I made 27 of them. There was some sort of political march on, and the police, instead of watching that, began watching this game of cricket, big crowd forming.' He grins, delighted by the recollection. 'They love cricket, although you'd need a stronger word to describe it properly. Knowing we had a shared interest, the kindness they showed me after that, inviting me for tea, wanting to take me to their house... I love travelling.'

But no, despite the claims of certain Cumberland teammates, he does not know his way around a surfboard. 'It's just the way I look! I've given surfing a go a few times, but that is one tough sport. I do like my music, outdoorsy stuff, and am definitely not obsessed with the game. I've got other interests in life.'

'Ross!' Slacky yells from the middle. 'Can you move the sightscreen, please?' His teammate though is again lost in music and a pair of Cambridgeshire outfielders are drafted in to do it instead.

Cumberland level the scores with four byes in the 16th over and by tea have crawled on to 34 for 1. The break, however, plays havoc with Slacky's concentration and he is out with just five runs added on the return. Dutts is in next and unwittingly contributes to the fall of Sempy with only one subsequent run on the scoreboard. His straight drive hits the bowler's finger and catches the opener, backing up, out of his crease – run out. At 40 for 3, already there is only one game plan viable. Attempt to bat until lunchtime tomorrow and take as many overs as possible out of the game.

Someone, however, forgets to tell Jacques, who comes in and immediately hammers a four. With him and Dutts at the crease, who knows, there could be fun and games yet. Both are by nature shot-makers but Dutts, having hit a couple of fours of his own, sweeps one straight into the 'keeper's gloves and it's 64 for 4. 'Gladders, rest of the day please, mate,' captain Syds tells Tyler, next to venture out.

The youngster takes the advice on board, as both he and the South African find focus and build a healthy partnership. Yet shortly after it passes the half-century, Jacques is caught behind, one short of his own 50, and Cumberland are again under siege with a couple of novices holding the fort. Still, they battle on manfully and even when Tyler falls, lbw, for 24 with 40 minutes left in the day, Boyney shows what a useful acquisition he'll be. The tail-end seems likely to collapse, but in an eventual second innings total of 189, it is Boyney whose bails stay unbroken, a personal haul of 42 runs including one of his side's only two sixes.

What is it they say about Minor Counties cricket? That it tests a person's powers of application? A lot more *is* learned about them in three-day games, more so than in T20. And they learn plenty too.

All in all, though, the visitors are now very much up against it, as even Ross would admit despite spending the back end of the innings reclining in a yoga position, soaking up the early evening rays. In fact, he had narrowly missed being hit by Boyney's six, snoozing in his bubble of Zen. If that was lucky, Slacky admits to having had some of his own, the ball having earlier looped into the air before landing on top of stumps that stayed intact. He and Toby are the only team members today who were part of Cumberland's 2015 Championship-winning side.

By common consent, the day has produced several dubious lbw decisions, among them Ben Howarth's dismissal for 8 with the very last ball. Long-form cricket tests the concentration of umpires too. With a day to go, Cumberland are 170 for 7 – just 148 runs in front. A result of some sort now seems certain. 'Cherry on top, mate?' says Toby to Ben's nemesis, as the bowler leaves the field, eliciting no reply. 'He knows, doesn't he?' he winks, the lad soon securely in his dressing room. 'Shithouse.' The entertainments officer laughs and goes to lounge with the boys and their beers in a little circle on the outfield. They discuss the day's play and wind down as the bells of St Peter's chime. Syds, limbs creaking perhaps, prefers a fold-up chair as Toby asks what everyone would pick as their identifying sting of T20 music. Scorer Geoff surprises everyone with a blast of industrial drum 'n' bass, as found on his phone.

Tonight, all except Jacques, visiting family, will head off to the Moghul for more team-bonding and a curry, the greater part of it paid for by the lads themselves. After which, taxis are to be booked back to the hotel. There is, though, a problem with that. On Saturday alone this week, the town experienced a drugs bust, stabbing and acid attack – as explained by the taxi driver on the way in. There would be no chance, he said, even on a Monday, of any of his colleagues risking pick-ups in the centre after 10.00pm. Thankfully, everyone will survive the subsequent 40-minute walk, not least because Jacques – by now returned from his trip – picks everyone up from the roadside, four by four, having rescued his teammates with a impromptu late-night shuttle service.

*****

The South African is among the early risers next morning, his tinted wrap-around shades again set to be put to use. Over an expanse of eggs, bacon, beans, sausages and black pudding, Toby confides that if Cumberland are to stand any chance of victory he is going to have to win this one today. With the bat, he'll need to help add 30 or 40 runs and then his spin must do the rest. Outwardly, he wears his responsibility lightly. His head may be another matter. Tomorrow he will be back in his office job, and at Leigh again on Saturday.

At the ground, the only batsmen yet to fall – Toby, Greg, Syds and Boyney – face Jacques and a plastic dog ball launcher in the nets. When play resumes, nine runs are added before Greg scoops one to short midwicket. Toby, hoping for a lead of 200, is off the mark with a leg bye, survives an lbw appeal, but is then out as the ball rattles his pads – 183 for 9. Some grumble darkly about 'umpire's revenge', Alan Wilson apparently having removed the fellow from some panel or other back in the day. 'He's getting his own back.' Toby is seething. 'Wankers!' he says, stomping into the clubhouse.

The innings culminates in another duck and hotly-contested lbw. Last man Syds, indulging in some elaborate forward defence, stretches forward and is clattered on the pads. The digit again shoots up as if its owner has a train to catch. They have just about lasted an hour, the upshot of which is that Cambridgeshire now need 170 runs for victory, with plenty of overs – at least 64 – in which to find them. And more are available in the last hour should they be required.

'They've had more appeals than Oxfam,' says Toby.

Back out there, Syds opens the bowling as Howgego and Lewis begin the hosts' chase, although in this heat Toby is a sensible choice in rotation. For now, at least, he maintains his attacking mindset and soon raps the pads of the Cambridgeshire captain, alas to no reward.

'How much are you paying these bloody umpires?' Alan asks the Wing Commander.

'I could see from the bar, it was a good decision,' says Derek.

In the Minor Counties, competitiveness ought only to be taken so far. Yesterday was Alan and Angela's 52nd wedding anniversary, so last night their friend took the couple, with Rob, Lesley and John, to the King William IV Country Inn and Restaurant at Sedgeford in Norfolk – 'miles away, but worth it' – their longevity toasted with a bottle of claret from the Getty estate.

Having located a canine-friendly hotel for £20 a night, Mike Latham is here again with Toby (the dog), 'good as gold' reportedly.

'Did the £20 get him a towel,' asks Steve, father of Toby (the cricketer), as the trio shelter by his car in the shade of a beech.

'More to the point, was it a double bed?' says Alan.

Steve Bulcock knows his onions. 'Good length on a Bolton wicket, that – here it whizzes through,' says a man who, as confirmed by Ross Zelem, has coached many a Lancashire county youth side and been partly responsible for the development of big-name talent. Suddenly, there is an appeal and Cambridgeshire's first victim falls, Charlie Lewis snaffled by Bulcock Jr, leg before wicket for 8.

'He's given it!' says Alan. 'What a bloody good umpire he is.'

Having played cricket himself as a youngster, Steve, with two lads of his own, later turned to coaching as a way of instilling them with good habits. Relevant badges acquired, he took charge of the under-11s at Baxenden, the family's local club, before leading his sons through the age groups and eventually coaching a Ribblesdale League representative side, of which Toby and his brother, Dominic, were members. In 2000, came a Lancashire town teams competition featuring every red rose district and Steve took charge of theirs. 'I was fortunate to have a good set of lads and their success got people thinking it was down to me rather than the boys themselves, which is the truth of it. Toby and Dominic had also managed to get in the Lancashire county sides at under-11s to under-15s, so they asked if I was interested in running the under-13s.' He agreed.

That group was considered key to the county's future fortunes and therefore played heaps of fixtures, which for their coach meant a lot of time and effort. Fortunately, he worked at Holland's Pies: '...which meant that with a 5.00am start I'd be finished at 11.00am, so had my afternoons. I got into the system, researched what was required and went watching numerous matches, all over the show.'

Soon, this stocky bloke with a drawling Accrington burr was inundated with young prospects, recommended by the sort of coach he'd been, in the Lancashire districts, chasing a place for their best in the county under-13s. 'So we arranged trials at different grounds to have a good look at everybody and had them bat seven overs in pairs, twenty-four at a time, three of spin, four of pace. If they got out, they'd swap ends. I built a five-man selection team.'

Of one hundred applicants, fourteen made it into the squad each year, though opportunities remained for late-bloomers. 'We'd play Nottinghamshire, Yorkshire, Warwickshire, Cumbria ... and at the end of the season there'd be a festival at Taunton. Twelve teams went down, bunked overnight. It was fantastic, really tough, put a lot of pressure on the kids.' Numbered among whom were the likes of Jos Buttler and the Curran brothers, with Marcus Trescothick or Darren Gough or some other celebrity presenting prizes. 'You wouldn't have known some of those lads were going to be stars, some you definitely would ... Haseeb Hameed ... Ben Stokes ... they went to Taunton. We had six pitches going at once. Families all over the place, barbecues, it was unbelievable, really well organised. It's still going – as soon as school term finishes, under-11s upwards.'

It is therefore against such a backdrop that Toby and Dominic (now playing semi-pro in Melbourne, having emigrated in 2010) developed their attitudes to the game. Cricket should be fun, yes, but be underpinned by principles of effort, integrity and purpose.

Steve coached at Lancashire for seven or eight years before domestic changes meant he could no longer offer the same level of commitment. 'If I couldn't give a hundred per cent ... at the ground before the team, setting everything up ... I'd be setting a bad example. How do you tell a lad to get there an hour beforehand when you're not doing it yourself? I'd have loved to carried on but couldn't.'

Nowadays, he is purely a spectator. He might visit Old Trafford occasionally but mainly, with wife Bev, follows Toby around. Highly regarded throughout the MCCA and beyond, ought his son to have made the first-class county ranks, climbing, as some suggest, to the heights of an England international spinner? Therein lies a tale with details hinted at rather than openly divulged.

'Rose-tinted glasses from a parent but, yes, I do. I've seen three or four lads who were really unlucky to have missed a contract when they were 18 and absolutely in the zone, and Toby is one. I mean, he captained Lancashire from under-15s to under-19s, and they won an awful lot of championships. Didn't even get an academy spot, when at any other county in England I'm sure he would have done. Whether there was something personal about that, I don't know. He's a wholehearted lad who wears his heart on his sleeve.'

It isn't necessary to be in Toby's company long before realising that beneath the comedic exterior, the game and team matter hugely to him. Cricket is everything. 'Oh it means a lot,' his dad continues. 'Even as a young lad, he'd put that much into it, win, lose or draw. It didn't matter if he'd scored a century or got five wickets, he'd almost be in tears at times, so eaten up with how the game was going.'

'*I am going to have to win this one today...*'

'Yeah. He feels that responsibility. With that mindset there is always a chance of getting on in the sport but, unfortunately for him, he's had trials and done well but, I don't know, maybe was unlucky. If you speak to him about it he'll say: "D'you know, I enjoy my cricket and might not have done." He's got a family of his own now too. He'll stay in the game in some way, give something back. He won't just stop and fall out with it. He's got a lot to offer somebody.'

Like his brother, Toby has played in Australia, at a place called Brighton, a coastal suburb in Victoria, and then at Dominic's current club, Westmeadows. 'He also had an offer in Perth, but didn't fancy that, so passed it on to a friend who also played for the Lancashire junior section. The lad still lives there and is married now.'

Mr and Mrs Atkinson having gone back to Penrith, Rob Cairns brings on the drinks – strictly no vino – but it's not long before Toby is pumping the troops up again. His is the voice you hear. 'One man army these, eh?' ... 'come on, fellas,' after every ball. His next over too is quite brilliant – how no wicket falls is confounding.

Syds bowls a maiden of his own as the duo continue to press hard, but there aren't many runs to play with and, after Jacques is given the over before lunch, Cambridgeshire go in for their bangers and mash on 39 for 1. Cue more banter from Derek and Alan.

'What was my highest score? 42.'

'Was that in one game or a season?'

Here is a friendship built over years, defying time and distance, precious yet not at all unusual in Minor Counties circles. The room behind the main bar in which lunch is served has the air of a cosy pub lounge, complete with fireplace, andirons and photographs of teams going back to Wisbech Town CC's official birth year, 1895, although Derek thinks cricket has likely been played in the town since the 1700s. The actual ground opened in 1926, with a match against the MCC. If and when 'The Crockey Project' hits its target, that story will remain even as the present bricks and mortar crumble.

A little wagtail on the boundary watches Cambridgeshire start the afternoon session, another appeal by Toby denied. It isn't long before Howgego is again among the runs, reaching 50 in the 31st over. A half-century is fitting, it being exactly 50 years since Cambridgeshire left the first-class county scene, the only side ever to have done so. In a field beyond, a group of schoolchildren form a circle and proceed to dance under a rainbow-coloured banner.

Tyler nabs a second victim, lbw, but by then Cambridgeshire are heading home with a flurry. When the target is passed for the loss of those two wickets, Howgego is 89 not out, having just been dropped by Greg Hall to rub salt in the wound. Just before 4.00pm, the sides are clapped off the field on the summer's hottest day so far.

Rather than miserable, the visitors look weary, their collective blood pressure low, and understandably so in such temperatures.

'First innings, fantastic,' says Syds, in the sheds. 'We could have applied ourselves better in the second. In three-day games you've to back it up. But we're at home next ... hopefully with local umps.'

'We lost that game ourselves,' says Slacky, cutting through the laughter. 'It's one of my pet hates, blaming the ref or whatever. Where we've lost that is middle order, second innings, no doubt.'

'We put our backs against the wall yesterday afternoon and evening, didn't we?' says Toby. 'But today shafted us.'

Ross, now upright, joins in: 'Three days of cricket, but one bad session can cost you the game, can't it? We've taken our eyes off it for one session and fucked it up.'

'But we learn from it, don't we?' says Dutts. 'So let's move on, get a beer and fuck off.'

Lap Two

The Garden of Eden

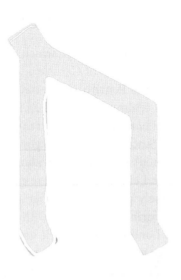

Mattie McKiernan has been offered a T20 contract by Derbyshire, which calls into question his availability not only with Cumberland, but also for Richmondshire. It would be for six weeks, so a gamble. His club side is going well and he may miss out on their success. Confident in his own abilities, he has nonetheless backed himself.

Mike Latham shares the news en route to 'Lakeland's northern neighbour', the Eden Valley, our latest lap of Cumbria's cricket scene. And this time we have a second guide with us, a book by John Hurst, author of Cumberland's original club history.

Published at the turn of the twentieth century, *Come Back to Eden* is more fine work by a man who had Cumbria in his veins. Beautifully written and unashamedly nostalgic, it champions a 'golden carpet' of a region, overlooked by day-trippers who favour the more famous spots. 'The appeal of Eden lies in a gentler, more subtle brand of beauty,' Hurst writes, 'typified by well-tended farmland, tranquil villages like Ormside and Warcop, Great Salkeld and Kirkoswald, and spectacular vistas which embrace both the sweep of the valley and the majesty of distant fells, be they the smooth-topped Pennines, to the east, or the more rugged Lakeland hills, to the west.' It is a description confirmed within minutes.

Eden's 'capital' is Penrith, Hurst's home town, but we've been there already and, anyway, are really here to explore the Eden Valley Cricket League, which nowadays extends beyond its initial footprint

– in the valley through which the river flows – out towards Keswick, the border city of Carlisle and, most recently, over the border into Scotland. Penrith, as we have seen, are in the Northern Premier League, although the 3rd XI is in EVCL Division 2 and destined to finish bottom this year, on minus 29, having conceded five fixtures.

Since 1974 and local government reorganisation, Eden District Council's brief has also widened, taking in bits of the Pennines and North Lakeland too. As a result, writes Hurst, this is England's most sparsely populated district: '...just 35 people to the square mile, comparing dramatically with the 18,657 crammed into a single area of a London borough.' He goes on: 'Native Cumbrians, of the Eden Valley and other parts, are seen as stolid unappreciative types. The truth is that with so much natural beauty all around them, so much grandeur and fascination, they see no need for outbursts of enthusiasm. Leave that to visiting strangers.'

Our first destination is Carlisle, whose first team host Cleator in the North Lancs and Cumbria today. The 2nd XI will win at Caldbeck, en route to a title-winning EVCL Premiership season.

There are few better venues in which to watch cricket than Edenside which, as its name suggests, is on a northerly stretch of the river, a vast bowl that may once have been an amphitheatre. Given the bathhouse excavated here in 2015, referred to at the Crooklands AGM by club secretary Mark Davidson, there is a definite link to Roman times. Our time today is precious, so more on that will have to wait until the county side plays its last game of the season here in early September, against Lincolnshire.

Carlisle, the city, reeks of antiquity, boasting such wonders as Tullie House Museum and Art Gallery, which in modern times have been extended, roots in the Jacobean era. It rests in the shadow of nine hundred-year-old Carlisle Castle, close to a stretch of what was once Hadrian's Wall, English Heritage flag flying. Tullie House holds a renowned oil-painting of a cricket match by Samuel Bough, circa 1844, in which Carlisle are said to be playing Newcastle, 'with Mr Howe umpiring at the far wicket.' The castle walls are visible amid a scene of tents, top hats and distant factory chimneys.

But then coming into town you also pass The Lanes – sizzling pink this sunny Saturday afternoon with bare-armed-and-chested shoppers drawn to its seventy or so 'specialist' retail outlets like bees to pollen. Exactly twelve months to the day the UK's then foreign secretary, Boris Johnson, made headlines in the *News & Star* upon 'stopping for coffee' just up the road. Staff and customers at a Brampton coffee shop were surprised to see 'the man who could become the United Kingdom's next Prime Minister' walk through the door. Linda Smith, a worker at Off The Wall, told the paper how the MP for Uxbridge and South Ruislip had happily posed for photographs, saying he was on a cycling break. 'He had two coffees and two cans of pop. He seemed nice enough.'

However such cordiality was in stark contrast to an earlier visit in 2005, about which Johnson, MP for Henley-on-Thames, wrote in the *Daily Telegraph* after a stroll down infamous Botchergate: 'Faces leered and weaved towards me, pale and waxy with drink ... everyone seemed to be hurling strange oaths and invitations, and, since I could find nowhere to sit and read my book, I fled to the railway station and sat shivering on the platform until the night train arrived.'

Having traversed a busy roundabout and crossed the Eden Bridge, turning left down a sharp incline a visitor is greeted by an altogether more enticing prospect. Edenside has a 'wow factor'. And despite its size inside, here is another ground you might never know was there – so unprepossessing is it from the road.

The other thing for which Carlisle CC is known is flooding, which it last did very dramatically in December 2015, only weeks after Cumberland won the Minor Counties Championship here. The damage was every bit as disastrous as at Keswick, Cockermouth and elsewhere. A line etched on the pavilion shows the height to which waters rose. That too though is a story for another day.

A game between first and third in the table begins a couple of minutes early. Cleator's David Watson, opening here as at Furness, hits a four in the first over, bringing applause from rows of benches on a hill to the right, shared with an unlikely dry ski slope. Edenside was a favourite spot of late Cumberland CCC patron Bob Bowman, who died in February following a decade with Parkinson's Disease. Indeed the funeral tea was held here, his name is on the gate. Mark Davidson calls the president's contribution: '...simply inestimable. We all owe Bob a huge debt of gratitude. He was a very talented cricketer for Carlisle and Cumberland and a lifelong supporter of both right up to the end.' In a varied life, Bob owned a chain of chemists before his retirement in 2009 and, as keen a patron of the arts as sport, became honorary president of the Carlisle Music and Drama Festival, a tenor soloist under the tutelage of distinguished Cumbrian soprano, Ena Mitchell, in the 1960s. In 2011, he received an OBE for services to music and the arts in Carlisle and Cumbria, although you suspect character-building days as part of the first Cumberland team to join the Minor Counties Cricket Association in 1955 – when he also represented the county in a draw with South Africa at Edenside – must have given him as much, if not more, pleasure. It's nice to see a framed photograph of Bob, posing proudly alongside Gary Pratt, with the Minor Counties trophy in 2015.

'Bob was here most weekends,' Mark will later recall. 'He'd drive down and watch the cricket, midweek too, latterly brought by his carer. He'd park his car by the boundary near the pavilion, come in for a cup of tea and a slice of cake. He was a true philanthropist and a great man, our patron and president for around a quarter of a century. Without Bob Bowman we wouldn't be standing here today. He kept the club going financially through all the bad times.'

The dipping entry road sweeps past former tennis courts, an unsightly mass of weeds and rubble now, beneath which those back-filled Roman remains await a decision as to what English Heritage intends to do with them. A pile of feathers presumably belonged to a bird carried off by some bigger raptor and, in front of that is the Jimmy Little Memorial Pavilion, a grand title for a redbrick structure the club intends to knock down and replace with a new pavilion on higher ground, the better to keep it dry.

Cleator skipper David Rooney – he of England's Barmy Army – watches from a bench on the banking, awaiting his turn to go in. From such a vantage point, the view is similar to that of the Samuel Bough painting in the gallery, although the castle, visible then, is one hundred and seventy-odd years later camouflaged by trees. All in all, though, those historical pioneers who favoured the place over Workington almost had it right. Were it not for its climatic problems, this would indeed be an ideal county ground for Cumberland.

As Cleator advance towards a 17-run victory, a group of non-batting players throw an Aussie Rules football about, stripped to the waist. It's another blistering afternoon, with a high of 27 degrees.

*****

'One of the county's three major leagues, the EVCL is traditionally associated with the gentle rolling pastures and green and fertile land that is the Eden Valley but, as from next season, those in the fourth tier will be playing their cricket in bonny Scotland.' Thus can be paraphrased the minutes of an AGM at Penrith in 2012, when a unanimous decision was taken to welcome Langholm CC to the fray. It is to there we now head, via the Carlisle-Edinburgh trunk road.

A club founded in 1858 had, since 1930, enjoyed membership of the historic Borders League before an exodus of sides to the East of Scotland League suddenly meant onerous trips to Edinburgh, Fife and the Lothians on a Saturday, rather than familiar rivals closer to home. The previous comp became a ten-team Sunday league only. By contrast: 'Road improvements and speed of access once on the motorway means they will reach many grounds within the hour,' the EVCL report said, explaining the appeal of its bottom tier. 'In fact, the journey to the Penrith meeting took much less.' The furthest trip now required would be Kirkby Stephen, around seventy miles south.

Castleholm – Langholm's base – is eight miles into Reivers country, a saltire confirming the border crossing into Dumfries and Galloway. Track the Esk to what is known locally as 'Muckletoon', turn left over civil engineer Thomas Telford's suspension bridge, cross a smaller stone one further on and the ground is at the centre of an overgrown racecourse, near the ruins of Langholm Castle, around a quarter of a mile from the centre. According to Scotland's *Gazetteer*, however, four 'flapping' race meetings, outside Jockey Club rules, are still traditionally held here every summer.

The switch to the EVCL has served Langholm well. Not only is the club in the competition's second tier, having won promotions in the intervening years, along with two senior teams they also boast a sixty-strong junior section. Today has been designated 'Ladies' Day' and the 1st XI are playing Nunwick from Great Salkeld, a village near Carlisle. Truth be told, the playing standard isn't great, but the bigger picture is something else entirely.

In making a case for entry into the EVCL, Langholm's Duncan Elliott, currently amassing 37 runs in what will be a 118-run victory, had described his club as ambitious and in need of a fresh challenge. 'We recently carried out £40,000 worth of improvements on our pavilion and are looking to extend further,' he told that fateful AGM. 'Visiting teams will receive great hospitality.' Fronted by clumps of spectators, seated on upholstered chairs around two laminate tables, Scottish accents in the majority, the facility certainly looks homely, a valued community resource. Inside, there is a good-sized bar and concert room and although everything is a little make-do-and-mend – no sightscreens, for instance – it has plenty of character and charm.

Here and there pink balloons are tied, strung in greatest number by a marquee signed 'Prosecco and Gin Bar'. According to posters, tonight there'll be a barbecue, with live music by Nicky Henderson – a local performer, not the celebrated horse racing trainer – and his band the 'Muckletoon Joggers'.

Ladies are indeed in abundance and two more drive up, their car raising dust, before they tip-toe in heels along the boundary and sip at something fizzy. Under another awning, a mother changes a baby just as a six is dispatched onto the racetrack, the ball lost in the long grass for a while. It is on account of such delays that Langholm's innings will last three hours, which risks over-running the league's 8.00pm finish stipulation. Happily, they are destined to see off their opponents with fifteen minutes to spare and consolidate their place at the upper end of EVCL Division 1.

England calls and as we make to depart it's so hot the square leg umpire pulls his shirt over his head, baking slowly among clumps of vivid daisies. As is now common at this level, the official umpire is at the bowling end, the batting side volunteering the man at a right angle. What we need is water and at our next port of call, Rockcliffe CC, that is a commodity they have in abundance.

*****

Wind farms and pylons adorn the drive north west of Carlisle, down narrow country lanes from where Scotland shrinks in the rear view mirror. We are off to where the Esk and Eden meet the Solway Firth, Mike fleshing out a league that has lost up to fifteen clubs over the last couple of decades. 'The Eden Valley was suspended in 2001,' he says, 'on account of the foot and mouth outbreak; it didn't get played. Since then a number of clubs have gone. Lowther, Shap...' He ticks off more of the fallen as an unintended 'short cut' takes us through private farmland and fields of maize, grown in abundance here for the feed that goes into beef and biomass for renewable energy.

Like the village the club represents, set on a marshy peninsula, Rockcliffe CC is reluctant to be found. Online, *Visit Cumbria* reveals that while this formerly busy commercial port has a solid maritime history, little of that remains but for: '...a few remnants of wooden jetties and a ship weathervane on the church spire.' That church is St Mary the Virgin, figuratively and physically prominent here since 1848, alongside a fragment of a thousand year-old Norse cross.

Seeking cricket, a regular might nip round the back of Church View cottage, a whitewashed roadside B&B, as that's where the club pavilion is located. To a stranger, however, that public footpath looks like private land, so we end up walking down a hilly lane as St Mary's rises higher alongside until even the gravestones are six feet over. As Mrs Spottsworth says in *Ring for Jeeves*, by way of Rudyard Kipling, it's the sort of place where: 'The dead, twelve deep, clutch at you as you go by.' At least we are in the open air and not yet food for worms.

Given the probable consequences, the height of this necropolis must be handy in times of flood – and it floods here a lot. The hill footings are cloaked by hanging trees, an unlikely chill on a day like this dispelled by a shaft of sunlight, before all again is fine. Turning left, a walker is beckoned by a fat finger of the Solway Firth in the near distance, beyond a smattering of cowpats and scrubland stream traversed by a wooden ramp. Nudge through a stile and Rockcliffe Cricket Club bobs into view, as if marooned on a coastal limb. Access there is none, the fortress encircled by a fence barring entry. The only seating arrangements are directly opposite, at the point where we *should* have come in.

Founded in 1907, the ground shares its name with the church, St Mary's, and the 1st XI are going well in the top division of the EVCL, its Premiership. Two further Rockcliffe teams play in the Carlisle and District Midweek League. Here, it's third against second and visitors Lanercost CC, from near the market town of Brampton, are making a meal of it. Opener Ross Wilson has contributed 51 of his side's running total of 79 for 5 after 28 overs, the following five batsmen failing to reach double figures. Their tail end rallies to take Lanercost to 130 for 8 once their 40 overs are up, but that won't be enough. Rockcliffe will pass that total for the loss of six wickets, needing only 31.4 overs in which to do it.

Hung over the fence is an England flag, Rockcliffe Cricket Club written in white on the red cross of St George. Beyond it, to the south, the jagged outline of parent peak Skiddaw and its offspring Colbeck, Saddleback, Threlkeld, Braithwaite and other such fells in Lakeland ... milky from this distance. Closer to hand, from its source to the east at Black Fell Moss, in the dale of Mallerstang, having cut through the valley that bears its name, the Eden itself meets the sea at this very spot.

Happily for Mike and his four-legged friend, it's dog-walking country and before long we are joined by a local doing likewise. When the river is up, he says, fields and buildings hereabouts are extremely susceptible, the pitch submerged with every high tide. The church alone – its spire poking over the top of trees at least 250 feet tall – seems to get away with it. 'The water hasn't reached that high yet.' Alongside us is an orange lifebuoy; not many cricket clubs need one of those. We won't either, unless it's to deal with excessive sweat.

The game proceeds watched by five men and four dogs, a pair of black Labradors among them belonging to chairman Robert Park, also vice-chair of Rockcliffe parish council. He says the land is owned by the Mounsey-Heyshams, who charge £25 a year in rent, one family member being club president. Prior to World War One, their games were played on marshland at Castletown House, part of an estate bought by Robert Mounsey in 1802. So much for Charles Darwin; Rockcliffeans surely ought to have evolved webbed feet by now. Councillor Park used to play here himself before hanging up his boots five years ago: 'It was just time catching up.'

Born and raised in the village, he elaborates. 'In winter, the ground floods twice a month. Three weeks ago, the wicket was under two feet of water a day after a new artificial one was laid.' In 2015, the place was wrecked. 'Worse than ever,' he says. Another major issue has been the closure of the Crown and Thistle pub, their HQ, currently up for sale while the village hall stands in. The chairman could be excused for feeling downhearted, but not a bit of it.

'There's a buzz we haven't had for a long time,' he says, a mood of positivity helped by winning games. 'The All Stars initiative is very successful. We average twenty-five schoolkids on a Friday night, which opens funding opportunities with the ECB. There's an issue with secondary schools, but family connections are what keep the club going. This is quite a small place.' A cheerful chap in a Standard Life insurance baseball cap, he does however admit to entertaining one doubt: 'There are times we think we should find higher ground...'

Proceeding in a southerly direction, next on our list is Staffield, a good stretch of tarmac away. Last season, with Lanercost, they won promotion to the EVCL Premiership. Today's opponents, Kirkby Stephen, came top of the entire competition and are going well now, destined to finish runners-up. Staffield, rock bottom alas, will be relegated back to Division 1, but all of that is for the future.

The Old Showground is in the manor of Kirkoswald, off the M6, junction 42 and along the A6, where we zip by the Eden Valley Visitors Centre in terrain John Hurst captured well. Here, crag and scree give way to rolling plains redolent of Tolkien's Shire, idyllic, beloved and fruitful. Dotted about are Brigadoon-like villages and hamlets preserved in a fug of interwar aspic.

Or as Hurst puts it: 'Stray thoughts float into the memory, most of them from a past era. Perhaps the fleeting vision is of an old-style bobby pounding his rural beat; the sight of newly-turned, chocolate-coloured earth, as ploughman and horse trudge across a field, hungry seagulls dipping low into the fresh furrows; a postman astride a pushbike, handing letters over a garden wall; a village showfield, full of activity and colour, with men and women in their "Sunday best"; or wind-driven rain angling down in silent repetitive waves, in harmony with the rise and fall of gusts, shimmering against the sombre backcloth of a mountainside.'

There is no gusty rain today lashing a landscape more redolent of Umbria or Tuscany. Just remaining clues as to those 'far off days' when, Hurst recalls, plentiful '...food and drink and the presence of pretty and elegant ladies all contributed to the enjoyment.' Days when press reports might detail the teatime menu at a cricket match and list the attending gentry, military bands providing music.

One such 'ghost' emerges on the way into Kirkoswald, namely the Midland Hotel, which fronts Lazonby and Kirkoswald station. The pub is at an angle to a bridge on which the Settle-Carlisle train passes, the Midland Railway having employed six-thousand navvies to construct the line in the early-1870s. There must be a scarecrow festival on somewhere too, given their ubiquity, but less easy to spot is Staffield's ground, down a narrow lane near three pubs – the Black Bull, Crown Inn and Fetherston Arms – packed tightly around Kirkoswald Cross, a memorial to the village's war dead.

It's a pretty little place. Kirkoswald won the first ever 'Cumbria in Bloom' competition in 1958. According to John Hurst, the judges were as impressed by the lack of litter, tidy bus shelters, phone boxes and notice boards as its contribution to the 'floral glory of Eden.' He quotes the *Cumberland and Westmorland Herald*: 'There are flowers in every available nook and cranny ... hanging baskets, window troughs and stone urns, tiny beds and narrow borders. Women householders have produced a riot of colour with a floral display of remarkable variety. Kirkoswald seems to make a feature of roses, for which this has been a vintage year, and the judges happened to pay a visit when the roses were at their best.'

Parking in the main street, Staffield CC is best reached by foot, between a wall and stone cottage and on past Kirkoswald FC's soccer ground, goalmouths taped up to ward off vandals. The penalty boxes have been reseeded for the summer. As for the cricket, all is silent as the grave. We arrive just as a four is struck off the last ball before tea, but even when the batsmen and fielders plod back to the only man-made structure in view, a wooden pavilion, it feels like something has been endured rather than enjoyed. There are no spectators, unsurprisingly perhaps given the boundary is fenced all around with only the top end open for casual viewing. It's as if we have stumbled upon some covert and solemn duty.

In a couple of summers' time, mid-Covid 19 lockdown, a day like this will be fondly recalled as the stuff of fantasy. But right now, there isn't anyone here who doesn't look like they would rather be at home watching Joe Exotic and his tigers on Netflix.

What-ho! Kirkby Stephen are destined to win by eight wickets, with three overs and three balls to spare. Heading back to the old five-seater is for us the work of a moment.

*****

'East Cumbria's quaintest ground used to be at Gamblesby, a village at the foot of the Pennines that could once field a team consisting largely of members of the Little family,' writes John Hurst, in *Come Back to Eden*. 'The ground fell away steeply on one side of the pitch, so that it was a masterpiece of anticipation if an outfield catch was taken. On the other side the wicket was close to a wall, so that ground rules applied – two runs if a shot struck the wall, four if it landed in the next field. In the 1960s, the Gamblesby ground was levelled and the uniqueness removed.' Also reportedly excellent were the teas, served in a farmhouse kitchen a six-hit or so from the field.

Those butterfly buns and egg sandwiches long since went down the hatch, but the venue remains as unique as Hurst claimed. If it truly was worse pre-1960s, it must have cut a sight indeed. Cumberland chairman Neil Atkinson had warned it was 'like standing on the top of the world', just four miles from Kirkoswald. Today the hosts face Carlisle's 3rd XI in a bottom-of-the-table Division 1 encounter. By August, the visitors will narrowly escape relegation, leaving Nunwick to fall into Division 2 alongside Gamblesby instead.

Alston – at one thousand feet above sea level the joint-highest market town in England with Buxton in Derbyshire – isn't far from here either, ten miles over the moor that bears its name. Originally a lead-mining community, it seems not to have its own cricket club, although does have another claim to fame. According to Mike, its male-female ratio is higher than anywhere: '...a ratio of ten men to every woman in the town.' He is joking. Probably. Apart from retaining its medieval stocks, Gamblesby cannot compete with that, although in terms of oddity its cricket club gives it a go. It is hard to imagine why anyone would come here for any other reason. The sense of isolation in what feels like the middle of nowhere must be even more potent and, for youngsters you'd imagine, claustrophobic during the winter months. It's also another bugger of a ground to find, squirreled beyond drystone walls and the stone cottages that line horseshoe lanes with blind bends eyed by murderous crows.

Signs to nearby villages ... Renwick (formerly Ravenwick) ... Melmerby ... Skirwith ... hang on black-and-white-striped poles of a type Miss Marple might pass on her way to investigate a poisoning at the parson's duck race. It's the sort of landscape John Hurst at his most nostalgic had in mind, where butchers with flea-bitten sheepskins in the window ration chops wrapped in brown paper. Mike's satnav says 'destination reached', but the ground is nowhere to be seen. Is it set to the right century? But then suddenly, as we reverse to let a tractor pass, there it is, a flash of white in a cow field, one of Gamblesby's two hundred or so inhabitants in his cricket gear, giving the game away.

Even then the entry is a tease, via a farmyard. The effort though is worth it, a charming sight, the epitome of village cricket in some ways, though with an open aspect that would in less amiable conditions appear stark rather than pretty. The field rests on a plateau and all around it are short boundaries such as Hurst describes; indeed a six is hammered the moment we walk in. There must be a lot of that about.

'Stick it down as a four and make a game of it,' says the 'keeper, heard by five people watching, not including ourselves, the waiting batsmen and the odd bovine observer nonchalantly munching in an upper paddock. We opt for a lap of the boundary, though with a certain trepidation. The vertiginous drop is still there at the bottom end, where the rest of Cumbria rolls off into the distance. Added to which a stiff breeze rises, entirely out of keeping with the day so far.

As at Langholm, the square leg umpire is from the batting side and, at one point, has to be told by his colleague that the over is up. He is standing feet from the boundary, close enough to say 'hello' to walking by. This raised and flattened earthwork is some feat of civil engineering, the notion of shuffling backwards, eye on the ball for a catching chance, intriguing. Sadly, the scenario doesn't arise. The hosts do however bag a wicket at the exact moment the umpire's hat blows off. Gamblesby applaud the incoming batsman on his way *to* the crease, a tradition now seldom seen. Cameron Westmorland, whose ancestors presumably didn't roam far, is caught Dan Martin, bowled Darren Coleman, for a golden duck. It puts 'Daz' on a hat-trick and his teammates get suitably excited.

The chap in next was last seen sat on the ground by the gate, back against a painted shipping container serving as a pavilion. He had been messing about on a laptop, presumably updating the scores as Geoff Minshaw does with Cockermouth and Cumberland to *playcricket.com*. In which case, the task will have to wait. Entering to a slow handclap this time, he not only survives a run-out first ball, but will almost reach a half-century in an eventual five-wicket victory. Impressive. It's good to know too that they have a broadband signal here and he doesn't have to file his reports by carrier pigeon.

This is a part of the world where sheep and cattle might graze on outfields through the week, with the natural product of that arrangement removed on Saturday morning. It's also a place where spectators might lean on a wall rather than enter the ground or, in some cases, get a little too close. Hurst tells of when Penrith met a team of Ullswater farmers at Watermillock. On going in to bat, their captain noticed twelve fielders. Don't worry, the 'keeper said, 'that's only Old Joe in the slips.' He wasn't playing; he just liked standing there to get a better view. No need to do that at Gamblesby.

Our final stop on another packed Saturday is Temple Sowerby, a.k.a. the Thunderdome. Only the Gods know why, since there isn't a dome at this the most exposed spot yet. It is easy to imagine thunder in the surrounding hilltops, though that may be due to the rumble of traffic traversing what would once have been a pasture below. Temple Sowerby has the epithet 'Queen of the Westmorland Villages', though its cricket pitch on her outskirts is far from regal, midway between Penrith and Appleby on a stretch of the A66.

Our journey here took us through Langwathby who, with Edenhall a mile away, are one half of EVCL Division 1 side Edenhall and Langwathby. Alas, they were busy losing to Keswick's 2nd XI in Lakeland, so there was no game to see. The place did though allow for a comfort break at a station that would once have been the sort of place Hurst describes in *Come Back to Eden*. 'Before Dr Beeching's axe fell on rural railway lines,' he writes, 'the appearance of village stations was also a cause of pride. Stationmasters and porters devoted countless hours to rose beds and flower borders...' The days of Langwathby winning the sort of prize Kirkoswald did are gone, although it does have a 'Brief Encounter café'. That too was shut. Through a window, a young woman sat at a table, gazing sadly at an open laptop. A modern-day Celia Johnson tweeting her 21st century Trevor Howard? Or was she just searching for updates from Gamblesby? 'Nothing lasts really. Neither happiness nor despair.'

We also passed through Culgaith, temporarily home to EVCL Division 1 side Appleby Eden while their own ground, wrecked by the 2015 floods, is repaired, Culgaith having since folded entirely.

When we show up, Temple Sowerby are 65 for 4, chasing 252. Braithwaite are the visitors and one of their fielders, white-haired, his glasses tied on with string, says: 'The coin came down the right way and we had a bat on a sunny day.'

Hurst's book contains an anecdote from 1992 in Workington, where Temple Sowerby, back then visitors themselves, closed in on victory in a tight finish – twenty runs needed, five overs to go, two wickets left. Their concentration however was broken by an invasion of '...youths taking part in Workington's Uppies and Downies ball game, an annual outbreak of local tribal warfare dating back several centuries.' The umpires stopped play while the unruly were cleared: '...but the damage had been done and Temple Sowerby's victory bid was thwarted.' The outcome will be nowhere near as memorable today, the hosts running out of steam and falling short, 174 all out.

Every ground visited in the Eden Valley League has had its own distinctive personality, even eccentricity. A garden of Eden, it's true, in a land that time cannot forget.

CHAPTER SIX
MEN OF KENT

Jacques du Toit tugs on a Marlboro Light, calm in the eye of a storm. 'If I got hit,' he exhales, words and smoke entwined, 'anyone could. A youngster might have turned his head and that can be serious.' He is referencing Phillip Hughes, the 25-year-old Australian batsman who died in 2014, two days after being struck in the neck during a Sheffield Shield match at the Sydney Cricket Ground. 'First one hit me on the glove – noise made me think it was broken. Second one was lethal, off a length. You train to keep your eye on the ball, so I'm happy with how I played it.' Drop of the bat, straight to ground. 'But you don't wait for something bad to happen, do you?'

It's day one of Cumberland's second Unicorns Championship match of the summer, a 'home fixture' at Netherfield CC in Kendal, against Staffordshire, Moeen Ali's brother Kadeer and all. Locals call this the Auld Grey Town, due either to the colour of its buildings or the 'Scotch mist' that frequently shrouds the place, blowing in off its surrounding fells. There is no chance of that today. The temperature is again punishingly high, outfield scorched ochre. The wicket is dry as tinder and cracked to the extent that, after a rocky start, the game's completion is suddenly in doubt with the Cumbrians 96 for 4.

'It's not the groundsman's fault,' the South African sympathises. 'Great wicket here and how much do you water it? It's hard to know.'

There is it seems the possibility of switching pitches; the track below is marginally greener. Might the morning's play be scratched and a new game begun after an early lunch? The umpires try to contact MCCA secretary Phil Caley, no one quite certain of the rules and precedents, initially without success. The chap from BBC Radio Cumbria remembers a game once when they went somewhere else the next day – Old Trafford – and had a two-day match instead. All agree that things cannot continue as they stand.

Well, almost everyone. As one spectator, who must moonlight as a magician, prods a playing card up his nose before pulling it out of his mouth at one bench table, Netherfield's secretary, Ian Heath, says the groundsman Jacques refers to can't see what all the fuss is about. 'In his view, the umpires took too quick a response to two balls that hit somebody,' he says in the clubhouse, as trays of lasagne are wheeled out and matters assessed. 'He's disappointed. It's a wicket that will get harder and faster, but those who play Minor Counties will be used to that. You see first-class pitches with a lot more cracks. Whether they are just being over-cautious I don't know.'

*****

It is early July, a month that would have begun with a Knockout Trophy semi-final had Cumberland still been in it. They weren't, so the squad hasn't met for a fortnight. Not that individually they have been idle, fulfilling commitments with their various clubs.

Gary Pratt's Richmondshire beat Stokesley, near Middlesbrough, by ten wickets in the semi-final of the North Yorkshire and South Durham League Cup, the skipper and his fellow opener, Bob Carr, both scoring half-centuries. The final is on August 5, so although Gary is back in the Cumberland side today, he will miss the fourth three-dayer in Bedfordshire. Teammate Mattie McKiernan, despite impressing in a number of 2nd XI fixtures with Derbyshire, still awaits his Vitality Blast debut. Word is it may be on Friday in an eagerly anticipated East Midlands derby with Nottinghamshire Outlaws. Yet despite the Falcons having lost both T20 fixtures prior to that, it will turn out not to be the case. In fact his chance will come on Saturday 14 July against Lancashire at Old Trafford. In a fourth defeat, Derbyshire will go down by 12 runs, the 24-year-old recording figures of 0-27 with the ball, 1 not out the bat. A day later, he will receive permission to play for Richmondshire in an ECB

National Club Championship fifth-round tie at Doncaster Town, scoring 81 not out and bowling five overs for one wicket and seven runs. There's also talk Mattie may play in Cumberland's next Championship clash, with Hertfordshire, since neither Derbyshire's Vitality Blast side or Richmondshire have a game that Sunday. Yet, in an ever more frustrating month when he is once again overlooked for the T20, that release won't come either. It ought to go without saying therefore that he is absent today.

At a less exalted level, Leigh CC managed a hefty 288 for 5 at Lytham in the Liverpool Comp the other Saturday, to which Toby Bulcock and Ross Zelem somehow contributed ducks. And earlier in the week, Sam Dutton represented the Unicorns against England under-19s at Loughborough – as wicketkeeper. 'Hands were red raw,' he said. 'Gloves had no inners. Couldn't bat afterwards...' In today's aborted innings, however, he'd done okay. Despite boundary pundits querying the wicket from the start, the little fellow had batted freely, knocking over a dog's water bowl with one well-struck four.

Away from cricket, the big sporting topic is football, namely England's 2-0 quarter-final victory over Sweden yesterday, having lost 1-0 to Belgium in their group and then registered a first World Cup penalty shoot-out win, against Colombia, in the last sixteen. Gareth Southgate's side will now meet Croatia, impressive so far, at Moscow's Luzhniki Stadium on Wednesday. Should they win that, they will be in the final next Sunday – the day Cumberland are due to complete their Twenty20 obligations at Workington. Given that not a few of his side would be eager to watch such an historic occasion, it's another scheduling irritation for Steve Sharp although, for now, he faces more immediate disruption. Would this second Championship match, entered into with optimism, be scrapped?

'Good wicket,' chairman Neil had said, bucking the trend, while the OAPs of Netherfield Bowling Club packed the equally frazzled greens alongside, as Cumberland got reacquainted on a gorgeous Sunday morning. 'A few cracks and there'll be something in it to start with, but when it flattens...' The sort of conditions, the chairman had predicted: '...when you want to be batting all day.'

Even at that stage, Toby Bulcock wasn't so sure: 'Well yeah, but you wouldn't want to be batting fourth on it, would you?'

As the weather was lovely, so too the vista of a one-time rubbish tip re-commissioned for cricket in the 1920s. Netherfield CC was inaugurated in 1892 (at Murley Moss, opposite the current site) by the Somervell family, owners of K Shoes (nowadays Clark's), for years a huge employer hereabouts. Netherfield though have never been the 'town team'. That honour went to Kendal, whose reputation as a gentleman's rather than worker's club doubtless accounts for a keen rivalry still. Looking back towards the pavilion and main road is a Norman castle, well, its ruins, atop what is effectively an earthwork grandstand – a tier cut into the hill beneath a plateau on which cars are parked, a terrific vantage point, with two more fields behind.

Accommodated at nearby Stone Cross Manor, a valued sponsor of Cumberland CCC and former old folks' home – '...still is,' quipped Eric – the players and officials had assembled in good time, Gary winning the toss and opting to bat. Ross and Sempy were again to open, Slacky at three. And with their skipper back the batting had greater depth, Gary in after Dutts at five and Jacques at number six. No reason why they shouldn't bat as long as the chairman envisaged then, although his chipper mood may also have owed something to a Baltic cruise he and Mrs Atkinson were soon to take ... Sweden ... Finland ... Russia ... Estonia ... Latvia. When everyone else was off to Workington, they'd be flying to Stockholm. But such optimism hadn't lasted long. Unexpectedly, the ball reared and undid Sempy, caught for four. As the opener trudged off, Ross and the umpires prodded at a rock-hard track as though it were hiding a rattlesnake.

'This will be called off for a dangerous wicket,' said Toby.

Rob Cairns seemed unperturbed. 'Look at this for teamsheets,' he'd said, striding by and drawing attention to a plastic folder stuffed with fivers and one pound coins. 'Record week, £200.'

The bowling had been pacy but, from the off, unpredictable, startling the Staffordshire 'keeper as much as anyone. At other times, the ball kept low. After ten overs Cumberland were 29 for 1 when Matty, whites removed, jogged on with drinks. The ball, he reported, had hit him on the arm although Eric, back in the fold after Wisbech, sympathised as ever with the duo in the middle: 'Hard to see that.' Slacky, settling in it seemed, edged a lucky four as clouds began to bubble, the day hot but increasingly humid.

Another unruly bounce saw Zelem replaced by Dutts, who hit a classic straight drive on arrival that finished up bouncing between cars in the road, the fate of many a ball at Netherfield. And the new pair crafted a decent partnership until one again skidded through to leave Cumberland 73 for 3, Slacky prey to an instinctive diving catch in the slips. Not out for many ducks, Gary was next in, but thanks to the slightest of nicks he fell for one here. Then came Jacques, whose intention was to stay put. Someone had to, although on such a pitch the philosophy had its dangers. One bad ball and you were gone. Perhaps the best tactic was quick and plentiful runs, the outfield quicker than ever. Whatever the plan the South African first took one on the bum cheek and then the thumb, as the wicket threw up more fiery surprises. Soon he was walloped on a knuckle and then, most worryingly, on the head off a length in consecutive balls. Somewhat inevitably, both skippers were summoned for a chat. What would the umpires do? Staffordshire's coaching team was consulted on the boundary.

As deliberations continued and the MCCA view sought, ever more people milled on the wicket as phones were worked and a brief interlude became a long delay. A whiff of garlic did battle with the stink of drains running diagonally from changing rooms to the base of a tree while, in the pavilion, secretary Ian Heath wondered: 'What can they tell them down the line? Two balls popped?' Even scorer Geoff Minshaw had vacated his lair to chew the fat. Ian, from 'the blue side of Manchester', became a member here forty-two years ago and is the author of *A Century Under the Castle*, a history of this club from its Victorian origins to present times, published in 1994.

'The ground then always looked nice, but didn't particularly play nice, not like now,' he said. Given that the pitch is built on a tip, ensuring there was enough topsoil while digging down 'about six or eight inches' recently and re-laying six pitches, had been essential. The money was raised through takings at the bar. 'We've always invested in facilities. The boundary has been lengthened by going back into the banking and, over the last ten years, we've put down over a thousand tonnes of soil to level it off, as it can sink. Hot weather shrinks it and rain then swells it, so it moves continually. It used to be undulating on the far side; that's now a lot better. We've been working on this side these last few years, to get it flatter.'

It is due to this loving attention that Cumberland are so keen to play here and, historically, they haven't been alone in that. 'They know the pitch generally lasts three days,' Ian said, 'which some Minor Counties players struggle with. Our groundsman came here as a kid, learned under the original one, so knows it inside out in terms of how much moisture it needs and so on. It's a good ground. We've staged four NatWest Trophy games with first-class counties ... Derbyshire, Leicestershire, Lancashire and Sussex. Chris Adams was the captain of Sussex and said: "That wicket is better than some of the county grounds we play on." We take pride in that.'

Other star names have played here too, as club pros at the start of their careers mostly. 'We've been good at picking them,' Ian said. 'Jack Simmons, when playing for Tasmania, said he'd a lad who fancied coming in 1980, Trevor Docking. The year after, he asked if we'd like his cousin, who turned out to be David Boon.' Hard-drinking yarns abound though in reality, aged eighteen at the time, '...he was still trying to play Australian cricket on English green wickets and that was before we'd re-laid any. Just couldn't hack it. Leg-side shots, leading edges, caught mid-off, caught mid-on. He got so exasperated that on Friday night's he'd go to bed early...'

'Usually with a bird,' Alan Wilson interjected, all ears.

'Well, it didn't work. He had a score of 93 against Darwen, his highest in the league, and didn't get 500 runs in total.'

South Africa's Jacques Kallis was here in 1995, aged 18. 'Kallis made 900 runs in half a season, averaging 99 then had to go home as he'd been selected for an 'A' team tour. Duncan Fletcher was manager at Western Province and he said: "Okay, I will send you a replacement." That turned out to be Herschelle Gibbs, who was a rugby player too and hadn't yet made his mind up which game to play. They said he could have been an international in both. I'd never seen anyone like him. His batting was a class apart.' There have been others ... Kenny Benjamin ... Carlisle Best ... Colin Miller ... Zander de Bruyn ... Callum Ferguson ... and at the moment the next hot prospect, Jack Boyle, a 22-year-old fringe bowler from Canterbury, New Zealand. 'This season will hopefully bring him through. You need the right professionals, not someone who's just there to bolster your team, but who wants to improve his game and is learning from the pressure of being expected to perform. I can see that's starting to work for him. He's getting consistency.'

Lasagne devoured, Toby, basking in the glory of having been

proved correct, said he'd been involved with this sort of carry-on before: 'Two-day game at Southport & Birkdale, 2009. Lancashire under-19s v Yorkshire, as I recall. We'd made around 330 and they were 16 for 6 when the game was abandoned. That was down to it being wet, though. Skiddy ball and bowlers slipping around.'

Meanwhile, despite MCCA secretary Caley reportedly playing it with a straight bat when finally located, the umpires reached their decision. The game was to be 'suspended due to pitch concerns' and a new one begun on the 2nd XI's track. 'It's not a three-day wicket,' cautioned Ian, 'but it'll stand up to it. You can see a slight green tinge.'

*****

On Monday morning, the flag flutters over Netherfield's clubhouse: 'Northern League Champions', black lettering on gold. Day two will commence at 10.30am, to help make up the lost overs.

Yesterday, the new game began at 3.00pm and continued until 7.30pm, Cumberland again winning the toss and reaching 76 for 3 at the point when pitch stopped play. By close, that read 206 all out, Gary this time managing an unbeaten 76 not out as the poor bloody infantry tumbled. Ross had been the next biggest scorer, caught behind two short of a half-century. 'Could be a decent score on a used pitch,' says Eric, looking on the bright side. At one stage they'd been 1 for 1, Sempy caught in the slips for a golden duck.

Having survived the day's final six overs for an overnight total of 12 for 0, Staffordshire are in the nets with an hour to spare. The roller is out; someone dabs at a crease from a pot of white paint. There is more cloud cover and it's a little breezy, but still humid. Bit of swing you'd imagine for the bowlers.

As for spectators, there aren't so many in today, although it's early yet and Alan Wilson is here. Why wouldn't he be, living not far from third man? Great company, it isn't long before he's sharing a few stories, an entertaining after-breakfast speaker too it turns out. On the field, Cumberland's president was by his own admission: '...a middling middle order batsman, with averages nothing to write home about.' His talents lay in captaincy, a leader of men. 'That and availability,' he grins. A kid with a bedroom overlooking a cricket ground, he dreamed of nothing but playing for Netherfield CC; well, that or turning out for the football club further down the road. He was also an enthusiastic clubman in an era when raising a side for Cumberland was far from straightforward. He remains just as keen.

'Back in the 1950s, decent crowds used to come, not only to the cricket, but also Netherfield FC. My life's ambition was to turn out for both, which I went on to do.' A goalkeeper, he spent nine years at the latter, seven as part-time professional. 'We won the Lancashire Combination in 1964-65, a great season. I was in and out of the first team, but even in the reserves, as the club was so successful, the crowds were big and we won that league too. There'd be a couple of hundred at least every Saturday, and watching the cricket as well.'

As a 17-year-old he had trials with Arsenal, until his dad – a sales rep with K Shoes for fifty-one years – tossed a spanner in the works. In hindsight, Alan feels he was: '...probably right. The only reason I went is that I'd never been to London before. We played Crystal Palace and got beat, 2-1, I think. We had a tour of Highbury, fantastic, and two weeks later they sent a letter asking me to go back. "You'll bloody well do as you're told until you're 21," and that was that. It would have been a gamble. There wasn't anywhere near the money in football then as now. I just saw it as a test of my ability.'

No such opportunities arose in the first-class summer game, although someone did put him forward for a trial at Lancashire. 'You had a number on your back and got two overs. That doesn't test you much but, no, I wasn't good enough. Enjoyed myself too much.' He did though captain Netherfield for thirteen years on the trot, a name he pronounces– along with every other local – NetherFIELD, the stress on 'field', when a visitor's instinct is to place it otherwise: NETHERfield. That implies the name probably originates in the land's relationship to the castle on high, i.e. in its 'nether regions'.

As you'd expect from someone who has lived in its shadow, Alan knows a bit about that pile too. 'Henry VIII's last wife, Catherine Parr, lived there. People ask if they were around when I started.' It's anecdote time. 'When Bernard Reidy was professional at St Annes, he got the league record here, 184, although we did drop him twice. A fortnight later I walk out and one of the umpires says: "Bloody hell, Wils. Reidy's made a mess of your castle."'

Along with skippering Netherfield and the Northern League's representative side for seven years, Wilson's county career began as a 13-year old in the mid-1950s. That though was with Westmorland, not Cumberland, in a local derby between the two. In his late teens he made the switch when along with the likes of Northumberland and then minor county Durham, the second teams of Lancashire, Yorkshire, Warwickshire and so on were also on the menu. 'It was a tough school because you never knew who you were going to be up against, particularly as a batter, but my feeling has always been to give it your best shot. Do your best against the best, if you can. Bowlers like John Lever, Ken Shuttleworth and Peter Lee were top notch. Minor Counties fixtures were two-day games and I've seen me being home at two o'clock on a Monday – for an away match! If you played Durham, they'd have eleven professionals. Neil Riddell was the only amateur in the side, their captain. We played Durham at Hartlepool in the 1980s and Lance Cairns and Wasim Raja were playing, so it was no surprise when they joined the first-class ranks.'

This of course meant he got to play at some impressive venues. 'I remember my debut at Old Trafford very well because "Leapy" Lee was the bowler and Ian Winter from Carlisle got hit in the mouth and had to go to hospital for stitches. Don't know whether his teeth came out, but when I followed him to the crease I thought: "Where do I make my mark?" There was a pool of blood. Anyway, I lasted one ball and lost my middle stump.' Mind you, he did score 50 in the second innings. 'I was quite pleased about that.'

Cumberland too had some decent professionals however, one who arrived towards the end of Wilson's career being particularly memorable, not least because he helped the club to its first Minor Counties Championship title in 1986. England and Lancashire batsman, coach, first-class umpire, TV pundit and more latterly author, David 'Bumble' Lloyd was a hit from the start.

'When Bumble joined us with three lads from Yorkshire, we had a good side,' he says of an arrival that persuaded him to carry on for one last season as captain, having filled the role for three or four years. 'I'd been going to retire but we did well and Harold Millican, who was chairman at the time, said: "You'll have to stop on."' A then 42-year-old would be glad he agreed. Wednesday 4 July 1984 was destined to be a red-letter day – when Cumberland, in the prestigious Nat West Bank Trophy for the first time, were given a crack at a first-class county.

That opposition was Derbyshire, in a match played on this very ground. 'They reckon about 3,000 people were here and normally I was fidgety, had to do something, smoke a cigar or whatever. That day I just thought: "This is my swansong," calm as you like. Funny. We got a nine-wicket hammering. Not so funny. I strolled out and had a good look around to savour the moment before taking strike. The banking was packed but the umpires spoiled it, never gave us any leeway against the likes of Geoff Miller and Kim Barnett – we were 0 for 1 when Bob Entwistle was shot out, lbw, and ended up making 121. It was said in the Minor Counties that the umpires favoured the first-class boys as they kept them in a job. My wicket was last to fall – for ten, caught and bowled Barnett – but to play on my home ground in front of so many, and in my last game for Cumberland ... beautiful.'

No better time to go then, but he has continued to serve the county and game generally in non-playing roles since, particularly within the MCCA. 'The sad thing is a lot of players take plenty out of the sport – I suppose that's true of any game – but very few put anything back. I think it's important for people to do that.'

It's a sentiment 'Bumble' would doubtless endorse. 'He was a superb character, nice guy and fantastic cricketer,' Alan continues. 'I roomed with him in Cambridgeshire before his first match and he asked if I'd like him to say anything to the lads. "You've forgotten more than I'll ever know," I said, "just don't shift any fielders behind my back." One of the last times I saw him was at Lord's, at a Test or something, you get these invites connected to a county. I went to his book signing and queued up. When my turn came he looked up and said: "What the bloody hell are you doing here?" I said: "I've come for one of these couple of quid books you're selling." He wrote in it: "Best captain I ever played under..." A naturally funny guy everyone likes, great for team spirit.' Which could also be said for his son Graham, a Cumberland player himself and 'chip off the old block.'

'No, hang on a minute, my last game was at Hartlepool against Durham,' he suddenly recalls. 'We needed three team managers due to time-off-work issues and George Scott, president of the English Schools cricket association, was one. As I got changed he wanted a word. I thought I'd got the wrong travel expenses. "I'm finishing," he said. "My eyesight's not so good," and he nominated me to take his place. I did that for three years and quite enjoyed it. Soon, I was missing the dressing room banter, so it weaned me off playing.'

The job gave him insight into issues he formerly hadn't given much thought. 'First, you've to find a player who is going to be good enough and wants to take a step up from league cricket and test themselves in the Minor Counties. I've seen a lot say, "well, I can't handle that," too quick, too whatever, others can't get time off. We've the same situation today around work, but it's not just about locals. If somebody rings up – "I've been released by Yorkshire, any chance of a game for Cumberland?" – you tell them to come to the nets and if they're good enough in they go. People come into the Minor Counties, do well, and are picked up by the first-class game again.'

Such occurrences, of course, give rise to allegations around the Cumbrian scene that the county side is a closed shop. 'When Mike Latham was cricket chairman, I told him: "All the people you ring up, keep a note of them." It was amazing that list – "Oh, I'm injured" or "I've got no holiday left" and so on – and these are the people who say they can't get a game with Cumberland, yet have the opportunity. Quite a few are in for a couple of matches and then suddenly start to find excuses not to play. If you really had ambition and wanted to get on in cricket, you'd go the extra mile ... pester people ... wouldn't you? We've a couple at Netherfield who should be playing, but don't want to. It's something to moan about; tittle-tattle in my book.'

Of course nowadays all of that is Steve's territory, Mr Wilson is strictly presidential. 'It's a bit like the parrot. You climb up onto the perch and then fall off it. Situations just evolved. They were short of a chairman when Harold was made president, somebody always seems to say: "Wils, you'll have to do it." It was like that when I became Minor Counties cricket chairman too. I looked around the room, nobody said anything, and next thing you've got the job. After next year I'll retire and let somebody else have a go.'

By which time he'll have done five years. What does the job of president entail? 'Being nice to people. I'm a figurehead, there if anybody wants me. I started playing at Netherfield at 12 and finished here at 52, so I put 40 years in and you do pick up a tremendous amount of knowledge. But one of the things I always hated was hearing someone of my age going: "Well, in my day, we used to hit it out of the ground..." this sort of thing. If one of these lads asks me what I think about so-and-so, I'll give my opinion, otherwise I keep quiet. But really, the president's job, along with the chairman, is to travel and say hello,' which with old pals like the Wing Commander around is a pleasure. 'Derek and I played against each other when he was at Cambridge, that's a nice part of the game. One or two who you might have had differences with down the years you keep away from, but mostly...'

An area manager of Skipton Building Society who had, in 1971, 'started the Kendal branch from scratch', when Alan retired in the mid-1990s at the relatively young age of 55, he had time on his hands and took up a ready opportunity to spend it. 'At that point the Minor Counties had a representative side in the Benson and Hedges and needed a selection committee member from the north of England; everyone was south of Birmingham. We were only in it for a year and the first match was at Leicestershire. Hansie Cronje was out second ball and we beat them. I thought: "This is good." Trouble however was brewing, the current existential threat being far from the first one faced by the Minor Counties Championship.

The structure of English cricket was about to change. Lord MacLaurin was appointed chairman of the new England and Wales Cricket Board (ECB), which succeeded the Test and County Cricket Board (TCCB). 'That had been running very well with no more than twenty staff while, before long, the ECB had one hundred and fifty.' And when a document called *Raising the Standard* was published, the Minor Counties Association barely merited a mention. To cut a long and complex story short, the MCCA, harried by a group called the National Cricket Association, decided it ought to look open to a bit of modernisation. A reshuffle of officials was required and Alan Wilson found himself in the frame. 'The chairman at that particular time was a nice chap called Jimmy Smith, Cambridge blue in football and cricket, lovely man; too nice really. "Sir" John Pickup – chairman, president, secretary and just about everything else at Cheshire – got his job. The cricket chairman, Derek Bridge, was given the presidency and since they reckoned I'd the nous and clout to fight for the MCCA, I took chairman of cricket. I'd not expected it. I'd been sitting there minding my own business.'

To begin with, he admits to being terrified. 'The meetings were all at Lord's and I'm a kid from Parkside Road in Kendal.' At the first such get-together he had to chair, he was so nervous he couldn't eat a morsel of a lavish lunch, hard to imagine now. 'I was asked by someone at our table if I was ill.' And well he might have been. For this was to be a fight to the death, the only question being which organisation would survive and which would not?

The National Cricket Association was led by legendary Surrey batsman Micky Stewart, destined for an OBE three years later for services to cricket. Its intention was to revolutionise the amateur game. Amid skirmishes, Wilson found himself in committees and talking shops with a single end point – a ballot between this new NCA and, in that organisation's view, the archaic Minor Counties.

'When the vote came, we won it by the skin of our teeth,' Alan smiles, still savouring a delicious victory. 'We survived and the NCA were finished, no messing. I was in the mix, but the man who did it all was John Pickup and for the next fourteen years he was my boss. Many a time he saved my skin with his legal knowledge. When something upset me, I'd be straight in. John, typical lawyer, would say: "Alan, perhaps if we did it this way..." I loved working for him and learned such a lot. I'd just started as chairman of Cumberland as well and I'd watch how he conducted meetings at Lord's. He gave me great confidence. We are still in touch. I spoke to him only a couple of weeks ago. He's now president of the MCCA, a job I also did for three years after finishing as cricket chairman. It was a big battle, was that; a big battle.'

With the NCA seen off, a board structure of eighteen first-class and twenty 'non-first-class' county clubs was introduced, along with those Premier Leagues up and down the land. The MCCA's long-established knockout Trophy was briefly replaced by a thirty-eight club county board competition, a potential money-earner that didn't last long, and two-day Championship games went as well. Initially, these were replaced by Aussie-style 'grade games' for the MCCA and Premier Leagues alike, an idea that flopped badly. In their place came the current six three-day matches, still in operation.

Furthermore, criticised for having too many ex-professionals in its ranks, the MCCA amended the rules to limit each county to one player who had played forty or more first-class matches. Around a decade later, an incentive scheme to reduce the average age of nine players in each side to 26 and below also came in. And so developed an era – on-going more or less – of being policed at arm's length. In Mike Latham's 2011 update of John Hurst's 1982 history of Cumberland CCC, Wilson wrote of such flexibility: 'It is a constant battle to survive as we try to appease our paymaster. As I write, the MCCA are about to negotiate in the spring of 2009 for further funding over the next four years. I wonder what the ECB have in store for us this time.' And he concludes: 'I am often asked how I can be bothered trailing up and down the West Coast Line for seven or eight hours at a time to meetings in London. My answer is simple, some three hundred or more volunteers run Minor Counties cricket with the sole intention of preserving the game they enjoy.' Although no longer an MCCA official, it is a point of view he retains.

'The whole point is, you've twenty minor counties run by twenty committees made up of cricket lovers. None of them are in it for the money as there isn't any. That's the big difference these days. We can't afford to pay anyone. When I played we had wonderful professionals from Lancashire ... Bumble, Reidy, Bob Ratcliffe David Parsons ... but those days are gone and you've got to move on.'

Indeed you do, so how does the Cumberland president see the future of the Minor Counties Championship, now that the five-yearly begging bowl – a.k.a. memorandum of understanding – is out again? 'Well, hopefully they'll see sense. It's fantastic Dominic Bess got into the Test team; two years ago he was at Devon. Richard Gleeson played for Cumberland and is knocking on the international door. We provide this info but it's these boards who do the early coaching, up to 17. That's fine, but what happens then? What we ought to be doing is playing half a dozen development matches, but there's only enough money for two. They give us an insight into lads coming out of league cricket and we can put them in a better class of competition. You don't get the half-volleys and long-hops you do on a Saturday afternoon, you've to be more patient and work out where you are going to score. If you aren't in the stream to go into first-class and then international cricket at 17 you won't ever get the chance, which is ludicrous. What about the late developers? Graham Monkhouse was 25 when he went to Surrey and Gleeson was 27. And don't forget there's a level above the Minor Counties – the Unicorns. You could be playing Essex and Duncan Fletcher or someone is walking around...'

In his stride, he canters on: 'Anyway, we are only playing three-day cricket because the ECB told us to. They wanted us to make the game longer, get spinners on. This isn't our idea, likewise Twenty20. I'd like to think we'll get another five years' funding, but I can't tell you what's going to happen after that. This has been going on for years. We give incredible value for money. How else could you run twenty counties on our contribution without volunteers? They're not going to find a way to do it cheaper.'

*****

Padded up, Staffordshire's openers stretch and prepare for a new day. Alan, a Netherfield committeeman too, nods in welcome to Phil Oliver, who he has known since managing an England amateur side of which 'Olly' was part, a prior incarnation of the Unicorns. When the Cumberland president first played here the banking didn't exist, the field merely sloped up towards the ruins. That was the late-1950s when due to the tip underneath they had one problem they don't have any more: '...bloody cockroaches were everywhere.'

The county likes coming here, although sometimes gets the feeling its love isn't reciprocated. 'We try to share matches around. Ideally, if everything were kosher, we'd have one in Kendal, one in Carlisle and one in Barrow or Workington or Whitehaven.' In fact, the 1999 Minor Counties Championship was won on this very ground by Cumberland, a six-wicket victory over Dorset. Yesterday, though, hadn't been great and Alan had another clue as to why.

'It's unusual to get two months' dry weather, but the problem was the groundsman didn't have time to prepare it.' Due to the usual club games and a schools tournament with Lancaster, Morecambe and Kendal, there'd been cricket here on Saturday, Sunday, Monday, Tuesday, Wednesday and Saturday again, prior to the Minor Counties match. 'He only had Thursday and Friday to get it ready.'

As the morning progresses the attendance climbs steadily, in terms of numbers and eccentricity. One bloke in a cream Lancashire shirt, 81-years-old, legs brown as teak, sports a wide-brimmed hat, shorts, socks pulled up to the knee, a pair of plimsolls and a bum-bag. 'Follows cricket all over,' says Alan. Another fellow wanders by who used to work at Booths supermarket, stacking shelves, but has just retired. 'I worked there 30-odd years,' he says, eyes bulging like table tennis balls, 'and do you know what they gave me?'

'No. What?'

'Fuck all.'

Of more cheery demeanour is Mr Sunshine, so named because when he strips to the waist the sun always comes out. He does so. It does. And then there is Fruit Machine Ken – whose photographic memory of one-armed bandit sequences have seen him allegedly banned from every working men's club in Lancashire. Mike Latham is atop the hill with Toby (the dog) and Steve Bulcock. As might be expected, their conversation is of a tactical bent, surrounding what they consider a shortage of seamers. 'Just Syds really,' Steve observes, 'and he's getting on.' Liam Grey is no longer available or is at least slow in returning calls – word is he's had trials at Worcestershire.

'It's a season of rebuilding, isn't it?' says Mike.

'Aye,' says Steve, 'but we knew that, didn't we?'

'If this seven or eight locals rule comes in, we wouldn't be able to raise a team.'

'Well, we would, but it wouldn't last three days.'

On a wicket nowhere near as lively as yesterday's, Staffordshire make progress before a first wicket falls and it's 44 for 1, Sam Kelsall caught behind off Toby (the cricketer)'s bowling. Kadeer Ali, though, is in dominant form and motoring along nicely.

'Are you well?' says one half of a couple, juggling cups of coffee.

'Oh yes, it's lovely here,' says the target of their enquiry, a man in a salmon sweater, sat on his own, 'sweater' being the right word. He's a hefty lad. 'Ah, Minor Counties cricket...' he ejaculates, out loud and with volume, before taking a theatrical swig from a large plastic bottle of pink lemonade. This, apparently, is Peter Pullover.

Staffordshire wallop a couple of sixes, but with Bulcock and Syddall bowling the wicket-taking opportunities are evidently there. Peter Pullover says he is glad to be out of the house. 'Left the gas fire on for a day and a bit, only on a low light, but it cost us eight quid. I thought it were too hot, but then it has been hot, hasn't it?' To whom he is speaking isn't clear. Receiving no reply, he emits a mighty belch, truly the prince of burps. 'Beg your pardon,' he soliloquises, loudly, as Toby embarks on another over. 'Can't beat a bit o' Bully.'

One supporter who hasn't made it is Gilbert Johnstone, unable to drive due to his heart issues. He may need a stent fitting, missed yesterday and can't get here tomorrow either, which John Patterson describes as 'devastating for him'.

Sam 'Spud' Wood comes on to bowl and Gary misfields. That Staffs don't take two says much about his reputation. Twelfth man Chris Hodgson recalls how during his own Cumberland debut Pratt kept fumbling similarly at midwicket. "'What's he doing?" I thought. He was kidding the batsman who, before long, set off for a single only to see his stumps thrown down.' Cricket by way of *The Hustler*.

When drinks are taken, Staffordshire are 78 for 1, Kadeer Ail 49 not out. Thirsts quenched, Sempy is thrown the ball. Dust flying off a rock-hard outfield, the opener duly passes his half-century. Spud is also brought into the attack, has more luck, and batsman three, Zen Malik, is caught behind for 18 after nearly being run out by Gary, as predicted, and it's 81 for 2. A joiner by trade, Spud then sees one rear up off a length, rapping gloved knuckles, a worrying sign after 31 overs, shades of yesterday morning. But when Toby is tried at a different end, a huge six bounces off the main road and up the stoop of a house – not Alan Wilson's – before knocking on the front door. A woman in a dressing gowns peers out of her window, used to this sort of thing. Good job there were no passing motorists.

Better times for the spinner are just around the corner – Ali bamboozled and then brilliantly stumped by 'keeper Ben Howarth for 62. But Staffs aren't about to let up. Toby is dispatched into the road again, boundaries start to amass and the next partnership adds a further 106 runs, before Alex Mellor is caught and bowled, Josh Boyne, with the visitors 208 for 4. At the other end, Peter Wilshaw had been in powerful form, driving the score to 254 for 5 until caught by Gary off Spud on a personal 'Nelson' of 111, a shot that plummeted out of the sky like a Luftwaffe bomb.

Today's team contains three homegrown Cumbrians – Slacky, Sempy and Dutts – and either side of lunch they have their work cut out in the field, particularly off Toby whose 26-over stint comes at a cost of 131 runs. Cumberland sausage and mash consumed, sixes galore rain down, putting those passing vehicles at still greater risk, not to mention a blitzed bowling green. The OAPs are scattered in scenes that lack only an air raid siren and a rush for tin helmets.

Never one to surrender, Toby maintains his stuff upper lip,

keeps calm and carries on, although the enemy pass Cumberland's total shortly before Mellor's wicket on the last ball of the 59th over.

For the hot and sweaty fielding side, it has been a real slog. With the sun out it is once again roasting. However young Boyney – or 'Boing' as Dutts calls him – bowls very well indeed. His 20 overs of right-arm off-spin cost only three or so an over. Twitchy, lithe and with a spring in his step, there is something of the dancer about him.

Alan Wilson recalls hitting a flat six once for Netherfield 2nd XI, which bounced in the road and hit a parked car, setting off its alarm. "'That was funny," I said to the umpire. "It might be to you, Wils," he said. "That's my car." Got in *Wisden* did that.' It isn't long before the ball is pinballing on tarmac again, big John P clambering valiantly over the wall to retrieve it with admirable athleticism.

'An old woman was driving past once,' says Alan, 'and the ball went through her windscreen and landed in her lap. She was fine, although we had to be bring her into the clubhouse for a brandy.'

As phenomena go, cemeteries next to cricket grounds are far from uncommon. Indeed, owing to many clubs' shared history with churches, the set-up may even be in the majority. Given the dangers of simply motoring by, Netherfield's may one day come in handy. Partially hidden behind trees, this one is on the scoreboard side – the box in question being of the traditional variety, perched in an uppermost corner wherein Geoff Minshaw lurks. At the foot of the rise is a small electronic board, near a garageful of mowers, rollers and the customary antique contraption. Geoffrey, as per, squints into his screen and tells of another 10.30 start tomorrow.

During drinks – two jugs of orange juice – news breaks of Boris Johnson's resignation as foreign secretary, his protest at Government handling of Brexit. On the restart, Boyney weighs in with the final wicket of the innings before Staffordshire, intending to press the advantage and avoid a draw, declare on 333 for 6 and conclude their 75 overs with another huge six into a dressing room door, the ball almost bouncing back into the umpire's pocket. Cumberland are 127 behind with a lot to do if they are to avoid a second Championship defeat of the summer in as many games.

To begin with, it looks as if they might. Certainly openers Ross and Sempy make a strong start, surviving a tricky 30 minutes in the ten overs before tea. The ball is still whizzing through, though less unpredictably, which leads to more talk of wickets and groundsmen. Alan recalls one such, Angus Forsyth, who swore by cow shit. I bet that mixed things up a bit, someone says. 'Oh, it was faster...' Alan agrees, framing it in his mind's eye, 'but it stank.'

One further benefit of Netherfield's ground is its abundance of arboreal cover. Mike Latham, a mini-celebrity in north-west cricket as we have seen, partly due to his weekly radio show, chats about the latest episode beneath one such bough with 'Mr WC Nicholson of Plungington Road' (presumably that's how he announces himself when calling the show), a genial fellow who follows Cumberland up and down the land with his just as enthusiastic wife, Mrs R Nicholson of Plungington Road. Both Mr and Mrs Nicholson of Plungington Road are amiability personified, but other listeners have been known to buttonhole Mike with no hesitation in 'putting him right'. One bloke told him off for having a cricketer on from the Palace Shield who, after a disciplinary hearing, had picked up a six-week ban.

'He said that by choosing a guest like him we were condoning bad behaviour. I asked when the offence in question was committed. "Oh about twenty years ago," he replied.'

After 30 overs, Cumberland's openers have moved the score along to 80 for 0, but neither is destined to reach his half-century. Sempy is first to fall, caught behind three runs short with around an hour left of what has been a very long day. Six overs later, Slacky goes the same way having contributed two. And when Ross then falls to a terrific slip catch for 43, captain Gary at the other end, it's 111 for 3, the hosts still 16 runs short of parity.

Tomorrow may be shorter.

Staffordshire celebrate that third wicket like they have just won the World Cup, sights set on topping this year's Eastern Division at least. Their excitement only builds when Dutts is out, caught behind, Cumberland's hopes well and truly run ragged, 123 for 4. With only ten minutes to go, it's not a great time for any batsman to enter the fray, although few are cooler than Jacques. He hangs around safely as four byes edge his side into the black. At close, the Cumbrians are 144 for 4, an overnight advantage of 17 runs.

*****

Fed by its tributaries, the Sprint and Mint, in normal times the River Kent courses through the centre of town. Today, it is barely a trickle. Ducks can't paddle so they sit on rocks, as an oystercatcher tracking the inlet from Morecambe Bay soars above. It's a far cry from 2015, when Kendal CC's Shap Road home was under water. Perched on higher ground, Parkside Road went unscathed.

Jacques pads by in flip-flops, having arrived like most of the Cumberland team half an hour before play. This morning it is cooler right across the country – upper teens or lower twenties – with cloud cover to boot, especially welcome for those hoping to swing the ball. That will be one more hurdle for the South African and Gary Pratt to leap once they resume at the crease and try to make a game of it.

A motorised roller works the pitch, Staffordshire already in a huddle, well-drilled and discussing how to get the job done. Does that mean Netherfield are showing an interest? Maybe. There were no keys for the nets first thing while, last night, Steve and Alan had to pull the covers on themselves with no one from the club about. It's certainly true that, more generally, Kendal – historically part of Westmorland – appears to fight shy of seeming too closely associated with Cumbria cricket. Its two main clubs have been in the Northern Premier League since the 1950s, although Kendal CC are this season in the Palace Shield having been relegated last year. Netherfield tried to gain entry to the Lancashire League in 2015, but were rebuffed. On the other hand, when Kendal were asked to host Cumberland's Knockout Trophy games from 2013-2015, Netherfield got the hump.

Yet Kendal, once the county town of Westmorland, *is* now part of Cumbria whether anyone likes it or not and such identity crises present the county in microcosm. Here 'fake news' has thrived for centuries, legend taken as fact, truth as myth. Currently, the County Council is under the control of a Labour-Liberal Democrat alliance, but the Tories are the largest single party and Cumbria is small 'c' conservative to its core. Cumbria is also a very 'white' county in which people of colour are rare. Touring its cricket grounds, that's all the more noticeable. Any non-white individual is likely to be the club professional. Only among the Lakeland day-trippers might that not apply. In 2016, Kendal's was the only area in six to vote to remain in the European Union, with pro-Brexit majorities in Allerdale, Barrow-in-Furness, Carlisle, Copeland and Eden.

Anyone of South Asian descent today is on a Staffordshire side that, to a man, is focussed purely on ensuring its second win in two games, having dispatched Suffolk a fortnight ago. Cumberland aren't so single-minded. One player rolls up with ten minutes to spare and others have family in tow, with whom they will sit when not directly engaged with events on the field. Some would see that as having your priorities right; others may detect a lack of focus.

In the middle, Pratt and du Toit reach 158 for 4 when the first chance comes, Gary dropped at slip. Anyone hoping for a full day's cricket would view that as a relief; this partnership apparently the last genuine hope. By now, Jacques, uninhibited as ever, has already cracked a six and there remains a sense that the game could yet be anything. More boundaries follow, including a glorious straight drive and five handy overthrows, as the duo take control. Gary, according to Steve Bulcock, is an 'eye cricketer' and therefore bucks the trend at his age. 'They usually start to go by their mid-30s, as the eyesight starts to diminish.' Batsmen who rely mainly on technique traditionally extend their career longer.

You can learn a lot, overhearing conversations at the cricket. One reveals that Cumberland and the Cumbria Cricket Board are indeed not getting on: 'Relations are at an all-time low.' Two lads who couldn't get into this Staffordshire side played for Derbyshire's 2nd XI yesterday. 'Minor Counties are scouts for first-class counties, aren't they? Picking the best eleven in a region for them to look at.'

Leanne Bell, a Cumberland committee member herself and midway through a pregnancy with a November delivery date, prefers the shade of an oak, from where she joins the applause as her partner Gary passes his half-century. This will be the couple's first child and she has known its father since secondary school. 'Aye, since he was eleven.' Fresh of face with a pleasant demeanour, she too is a product of County Durham and has the accent to match. 'I've always known he's into cricket and accepted that. I learned to love it myself.'

That's just as well since it's hard to imagine putting up with a schedule like Gary's if you didn't take an interest. 'He used to get out of school quite a lot, to go play for Durham, the academy and things, so I realised what I was getting myself into.' Nowadays Leanne follows him all over, work permitting, and with Richmond too, home and away. 'I absolutely love it. On average that means two games a week, depending on night matches and what cups they are in, but certainly every Saturday and more often than not Sunday. It takes up a lot of time, especially the three day games, but I wouldn't want to stop him doing it.' They talk cricket at home. 'Gary is constantly on the phone of a night. As soon as he finishes work, if I try to get hold of him, he'll be on it talking to someone about cricket until half-ten or eleven o'clock sometimes, sorting stuff out. It does take over your life, especially when you're the captain of two sides.'

Which raises the question of what he will do when the curtain finally does come down. It won't be coaching.

'I know, it's a worry for me really. I don't know what we'll do. On our days off, when Gary's not playing cricket, we'll go and find a match somewhere. He doesn't enjoy coaching and I don't think he'll go down the umpiring route. A cricket manager like Steve and Mike is an option...' And then there are the friendships, high among which is that with treasurer Eric and his wife, Margaret, their 'adopted parents'. Leanne says: 'It's been lovely growing bonds with people. We see them in the winter, holiday with them and things, so spend a lot of time together. But when the season comes round you look forward to seeing everyone on the committee.'

The current game has been a bit of an effort, what with Sunday's false start and everything, even more so you'd imagine with a baby on the way. Unsurprisingly then, here is one Cumberland member who much prefers short-form cricket: '...where you get a result rather than spend three days playing for a draw. He doesn't understand what hard work that can be, watching all that time. I'm always tired on the way home. He's played Saturday, driven down to Oxford or somewhere for Sunday, Monday and Tuesday and then it's me that's asleep in the car!' Leanne is about to share her account of when Gary met Ricky Ponting – 'I was out shopping, came home, turned on the TV and there he was...' – when suddenly there is an appeal and he is out, caught, for 56. Cumberland have progressed to 215 for 5, still only 88 in front, so that's a blow.

Game over? Not quite.

Prior to his skipper's dismissal, Jacques smashed two more sixes to move within five runs of 50 himself. Much will depend on his calming influence over Josh Boyne; at least that's what it says in the script. Sadly, having accumulated just three more, Jacques is then caught behind on 48, his new batting partner not yet having scored. A calming influence he was not.

Young league cricketers often struggle to play spinners, even when they are spinners themselves. Staffs have made plentiful use of theirs, Paul Byrne again set to let rip having already bagged six first innings wickets. With Sam Wood now at the crease there aren't many who expect a show of resistance yet that is exactly what they get, from one end anyhow. It isn't long before Byrne gets Spud and next man in Ben Howarth falls for a duck after drinks. Experienced tail-enders Toby and Syds, however, split 29 runs between them, which gives Boyney time to show what he can do, his 36-run contribution helping Cumberland to 285 all out. His dismissal too causes a degree of controversy: 'He's not hit it,' says Steve Sharp. Still, it's in the papers, or would be if they took any notice. The bottom line is Cumberland have somehow staggered to a lead of 158. It is a target, though not much of one. Cumberland's bowlers will need to strike early.

The original wicket now resembles a Roman mosaic and, while digesting his lunch of Lancashire hotpot and beetroot, Jacques is reminded of the climate in his homeland. 'We had the weather, so played a lot of sport,' he says, though rugby was the main one. 'We'd play an hour of that, then an hour of cricket, then an hour of something else.' His father played union for Eastern Province and then began running ultra-marathons. 'He tried to get me into it, but I've never liked long-distance running and never will. Anyway, the rugby season had just started and I got injured halfway through, which is when I turned to cricket.' Signed aged 16 by Easterns, not far from Johannesburg, his contract stipulated: no more rugby.

Born on the coast, in Port Elizabeth, he and the family soon moved to Bloemfontein in central South Africa: '...which is all farms and open fields. That was with dad's work, he was in the army.' And from there they headed north to the nation's largest city. 'I won a full contract at Easterns, but stopped at the end of the 2000 season as I wasn't enjoying my cricket. We came to a mutual agreement. I'd made my first-class debut as a bowler and it was bowl, bowl, bowl... never got a bat. In South Africa they have you bowling in the nets for three hours at a time and I got bored, needed a break. When you did bat it was for five minutes. We'd a good side. Easterns are a provincial team and we won the championship, did well in the one day cup, but personally I was stagnating.'

In 2004, after a period of drifting, he travelled to England for a stint as club professional with East Anglia Premier League side Cambridge Granta, a move that rekindled his appetite. South Africa though wasn't done with him yet. Impressing with 'a few big scores', Cambridge asked him to return the following year but he still had a contract with Easterns and the province put its foot down: 'If I wouldn't play for them, I couldn't play for anyone.' So back he went again until the contract ended and, in a subsequent English stint at Godmanchester Town CC, no less a figure than ex-England women's captain Charlotte Edwards recommended him to Leicestershire.

'It just happened that she arrived as I was batting in a game in Huntingdonshire. We were in trouble – about 16 for 3 – and I got 223 not out. I didn't know who she was. They introduced us and she asked if I played county cricket. I said no and the rest is history...'

After a trial at Kent, for the first few seasons du Toit figured chiefly in Leicestershire's 2nd XI and academy games, having to wait until 2008 for his eight-year stint at Grace Road truly to take flight. To begin with he kept a toe in the East Anglia Premier League and then dabbled in the Leicestershire Premier League too, with Lutterworth, even as his first-class career built momentum.

A maiden County Championship ton – v Northamptonshire – was followed by his highest one-day score, 144 from 119 balls against Glamorgan at Colwyn Bay. In 2010, his contract was renewed after an impressive season in which he amassed 899 runs and was voted Leicestershire Supporters' Player of the Year. In hindsight, he thinks not moving on then may well have been a mistake. 'I played against Warwickshire and scored 180 in the first innings, 70 in the second. They asked if I'd trial there, but I thought I'd be loyal to Leicester. Looking back, I don't know. It would have been a good set-up, Warwickshire.' In 2011, he also wintered in Colombo, travel in the blood. With no English ancestry, he is now eligible for Cumberland – and therefore England – on residency grounds.

The 2010 season at Leicestershire was particularly enjoyable, he says, because overseas pair Andrew McDonald and Brad Hodge came on the scene. 'Every player is different and they knew what was needed. I knew what worked for me but was being made to do things that didn't. McDonald and Hodge told the coaches to leave me alone. It wasn't about letting me do what I liked, you've to respect the rules and so on, but for instance I don't like having a net, yet was forced to do so. I like to have throws, work on drills and know my game is in place. It became hard work because the coaches weren't man-managers. To get the best out of people, you need that.'

Jacques was released by Leicestershire aged 32, the prime of his career behind him, but with gas still in the tank. 'I'd three or four years' first-class cricket left in me, but I probably stayed a year longer than I should have. I wasn't enjoying the environment.' After which he took another cricketing hiatus – for eighteen months this time – before ending a brief spell at Sleaford in the Lincolnshire Premier League by heading up the A1 to Newcastle upon Tyne. 'I liked the outskirts of Leicester, but not the city itself. The first time we played in Durham I fell in love with the North East, especially the people. At the beginning of every season I'd look at the fixture list and say: "When do we play Durham?" I always had a great time and knew that if I didn't move back to South Africa I'd go live up there.'

In 2013, Jacques helped Newcastle to fourth in the North East Premier League, their highest position yet in a competition founded in 1999. The following year, he was captain. The switch also led him to the Minor Counties Championship with a Northumberland side that had been struggling but improved their form on the twin arrivals of himself and former Durham coach Geoff Cook. He wasn't exactly a stranger to this level, having played for Huntingdonshire from 2005-2007, though they by then only played informal matches and no longer compete in any official Minor Counties competition.

Off the field, there is that meat delivery job mentioned at Oxton during the Trophy game. He's supposed to spend five and a half days a week doing that, although gets Saturdays off for cricket. To play in the Minor Counties he is forced to take holidays. 'When I went to Northumberland five years ago, it was all good; we had a great time. They hadn't won a game in years, yet in 2013 we reached the semis of the Knockout Trophy, where we lost to Berkshire. In 2015, they made me captain and we won through to the final, against Cornwall. I tore an ankle ligament in the warm-up but thought: "Do you know what, might as well play." The 12th man couldn't for some reason, so I had to. I just bandaged it up.' That same year Northumberland won their first three-day match in thirty-odd games and never lost another, only missing out on the final due to run-rate. 'We made a team follow on twice in a day because it was raining on the second,' Jacques sighs. From such heights, however, issues last winter arose.

'A lot of players decided they weren't going to play this year because of work commitments and girlfriends etc, which is fine. That happens in life.' The club had endured a tough 2017, rock bottom of both a qualifying pool in the Trophy – just behind Cumberland – and Eastern Division in the Championship. 'They asked what my plans were. To be honest, I didn't much fancy it. I knew it was going to be a slog, rebuilding phase, but didn't want to let them down. I'd had interest from other minor counties as well but thought: "I'll just play. It's the right thing to do." Then in December I got a call saying they wanted to change the captaincy. I told them okay, I don't have a problem with that, but asked for reasons and they said they'd rather have a local Northumberland lad. Again I said fine, but warned them that it was going to be a tough one after five seasons of playing good cricket and reaching big games. I then phoned Geoff Cook, the most respected guy in cricket I know up there, and he told me: "No way should you do that. Why don't we organise a meeting?"

Cook spoke to the committee about it and then went off on holiday. 'He'd gone for a three-week break to Australia but no sooner had he landed than I got a call from one of the players: "I don't want to play for Northumberland if you're not going to be captain." I said it wasn't decided yet and that it wasn't a big issue, I'd still be available to play. He went: "No, no, I've heard you are not captain." So I rang a committeeman, who confirmed it. I said I thought we were going to meet about this. "No, that's the final decision," and that was that. If that's how they handled things there was no way I was going to play. I hadn't wanted to walk away after a bad season. If you change things for the wrong reason you start again from scratch and I can't play for someone I can't trust."

But why come to Cumberland? 'Me and Gary always got on and he contacted me to see if I was available. He said we'd like to have you on board, so here I am. Yeah, there's a lot of travelling but I'm used to that. There always has been. Even in the East Anglia league, a lot of the teams were from Norfolk, so a good two-hour drive away, and the games started at 11.00am as well. Long days.' He is enjoying himself though. 'We could've played smarter cricket at times, but we've got a good bunch of youngsters with talent coming through. They just need the right people around them.'

*****

Yesterday, few would have predicted that the game would even reach lunch on the third day never mind go into the afternoon, but that's cricket for you. Just when you think you're out, it pulls you back in.

Had the death rattle sounded earlier, a seventy-mile drive around the Lake District National Park would have made watching day one of a two-day Cumbria v Scotland under-17s fixture a real possibility, or part of it at least, a fixture destined to end in defeat for the Cumbrian youngsters by an innings and 15 runs. Not to worry. Another chance to gauge county board activities will come on Thursday, when the sides meet again in a one-day cup match at Slacky's club, Wigton, up in Allerdale. Besides, events here have the potential to be intriguing should Cumberland strike early.

Toby bowls the opening over, a maiden, before Staffordshire's first four of the innings zips tantalisingly over his head in the slips, off Syds, and the visitors progress to 21 for 0 after five overs.

High on the hill, an assortment of Duttons – mum, dad and sister – are here to watch Sam from a bench accessorised with a floral quilted throw, on which the matriarch crochets.

On the level above that, a couple of friendly Staffs supporters enquire about the best Kendal pubs for real ale and point out another spectator sat peaceably by the pavilion amid a sizeable ensemble for a Tuesday afternoon. His name is Zigger Zagger, a reformed football hooligan by all accounts and presumably named after Peter Terson's play that, in 1967, became the first new writing commission of the National Youth Theatre. Back then, the *Observer*'s critic wrote that Terson had: '...expertly concocted a Brechtian morality designed for playing on a bare stage in front of an enormous and vociferously involved chorus,' which seems about as far removed from Minor Counties cricket as it is possible to get.

Football, though, is still on the minds of many and its likely impact on Sunday's final T20 game at Workington. Four of today's squad – Pratt, Wood, Carr, Cowling – will be with Richmondshire in the last sixteen of the ECB National Club Championship. Mattie McKiernan is still away, trying to make in-roads at Derbyshire, and 'keeper Ben has booked a holiday, having failed to realise there'd be a T20 game in between two Championship three-dayers as that just doesn't happen usually. Adam Syddall, Josh Fellows and Jamie Smith will be at Edgworth – 'a moneyed part of Bolton,' someone calls it – for the Greater Manchester League's own T20 finals day ... and even those who are there in person may well be elsewhere in spirit.

Then, as a clean half-century approaches, attention snaps to the present as Jacques takes a catch that delivers Toby and Cumberland's first wicket. Not long after, Staffs are 68 for 2, Boyney engineering Kadeer Ali's caught behind. Breakthrough? Come drinks at 3.00pm that total has moved on to 94 for 2, but then Toby is straight-driven directly into Slacky's midriff to give Dutts – growing bored no doubt – an opportunity to leap flamboyantly into the fielder's arms. Soon after, a looping shot off Toby passes just out of Sempy's reach. Gary pouches a scooped gift as Staffordshire's fourth falls to the bowling of Sam Wood and a 56-run race against the clock is on. When Toby reacts superbly at deep gulley, Boyney claims Staffs' second victim and they are 125 for 5 at tea, just 31 runs behind. A lost cause has become a decent effort that, nevertheless, never quite looked like being enough, an impression confirmed when instead of two wickets from decent appeals, a pair of mammoth sixes welcome the restart and Staffordshire come home with a flourish.

There is still time for Toby's third wicket, but their opponents meet the target with ease, 159 for 6 in only 43.5 overs, the final four taking an unlikely route through the otherwise super-safe hands of Gary Pratt on its way to the rope. With more middle order runs, who knows? It's another one that got away. With Workington to arrange, secretary Rob asks Steve when he can have Sunday's team.

'As soon as I can find one,' the chairman of cricket replies.

*****

Childhood home of author, broadcaster and Labour life peer Melvyn Bragg, Wigton is a town of bygone idiosyncrasy. Its varicoloured market square is actually a triangle and a distinctive bell tower on the skyline once belonged to 'orientalist' mansion Highmoor, whose parkland was stocked with flamingos, wallabies and llamas. At some point it was requisitioned for social housing, flats by the look of it, although the estate's original iron railings, long since gone to rust, continue to line the fields en route to the cricket ground.

This is a green and pleasant part of England, more Cotswolds than Cumbria on such a summer's day, although an experience less bucolic in bleak midwinter you'd think. Entering Cumbria by the M6, leave at junction 41 a mile or so north of Penrith and track the charming B5305 west, braided with little waterways that may explain the verdant landscape ... Peel Gil ... Rush Gill ... Whale Gill ... Oaker Gill ... Cockley Beck ... Fellican Beck ... and stunning long-range views. One handmade sign offers free-range eggs, another 'Ladies Hats [sic] – For Sale or Rent'. On you go, up innumerable lumps and down with a bump, heat shimmering off the tarmac at every dip and rise, over the River Caldew, bypassing more becks ... Chalk ... Wiza ... and settlements evocatively named – Unthank, Hutton-in-the-Forest, Sour Nook, Sebergham, Rosley, Warblebank – before traversing the A595 Roman road and landing at Wigton RUFC, the Highmoor sentinel on one side, a rugby ground with which the cricket club shares facilities opening out northwards on the other.

It's another glorious day of blue sky and red admirals, ten overs having already been bowled as the latest Scotland wicket tumbles, the visitors 54 for 4. 'Come on, Henry,' someone says with a heavy Caledonian accent, as the latest youngster walks to the middle.

The ECB's under-17s cup and championship competitions are arranged in groups of eight, each team administered by its relevant county board, in this case Cumbria Cricket Ltd. For practical travel reasons, both are played in three-day blocks, championship two-day game first, then cup-tie with the same opponents. Cumbria under-17s are in Divisions 1B of championship and cup – alongside Cricket Scotland, Leicestershire & Rutland (one team), Lincolnshire and Northumberland. Other age groups play one-day games only, but are similarly organised. Teams from under-11s to under-15s (there's no under-16s), any open-age development XI and Chief's 'Hobblers', the over-50s team last seen playing Durham in Keswick, are pooled too, before progressing to a knock-out structure and finals.

Of the twenty or so spectators, most appear to be the boys' family members. Scotland wear dark blue, while Cumbria are in black tracksuit bottoms with green top, black sleeves and yellow shoulder piece, not dissimilar to Cumberland's one-day 'Green Man' clobber. Known as the 'shooting gallery', this ground has a reputation for being among the world's worst places to watch cricket – high winds gust through unimpeded – though sunstroke not hypothermia is a bigger threat right now. It is pleasant indeed.

So pleasant, in fact, that hardly anyone appears to be moving. On the field, there are the same half-hearted gee-ups as can be heard at open-age level, a way to keep teammates awake perhaps: 'Keep building it, buddy.' The encouragement does the trick, mind. The bowler responds and Scotland are 69 for 5.

Carlisle secretary Mark Davidson is here to watch son Jonathan represent Cumbria. Amid a cluster of beer garden benches beneath a tiled triangular dormer scoreboard, he introduces Arthur Brown, chair of Cumbria Cricket Ltd, under-17s manager and Cumberland's *bête noire*, the feeling mutual if the Mike Latham episode at Lindal Moor was any indication. Despite his advanced years, Arthur is clad in black storm jacket, training bottoms and a baseball cap with tufts of white hair poking through, unconventional. His side's kit, it ought to be noted, is supplied by Lorimers of Bishop Auckland. 'There goes the famous Wigton wind,' he says, an unlikely breeze bringing relief. 'It's not usually like this. It's hell. There's nowhere to shelter.' And off he goes on a lap, pet pooch at home, presumably on account of the 'No Dogs Allowed' warning sign outside.

Cumbria Cricket Ltd's director of cricket Bob Simpson is here too, black shorts, green top, 47 years of age. The epitome of a clean-cut company man, finishing touch of tennis socks and trainers, he agrees to chat but, after being distracted by his phone, nips off to catch up with Arthur; perhaps the lap will be a chance to agree on a party line. Five overs later, the 100 comes up just as five non-batting Scots wander off with a football. 'I'll show ye the skells,' says one of South Asian heritage, as young Davidson takes a superb catch, unfortunately off a no-ball. As a youth his father, Mark, played hockey and is on his way to being a top referee. His two boys though are cricket through and through. With Carlisle, Jon comes in at four or five, while eldest son Ben, 20, opens the batting. By way of complication, there's a Ben Davidson in today's Scotland side too.

The visitors are soon back in the groove, one lad clipping a four that travels the length of two pitches, this one and the rugby paddock next door. Youth cricketers they may be, but there are some powerful hitters on display. It really isn't kids' stuff. This is a 50-over game and there are 15 left when Scotland reach 150, though by then a further three wickets are down. No matter, the heat makes it tough for the bowlers and the tail-enders dig deep. They add five more runs an over before bowled out for 207, two runs off Cockermouth's Sam Thompson – like Ben Davidson part of Cumberland's development squad and chaperoned by his dad – nudging them past the 200.

Two young Scottish women in hijabs, here to watch a brother of one, stand on the bottom boundary during the pause in play. 'Can we cut across the field?' one of them asks. 'I want to have a look.'

'Why?' says the other. 'It's the exact same sort of grass.'

'Are we allowed onto it?'

'Och, no,' she says, as the wicket is swept and silent dust flies.

Lunch is a childrens' party-style buffet in the adjoining rugby club, after which Bob, short and stocky, sits down to talk business. Born in Manchester, he moved to Shropshire when his mother remarried in 1978, played club cricket with Whitchurch CC and took the job here in Cumbria in October 2002. It's a task he takes seriously. Furthermore, it turns out that his 16-year-old son, a spin bowler, is in today's side also and that lads from outside the county can represent it too. 'The guys are from a variety of clubs ... Penrith ... Carlisle ... Whitehaven ... my lad plays for Coniston ... North Lancashire and Cumbria League, a couple of Northern League clubs and two from the Westmorland League. Adam Murphy plays at Shireshead & Forton, a club near Lancaster, but they are affiliated to Cumbria Cricket.'

The under-17s season has been a mixed bag thus far, he says, although up to now they have only played friendlies. 'We didn't turn up yesterday and losing so heavily was disappointing, but this is a one-day game and they are performing a lot better. We've had issues with availability, but that's getting harder generally. Arthur has found that there's not the same amount of commitment, purely because society is changing and there's a lot of other things you could be doing. You'd find the same scenario if you were in Devon or Suffolk.'

Helping in the battle are three ECB growth initiatives. 'Well, four, but one is aimed at South Asian participation and we don't have many South Asians in Cumbria, it's just the demographics.' Indeed, the only Asians here are with the Scottish party and while Bob and Arthur were joined on a lap earlier by a man of Asian appearance, he turned out to be Whitehaven's Habib Baloch, who arrived as a pro but is nowadays an amateur, having settled in the town.

'Our age groups from under-11s are linked by performance programmes [EPP] over the winter, in which the better players get specific training and coaching. Chris Hodgson delivers a few of those with Lee Conroy, our performance director, who also works with Lancashire and Durham to ensure our kids have a route to the first-class game.' Conroy is also Cumbria Cricket Ltd's representative on the Cumberland committee, although he didn't show up for the AGM in March and neither is he here today.

'There are six districts in Cumbria but, because there's not a massive amount of players coming through, we split them into four. There's the west, Workington down to Millom, and the Barrow area. You've also got the South Lakes, east of Ulverston all the way up to Shap, and the east, which goes from Carlisle down to Penrith. That mirrors where our four development officers work. Their main aim is to get kids interested in cricket from primary school age through the ECB charity "Chance to Shine", and then transition into clubs.'

Bob reckons there are eighty-five board-affiliated clubs within the county and says the organisation's role is to: '...administer the recreational game and introduce as many kids to it as possible. I must say, "Chance to Shine" has been fantastic with the year-one-to-year-three key stage. It's a bespoke programme for younger kids – cricket, but you wouldn't recognise it as cricket. We ran it for the first time this year and they loved it. We are introducing them to non-traditional as well as traditional cricket and working more closely with 'All Stars'. You are getting parents who have never been to cricket before, bringing their kids down.'

Funding all of this isn't easy, money perpetually in short supply. Again, though, Bob isn't interested in making excuses.

'We have done particularly well for a small county stretching over a massive area. I don't want to reveal the actual amount we receive, but it's based on a figure the ECB has worked out based on the total number of schools and clubs per population; so for example, Yorkshire get far more than Lancashire and rightly so. In the end, it all comes down to chimney pots. But that doesn't stop us wanting to grow the game and being the best we can. Part of my role is to try and secure additional funding so that we can staff the organisation properly and deliver. Capacity-wise, we are flat out. Give us more, whether that resource is financial or human, and we can deliver more.'

One ambition is an increase in club-based activity.

'This is a conversation I've had with the ECB – at the moment our guys work hard to deliver in schools, holiday camps and so on, but ideally you'd have a school development officer, a school/club transition officer and also a club support officer. You've to remember, clubs are run by volunteers and the game's strength is dependent on them. It's crucial that we try and support them more.' All of it leading to this sort of representative team in Wigton, before further advancement, in theory, to the Minor Counties. How are players selected?

'Every year we have assessment days for our four area squads, at under-11s, under-13s and under-15s. They train in winter. Then we have our county age group squads based on nominations from area squads. They then train and play in the programme. The under-17s have three or four friendlies, then play the likes of Durham, Leicestershire and Northumberland... fifteen or so fixtures a year.'

There is now a growing women's programme too, including a softball festival that is: '...another brilliant initiative from the ECB. It gets sporty and non-sporty females playing, breaks down barriers, turns a game that takes forever into a fun and informal opportunity to run around, smack a ball, but most importantly have a good social.' The female age groups are under-13s, under-15s, under-17s and senior. They too all compete in an ECB programme of fixtures.

'The women's senior team have finished for the year and did all right. The issue we have is we produce female players and they go to university, move out of the area, then it's a fight for numbers. It's why we're looking to set up more female hubs.' The imaginatively named South Lakes Maidens at Lindal Moor are Bob says: '...a model for us. They've got a junior team and senior one as well but, at the moment we haven't got it replicated. We are working on that. The likes of Cockermouth, Egremont, Carlisle and Temple Sowerby are looking at establishing hubs. Once that's set up there'll be a league structure. You don't want to be training people up with no fixtures to play in.'

As for the male under-17s, where are they likely to go after this? Local club scene? Cumberland? A first-class county side somewhere?

'In the past, we've worked with Cumberland on development games, jointly-funded. This year we've both done our own, in our case off the back of the EPP. We want to work with them on that basis, but for a variety of reasons it hasn't happened. The ECB though is now basically saying county clubs and boards must work together, with a central partnership agreement between county and board in terms of pathways. That should be pretty simple, in my eyes. County age group stuff all the way through to the Cumberland first team – and branching off that you've got your first-class academies and your performance programmes in house. Lee is doing a great job with Durham and Lancashire to make sure that's getting better and better and we've noticed that Lancashire have become a lot more proactive in supporting what we are trying to do. Durham are very good too.

'We recognise – as I'm sure Cumberland do – that we have to get closer. If we can support a common goal, look at a permit system for the league structure, say, so the best players stay in the county, then by a process of natural selection you would hope a higher standard of club cricket would emerge in Cumbria. That's then a selection process, where future Cumberland teams will come from. I think that's what the ECB are saying: "Hang on, let's have a look at the Minor Counties. How many first-team players are coming from within Cumberland, Northumberland, Suffolk or Devon pathways?" That's a clear bit of working through at the moment.'

Cumberland's counter-argument, of course, is that those doors are already open, they just can't get players to commit and show the ambition to go the extra mile. But maybe that point in itself is reason enough to form an aspirational Cumbrian Premier League, building a positive out of local rivalry and even personal grievances.

'We've had league association meetings at which the North Lancashire and Cumbria League were proactive in recognising that participation is dropping – so how are we going to sort it? They've got the clubs involved in a consultation process. There is a want for that. If you talk to their chairman, Gary Postlethwaite, he'll say, look, we're not bothered what it's called, we just want a structure in place to promote the best cricket and enable it to survive. We recognise other leagues will want to retain their independence, but there still could be promotion and relegation. There are ways of working it. Leicestershire have done a pretty good job with that. Ideally, you'd have a seamless and very easy to understand pathway.' He gives an example. 'Kid comes in, experiences "Chance to Shine" at six years of age, then transfers to an "All Stars" centre. He joins that club and is nominated for Barrow area under-11s. Gets nominated for the county under-11s and goes all the way through to Cumberland or, if good enough, first-class academy. Simple.'

To an outsider, that all sounds perfectly reasonable and indeed even obvious. But this is Cumbria, isn't it? 'In an ideal world, if we, collectively, Cumberland and Cumbria Cricket Board, have such a plan to work towards, to get this seamless pathway and support recreational cricket in getting better and better, in fact to allow any player to operate at a standard that they are good enough to play at, hopefully funded through the ECB, away we go.' Yet the likelihood of success may hinge on one question. Does Bob see this happening via a partnership or one single unified organisation? 'Whatever works best within Cumbria is fine. Everywhere is different. But if you could remove history and politics it would be so much easier.'

What is an average working week for a director of cricket? Not nine to five, Monday to Friday, presumably. 'You are working with volunteers so, understandably, they will email or call at the weekend or evenings and you've to be careful how you manage that. Again, with more staff it would be easier. When the ECB puts out a new initiative, we've to deliver it whether we've enough people to do it or not. We find a way. It may not be the best way, but we do find a way.'

And as for that relationship with Cumberland: 'I am absolutely not saying there's an issue with them and hopefully they would say the same. Let's start the process of working together. Since I took up this post with Cumbria Cricket Ltd in 2002, there has been massive change. We've development officers, a team of people, it's no longer just me. That takes time. These things don't change overnight.'

Bob's son Ted having taken two for 58, Cumbria re-emerge with fire and Rice Krispie-buns in their bellies. The afternoon is still and clear, heavens marred only by vapour trails left by an RAF jet.

Coming in at four will be Theo Manihera, son of veteran rugby league stand-off Tane Manihera, a New Zealand Maori who played for Workington, Barrow, Whitehaven and even Carlisle in his time – the Cumbrian full house, before settling here. Along with cricket, Theo plays for Newcastle Falcons' rugby union academy, so presumably a Ben Stokes-like career choice lies ahead. He's a hefty lad who, as Cumbria's openers Will Atkinson and Henry Marshall take the field, makes his way through a bar of chocolate.

'Happy with that?' he is asked, about the first innings score.

'Could be better,' he replies, between munches.

The two though make a solid start, 45 runs on the board after 13 overs, at which point skipper Atkinson hammers one down a fielder's throat and Jonathan Davidson enters the fray. Alas, the incomer lasts but five balls before he is caught behind for a duck and the wicket tally is doubled without gain. The Scots scent victory and their yells of support grow louder, 'buddy' the epithet of choice. Enter Manihera junior, shoulders whirling, no hiding his intentions. He survives two sticky early moments. The first is a wild – and unintentional – beamer that he does well to duck beneath. The second comes when he is almost cracked on the head again after the fielder who cuts it off at the rope hurls the ball back over the 'keeper. By way of response, he belts the four that takes his side past 50, en route to a personal half-century achieved in only 59 balls.

Thereafter, with support from Marshall and Mark Wharton in particular, a tight and exciting game finishes in Cumbria's favour, the runs knocked off at a cost of eight wickets with ten overs to spare. By season's end, Scotland and Cumbria will sit respectively third and fourth in Group 1B, both missing out on the Cup's national stages. In the under-17s championship table, Cumbria will finish bottom.

*****

Three days later, around twenty miles south west of Wigton, in Workington, the calculator is again in use, this time to work out what Cumberland's Minor Counties side require if they are to qualify after all for the final stages of the Twenty20 competition.

One complication at least has been resolved; England went out of football's World Cup on Wednesday, losing their semi-final with

Croatia, 2-1, in extra-time, so won't face eventual winners France in today's big Moscow showdown. And that's just as well. A request to Northumberland to move the game forward was knocked back, so the original noon start remains. Gary Pratt, meanwhile, also refused to begin Richmondshire's National Club Championship tie any later.

That potential controversy dodged, news from Staffordshire did raise eyebrows, Staffs docked points for fielding an ineligible player against Northumberland on May 27. The two-point deduction could not affect qualification, however, as they were level with Cheshire at the top of Group 1 with an inferior run-rate, both sets of fixtures completed. Mathematically, only Cumberland or Northumberland can now deny Cheshire's progress.

Jacques du Toit will captain the side against his former county – which at any other level of cricket would inspire headlines re score-settling. In a further spin-off, there will be no fewer than eight home-grown Cumbrians on display, unprecedented in recent years. Only du Toit, Bulcock and Boyne are outsiders. Hands still sizzling from his Unicorns experience behind the stumps, Sam Dutton is to fill in for Ben Howarth and Matty Cowling, while there will be debuts for Cockermouth pair Marcus Stables and Alex Grainger, and Minor Counties returns for Glen Weightman – a rugby-playing batsman from Keswick – and seamer Matthew Lowden on his home turf. The prize at stake: spot number four alongside Devon, Berkshire and Norfolk at Wormsley on August 26. To dump Cheshire though, either Cumberland or Northumberland will need to win both matches and improve their net run rate substantially. One victory apiece would spell failure.

The Ernest Valentine Ground is named for the fellow who bought a site that's been home to cricket in some form or other since 1865. The present club was established here circa 1895, when the first game with neighbouring Whitehaven was recorded that May, in a part of town known as the Cloffocks. John Patterson is a Workington CC man and sits chatting in front of the pavilion with the club's scorer, Tim Kempster, who has filled the role since 1996, over five hundred games. Behind them is a more eye-catching sight, an eccentrically painted ex-brewery whose green maltings tower and domed cupolas say apocalyptic Tyrolean zombie death trap. In fact, since the mid-2000s, it has actually been used for social housing, accessed via the forecourt of a police station that might itself be mistaken for Stalag Luft III. It is shielded by mounted surveillance cameras, while barbed wire fencing completes the homely touch.

'That was Workington brewery,' John says of the first building, 'it's now basically a block of flats. It closed as a brewery in the early 1980s.' Subsequent research reveals that to be correct, Scottish and Newcastle back then the owners of land on which beer had been produced since the late 18th century, doubtless making use of the Derwent that flows past the bottom of the ground, occasionally to devastating effect. In 2015, floodwaters impinged here as elsewhere, though wreaking less havoc than was caused in 2009. As at Carlisle, a plaque in the pavilion shows the level the waters reached that year, several metres high, leading to the old clubhouse being demolished and a new one built in its place, 're-opened' by Ian Botham in 2011.

Also that year came a new footbridge over the river that looks a long way from flooding today, even beneath skies cloudier than of late, the original 'Navvies Bridge' wrecked by the torrent. Each of the town's major sports teams are based hereabouts. A little further downstream, a crossing by Workington's football ground collapsed too, killing a policeman who was standing on it at the time.

Set against such tragedy, the state of the cricket club's outfield a decade or so on is small beans, though it must be said it's a mess. 'It undulates' says Tim. 'We don't know what's underneath it, though have tried to improve the drainage in recent years.' Its issues aren't completely down to floodwater. 'In 1990, a huge hole appeared and the slopes have got worse over the years,' the scorer adds. The surface is awash with dips and mounds, each one a potential ankle-turner.

'They tried to lift it a bit last year,' John says, 'but with the summer we've had it hasn't settled in as well as it should have.'

President of Workington RUFC in 2018, having filled the same role with the county side two years ago and also been on its selection and disciplinary committees, this faithful Cumberland CCC follower played cricket here and looks thoroughly settled in himself. 'I was one of the poorest players in the first team, so it was just third man to third man, to long-off, you know. I ended up going to the local steelworks and played at work, batting middle order, so at least I got some time with the bat, which I enjoyed. I did that until I was about 35.' His involvement with Cumberland came through Eric. 'He'd see me watching at Workington and gradually, on retirement, I started going to away games and joined in with the good group they are.' Aged 72, he continues to insist his committee days are behind him. 'I just like to watch. I'm sure Eric would find us a job if he could, but I keep putting him off.'

Beyond sport, John eventually took charge of outside inspection at British Steel. 'We used to design and build the casting plants around the world. One of my jobs was to visit all the sub-contractors. In 1992, the firm moved to Sheffield and I took the opportunity to leave.' Mrs Patterson was a ward sister at West Cumberland hospital. 'We found we could live on less money, so I ended up working for a small engineering company in Workington and lasted in that until I was nearly 69, three years ago.' Hence more time for cricket and holidays, including trips to Portugal every year. 'We are travelling down the east coast of Italy soon, for seventeen days. I'll miss Bedfordshire, but will be back in time for Newcastle.'

In a squad finalised after the World Cup semi on Thursday, Steve Sharp opens with Dutton and Grainger, though Dutts is soon stumped, Cumberland opting to bat on winning the toss. Boyney is caught at mid-off and the hosts are 14 for 2, with Grainger still to contribute. As starts go it's not promising, but his subsequent 31 runs in partnership with Sempy moves the side on to 72 for 3, before Sempy, Weightman and the unbeaten du Toit drive the Cumbrians home for 107 for 4. The low total is partly explained by the lack of the usual late flourish. Only sixteen overs were bowled.

Everywhere but here, the British Isles are enjoying another beautiful summer Sunday. The journey north was as usual glorious, the switch westward not so much. Coming into Workington, cloud began to descend that even produced a few spots of rain, the sort of day when a fleece and umbrella would have been a good idea. On arrival, one woman handed Eric a raffle prize, chocolates in an M&S carrier bag – Thornton's Exclusive Collection. 'They were on offer,' she said. 'I don't suppose whoever wins will notice.'

Asked if Cumberland could achieve the run rate to progress, he'd replied: 'We'll give it our best shot,' but with no great conviction.

Had England reached the final, due to its flat screen telly the bar would have done good business, but they hadn't. France versus Croatia went largely unnoticed. Of more immediate concern was a darkening sky, beneath which a cricket match had done its best to get going, as confirmed by the occasional blast of tinny music from awnings on the cop shop side, the club trying hard for the T20 spirit.

The first interruption for a heavy shower had come with three Cumberland wickets down in the 13th over – covers on, players off, clubhouse suddenly abuzz with shelterers from the rain.

Happily, one of those was Gilbert Johnstone; club tie, green fleece, ready smile and rose-veined cheeks under a sprightly thicket of silver hair. The DVLA currently holds a letter from his specialist re his ability to drive, a matter unresolved. Coming to this game was not an issue at least; the 77-year-old lives just up the road.

*****

Born at Benwell, Newcastle, on 12 March 1941, without wheels Gilbert may be, but he still walks at least three miles a day. Quite often that's to Workington library, where he is currently compiling tables and batting and bowling averages for the North Lancs and Cumbria League, going back to that competition's very foundations.

Given his Northumberland roots, 'I'll be in my element today,' he'd said during the interlude, though truth be told the Johnstones weren't long on Tyneside, the family moving to Branthwaite, some five miles from Workington, when Gilbert was four years old. Nor was it long before cricket weaved its spell. While at secondary school, he'd come down to this ground when the players were netting. 'We never batted, but were happy retrieving the ball when it escaped.' One such player, Mr Hudson Schofield, a local bank manager, used to complement his whites with a dashing cravat. 'He'd place a coin on each of the three stumps and bat against us youngsters, who would endeavour to knock over the stumps. If you were successful he'd give you the coin from the removed stump.'

Gilbert's eyes twinkled at the memory. They do that a lot. A man who could not imagine life without cricket has a lot of stories to tell, about matches seen, people met and admired. 'I follow Yorkshire for my sins and really do enjoy it. I've met lovely, lovely people.' Some of them famous. 'Sir Colin Cowdrey, Derek Randall ... I mentioned to him about running Geoffrey Boycott out and he said: "We won't go there" ... I've had a wonderful time.' The highlight, he said, was half an hour in the company of spinner John Emburey who, aside from an England career shortened by two rebel tours to apartheid South Africa, also had a stint at Bedfordshire in the Minor Counties, Cumberland being the visitors on one occasion. 'He sat opposite me and Vera, a true gentleman.'

Gilbert has an old photograph somewhere of himself as a ten-year-old amid the footings of a soon-to-be new pavilion in the early 1950s, the building prior to this one, erected after the floods. He was destined not to be a Workington CC member, but remained a follower of the club and was once called upon to field for ten overs at Barrow, until a missing team member arrived. Like many of his generation, works cricket was his primary competitive arena.

'I started work on 19 August 1957,' he would later confirm in an email, intent on getting his facts right, as would any statistician worth his or her salt. 'The factory was Hornflowa, better known as the "Button Factory". There I completed my apprenticeship as a draughtsman. I worked with a man called Tommy Hardy, who asked if I was interested in cricket and would I like to join Dovenby Hall CC. I joined a year later and stayed until the club disbanded in 1969.' He then played for three years at Maryport CC, alongside some ex-Dovenby players, before his job at Post Office Telephones took him to Carlisle in 1974, where he played in a Civil Service side until 1982 in the former Cumberland Senior Cricket League. 'Dovenby won the second division title and Junior Cup [now the John Scott Trophy] twice each. I appeared in a further four finals and lost in them all.'

The road to the Minor Counties and Cumberland began on his retirement from what was by then BT on 29 July 1992. 'On the Sunday, Vera and me went down to see them play Bedfordshire and the following year watched almost every game.' Upon moving to York, 1994 was wiped out but the pull remained and thereafter back he went, Vera often in tandem. 'At Grantham in 1996, Harold Millican, Barry Parker and Alan Pemberton were doing a lap of the boundary and stopped to ask if I'd like to join the committee. Still living in York then, I couldn't see what value I could offer.' The trio pointed out that it didn't seem to prevent him watching the club home and away, so he accepted and was the following year elected. 'I used to travel from York to the Shap Wells Hotel for the meetings.'

Since when, there is scarcely a role with the county that Gilbert has not at some time filled. 'I have been committee member, team manager, secretary and raffle ticket seller,' he said. 'I have scored for them in emergencies and umpired at square leg – five overs – at Southgate versus Middlesex CB in 1999.' He has umpired for rather longer spells in the Ribblesdale and North Lancashire leagues too, and was keen to point out that once, while on holiday in Benidorm, he oversaw a game with Mike Hendrick, ex-Derbyshire and England fast bowler.

This faithful servant still helps out when required, though is keen to take things easier, time-consuming historical research apart. In recent years he has taken it upon himself to gather full scorecards for every single game Cumberland have had in the Minor Counties, along with similar for Cumberland and Westmorland prior to them joining the MCCA ranks in 1955. Unsurprisingly, such devotion to historical archives endears him to such as Mike Latham.

Though cricket is his greatest pleasure, Gilbert is also a staunch supporter of Workington Reds soccer club and 'for pocket money' could list a further array of jobs-on-the-side, in the unlikely event a CV should ever be necessary. 'I have cleaned windows, served petrol, fitted tyres and driven taxis.' This latter job reminds him of the time he had to drive a hearse to an undertaker's. 'As I pulled up, he asked me to help him get an empty coffin in the back, which we then took to an old folks' home and carried upstairs. It was for a dead body on a bed. The undertaker said: "Do you want legs or shoulders?" I took the legs. We got him into the coffin all right, but he was too heavy to carry far, so we went to use the lift. Trouble is, it wasn't very big, so we had to stand the thing on end as we went down. Having driven to the mortuary we were met by a white-coated gentleman, who took down the dead man's details and attached them to the body before opening a big door with a sign that read: "All bodies to be placed feet first". I told the taxi owner not to send me on any more jobs like that.'

An even more macabre tale features a second body that on this occasion belonged to his stepfather. 'My dad died at Wembley in April 1967, watching England play Scotland, and a few years later my mother remarried. One night I got a call saying her second husband was dead so I went to her house, where she was obviously distressed. I asked if she'd like a cup of tea, and she said yes, she would, so I went in the kitchen to make it. Thing is though she hadn't told me his body was still laid out, on the floor. The doctor had certified him dead, but the undertaker hadn't yet taken the body away. I got quite a shock.'

His chauffeur today is John Patterson, whom Gilbert lived next-door-but-one to in his youth: 'He has offered to take me to Furness next week.' Given that John is holidaying in Italy, the game after that in Bedfordshire is a no-go. He'll take Gilbert to Newcastle for game five, though, where he and Vera will stay for all three days. 'Carlisle I can manage on the service bus.' Driving licence or not that's the rest of the Championship season sorted, although there may yet be reptilian trouble in store.

Perhaps coincidentally, Toby Bulcock entered the conversation as the heavens brightened. Barrow may not be straightforward after all, because Vera has agreed to babysit next-door's tortoise. 'Tortoise, eh?' said Toby. 'I've one of those in a vivarium at home who's looking for a girlfriend.' The lovelorn beast has hit maturity and is constantly humping a stone replica, he revealed. 'I'm forever wiping spunk off.'

Upon the restart, Jacques du Toit slapped an immediate six, frustrated by news that this first game was now shortened to the tune of four lost overs apiece. There seemed little reason for it; the day was young, sunshine back, the light not in doubt. But as ever in this sport, rules is rules and the umpires' hands were tied. Cumberland's earlier batsmen hadn't had the time expected and when Sempy was stumped so were his side, scant overs left for miracles. If the run-rate target was confusing before, it was more so now with new convoluted equations to be solved courtesy of the Duckworth-Lewis method. This in a 'simplified format,' accessible to new audiences.

'We'd been pacing ourselves for a big finish,' said Jacques as he came off the pitch, a total of 107 for 4 revised to a 114 run-chase – life way too short to work out why. Back on the field, however, he soon gives his teammates a boost. His over-the-shoulder acrobatics off Slacky ensures the scalp of former Durham, Gloucestershire and England one day international Phil Mustard, out for a first ball duck. Yet not long after, 1 for 1 reads 18 for 1, as Jacques is belted for three boundaries and the Geordies forge on to just short of the half-century before a second victim falls, a Dutts stumping giving Chris Hodgson his first Cumberland wicket of the season.

The crowd roars – for a rugby league derby at nearby Derwent

Park, where Workington Town simultaneously face Whitehaven, a reliably raucous affair however far those clubs have fallen in the food chain. John Patterson points to a hill yonder, upon which the farm of a former Workington Town chairman once sat. Along with advising the Ministry of Agriculture and counting Nikita Khrushchev, King Farouk and Pablo Picasso among his many acquaintances, the inimitable Tom Mitchell, before his death in 1998, was a legend in these parts. 'You could always tell when Town were about to sign a new player,' John quips, 'because his barn would burn down.'

League legend Ike Southward too once played cricket here and, in his later years, parked his car along a boundary that is now the source of T20 music. Hodgson is smashed for six off the pavilion roof and a sting of Queen's 'Another One Bites the Dust' rents the air. Midway through their allocation, Northumberland are 61 for 2 and well on course for victory. Dutts then takes a catch as Sempy makes it 68 for 3 in over nine, but wickets-wise that's that.

There is another brief hold-up as a billowing section of black tarpaulin –a makeshift sightscreen held together by gaffer tape and weighed down by ladders and scaffolding poles – is replaced in a stiffening breeze. As grounds go it may not be pretty, but no one is worried by that as runs get hard to come by and the game suddenly finds a competitive edge.

Local bowler Matthew Lowden comes on for an over, earning a cheer from a group of admirers under a red-brick wall. He does well too, before going for six on the last ball of his over and then is really unlucky to be denied a maiden by a fluke four on the last ball of his second. Northumberland now need 12 off the final two overs – a run a ball with seven wickets in hand. They manage it with two balls to spare, four byes the *coup de grâce*. A little unfortunate today and clearly understrength, it's nevertheless the tale of Cumberland's year. In need of a bang, they end on a whimper. A competition they were never much interested in is finally out of its misery.

Well, not quite. There is one fixture left and while Cumberland are definitely not going to Wormsley, Northumberland may yet do so, although the omens aren't good when their opponents again win the toss, bat first, and this time make 127 for 9, Dutts top-scoring with 30. Eric, as good with numbers as you'd hope, works out they'll need to reach that total in twelve overs if they are to get the run rate.

In launching a reply, Northumberland, watched by Geoff Cook, see Mustard fall cheaply to Slacky again, although before long none of that matters. Given twenty overs in which to notch any old win, they will require one ball fewer than sixteen to pass Cumberland's total in an eventual five-wicket victory. Long before which point it has become clear that the mathematical requirement for progress is beyond them and Cheshire, nervously refreshing *playcricket.com* no doubt, are able to breathe a sigh of relief.

There is relief at the Ernest Valentine Ground, Workington, too, as an afternoon that has swung between cloud and drizzle concludes in belated sunshine and Sherbet's 1976 hit 'Howzat' provides a fitting coda to Cumbria's last T20 encounter of the year. Gilbert has good news. The trip to Barrow next week is back on the agenda.

Vera has found another tortoise-sitter.

Lap Three

Go Westmorland !

Forty years ago, the author Geoffrey Moorhouse, whose other works veered from rugby league to a trek by camel across the Sahara, set his sights on the Minor Counties. Well, not just the Minor Counties. *The Best Loved Game*, published in 1979 and updated in 1987, was his response to cricket's imminent demise. A moment the back cover blurb saw as ideal: '...to take a fond look at the game he had loved since childhood and to see how well it was surviving amid the frictions and uncertainties of the Packer era.'

Moorhouse spent the summer of 1978 taking soundings from Eton v Harrow, to the Lancashire League, to an England Test with Pakistan, a Village Championship tie in Oxfordshire and even the Hambledon Game, opposite the Bat and Ball Inn at Broadhalfpenny Down, which some consider cricket's birthplace (it isn't).

He settled on Staffordshire as the venue for his Minor Counties chapter, Cumberland's opponents here at Netherfield a fortnight ago. Today, we are back in Kendal ahead of our latest lap of the Cumbrian club scene – a tour of Westmorland – in Mike Latham's trusty Skoda Yeti, and Minor Counties advocates have reasons to be cheerful. Four, in fact. That's how many players of recent MCCA experience have been named in England's under-19s squad ahead of three one-dayers v South Africa: Staffordshire's Liam Banks (Warwickshire), Berkshire wicketkeeper Jack Davies (Middlesex), Oxfordshire's Ben Charlesworth (Gloucestershire) and Harrison Ward (Sussex) the chosen few. Yet Moorhouse's observations, penned all those years ago, reveal that really, at the sharp end, not a great deal has changed.

'It took half an hour this morning to find anyone who could tell us where their county cricketers were playing,' he writes. 'The game began yesterday, but it might not be happening for all most of the locals seem to know or care.' The two-day match at Lichfield CC sees Staffs face Northumberland and it is at an exciting stage, a win there for the taking: 'Yet I doubt whether twenty people have turned up...' Moorhouse blames two things for this 'bare quorum'. First, the fact that Minor Counties teams: '...occupy a curiously ambiguous position in the pattern of English cricket. They are not regarded as intrinsically first-class by the legislators.' And second: 'When cricket watchers had to consider bus timetables more than they nowadays do, minor county teams reaped a partisan reward. The motorised age has damaged local loyalty at this level perhaps more than at any other, vastly increasing the temptation to visit the nearest first-class ground instead...'

In our very own motor, Toby (the dog) reclining in the back, Mike hands over a pork pie from Stuart Smith & Sons, Milnthorpe, renowned fifth-generation purveyors of fine foods, and concedes that there is no need really to include Netherfield on our latest jaunt as we have been here already. Geographically, however, Kendal is as good a spot as any to stage base camp for a tour of the Westmorland League and here, at the town's 'second' club, there is a decent game on, albeit in the Northern Premier League. Penrith are the visitors, by now in a relegation battle with a drop to the Palace Shield lurking.

Arriving via Settle, Giggleswick and Clapham, having climbed into a patch of cloud at Goat Gap before dropping into Ingleton, Yorkshire's sole Westmorland League club, and going on past another Westmorland League set-up, Kirkby Lonsdale, with its Devil's Bridge, an otherwise bright morning has turned overcast. There is even the odd spot of rain, although the temperature is mild and the car share as convivial as ever. Typical really. The schools broke up for summer yesterday, so no doubt the heatwave of 2018 is at an end.

Having walked up the Netherfield hill, we bump into Penrith's chairman, Andrew Hall, father to Cumberland's Greg, who was last seen tending the wicket with Greg's mother on Staffordshire's visit to Tynefield Park in the T20. His son is bowling as we chat, home side batting first. Yes, going down would be tough to take, Andrew admits: '...but overall, relegation is good for cricket.' In contrast to the recent county game, it's chilly today, fleece weather. Mike is again collared regularly as we stroll and talk turns to Cumberland where, despite earlier claiming not to be interested in T20, it is suggested that Toby (the cricketer) is upset because Gary Pratt hadn't made himself available for Workington.

Ominously for Penrith, Netherfield are soon 32 without loss, Greg unlucky to see the opener dropped off his right-arm medium pace. They are on the track Cumberland were supposed to play on, though it is now behaving itself. Behind us, a third tier game featuring Netherfield's 3rd XI and Cartmel's 1st XI is on, first versus second. In that one, players seem either to be of school age or near retirement. With Geoffrey Moorhouse in mind, maybe they all came on bus passes. One umpire is Tracey Williams of the Westmorland League management committee, whose husband Kevin is Cartmel's opening batsman, currently amassing 40 runs in an eventual 65-run win. Fortunately he will be caught out, not given lbw by his missus.

Among those Mike bumps into are two Netherfield cricketers, on a lap themselves: left-arm bowler Matt Jackson and ex-Blackpool and Morecambe goalkeeper and now wicketkeeper Lewis Edge. The foe tomorrow will be Liverpool Comp giants Ormskirk, who they are to meet in a Lancashire Cup quarter-final. Among their number is Scott Lees, a one-time Cumberland player – in fact he was in the 2015 Championship-winning team – and notorious practical joker.

Factotum Mike lets slip that Scott is about to take accountancy exams. Helpfully, he proffers a handy 'sledge' that might just disrupt his game. If that sounds mean, it ought to be noted that a Wikipedia search for Lewis Edge (possibly deleted) reveals how: 'Throughout his twenties Lewis was recognised as a potential UK table tennis champion but after many attempts for the crown became somewhat disheartened by the sport and focussed his attention on a sport nobody likes or plays called Cricket. In the summer of 2017 he was challenged to a game of table tennis by his idle [sic] and former 1990s teen sensation Paul Wilson but alas he bottled it again and never turned up, citing nerves and lack of practice time.'

Banter, obviously. Anyway, the dastardly scheme won't work because Ormskirk are destined to win by 106 runs.

Meanwhile down below, their Netherfield teammates pass the half-century, comfortable against a side with two Cumberland players of the late-1980s in its ranks, left-arm spinner Richard Elwood and Chris Stockdale, a golf buff with links to Malaysia, apparently back in England for a while. 'I'm getting too old for this,' says Elwood, as he slides to stop a boundary. Greg's brother Sam also bowls spin and exactly midway through the visitors' 50 overs he gets the first wicket. At 85 for 1 it's time for us to depart, with a promise to pop back later as a final stop, should the game last that long and the opportunity arise. It's time to get a proper look at the Westmorland League.

*****

First up, Sedgwick, this year in Division 2 but set to win promotion to the top flight. Visitors Shireshead & Forton 2nd XI will just escape relegation, Bolton-Le-Sands and Ingleton tumbling into Division 3 instead. The Westmorland League encompasses four divisions of forty-six teams from twenty-six clubs, with various junior leagues from under-9 to under-19, split north and south, hard ball and soft. If not quite thriving these days, it is very much battling on.

There's been a competitive league structure south of the Lakes for well over a century. Indeed a book to celebrate its one hundredth anniversary, John Glaister's artfully lower case *of smittle spots and sticky buns* was published by the *Westmorland Gazette* in 1994. Originally known as the South Westmorland Village Combination, it later became the Westmorland Cricket Combination (1907-1925) and the Westmorland Cricket League (1926-1974), at the latter end of which period a contemporaneous breakaway 'Super League' of leading clubs occurred. That acrimonious split gave rise to the South Westmorland Cricket League (1965-1974), although the discarded clubs substituted other monikers, 'none of them printable,' Glaister now jokes. Despite limping on for a decade, it was obvious within two years that the division was doomed and in 1974 the two groups kissed and made up. That coincided with the boundary changes that sought to render entities like Westmorland, Cumberland *et al* redundant and so, in finding a new name for the reunited competition, the politically correct South Lakeland Cricket League

(1974-1996) got the nod. Traditionalists were never going to be happy with that and, as a new millennium reared, a reversion to Westmorland Cricket League took place in 1997. Thus it remains, with boundaries stretching from Coniston in the north to Forton in the south, Ingleton and Sedbergh to the east and Cartmel out west.

Sedgwick CC, four miles south of Kendal, is just about central to all of that. At a micro-level it is in a novel position, tucked away behind modern housing in the former grounds of Sedgwick House estate, the roar of a motorway over adjoining fields heard here as a vague hum. Travel far enough into Lancashire and you may well end up at the M6 services that bear the latter half of the visitors' name, Forton being a village in the vicinity, Shireshead, despite its primary billing, a mere hamlet. This is a cosy little spot tailor-made for cricket, compact and awkward to find though it is.

In 1902, during the league's first incarnation, Sedgwick were crowned champions, but that was as good as it got title-wise. In 1894, the inaugural winners had been Gatebeck, historically linked with Sedgwick – indeed they occasionally joined forces on the field. And in a comp that began with just eight teams (Arnside, Burton-in-Kendal, Gatebeck, Holme, Levens Hall, Milnthorpe, Netherfield and Sedgwick) and finished with six, it was when Sedgwick withdrew to leave an unwieldy five that the original Combination drew stumps in 1905, before resuming under its new name in 1907. Long before, however, there were signs that the people who owned the club were less than enamoured with the idea of an organised league structure.

It wasn't that they were averse to the wider encroachments of competitive industry – far from it. As Glaister says: 'By the 1860s this tiny rural community encompassed all that the Victorian work ethic stood for.' A decade earlier: '...one of South Westmorland's richest and most powerful families moved their gunpowder works from Sedgwick to the Peasy Beck site at Gatebeck.' That family was the Wakefields – Quakers with a fortune made in banking and wool. A convenient outcome of the switch was that, in 1867, a prettier setting was left behind in which to erect a brand new mansion.

Sedgwick House, with its pitch in the grounds, soon became a noted venue for country house cricket. According to John Glaister: '...a statement in itself as to the stature the game had reached in

South Westmorland.' As he further points out, however, a formalised competition was still a quarter of a century away, when the game would begin to move on from 'the gentry and their lackeys.' In July 1880, Westmorland played their first county game against ten-man Cumberland at Penrith, and three years later with league cricket on the way, the latest Wakefield to reside at Sedgwick House, Jacob, told the hundred or so attendees at the annual dinner that he liked to see friendly rivalry: '...but deprecated village clubs playing in league matches.' He was very much on the wrong side of history.

According to *of smittle spots and sticky buns*: 'The country house cricket that had been played at Sedgwick House in the golden age between 1892 and 1914 had been some of the finest in the land.' Then World War One intervened and by the time a Sedgwick side was able to return to what was now the Westmorland Cricket League some thirty-five years later, World War Two had also passed. They had a new ground too, in a field near the Heaves Hotel. 'Jacob,' writes Glaister, 'would have turned in his grave.' In 1955, though, it was back to Sedgwick House where the old pavilion once again 'welcomed the smell of linseed oil,' although the sacred turf was now a hayfield. 'Nearly sixty tons were removed to reveal the precious wicket that Mr Wakefield had paid good money to have laid.' Lovingly tended it had been – 'probably the first genuine square laid in the Westmorland League' – but there was no longer any such attentiveness. The house and its grounds were in the possession of Lancashire County Council and refashioned as a residential home for schoolchildren. 'It took delicate dealings, often with faceless bureaucracy, to re-establish the village team on its own midden.'

Today, observing an idyllic scene from a bench alongside the now grade two-listed pavilion, it is easy to conclude that the battle was not in vain. And by coincidence Tony Hutton and his wife, Jennifer, last met on the boundary at Wisbech, are here too. They are on their way to Barrow, for Cumberland's Minor Counties game with Hertfordshire at Furness CC tomorrow. Being groundhoppers like Mike, they have already been to Arnside and will pop in at more grounds due west, such travels forming the basis of Tony's enjoyable online blog. In fact, he lays claim to seeing Cumberland's first ever Minor Counties game, a loss by an innings and 35 runs to Yorkshire's 2nd XI in May 1955 at Edenside, Carlisle. Promoting a book in 2007, he described Jennifer to the *Yorkshire Post* as: '...not really a cricket person, but she's happy to sit in a deckchair when the sun is shining.' By the look of it the intervening decade has seen her interest grow, but in any case, after its overcast start, the day is brightening up.

On the field, there is a repeat of the phenomenon seen on our Eden lap, the batting side providing the square leg umpire, here clad in shorts, a common frustration for groundhopping photographers apparently. Shireshead & Forton are at the crease and a third of the way towards a total of 146 for 8 that will be reached at the cost of four wickets. Time advances and so do we, taking a clockwise route past the now truncated gardens of Sedgwick House, gone to the wild as a copse of woodland behind raspberry bushes. Indistinguishable once from the manicured swathe beyond, it is now home to the bees that fuss and buzz on purple thistles and many a scavenger and rabbit, as betrayed by scattered pellets on a carpet of ivy. Down here, the scent is of mint and conifer, not linseed.

Holme is next on the agenda, a boon no doubt for punning sports desk sub-editors. It too is a Westmorland League founder, although its ground is more municipal than village green. Runners-up to Gatebeck in seasons one and two, achievements thereafter were regularly plentiful, though rare now. Title wins in 1935, 1936, 1957 and 1958 are among its twentieth-century accomplishments.

A more poignant clue to past glories is to be found at the top of the lane on which the cricket club sits. It is there that a stretch of the Lancaster Canal lays stagnant, obsolete now but a vital part once of what would one day form a transport triumvirate with the West Coast railway line and M6 motorway, taking advantage of Holme's position in the landscape. Originally a dot in the parish of Burton-in-Kendal, this once rural community grew like many another such settlement in the early nineteenth century, in its case on the back of quarrying. As a Virgin train suddenly shatters the tranquility in the middle distance, just such a crag looms high to the east, from where limestone would have been extracted before being carted to the narrowboats and barges that then lugged their loads south.

Today's opponents, Burneside, are of equal vintage and actually Westmorland's most successful club. Winners in 1896 and regulars at the top table thereafter, they were triumphant nine times in the South Westmorland League during the 1965-1974 split, Holme, in

1967, being the only other such champions. Come reunification, Burneside were then eight-time winners in the first ten years of the new South Lakeland League. That though is in the past. Neither club is setting Division 1 alight and indeed Holme haven't been in the top flight since 1996. Burneside too have more recently struggled, now navigating a second summer of what is seen as mid-table improvement. Holme will conclude the 2018 campaign rock bottom.

The sun now shines openly on a population of 1,500, although not many of those are at the cricket. As in the Eden Valley, this is another spot with a 1940s feel where, in modern times, raising a side seems like a minor miracle. If all you desire of life is a general store, social club, church and pub – The Smithy Inn – it could be the place for you. If that sounds too dull, there are hourly buses to Kendal, Carnforth and Lancaster. We park next to a playground overflowing with happy and noisy children and gaze over a soulless concrete wall – 'No Football. No Golf. No Dogs' – where Holme are trotting along nicely, 79 for 1 after 22 overs. This, Mike says, is a family club; a point proven when a second wicket falls and the female scorer's brother comes in. 'Their mother is the chairman,' adds our guide. The Holme skipper meanwhile, Liam Teasdale, is a grandson of 'Mick' Fawcett, one of Westmorland's all-time greats.

At the top of a sloping plot on which the first recorded game took place in 1888, a single-storey cream pavilion is fronted by a row of plastic chairs, reached via a gravel path beyond a farmyard-style metal gate. Unable to enter with Toby, we loiter outside long enough to see 50 runs added in what will be a rare home win. Crossing the canal via what a sign calls 'a weak bridge', we then head to the market town of Milnthorpe, three miles to the south.

The standard here ought to be higher. Visitors Westgate are targeting what their local paper, the *Lancaster Guardian*, calls the 'Holy Grail of a hat-trick of championships.' If successful, they'll be only the third club ever to pull it off. Alas, it is not destined to be. They'll have to make do with fifth, Carnforth taking the top honours.

Having been reached by narrow country lanes, Milnthorpe CC is in a setting more urban than pastoral. A ground sloping towards the sea is shared with a football club – a little wooden grandstand says 'Corinthians' on the roof – while waggle-dancing youngsters in a playground alongside squeal with delight on swings, slides and roundabouts, no interest in deftly-taken singles. In a public car park are colourful maps of the Cumbria Coastal Way, a long-distance footpath around what at this point is a winding coastline: '...the best way to discover scenery ranging from sandy beaches and rocky headlands to coastal mudflats rich in bird and plantlife.' Wading curlews are illustrated, along with bar tailed godwits on the shore at Drumburgh, Ravenglass railway, a natterjack toad and a panoramic mountain view from Muncaster Castle. Such close proximity to Morecambe Bay – around a minute away – is not however without dangers. In 2015, the river heading for the Kent estuary broke its banks and floodwaters rose as high as that football stand roof. No danger of that today. Westgate are at the crease and on their way to 151 for 9. Milnthorpe will pass that for the loss of two fewer wickets, a victory we will not be around to see. Perhaps they celebrated with some excellent pork pies, courtesy of Stuart Smith & Sons.

✳✳✳✳✳

To head north on the Cumbria Coastal Way is to pass Grange-over-Sands, Barrow, Seascale, Whitehaven, Workington, Maryport, Silloth and the like, before heading inland to Carlisle. We take the southerly track, through Milnthorpe and Sandside (well named with the tide out) before arriving in Arnside, our next port of call.

Once upon a time, Arnside – and Morecambe Bay generally – was the holiday resort of choice for the heavily industrialised city of Bradford, West Yorkshire. That this should be so owed everything to the rise and dominance of a railway connecting such contrasting parts of the country. For similar reasons, the people of nearby Leeds tended to flock east, in their case to Scarborough. In his elegiac 1933 book, *Now a Stranger*, Bradfordian poet and man of letters Humbert Wolfe reminisced about boyhood trips from Manningham station on the Midland line, escaping day-to-day Victorian soot and grime first through Bolton Abbey and then north-west via the 'gateways of escape that were [the junctions of] Hellifield and Carnforth ... One hour in Yorkshire, the next in Westmorland – and beyond into distance always deeper, country ever greener.'

Motorways and overseas package holidays would put an end to all that, although Arnside can still boast No 43, a five-star B&B

on the water's edge, which former Prime Minister Tony Blair among other luminaries is said to have favoured. It has striking views of an iron railway bridge that still crosses the estuary, Grange-over-Sands and distant peaks of Helvellyn. A pretty ribbon of a promenade is abuzz on what is now a glorious Saturday afternoon, a scene looked over by the 'tree covered hump' of Arnside Knott, a hill Wolfe calls 'Lovers' Knot', due to the pair of larches planted and entwined there by an amorous couple in bygone days, 'thus plighting their troth.'

As for the cricket, the town team is currently leading the Westmorland League and today's visitors are Silverdale, who live just down the road, so haven't had far to come. This pitch is next to yet another children's playground, currently vying with cemeteries by way of an appeal to both ends of the market. 'Owzat?!?' howls Arnside's roly-poly keeper in timely fashion, but the umpire blanks him. The hosts have amassed 140 runs batting first and their neighbours, flirting with relegation at the foot of Division 1, are 19 for 0 after three overs. Might a shock be in the offing?

No. As a sudden chill wind whips in with a whiff of fish and chips, and a group of young mothers share a picnic with their toddlers, the well-nourished 'keeper snags a catch to deliver the opening wicket of an innings set to deliver 113 all out.

Leaving a venue dedicated to '...those who served their country in 1914-18 and 1939-45', the short hop to Silverdale means crossing the boundary into Lancashire, where the 2nd XI reverse fixture is in going on. Again, the views across the bay are spectacular, among the UK's most under-rated. Through a patch of trees at the far end of another compact ground glinting sands can be glimpsed, a fitting backdrop to an outfield that crests and falls like ocean waves.

Here, Arnside also batted first and compiled 135, so an equally effective bowling stint will be necessary from their 2nd XI. Six overs in, the hosts are 26 for 1 in a game watched only by members of the home side in front of a wooden pavilion, next to which is the rare and reassuring sight and smell these days of a new scorebox under construction, sawdust and all. Sheep penned behind drystone walls in adjoining fields take no notice. Given the absence of any obvious residential housing – it must exist, comedian Victoria Wood once lived here – the question of where such clubs find enough players for two teams again strikes one as a mystery. They must come from somewhere and a banner advertising the ECB's All Stars campaign hints at a new generation too, enticed to a distinctive venue whose topography suggests cow patch rather than cricket field, with bumps and divots to match. It isn't long before the tins on the 'wkts' hook are called back into use, but not regularly enough for Arnside to avoid defeat by two wickets.

On we go to 2018's eventual Westmorland League champions, Carnforth, some five miles inland, a Lancastrian town with a history in and out of the various cricket competitions betwixt and between, but more widely known as a setting for David Lean's stiff-upper-lip satire – yes, satire! – *Brief Encounter*, last encountered at the café in Langwathby on our Eden Valley lap and based upon Noël Coward's play *Still Life*. Which brings us back to *Now a Stranger* (published some twelve years before the 1945 film), in which Humbert Wolfe waxes nostalgic about his twenty-minute waits en route to Arnside: 'Carnforth, like Hellifield, is a junction, but a whale to a sprat. Here the London and North Western expresses thundered magnificently on their way to rich destinations. The local train drew up, panting and humiliated, by their side, as though a dray-horse had clumped up to peer over the rails at the elegant line of starters for the Derby.'

On our own excursion, 'Jeeves' Latham shares another point of order as we pass by the tiny village of Warton. They too have a team in the Westmorland League and are Carnforth's great local rivals, but their real claim to fame is as George Washington's ancestral seat.

In Carnforth, it's gala day and as strings of flags flutter it is easy to see why Lean saw it as his ideal Milford Junction. Original period features are still evident, the station nowadays hosting a heritage centre. In the August 2018 edition of *The Oldie* magazine, upon the 50th anniversary of the demise of steam trains, Paul Barnes wrote about Carnforth's links with *Brief Encounter* and recalled how its engine shed had been home to some of the last few:

They had shot the film in the bitter cold of February 1945; it was just as bitterly cold when I turned up there at one o'clock in the morning, 23 years later. Apart from the posters, nothing had changed. The deserted platforms with their massive Victorian benches and sturdy, wooden, sit-up-and-beg porters' barrows were gloomy in the gaslight. Between the rails, the sleepers were white with frost; icicles hung from the water columns at the platform ends.'

That was in February 1968 and, having gained permission to make his own film, he spent six weeks in the town as: '...steam retreated and diesels and overhead wires advanced. Nobody was glad that steam was on the way out. Train driver Jack Simpson said being under those advancing wires was like "driving in a bloody birdcage."'

Yet some were intrigued by the changes. Barnes recalled how:

> The engine shed was a retreat from the freezing night, warmed by the eighteen engines, six rows of three, simmering quietly as steam drifted upwards, their boiler pressure rising slowly ready for the morning's work. In the drivers' lobby there were faded, typewritten traffic instructions, and safety notices. One was a prophetic drawing of a diesel with two men beside it: "Don't let interesting new equipment endanger your life."

Carnforth CC is not averse to change despite having just celebrated its 150th anniversary. Six years ago, in 2012, when the club chose to leave a Northern Premier League joined in 2006, Cumberland's Toby Bulcock had been their final professional player. Pragmatically, the club decided it could afford either a professional or a groundsman, not both. In 2013, they joined Westmorland Division 4. Successive promotions later they are in Division 1, currently second in the table and about to move upwards, crowned champions last year too.

Today, however, the 1st XI is without a fixture due to the withdrawal of Windermere CC, the second most successful club in Westmorland League history after Burneside. Founded in 1857, a player exodus has damaged Windermere severely enough that they have been forced to regroup in Division 4, where a young side now plays as the 1st XI, a development one newspaper called: '...a seismic event that has sent shockwaves through local cricket.'

All seems calm in Division 2, where it is Carnforth 2nd XI's turn to take the stage, having declared on 234 against Bolton-le-Sands 1st XI. Visitors from a couple of miles down the road, they'll be relegated at season's end. After 14 overs, they cling on stubbornly, 23 for 1, which leads the few spectators correctly to predict a draw.

Given the lack of 1st XI action, more people might have been expected at this latest hard-to-find venue, squeezed in behind a plant hire firm. Lodge Quarry, as it is known, is hardly bucolic yet has a quirky charm. If grand, it is self-made scrap merchant grand. Three coiled letter 'C's are welded to the metalwork on the entry gate, for example, and also top decorative iron railings.

Most impressive is the view of Warton Crag from a part of the ground called the 'One Pint Wall End', named for the then chairman who painted the wall there white and whose moniker 'One Pint' hints at his drinking capacity. In fact, the chap in question is seated with the current chairman on another odd feature, the raised soil banking that offers an elevated view of an immaculately tended square and outfield which inclines sharply in its top eastern corner.

The groundsman decision clearly worked, but the side too is doing well, according to the two chairmen. 'We've got three senior teams, ladies sides, junior teams, this is a thriving club,' says One Pint, presumably saving his one pint for later. It's good to hear although as this game is far from thrilling, conversation soon turns to last night's rain-shortened T20 encounter at Old Trafford, where Lancashire beat Yorkshire by one run, former Cumberland player Liam Livingstone in the thick of it. 'Did you see those crowd scenes? It was wild. Like watching another sport.'

*****

'Kendal Cricket Club was formed in the year 1836, the first secretary being Mr. Frank Pearson.' So begins *History of Cricket in Kendal – 1836 to 1905*, a hardback labour of love compiled by member James Clarke and published in 1906. It's a start date so long ago that Kendal Mint Cake, 'the world's first energy bar', didn't yet exist, that happy accident of confection being invented in 1869. Since when it has been nibbled by Sir Edmund Hillary on Everest and Sir Ernest Shackleton on his ill-fated Antarctic crossing of 1914-17. In fact it continued to be enjoyed everywhere but 1950s New York, where customs officers are said to have dumped a shipload into the Atlantic when it failed their 'cake test' by containing no flour or eggs. Fake news perhaps.

Clarke's story, meanwhile, is fascinating, as only a book certain in the knowledge that it is ahead of the great sweep of time can be:

To the present day cricketer, but more especially to the present day Cricket spectator, the scant records of the Club during the first dozen years of its existence cannot appeal very strongly. For the glamour of the "League" had not yet fallen on the game; the keen fight for position in a league table, and the crude wit of a league crowd, were still things of the future.

The author continues:

And yet each one of us who lives Cricket for its own sake must have a warm corner in our hearts for those worthy "old boys", our grandsires, who for twelve years could meet in the long summer evenings, or on holidays, and put as much zest into a sides' game as we moderns do into a league match.

Awash with scoreboards from such fixtures as Mr. W. Willison's Side v Mr Hibbard's Side (won by Mr W in 1852), a loss for Kendal Carpet Works to Burneside six years later and a one-run defeat for Married versus Single in 1866, it is a window into earlier days from which it is impossible not to harvest quotes, both with respect to historical achievement and the extent to which it reminds us that past, present and future have forever and will forever be inextricably entwined.

An occasional match with some neighbouring club probably did take place during [the very earliest] period, but no record of any such has come down to us. In 1847, however, things did begin to look up, and the members ventured on a journey to Arnside, with the avowed object of playing a match on the Sands. Whether the match was actually played or not the writer cannot vouch for; possibly the journey itself was sufficient for one day; at any rate, no scores have been preserved and legend has it that the incoming tide washed the score-book away.

In 2018, Kendal are in the Palace Shield Premier Division having been relegated, with Lancaster, from the Northern Premier League last year, when those two competitions were amalgamated. Come season's end they will be going back up, with Longridge of the Ribble

Valley, but they don't know it yet and times have been tough. The Westmorland League behind us, we've opted to end our latest lap here for the same reason we began it across town at Netherfield. And after a long hop up the A6 to Shap Road, the hosts are revealed to have reached 123 for 2 in chasing a target of 184.

This is a proper 'town ground'; a couple of rows of benches front a car park down one side, open rolling hills to the left, a line of tin-roofed industrial warehouses directly opposite, and a two-storey white clubhouse with attached changing rooms to the right of an elaborate entranceway, over the road from the Duke of Cumberland pub. Padded up in front of said pavilion is Terry Hunte, a club legend back for one last go-round, who Mike is very keen to see. Having originally joined Kendal as its professional in 1987, Hunte long since became the highest scorer in Northern Premier League history, over 20,000 runs to his name.

After 31 overs, however, there is still no sign of his services being required, Kendal moving on to 136 with little resistance from Preston-based opponents Vernon Carus, that rare thing these days, a works team, whose ground is appropriately on Factory Lane. As every league in cricket seems to be structured differently, this is a 45-over match but any hope – for the neutral – of an exciting climax is soon put to bed. Only four overs later, the home side has motored to 160, leaving a requirement of just 25 runs.

Kendal captain Chris Miller wanders by and reveals that when the club went down he had chances to move elsewhere. 'But then you start playing cricket for the wrong reasons, don't you?' His side has clearly regained its mojo, with or without Terry Hunte. Building upon a half-century from 14-year-old Sedbergh schoolboy Tom Aspinwall, two further quick 50s – from Australian opener Lachlan Stewart and wicketkeeper Ben Phillips, both unbeaten – guide the hosts home with a comfortable eight wickets and six overs to spare. Before long, a victory song rings out from the dressing sheds, the first such audible eruption of passion witnessed this season.

Mike suggests we meet the club's scorer, David Sykes, an Oliver Reed lookalike who having clambered down from his wooden abode accompanies us across the field while discussing the fall-out from Storm Desmond. Netherfield may not have been flooded but Kendal certainly was, to heights of seven feet. Around 1,500 properties hereabouts were wrecked. One belonged to David. 'I was close to a breakdown...off my head,' he grimaces. 'Some families in the centre of town aren't back in their houses yet.' Being relegated to the Palace Shield was a disappointment, but hardly on the same scale.

'Losing had become a habit,' says David, who looks more like a bearded heavy metal roadie than stereotypical cricket scorer in this, his 32nd year at Kendal. 'They forgot how to win. The hangover lasted into this season for a while, but then we began beating teams and beating them with ease. Terry Hunte coming back has created a buzz too. He's a legend.'

'Is he still on the bins?' Jeeves enquires.

'Household recycling,' says David.

Our busy day is done, but there is still just enough time to pop back to Netherfield – or 'the filth' as David calls them – to see if their game with Penrith is done and dusted. Not a bit of it, in fact it is at its most rousing stage.

The home side's innings concluded on 225 for 8, a chase that for the visitors seems achievable. What's more, at the batting end is Cumberland's Greg Hall. His two sixes in the final two balls of the penultimate over leave his side needing 14 from the last. At least one more boundary will be required and it comes off the very first ball, a four, followed immediately by another. Six runs are now wanted and Penrith have four balls in which to find them. Ball three, though, results in only a single, which again gives Greg the strike.

Five runs in three balls, he can do that, can't he? What a boon for a side staring down the barrel of relegation. In the event, however, he has a rush of blood to the head and tries to smash one into Alan Wilson's front garden, only to be clean-bowled going for the big hit. Not the wisest course; the new batsman now needs five runs in two balls. He scrapes a single, leaving a last ball target of four. It doesn't happen. Penrith are able only to scramble another single and a relieved Netherfield escape with a winning draw.

Nor, if that was unlucky, are Penrith's fortunes set to improve. Three weeks later, against fellow relegation battlers Barrow, they'll be 160 for 3, chasing 210, when the rains come and turn a priceless sure-fire victory into yet another useless draw.

CHAPTER SEVEN
HERTS AND MINDS

'Heatwave!' scream the Sunday papers, hot for a forecast that the driest summer since 1961 will last for at least this coming week longer. Barrow's skies however are bleached white as bone, the sun refusing to burn through. One patch has the effrontery to suggest a storm may be brewing, as Gary Pratt loses the toss and is invited to bat.

Cumberland are at Furness CC, set to return to Minor Counties Championship action. A handful of spectators are in at the start, just about all of them out-of-towners, so the place is friendlier than it felt on our lap and the attendance soon builds. Hertfordshire are today's opponents, a youthful side. 'But that's the way the Minor Counties is going, isn't it?' suggests groundhopper Tony Hutton, here as he'd promised at Sedgwick, with Jennifer, his wife.

Cumberland field a Championship debutant, Marcus Stables, 19, of the development squad. He and Tyler McGladdery, 22, who started at Wisbech, will bat at four and three respectively, thrown in at the deep end. Jacques du Toit is unavailable for family reasons.

Ross Zelem starts briskly, two fours off the opening two balls, but it isn't long before Tyler is called into action, Ross trapped plum, leg before wicket. Nor does the new left-hand partnership last long. Sempy soon clips one to the 'keeper and it's 18 for 2. Will this game even last the three days?

Defeatism is premature. Stables joins McGladdery at the crease and the inexperienced pair exert control, to the surprise of some beyond the rope who had expected an older head to be shunted up, under orders to steady the ship. Tyler in particular plays confidently and comfortably, but it is Stables who belts a mighty six into Oxford Street for his first Championship runs. The two are going nicely at a rate of five an over when Tyler's concentration slips and – bowled by a left-arm spinner – it is 85 for 3 in the 17th over.

Next in is Sam Dutton, on his home midden. He settles into an even more effective partnership worth 132 runs. A run from Marcus brings up Cumberland's 100, five overs later, bringing applause from Steve Sharp and John Patterson, who watch play unfold by the nets. At the pavilion end, Eric and Rob are busy with various duties in the absence of chairman Neil, still away on his cruise.

Seagulls circle as Marcus's individual 50 arrives ten minutes before lunch, quite an achievement on debut, and when his gloves are removed en route to some Cumberland sausage, Dutts is just five runs shy of his own half-century, the team 148 for 3. 'Nice to see two Cumbrian lads walking off,' beams Eric, as they mount the steps to the changing room. Pads removed, they descend to a clubhouse that has the air of a WW2 village hall, in Walmington-on-Sea perhaps.

Second eldest of Cumberland's old guard is 38-year-old Adam Syddall. Born in June 1980 and so six months younger than Jacques, he makes light work of his feed and flops down for a chat amid the rows of benches outside, a turn in the weather for the minute at bay. 'I've been thinking about this year being my last,' he confides, behind shades that can't hide a shy smile. 'If I do play next season it will definitely be my last.' Apart from his advancing years, another big motivation for retirement is his six-month-old son, Arthur, who is being indulged by his grandparents and mother, Ruth, further along the boundary. 'At this age he doesn't really know what's going on and is fine parked at the side of a pitch, but as he gets older, not so much.'

This left-arm medium fast bowler and lower order right-hand bat began as six or seven-year-old at Heaton CC in his hometown, Bolton, where he stayed until the under-18s and made his first team debut aged 16. From there he spent four years at St Andrews in Fife, third oldest university in the English speaking world after Oxford and Cambridge, gaining a Masters degree in Modern History. While studying, he'd nip back and forth to open the bowling for Lostock, another club in Bolton, when not captaining the St Andrews 1st XI, or playing in the Scottish Universities side against the English, Irish and Welsh in a home nations tournament that no longer exists.

During his first year at uni he was also selected for Lancashire under-19s and then, in 1999, bowled well during a 2nd XI debut for Lancashire against Middlesex, at Southgate. Ex-Aussie Test cricketer Peter Sleep (nickname: 'Sounda') was in charge. 'He was very keen for me to do a pre-season with Lancs the following year, but then he left and Mike Watkinson took over. We played on a flat one at Hinckley, against Leicestershire, and like the rest of the bowlers I went around the park ... the end of my Lancashire career.'

That wasn't quite that though. John Stanworth, then director of the Lancs academy, put Syds in touch with Hampshire, where he went to play for their seconds and then moved on to Worcestershire and Glamorgan all in the same year, 2000. 'I was still at university then, only 20, but it was good fun and I enjoyed it. I bowled very well for Glamorgan, took four wickets against Lancashire actually, but no contract was on the table so I just went back to club cricket.'

Until in the summer of 2002, and having only just graduated from St Andrews, a still youthful bowler suffered a stress fracture of the back, putting paid to physical activity. 'I was in full body plaster, pretty grim,' he says, wincing at the memory. 'I couldn't sit because this leg had to be kept straight, only stand up or lie down. If I went anywhere by car I had to lay across the back seat. I'd a special fitment for going to the toilet and this went on for eight weeks.' None of it put him off cricket. 'I realised then that to be a fast bowler, if you wanted to maintain any sort of longevity, you needed to maintain a decent level of fitness.'

Out of plaster, Syds didn't bowl for pretty much a full season, spending time in rehab and remodelling his action with Barbadian coach and former West Indies cricketer Ottis Gibson, then based at Old Trafford. 'He helped me quite a lot and got me bowling as quick as I ever had. I got offered a couple of pro-ing jobs and ended up at Edgworth, where I'm now in my second spell as professional and captain.' This undemonstrative man with an engaging personality takes in the scene, noting that he has played here before, in a three-day development game against an India touring side in 1998. He hasn't been to Furness since, involvement with the Minor Counties having begun as a 24-year-old at Cambridgeshire in 2005. He was drawn there by captain Ajaz Akhtar, whom Syds had met while with guesting with the MCC – '...a touchstone for those whose greatest fear is the erosion of traditional values,' as that team has been called and with whom he remains active, for and against, being a regular member of the Minor Counties' Unicorns side too. Indeed it was MCC men who then tempted a wanderer who has also squeezed in three seasons in Sydney to his next destination – Cheshire Premier League club Bowdon. That route led to selection for Cheshire itself, at the urging of a feisty and persuasive Scot. 'Sandy Scrimgeour was his name,' Syds smiles. 'He umpired in that league and also ran Cheshire Minor Counties. He said I was daft to keep travelling all the way down to Cambridgeshire.'

Throughout Sandy's tenure as manager and beyond, Syds and teammates enjoyed great success; Cheshire beating Northumberland at Jesmond in 2007 to win the Championship by an innings and four runs. 'We had a good team and I went on to spend nine seasons there. We got to a one-day final at Lord's that same year, but lost to Suffolk, and won the Championship title again in 2013.'

The move to Cumberland came in 2016. 'I'd started playing at Nantwich, which was a bit too far to go every week from Bolton – driving an hour and a half each way on the motorway at the age of 36 wasn't what I wanted to do anymore.' Nor was it just weekends. 'There was netting of a midweek evening too, so I decided to move back to Edgworth and play more locally.' And since Cheshire had a policy of only selecting from the county's Premier League, that meant a change in Minor Counties side too. 'Cumberland picked up on the fact and said: "We need some seamers, come and play for us."'

Now in his third Cumbrian season, he and his family feel right at home, his mother, father, wife and baby boy as dependable a part of this travelling band as Syds himself. Away from the game, he is a fully-qualified partner in his father's Bolton firm of chartered accountants: '...so I think that will be me after the cricket.'

What about those Modern History studies? Will his hard-won knowledge of French absolutism, among other such handy subjects, be called upon in shaping his future? 'Not in any way, shape or form,' he laughs. 'People ask why I didn't do a maths degree – I didn't know what I wanted to do then, apart from play cricket.' It does, however, whether he realises it or not, seem to have instilled an awareness of the bigger picture. 'I see where the young players are at now and this is the best cricket for them to be involved with, to be put on show, because people do still get picked up from here. In the last ten years, about a hundred of them have got a first-class county contract from being in the Minor Counties.

'There are people on the ECB who would like to get rid of it, but it provides a huge stepping-stone and bridge. You get to know the people who are keen and want to make it, because they are giving up days off work or taking extra holidays to play. Younger lads might not have jobs, at uni or whatever, and so you get to see who is really keen. That's a massive thing. In club cricket, it's mainly 50 overs, often with a fielding ring, so this is the only opportunity outside the first-class game to play the longer format. Of course it has a place.'

*****

Play resumes and before long Dutts has his 50, his highest score at Furness this year, a sweet personal moment. As Cumberland pass 200 both batsmen sail on, shots flowing. By the 52nd over, Sam has reached 80, Marcus trailing him narrowly on 67. In fact the latter really then ought to have been caught out, his dipping but catchable stab unaccountably dropped at midwicket one run later. No such luck for Dutts who, having failed to complete a century in the away game at Wisbech, endures similar disappointment here, caught – with a spot of juggling – at slip for 87, Cumberland now 217 for 4.

Gary Pratt takes the steps from the changing room a couple at a time and then jogs on to the field, keen to get out there by the look of it. And why wouldn't he be, having registered a century of his own for Richmondshire yesterday at Hartlepool? There have been signs that, unused to long-form cricket, 19-year-old Marcus may be losing concentration, but his skipper is a steadying partner and the pair soon pass 250, scoring just as quickly on a now sunny afternoon.

Ticket 657 wins Rob's raffle – a flavoursome bottle of Scotch – as Marcus closes in on his ton, the 100 coming from an overthrow that sees Geoff rattle up 294 for 4 on the scoreboard. Is the youngster tired? The huge six that takes him to 115 suggests not, sailing over the boundary where Sam Dutton is shrugging off his own failure to reach the magic number. 'Not here for a long time, here for a good time,' he says. Two runs later, Sam's fellow Sedbergh School product is caught in the deep going for another big hit.

At the age of 19 years and 159 days, Cockermouth's Geology student has become the youngest player to score a century on debut for Cumberland, and only the seventh-ever amid a roll call of such talents as Steve O'Shaughnessy, Ashley Metcalfe and Graham Lloyd. He is also the third youngest player to bag a century for the county full stop, the overall record still claimed by a then 18-year-old Alex Atkinson, son of chairman Neil, against Buckinghamshire in 2010.

Alas, as so often when such a partnership is broken, 317 for 5 is soon 317 for 6, Boyney caught behind for a golden duck. Gary, on 47, is joined by North Yorkshire and South Durham Premier League clubmate Sam Wood, who plays one off his toes to deny Ben Waring, *Wisden*'s 2016 Schools Cricketer of the Year, a hat-trick, though the Herts left-arm spinner will go on to collect seven first innings scalps. As Gary passes his half century, it isn't long before 'Spud' is cracking sixes of his own and soon Cumberland have made 355 for 6, four bonus points in the bag. Mainly, though, runs are now coming in singles, as noticed by Sempy and 12th man Chris Hodgson, tasked with pushing the sightscreen to and fro, for left and right-handers.

As tea is reached with ten runs added, there are reports of Slacky having got wickets for Wigton in their County Cup semi-final with Workington, while Mattie McKiernan is in Derbyshire's four-day squad, accounting for his continued absence in this fixture.

On resumption, Gary is caught almost at once. As he trudges off the field, some wit says 'oh, he dropped it,' and the skipper whirls back around to much laughter. One run later, Spud too is out, clean-bowled Waring, and it is 369 for 8. Can they reach 400? No. After Toby Bulcock is caught on the boundary, Syds comes in as last man and Ben Howarth is stumped – metaphorically and physically falling over – 376 all out. If the end of the innings had an element of farce about it, decent foundations have nevertheless been laid.

Preparing to retake the field, Toby tells Syds chummily: 'Green grass and lots of cloud cover, Sidney. What more could you ask for?'

Not a lot, he might have replied, though when Hertfordshire's first wicket falls in over two, it is Sam Wood who finds the slightest of nicks before the ball thumps into Ben's gloves. When Syds clean bowls Hertfordshire's other opener, it's 10 for 2 in only the third over and there are echoes of the start this morning. Contributing to the high spirits, Dutts bobs here and there inviting people to a barbecue at his parents' home, near the top of the ground beyond some trees. As cotton wool clouds pattern an otherwise unblemished sky, it is an agreeable prospect that will pass without a hitch. Just as well, given how both umpires are on the guest list, exemplary behaviour guaranteed.

The ball is tossed to Toby for more immediate fun and games. 'Southern mentality, boys,' he sledges. 'No temperament.'

A big appeal is survived in the 12th over, but Herts have a luckier escape when Ben can't quite take advantage of a thick edge engineered by Syds, diving in vain. But consecutive sixes off Toby which thud into the same garage door up the street confirm that the visitors have overcome their own early blows, the latter clattering the house door too by the sound of it. In fact Toby gets still more expensive and his mood isn't brightened when Tyler, close in, drops a shot hit straight to his midriff. Reaction stuff; it either sticks or it doesn't. As Herts pass the century mark though, Syds, fielding at fine leg, takes a superb over-the-shoulder catch off the big fellow's spin and the visitors end day one having amassed 125 for 3.

*****

Monday will be the hottest day of the year, recording temperatures of 33 degrees Celsius – 92 degrees Fahrenheit in old money. That though is in Santon Downham, Suffolk. On the Furness Peninsula, drizzle is forecast, belying a beautiful turquoise dawn.

An hour before play, the teams warm up ... bowling at a single wicket ... batting practice. Dutts mimics Geoff Minshaw's air-raid warning re Toby's bowling at last night's barbecue – 'Heads!' As ever with Geoff, the anecdotes had flowed: 'I'm not telling the one with the false teeth,' he'd said. 'There's ladies present.'

Unsurprisingly, there are fewer spectators in than yesterday. The pavilion is quiet, but family members like Josh Boyne's parents and girlfriend dot the boundary. President Alan Wilson arrives in smart shirt, jacket and county tie, Mike Latham and Toby (the dog) close behind. When Cumberland's fielders and the Hertfordshire batsmen trot over the rope, the welcome is half-hearted in a ground still rubbing sleep from its eyes. Syds takes the first over, a maiden. The second from Toby (the cricketer) is equally uneventful until Ross drops a slip-catch on the very last ball. Uncharacteristic. Tobes isn't deterred. In his next over, a low one traps its victim lbw and Herts are 136 for 4. Then Marcus adds a slip-catch off Syds to his debut gains and the innings of free-scoring Joe Cooke ends on 79, a decent start to say the least.

With five scalps to their credit, Cumberland are really making in-roads, but with new batsmen at the crease there is a sudden spit of warm rain. Handy then that wickets should continue to tumble, the first caught behind and the next allowing Ross to make amends to Toby, who will complete the innings with a 'five-fer' at a cost of 73 runs. With Hertfordshire 147 for 7, talk turns to the wisdom or otherwise of enforcing the follow-on, the opportunity arising if the visitors fail to reach 227 – a required 150 behind Cumberland's score. And the heavens now look menacing. 'It's gonna rain, don't you worry about that,' mutters the groundsman, orange numbers on the electronic scoreboard fluorescent in the gathering gloom.

Dutts tries to raise spirits, his every piece of fielding topped by a roly-poly tumble, but the umpires look concerned. For a while they stay on and, for the hosts, good thing too as Toby pins another victim to his lapel, lbw. But with eight wickets down, spit turns to drizzle and a sea mist descends. Having completed only 50 minutes, the sides leave the field.

Given the weather elsewhere it's particularly frustrating, but the time is ripe for that promised trip to Ulverston and its Laurel and Hardy museum, before a return via the coast road and diversion to Roa Island, which is actually attached to the mainland. Prior to 1847, the only access was at low tide, by foot over the sands, since when a raised causeway has made for an easier approach. The spot is also home to the Piel Island ferry, a supposedly daily link to an actual island half a mile off the Furness Peninsula's southern tip. 'NO FERRY TODAY,' someone has scrawled on a block of wood. With views of the Barrow submarine base yonder, water laps at the sort of grassy inlets and rust-chewed derelict boats that would be an ideal setting for bleak ITV drama, serial killer optional. And as for Stan and Ollie ... what a delight to see children laughing heartily at supposedly old-style silent comedy in the museum's movie theatre.

From bowlers of one variety to bowlers of another. Motoring back, Mike points out that Cleator-born Jordan Clark, who played for Cumberland in 2006, collected a hat-trick for Lancashire against Yorkshire yesterday. Liam Livingstone, alas, broke a thumb. Clark, like Dutts and Marcus, is another Sedbergh School old boy. When play resumes at 2.30pm, Marcus swoops for Hertfordshire's ninth wicket, again with a catch off Syds. The heavens however stay heavy, so when Ross then pulls off an amazing dive in the slips to leave Herts 176 all out with damp in the air, it is met with joyous relief.

Will Gary enforce the follow on? In unpredictable conditions and Herts exactly 200 runs behind, the skipper must be tempted, but decides to the contrary. He could still declare at any point, of course, but light drizzle returns before Ross and Sempy have posted so much as a single run. Tacticians reckon he will try to bat until 6.30pm and put Hertfordshire in for the last hour, to see if they can chase what's on the board. Toby doubts their ticker.

'If we come off now, we won't go back on,' says Steve Sharp.

Josh, who has a look of Stan Laurel, come to think of it, sits on a wall. Last Friday he got a 2:1 in physiotherapy at Leeds Beckett. He is jetting off to play in Perth, Western Australia, this winter and may do a Masters degree in 2019. He's already got the thongs, or flip-flops. As play proceeds hesitantly, Toby, Mike and Steve reminisce.

Toby: 'What was he called, who I had a bit of a to-do with?'

Mike: 'You'd have to be more specific.'

Somehow, ten overs are got through and without loss at that, Ross 27, Sempy 18, as Cumberland pass the half-century.

Hertfordshire's team manager wanders by, joking that their committee has a combined age of 932. The Minor Counties '...ought to have an age qualification on committees – average age 90 perhaps.' Cumberland are staying in Barrow, in rooms above Wetherspoons, where locals this morning were seen breakfasting *al fresco* on bacon, eggs and pints of lager. The Herts squad has digs on the outskirts of town, although their hotel too has a certain ambience. Down in the car park at about 1.30am, someone in a back seat was strangling someone in the front, while a third person in the back pummelled the assailant with his or her fists. 'Otherwise everything is fine.'

By the sound of it, Toby still has the hump with Gary and now Slacky for no longer putting Cumberland first, Wigton as it happens

beaten by 20 runs yesterday with today's absentee out for a duck. At
the wicket, Sempy survives one lbw appeal only to fall on the next,
having contributed 32 to an ongoing 79 for 1. Tyler trots out and
does a few stretching exercises, bat held flat to the grass. He sees out
his first over and gets off the mark. With around three hours left and
the threat of rain again lifted, the stage is set for a late flurry, but he
doesn't last long. A rash sweep sees him out lbw too and he kicks
the turf in disgust.

Soon, it's 93 for 3. Marcus, unable to repeat his earlier heroics,
is fooled by the speed of a full-length delivery. Dutts is told by Gary
to 'try and stay in until tea' and does so, Ross four runs short of 50.
Both landmarks are passed on the restart, but Dutts is soon caught
out, passing his captain on the way back to the sheds. Gary, having
added a brisk 11, then clips one to the 'keeper and it's 135 for 5. They
are still 335 runs ahead, though, which ought to be enough.

There are few histrionics therefore when Josh is judged lbw,
even as the player himself swears to an inside edge. And Sam Wood
isn't overly disappointed when his golden duck makes it 147 for 7 –
his moment is yet to come. Ben Howarth will face the hat-trick ball,
but not before a cruelly-timed drinks break. After which he survives
– just – with two from a nudge behind. A single from Ross brings
up the 150, although soon after he too goes leg before wicket, for 76,
a century having been there for the taking. No matter, from 153 for 8,
Ben and Toby take their side past Hertfordshire's first innings total,
a mammoth six by the 'keeper and reverse sweep for four from Toby
the highlights of an entertaining late spell. Seven runs later, Gary
waves them in off the balcony, 184 for 8 in the 54th over.

A lead of 385 is surely plenty and, like a cruel Roman emperor,
Cumberland's captain gifts Herts a now chilly and awkward fifteen
minutes with the bat. Fielders crowd in, but the visitors are equal to
the pressure. By the close Herts are unbroken, five runs on the board.

*****

As the rest of the nation basks in sunshine, Furness CC is overcast
when Rob Cairns and Steve Sharp rendezvous on Tuesday morning.
Rob squeezes into the passenger seat of Steve's Mini and off they go
to the Ernest Pass Memorial Ground, a stone's throw up Abbey Road.

Among day two's spectators had been Barrow CC president and Conservative councillor Alan Pemberton, heard complaining that Cumberland don't take games there anymore. In his wallet was a newspaper cutting from the late 1950s or early 1960s when he played for the county, once contributing 39 runs at Edgbaston. A week from now he'll be quoted in the *North West Evening Mail* on the death of 101-year-old Dr James Rogerson, hailing a man who was part of Barrow's North Lancashire League-winning side of 1954 as: 'the life and soul of the club.' In just a fortnight, Barrow's 2nd XI will be unable to raise a team for a game at Egremont. Two weeks later, they will be 81 all out to Seascale's 282 for 2 declared. In 2017, Barrow scrapped its 3rd XI. Is this a club whose best days are behind it? That 2nd XI is rock bottom of the North Lancs and Cumbria table. For sure they are doing it tough, very much the poor relation to Furness.

Steve swings into the car park and squints at a triumvirate of lawnmowers – it seems he is expected. Barrow's upset at a perceived snub has been no secret. The county's own view is that while it would prefer to take games to Kendal, Carlisle, Sedbergh and either Barrow or Furness in alternation, the quality of the pitch at the Memorial Ground has for some while simply not passed muster.

'Down in Wisbech,' Rob says, 'Rod Heywood, who follows Cumberland home and away and used to be Barrow's groundsman, told me the club was upset with us for not using them. But it goes back to 2014 when our last game here, against Buckinghamshire, was over in two days. The umpires made a comment that before we came back Barrow would have to improve the wicket. We told them so and ever since I've given updates to a guy I thought was chairman but no longer is, waiting for a response that never came. Having realised this I came to see them on Saturday and had a word with a couple of committee members, which is why we are here today. We are actually really keen to use the place again as long as the wicket is up to scratch because it's a fantastic facility. They have spent a load of money on the clubhouse. Hopefully, one or two of them will come across to Furness later and we can make total peace.'

As the duo walk on to the field, the mowers on the square buzz like angry wasps. There are in fact three wickets laid and each looks fine, if a little too green perhaps. The outfield however is far from a carpet and certainly not a patch on the swathe at Furness.

'What do you know about bloody wickets?' jokes the elder of the trio as Rob approaches, a wiry and elderly club stalwart who has a look of Groucho Marx about him, albeit in long shorts, T-shirt and baseball cap rather than Captain Spaulding-style safari pith helmet. The main man sits on a motorised roller and stops for a chat with Steve – quite a coincidence, all this Tuesday breakfast-time activity. He wasn't here in 2014 and does indeed appear to have done a good job since. More runs have been scored on it this summer than for some time, he points out, though the dry conditions may also have had something to do with that. In the car on the short hop back, it is decided that Steve will see how it performs in a coming league match and take a more informed and reasoned view after that.

At Furness, Toby, in a bit of a huff, predicts a draw. Added to yesterday's complaints about commitment, it appears he also has cash issues or is at least showing that he too can be difficult if that's how the club wants to play it, jibing Eric about needing a new car.

'Are you going to knock them over?' asks faithful Cumberland follower Peter Lingard, last seen in Cambridgeshire.

'Can't someone else do it?' Toby replies.

Play commences on time at 10.30am and again there is spit in the air, though sunshine is promised. Despite his complaints, Toby takes a first over watched only by the hardcore support, Tony and Jennifer Hutton, Gilbert Johnstone and the Syddall clan among them. As the day progresses more will come in, 'Blackpool Ken' among them, of the ground-hopping fraternity. Upon hearing of yesterday's Ulverston detour, he'll share an anecdote featuring his friend Colin, from Radcliffe, near Bury, who knew Pasan Wanasinghe, a former Sri Lankan professional at Radcliffe CC. 'When Pasan moved to Barrow, Colin would come up to watch him. One week, there must have been a Laurel and Hardy convention on because the train was packed with folk singing "The Blue Ridge Mountains of Virginia".'

John Patterson browses the *Daily Mail*, on whose back page the death of former Leeds United footballer Paul Madeley is reported. On TV last night, news broke amid nostalgic photos of the stars of the Don Revie era. 'Makes you realise that time is passing by and you've got to make something of what's left,' someone says, just as Gary Pratt almost forces a run-out, fielding a bouncing ball superbly before just missing the stumps, the visitors 18 for 0 in the tenth over. Baby Bulcock turns up with her mum and grans, drawing another off-stage comment re the place becoming a crèche. With Pratt junior also on the way, next year should be lively. As it is, Toby's daughter begins to wail and is whisked off by her mother for a nappy change.

Herts gets the best of another run-out decision three runs later, the umpire's view blocked by fielders, though the target scampered home anyway. Otherwise, under a looming raincloud, the body language of some on the fielding side is too casual for comfort. 'Everyone up lads, come on,' shouts Dutts in the deep. 'Give it a bit of Cumberland sausage.' Offbeat motivation but it serves its purpose, 'Spud' Wood tempting the left-hander into a caught behind just as the pair are looking settled. He then knocks leg stump out of the ground for the second wicket and bags the third too, former England captain Nasser Hussain's nephew Reece caught behind on a duck egg. The visitors are rocking on 46 for 3.

Worryingly however, the specks of rain in the air suddenly turn into great fat drops, just as the day simultaneously starts to brighten up. That's Cumbria for you. Off they all trot while Gary Pratt glowers at the heavens, unamused. This wasn't in the plan.

It's only a squall. Two overs are lost, but Spud is again soon bowling well. It is now that Blackpool Ken rolls up, with a resigned glance at the scoreboard. Three wickets down, eh? Still, it's not as bad as the time he went all the way to Northumberland only to find that the batting side was chasing four runs. 'I had a Day Rover, so jumped on a train and went to Carlisle instead.'

The sunshine is now sustained, but Herts benefit most from the overdue burst of serotonin. To mix things up, Boyney bowls around the wicket and Toby switches ends. Herts opener Steve Gale, a useful batsman indeed, has notched 18 runs in 32 overs, intention perfectly clear. But then with the approach of lunch the breakthrough arrives, Gale out lbw, bowled Bulcock, 93 for 4.

Tempering the rising heat somewhat, there is now a stiff breeze. The Cumberland flag that began the day drooping like an old rag on a pole, now flutters with gusto over the pavilion, loud and proud.

*****

On his BBC Radio Lancashire show *Inside Edge* in May, Mike Latham described Toby Bulcock as the 'best left-arm spinner in the country.' Hyperbole? Perhaps. But there is no doubting his ability.

'He's played alongside several current members of the England side,' the introduction went on, 'is the star of Cumberland's Minor Counties team and has played in virtually all of our local leagues. He took on the arduous role of being a club professional as a teenager and that responsibility has taken him the length and breadth of the country, not only in league cricket but also extensively in Lancashire age groups to under-19s, and for recreational cricket's key side, the Unicorns, a level below first-class. Currently, he plays professionally at Leigh in the Liverpool Comp, having previously played for Accrington, Baxenden, Rawtenstall, Elton, St Annes, Carnforth and Richmondshire in the North Yorkshire and South Durham League.'

Teammates were evoked who were destined for greater things, like Somerset's Dom Bess ... Ben Stokes, with whom he represented the North of England ... Keaton Jennings. Did Toby ever see their progression, Mike wondered, and think: 'Why wasn't that me?'

'Yeah, it takes a while to accept. It's easy to become bitter, very easy to think ill of other people's performances and be cynical. But they're lads I've grown up with. We are friends, part of the cricketing family. These are people you live your life with. You're married to the game essentially, so to see them doing well ... the only thing better is to do well yourself. These things work themselves out.'

And how about Stokes? How early was his talent and potential obvious? 'At under-14s it became crystal clear. It was Cumbria versus Lancashire, him being a Cockermouth lad by proxy. He got 65, which doesn't blow anyone's socks off but it was full of blistering shots, hit like a man. He cleared the clubhouse. Fourteen-year-olds don't clear clubhouses. Ben did. Do that, you open some eyes. At the same time, he never did himself any favours off the field. We've seen how he's took a battering for that, but the [cricket] talent that is Ben Stokes is still there and that's what England desperately need now. My worry is that through the media trauma, maybe a bit of that charisma and character, what makes him a renegade, is battered out of him.'

Having devoured his corned beef hash and mushy peas at Furness, Toby fleshes out some of the biographical detail heard on the radio and alluded to by his dad, Steve, in Wisbech. 'I started when I was six. Our house backed onto Baxenden, so it was in us from the off, a natural thing to do.' What grabbed him most forcibly about cricket was its mind games. 'The fact it wasn't just an exercise in physique or brawn; there was a thought process. Even then I enjoyed trying to out-think the opposition. The higher up the spectrum you go, the more cricket becomes like chess. Field position, what shots to play at what times, what shots they'll play...'

At Leigh, he's vice-captain, not captain. 'It's my first year there; in your inaugural year you never lead the group, generally speaking, because you don't know the lads inside out.' The club with which he turned professional was Elton CC, then in the Bolton Association, the oldest cricket league in Lancashire until it folded in March after one hundred and thirty years, two-and-a-half of those in suspension following its final playing season in 2015. And this after the following was written ahead of the season before, now archived at play-cricket.com:

> After 125 years the Bolton Association is arguably as strong as it has ever been [with] an 18-team competition in 2014 [and] five thriving junior sections, testament not only to the hard work of the current committee but also that all of their predecessors. One wonders what the founding fathers back in 1888 would make of it all? Surely their chests would fill with pride.

It was also then that Mike Latham brought him to Cumberland, his professional career thereafter advancing via Carnforth, St Annes and with Gary Pratt at Richmondshire. 'I did two years there. If you're a club pro and only do one it tends to suggest you've not done well or that there have been problems. If you've done two you've progressed ... that's how my brain operates anyway.' At Leigh, where he moved to be closer to home 'when the missus fell pregnant', he is now a pro among many, the Liverpool Comp being an open competition.

Cricket may not have been about brawn, but he had plenty. 'I was an early starter, the way I grew, a six-footer at ten years old. I was strong, so ended up playing representative level at pretty much every sport I turned my hand to. I'm not being an egomaniac, that's just how it was.' Cricket though was always his first love. Not exactly an obsession, he claims, though very definitely his life. 'I'm married to it. My dad was married to it. I was born into that world. From April to September, nothing else existed. We never went on holiday during the cricket season. I never go to weddings. I'll be able to do that when I'm old. Although I probably still won't go on holiday then as I'll want to watch it, especially if my kids are playing.'

He likes watching cricket, though denies he's what he calls 'a badger'. 'Mike is a badger, someone who keeps an eye on and has a vested interest in everything. That's not me. But I do like to watch friends, whether they are rubbish or great, playing on TV or in the third team; I like to see old pals.'

And how does he see those days in the Lancashire youth teams now, as described by his dad in Cambridgeshire? The time when his hopes of a first-class cricketing career were effectively thwarted?

'I was in quite a unique position really, one that won't have been seen many times. There were three players capable of playing for England, bowling left-arm spin for a county. They all represented England at some stage, but it got to the point, under-19s, where even though I'd had an exceptional season there was no room at the inn.'

How did it feel not to make it?

'I was an immature person who grew up very quickly. I might still have my immature moments now, but while I did find it a bitter pill to swallow, I never wished ill on those who did make it. That would have been sour grapes. Lads I captained year in, year out have gone into the county game and been prolific. That's good to see.'

What about his dad's point that although the really big break didn't come, Toby is nevertheless enjoying a career most wannabe cricketers would love? And that he might not have enjoyed the game as much at its uppermost levels? 'Yes, cricket is the be all and end all for some and I'm in a fortunate position. It's my life, but I've also got fingers in other pies, still young enough to do what I want. I've got a career as an accountant and that's going to take me on.'

There is also the fact that, actually, there *was* once an offer of first-class cricket, from Glamorgan: '...but, monetarily, it just wasn't viable. The money offered was not enough to uproot the missus and myself from our jobs and take off to Swansea or Cardiff.' That was in 2015, when Cumberland last won the Championship. 'I couldn't commit to it, because it wasn't right. You are probably going to have ten or fifteen years max as a cricketer, earning a steady amount. But then you're a 35-year-old man with no qualifications and no work experience after doing something that, in the real world, most people really aren't that interested in.'

So, at 27 years old, how does he see his future panning out?

'Definitely not coaching. I'd be a very poor coach, in the same way I'd be a terrible teacher. I could coach the best but that's it, which makes you poor. I could only educate the brightest, that's one of my limiting factors.' Bully by nickname, bullish by nature, his ebullience on the field is merely an extension of who he is off it. 'I've always been a bull in a china shop, loud and boisterous, to pretend to be anything else would be a lie. It's something I've had to embrace as a person and try and curb at times, but it does come out. I do like being the guy who bangs the drum and pushes us that extra per cent.'

Does it also show what Cumberland means to him as a club?

'For me, it's all about commitment. Without commitment to the cause, to buying into the idea of what it is and what it stands for and what it means to people ... it's what bloods the next generation. Commitment is everything. If you can't come into something full on, then don't come into something at all, that's my take.'

His mind goes back to a situation 'a couple of years ago' when he found himself double-booked – a cup semi-final for his club and cup game for Cumberland the same day. 'The club side was trying to be a little underhanded. It was written into my contract that if the two ever collided I'd take the Minor Counties option and they were trying every tactic to get me to stay, offering X, Y and Z. I had to explain that while, yes, money is a massive thing in my life, because I don't have any, this wasn't about that. It's about the fact that you'd be lying to yourself if you went and played and took however many pounds were on offer. They said: "We'll pay you a grand if you play this game." I said no and they docked me £500, so it cost me £1,500.'

All of which makes the complaints of Cumbrians within the various county leagues that Cumberland players are at best outsiders treading on local toes, and at worst a bunch of sell-swords with no real affinity for the place, all the more dubious.

'For me, it's about buying into the idea of what a minor county stands for,' Toby says, as play is about to resume. 'Where do we want to take it as a going concern? Cumberland is where my heart is. If

I'm not living in Australia in my latter years, I'd like to settle down here, in the Lake District or wherever. The people get to the point.'

*****

Hertfordshire pass the century soon after lunch, Reece Hussain making a round 50 before becoming Sam Wood's fourth victim and wicketkeeper Ben Howarth's third. With the arrival of blazing heat the venue fills up again too, at least one hundred along the boundary on a Tuesday afternoon, the majority hushed and still as though willing another wicket.

Sam Wood has been particularly impressive and continues to be so, producing his performance of the season by far. A gentle spirit who more often goes unnoticed, he is as enthusiastic as he is quietly loyal. Earlier, in the dressing room, he'd been saying how, like Toby, he sees playing for the county as an honour. 'As long as I get picked for Cumbria, I will play for Cumbria. I enjoy it.'

He too began young, aged 8 in Middleton Tyas, a one-pub rural village in North Yorkshire, a mile so from Scotch Corner on the A1 and five miles from Richmond where, having been taught by his grandad, he played his junior cricket and eventually met Gary Pratt. 'I was that kid you see hanging about at every club, missing holidays to watch the game, never mind play it. I was obsessed then – always wanted to be a cricketer – and am obsessed with it now. I go to four-day first-class county games now and then, where learning is a big part of it. You never stop learning, do you?'

Sam still lives in Middleton Tyas, has done all his life, his first season with Cumberland being that Championship-winning year, 2015. Brought in by Gary, he was nevertheless overlooked for the big one. 'I was lucky to be involved but didn't get picked for the final, which I admit I was annoyed about at the time. Looking back, I hadn't expected to play one game, never mind six, so it gave me an opportunity and I'm still here. Can't grumble, can you?'

Someone else's loss was his gain. 'Gary rang on the Thursday and said a lad had got injured, could I play? I'm a joiner, so I asked at work and they said: "Yeah, you don't get many chances like this." I made 66 and 40-odd as a batsman and only got four overs when I was supposed to be there as a bowler! It turned out pretty well.'

For Richmondshire, he opens the bowling and bats in the middle order, though that hasn't always been the case. At under-16s, when he represented North Yorkshire and Yorkshire 'B', he'd been a batsman first and foremost, yet at Richmond '...grew fast, got quicker and stronger and with four strong openers ahead of me realised I should concentrate on bowling, not just do it in the nets.'

Given his penchant for slipping into the background, hearing that Spud is vice-captain at Richmondshire comes as a surprise. 'I'd like to take over from Gary when he's finished. He has taught me loads. I'm 26, enjoy responsibility and like being alongside Gary. I would never have been able to captain a side if I wasn't under him ... how to place fielders ... when to change it up.'

Syds, by contrast, has looked under the weather and when he is called back into action Spud misses a difficult catching chance in the slips. Nor can Tyler conjure a breakthrough at the other end as the new Herts pair works methodically towards a 100 partnership that, for Cumberland, transforms the afternoon session into a sweltering struggle. There is the occasional flourish too, such as when Tyler is belted for a four and six in succession following a much-needed drinks break, the latter shot narrowly missing the Herts team manager, at which point it's Toby turn to wail like an air-raid siren. Joking aside, they long since began to look frustrated.

More worryingly, at around 3.00pm word sweeps around the ground that Gary is no longer here, 12th man Chris Hodgson having taken his place on the field. Leanne, some six months pregnant, has been feeling unwell, it is reported, and therefore any concern is only natural. After all, what does completing something as trivial as a cricket match matter in such circumstances? Very little, of course.

Without their talismanic skipper, Cumberland beaver away, in pursuit of more wickets. The finishing line of a game scheduled to end around 6.30pm (with a post-five o'clock minimum of 17 overs) is tantalisingly close, but they will need to get on with it.

Half an hour later, Sempy – under-employed as a bowler all year – strikes at last, removing half of the stubborn duo lbw and Herts are 220 for 6, still 164 runs behind. The anticipated collapse though does not materialise, the next man in also collecting a half-century in another stubborn partnership. By 4.00pm the hosts are decidely antsy and a pair of missed chances – catch and glaring run-out – don't help them to settle down. At tea, Hertfordshire are 260 for 6, now chasing 125, and an away victory no longer looks unlikely.

In fact, it has begun to look distinctly probable. And even more disconcerting are the rumours circulating that, actually, the reasons given earlier for Gary's premature departure were wide of the mark. He has actually left to play in an evening game for Richmondshire. This seems scarcely credible. Sam Wood is still here, isn't he?

Indeed he is and, when tea has been taken, he still has another wicket in him, which is just as well. In your average club game, you would be into the tail-enders by now, a mopping-up job. This though is the Minor Counties Championship where, as was seen at Wisbech, the batting talent is more evenly spread. So it is with Hertfordshire, whose nine and ten batsmen have both registered league centuries so far this summer. And a target of 120-odd in around 40 overs could be reached twice in Twenty20.

'We can do it,' says Josh Boyne, as the players descend the steps and head on to the field: 'Toby Bulcock spins Cumberland to victory.'

It doesn't quite work out that way. They resume aggressively, a huge appeal turned down when one appears to clip a glove going down leg side to Ben Howarth off Syds. Not long afterwards, though, the bowler takes his revenge, Dominic Chatfield out lbw for 72. Meanwhile along the top boundary, a flock of gulls circle and swoop, one with an awkward protruding feather it flaps wildly to dislodge.

Toby returns to the fray, hungry now, a point to prove by the look of him. The mind games begin. 'It will be 11 o'clock now by the time they get home and counting,' he shouts as the winning target drops beneath one hundred. The last three wickets are vital; a draw is no longer part of the equation.

Enter once again Sam Wood, 'five-fer' achieved via the middle stump, leaving the visitors 298 for 8. Eight runs later, Toby takes his second wicket, Alex Axon caught by a wildly celebratory Dutts for 55, Hertfordshire's four-man middle order having amassed 240 runs between them. At 306 for 9, it is surely now Cumberland's game.

Bang on 5.30pm, the potential last 17 overs kick in. Can this latest pair bat them out? Or less likely, hit the 80 runs still needed?

The new man immediately goes on the forward defensive, suggesting the former approach, before 12th man Chris nips off for a helmet. Moments later, crouching up close, the opportunity for a winning catch slips through his fingers, a significant moment in the scheme of things, though few in the ground realise it at the time.

The rest of the field too crowds in, Syds at one point having to scamper off and save a four, off his own bowling, on the rope. In the slips, he then drops another chance off Spud, the score 310 for 9 with no more than 14 overs remaining. The veteran has been battling sickness all day and doubtless feels even sicker now. But then who should step up but Josh Boyne, predictor of headlines, with a ball that Hertfordshire's last man doesn't play a shot at – and is out to – lbw. Cumberland has its first Championship win of the campaign, a victory that nudges the club up to mid-table.

It ought to be a sweet moment, but there has been high drama off the field as well as on it. The real reasons behind Gary's exit are soon made known and, should the revelation be authentic, there will almost certainly be repercussions.

'Best call the war minister,' chuckles Alan Wilson darkly, toying with his mobile phone. On the boundary: a seagull feather.

CHAPTER EIGHT
THE FLITWICK PAPERS

The distance from Barrow to Hartlepool, according to the AA route planner, is 127 miles; a two-hour and thirty-nine-minute drive. Gary Pratt set off at 3.30pm, so he must have landed at Park Drive around six minutes before Richmondshire's 6.15pm scheduled start.

Had he hoped to avoid detection? If so, that was never likely. The scorecard of every game in the country is immediately uploaded for scrutiny online, so his 35 runs and two wickets in 1.3 overs in a comfortable Premier 15s Cup victory were a matter of public record.

Even so, by Monday 30 July, around one week later, nothing official had yet been heard from the Minor Counties Cricket Association. Nor, just as surprisingly, had opponents Hertfordshire raised so much as a peep in defeat. Maybe both were keeping their powder dry, awaiting contact from Cumberland. Or perhaps, given on-going discussions with the ECB regarding the Championship's future, all concerned hope to avoid any damaging publicity.

At Cumberland, never had the lack of a centralised HQ been so manifest. Communication was limited to phone calls and a flurry of emails. The first such, sent on the evening of Wednesday 25 July, was a round-robin message ostensibly from Gary himself, in which he outlined his own position, having: '...been made aware of some negative feeling towards me for leaving the game at Furness early yesterday to play in a cup competition for my home club Richmondshire.' He went on:

I would like to make it clear that all parties who needed to know about my early departure were aware of the situation a week before the game. I did not feel it necessary to speak to the whole of the committee. I am disappointed that after more than 10 years this has caused my commitment to Cumberland CCC to come into question.

The captain reminded everyone that while he is contracted to play for Richmondshire, until this year he'd prioritised Cumberland. En route to the quarter-finals of the ECB's national knockout and final of the Kerridge Cup, a number of clashes meant missing three games thus far. He would also be unavailable for the next Championship game with Bedfordshire at Flitwick from Sunday 5 August:

This is the first year that anything like this has happened. I have never missed a game for personal reasons, through ill health or injury. If I could play [in every] RCC and Cumberland CCC game I would, but the fixtures are unfortunately not under my control. As always I remain fully dedicated to my cricket (for both teams that I play for) and if anyone would like to chat to me about my role within Cumberland CCC, I will be more than happy to do so either in person, by telephone or email.

After which, club officials batted messages back and forth, from which it could be gleaned that Steve Sharp had replied to Gary with 'a holding email'; an Extraordinary General Meeting was unlikely given the timeframe; and there was an urgent need to possess all the facts, preferably before the MCCA got formally involved. Chairman Neil Atkinson called their lack of contact so far 'good news', but stressed that, if approached, the club would need to organise some type of meeting quickly. 'Let's hope all remains quiet in the interim.'

Some hope. Rules on the use of substitute fielders are clear. For a start, it is up to the umpires to allow them and then only if satisfied that the player being replaced is injured, ill or absent 'for any other wholly acceptable reason. In all other circumstances, a substitute is not allowed.' Furthermore, if a fielder leaves the field during play 'an umpire shall be informed of the reason for his absence.' What reason were they given at Furness? The same one everyone else heard?

Surely the MCCA would hear about it, assuming they hadn't done so already. Even signing up to some sort of conspiracy theory wherein Herts, allegedly swift to kick up a fuss when wronged, had perhaps been persuaded to keep schtum in the wider interest, how could potential whistle-blowers be effectively silenced? What if the local paper, the *Hertfordshire Mercury*, got a sniff? It's hard to imagine any serious news platform ignoring such a yarn.

The following Monday, Mike Latham calls to say that Toby – on Cumberland's management committee with Mike and the likes of Chris Hodgson, Gary's partner Leanne Bell and scorer Geoff Minshaw – insists he will not play for the county again unless an EGM is called, accusing the board of trying to 'cover the matter up.' If so, it will be a sad end to a fine Cumberland career. In great form with club side Leigh in one of the most competitive leagues in the country, on Saturday he took five wickets against New Brighton and is now the Liverpool Comp's second-leading wicket-taker with 50 in 15 games. He is also said to be disgruntled at not being skipper in Bedfordshire this coming weekend, that honour going to the returning Jacques du Toit, with Syds his vice-captain.

It also emerges that Eric was so unhappy with having his leg pulled about money for cars at Furness he has 'put in a complaint', though to whom isn't clear. Underlying financial issues, it seems, cloud an already murky picture. Steve, meanwhile, will not 'have a gun held to his head,' amid suggestions that he and Eric are the officials Gary claimed in his round-robin email to have told of his proposed exit a week beforehand.

In fact, it seems that of the main officials only Rob Cairns and president Alan Wilson are close to being annoyed, while chairman Neil continues his policy of treading a diplomatic tightrope.

The scenario is tricky. In friendships forged over a number of years, good times and bad, when words like 'lies' and 'betrayal' begin to be bandied about, feelings will inevitably run high. The original indiscretion was relatively minor in the grand scheme of things, albeit something of a sporting taboo, but what will not be so easy to explain away is any hint of a cover-up. Mike's view is that the club ought to have informed the MCCA immediately once it became apparent that its captain had transgressed, not dilly-dally in the vain hope that the fuss would evaporate like steam on a pot of afternoon tea. Quite aside from anything else, reputations are at stake. It then transpires that Gary is available for Flitwick after all, wherein lays the latest example of how a chairman of cricket's life is seldom straightforward.

Originally, Sunday 5 August was to be the date of Richmondshire's Kerridge Cup final with Middlesbrough at Marton CC, but when the club qualified for the last eight of the National Club Championship, the ECB's quarter-finals took precedence and the North Yorkshire and South Durham League's big day was shunted forward to August 12. National Club opponents Ormskirk, meanwhile, were meant to appear in national T20 finals yesterday, but with the heatwave well and truly over that event was rained off and pushed on a week, meaning Ormskirk are no longer able to play the quarter-final until Sunday 26 August, so the 5th is now free. Confused? You should be. As a result, Gary and Sam Wood have again made themselves available for Cumberland, but Steve has nevertheless insisted that they will not be selected, having already picked and named his side for Bedfordshire.

The rest was for the rumour mill, impossible to verify. He said, she said. Gary and Toby had now spoken, the former apparently telling the latter that Eric and Steve knew he was leaving all along. But Alan has told Toby that Steve said he knew nothing about it. Steve is supposed to have spoken curtly to Eric when the treasurer was compiling the rooming list as usual, while Eric has said that if any action is taken against Gary he'll never speak to certain people again and, what's more, resign. Before the late fixture reshuffle, Gary and Leanne had intended travelling down to watch on Monday and Tuesday, but when Rob began to sort out the meals required he was supposedly told they would no longer be doing so since Gary's offer to play had been snubbed, as had that of the hero of Furness, Sam Wood.

Then word arrived that Minor Counties Cricket Association secretary Phil Caley has indeed got wind of it all and intends to get the Cumberland view at Flitwick on Sunday. At this stage, though, it is likely that Sharp, Pratt, Bulcock and Latham too, won't be there. It's being said that Toby could be persuaded to change his mind and play, but only on condition that he is made captain. Sharp, perhaps belatedly alert to the price of indecision, is putting his foot down.

As to who informed the MCCA, fingers are pointed primarily at messrs Bulcock and Latham – 'we are being ganged up on,' says Mike – although Hertfordshire would surely have picked up on the rumours buzzing around the boundary at the game itself.

Mike though does have his connections, and has learned from someone who spoke to one of the umpires that the reason they had been given for Gary leaving the field was an ankle injury, or maybe Leanne not feeling well, wires are crossed somewhere. But in either case, they were misled. How will *they* react? And another factor thus far overlooked is the extent to which the incident has soured the Cumberland dressing room as a whole. In the aftermath, such as Dutts and Tyler were forthcoming in their displeasure, but the rest? Gary held their respect; is his captaincy irreparably damaged? Toby was hugely popular, the maypole everyone danced around.

As July closes, the fall-out just could be terminal, the Slough of Despond deep. With no dog in the fight, it's clear Gary ought not to have been picked – or agreed to play – if unable to complete the fixture. But with that error made, nor should he have been allowed to leave before it was over, still less be replaced by a 12th man in circumstances the rules explicitly forbid. All else is obfuscation.

*****

August begins with England's 1,000th Test match – against India at Edgbaston, a game won by England in four days, Ben Stokes taking four wickets for 40 runs in his side's second innings. He will however miss the second Test at Lord's, his court case for affray due to get underway in Bristol the following Monday.

The month will also see the anniversary of Don Bradman's last innings in 1948 (out for a second-ball duck, leaving the great man with a Test average of 99.94) and the commencement of English football's Premier League season. Geraint Thomas becomes the first Welshman to win the Tour de France and the BBC reports how the French want boules to be made an Olympic sport in 2024. To create a more professional image, they are: '...encouraging players to take training more seriously and have banned them from playing in T-shirts and jeans.' In response: '...the chairman of a club in eastern France protested by turning up for a competition dressed as a clown.'

In the Minor Counties, accusations and denials continue to fly back and forth at Cumberland CCC; a weakened squad is almost certainly off to Bedfordshire. Piecing it all together would make Woodward and Bernstein blanch, but here's the gist.

First up, on hearing from Leanne that she and Gary would no longer be going, Rob sends another email to the committee asking for clarification on just what exactly is going on, what with him being club secretary and all that. The fissure between Steve and Eric may be widening, the latter having also told Mike he will never speak to him again if he says anything to Hertfordshire or the MCCA, even though they know now anyway and probably always have. Toby is officially dropped; Steve will not be told what to do. Toby's response is that not only is he a senior player, he is also on the committee, dropping the word 'dictatorship' into the mix. Jacques has offered to let Toby captain since he isn't bothered about taking the role anyway, but Steve said *he* picked the team, and that was that. Stable door open, the garrons have very much bolted.

Late on Wednesday, it emerges that an 'emergency committee meeting' has been called in the Romney Room of Stonecross Manor Hotel, Kendal, this Friday at Toby's request. It's not an EGM, but an informal gathering: '...to discuss matters arising from the recent Hertfordshire game in Barrow.' Establishing the truth, Mike tells Rob, is key: 'This could bring the county to its knees and tear us apart, so I'm confident you and Neil will do the right thing.' In the event, the only other committee members there are Steve and Toby, the details of whose conversation won't be revealed for a fortnight.

As for Gary, was he given permission to leave Furness early? If not, says Mike, 'he should apologise to the committee and players and be stood down as captain for the rest of the season, but be considered for selection,' adding: 'What Gary did was against the laws and spirit of cricket.' But if he *did* get the okay, 'the people/person who gave it to him must, logically, face a consequence of their own actions on similar lines.' Such apologies would, Mike believes, enable 'everyone to shake hands and move on,' especially as 'over the years, no one has given more commitment to the county than Gary.'

Midway betwixt Bedford and Luton, the town of Flitwick is on the river for which it is named, the Flit – as in moonlight – where according to Wikipedia: 'Eight species of sphagnum moss have been recorded.' The Hardy Vale, home to 'The Otters', cuts a glorious sight on a summer Sunday morning. Under a pristine sky by a tidy brick pavilion, the flag of St George stirs but lightly. The ground, next to a garden centre on the A5120, comes up on a motorist quickly, the road dimly audible inside. Birdsong competes with the mournful purr of doves hiding in the trees, shrubs and hedges that enclose the oval. Down south, the long hot summer sizzles on awhile yet.

'Welcome to Flitwick,' says a chap with a smile as bright as his bib. 'Park anywhere, as long as you don't block the right of way.' This is Richard Wigfield, club chairman, who'll later proffer a copy of *A Bowled Move – A History of Flitwick CC*, published to commemorate the venue's 30th anniversary in 2014, profits to the development of youth cricket. In it, a reader learns that although the club was formed in 1904, it wasn't until 1981 that the Vale staged its first official match. The land was bought in 1975 (the club appearing in the very first episode of BBC sitcom *The Good Life*, trivia fans) and the clubhouse opened in 1978, three years before that inaugural encounter.

Bedfordshire brought Minor Counties cricket here in 2003; the pavilion's decked seating area and patio arrived five years after that. Clumps of people are already availing themselves of morning gossip, with tea, coffee and bacon baps served inside. Along the pitch-perimeter are rows of green-legged benches backed by advertising hoardings, though not so obtrusively as to clash with the picturesque beauty of a classically English Arcadian scene.

Tranquility, of course, is not Cumberland's thing right now. Such a long trek is arduous at the best of times and these are not the best of times. Will the game last three days? Syds and Jacques apart, it's a youthful side and young cricketers aren't supposed to be capable of hanging around long, are they? At Furness, even debutant run-centenarian Marcus Stables had needed a steadying hand.

Richard has been here since dawn by the sound of it, 'sorting the wicket, cleaning the benches.' Amiable and chatty, he beams when complimented on the gorgeousness of the spot. 'We are proud of it,' he nods dreamily. He tells of plans to put another pitch on the cowfield next door, beyond a line of giant trees that, were they in a wood and surrounded by wildflowers might be danced around by pixies, a portal to the faerie realm. Work is scheduled to begin over the winter – a time of year that feels impossibly distant. 'The club is thriving. As well as men's open age teams, we have two sides at every age group level and a women's set-up that is even starting a rounders team, so two pitches will come in handy. Enjoy your stay.'

The Cumberland boys get here an hour before play and a few of them kick a ball about. The mercury is already high and only going upward. Jacques and Slacky, returned to the side, stroll out to inspect the wicket, joined by Sempy. Several players didn't arrive until the early hours, a motorway accident blocking all three lanes of traffic. 'Hard and low,' says the stand-in skipper, prodding an area short of a length. 'It will turn square here,' he predicts, of a track that is flat and dry with tiny tufts of green, but otherwise looks quick. Yes, Toby has phoned him to explain why he isn't playing, but Steve then rang with another story. 'I don't get involved,' Jacques says, 'and what surprises me is when other players do. I want to play cricket.'

The visitors seem chirpy, some two weeks on from the Furness kerfuffle. Clad in flip-flops and a green T-shirt, Dutts however looks glum for once, striding out to the middle with a couple of cartons of coffee. It could be down to lack of sleep or that his team, Furness, got walloped yesterday. 'I'm not enjoying it there,' he admits.

Eric and Neil, both in short-sleeved shirts and club tie, seem positively cheerful when they turn up at 10.15am. A united front is the order of the day, grins from ear to ear. The many trees provide welcome shade and when play gets underway several spectators have parked their car beneath their branches. A willow backs on to a milky stream from where future archaeologists will dredge many a cricket ball. The date on a little bridge confirms it as exactly one hundred years old this summer. When Rob Cairns arrives, it is to the peel of church bells in holy welcome. Eric unrolls the Cumberland flag and down comes St George as butterflies dance around a hanging basket of pink and purple geraniums, as if in celebration of Jacques having won the toss. He opts to bat and it pays off. After 10 overs, openers Ross and Sempy share 31 runs.

Sempy ducks under the second of two bouncers and a floppy-hatted Steve Sharp can be spotted, here after all, chatting with Neil on the boundary. Asked for an update, he plays a straight bat. Toby had been shouting the odds about not playing unless he was made captain. 'I said I wouldn't be dictated to. Gary isn't playing because when the team was picked he was unavailable. We can't just drop someone now.' And was the captain okay with that? Will he play again? 'We'll see...'

As ever, there is a family turnout: Syddall, Boyne and Staples. 'Marcus was chuffed with his century,' says Alan, his dad, 'although he keeps it to himself.' The Howarths are here as well. On a lap, Ben and Josh discuss the success of the ECB All Stars initiative – one hundred and thirty kids came to Flitwick the other day. At Blackpool they get eight. 'Yeah,' says Ben, 'but we don't need them, do we? We've got loads of kids already.'

Eric chats with MCCA secretary Phil Caley, here as anticipated, who had a twenty-eight-year playing career with Suffolk. Both scoff at the idea of the Minor Counties as: '...a retirement home for ex-professionals, as the ECB seem to think it.' Caley will be happy to discuss Cumberland's situation later, distracted for now by the fall of the game's first wicket. A lazy dab by Ross is punished in the slips, disappointing when all was going well, but it's a good excuse for drinks. After which, Slacky goes in and belts a four, only to see Sempy bowled in the 11th over and the visitors are 35 for 2.

If all seems calm off the field, the same can't be said for on it. Marcus is next in and almost immediately survives a caught behind appeal with the passing of the first hour of play. And although the new pair put a few runs on, it's soon 70 for 3 when Slacky hooks one high that is pouched at midwicket. Concentration issues perhaps, but certainly a gift for Bedfordshire. It's 71 for 4 when Marcus is next to go, victim of a tickle behind. 'Get your pads on, Syds,' quips Caley, as the veteran bowler walks by. Batting six, Sam Dutton cracks the spinner into the hands of a fielder in the covers: 74 for 5. They have only been playing an hour and forty minutes, 22 overs gone, as Jacques goes in to steady the Cumbrian wobbles.

Bedfordshire quickie Al Mahmud Hasan is doing most damage. He also plays for Flitwick and took five wickets yesterday to go with the 'five-fer' he'll get today. Hammering in at full pelt despite the sweltering heat, there is no stopping him until his captain takes him off for a rest. Twenty-five minutes before lunch, there is a screech of tyres and ominous crunch outside. Witnesses report a narrowly-avoided crash, as good a metaphor for the Cumberland innings as any when Tyler is simultaneously dispatched with the scoreboard reading 89 for 6.

Next in is Liam Watkinson, last seen at Oxton in May in the Unicorns Trophy clash with Cheshire. Selected chiefly for his bowling, the son of former Lancashire great Mike is the man of experience needed right now to settle in with Jacques and build a partnership. While his skipper goes on the attack – the game's first six coming via the South African's bat in the 30th over – the Boltonian is a calming presence at the other end. He enjoys a piece of good fortune when Bedfordshire's spinner misses a caught and bowled, the ball dipping at his fingertips. But having survived, the pair go off for lunch with a platform at least, 126 for 6.

A fine spread it is too, served amid convivial tables, hospitality and bonhomie overflowing. So enjoyable is the fare for both sets of club officials that when Jacques is immediately caught off Hasan's bowling on the restart, an unlucky 13 short of his half-century, most are still devouring their cheese and crackers.

Josh Boyne is next in, the score 130 for 7, with Beds focussed on clearing up as swiftly as possible. As ever, though, that's easier said than done in the Minor Counties, where batting orders are scant indication of aptitude. Liam, entirely comfortable, reaches his 50 in as many overs and it is his six that, a handful of balls later, brings up a once unlikely 200 for 7, Boyney plugging away well alongside.

The boundary in question plops into the stream at the bowler's end having sailed over Phil Caley's head, lost forever, or at least until those future antiquarians decipher it as an offering to the gods. Phil was coming to the game anyway, he says, but does intend to spend ten minutes with Steve later, just to get to the heart of the matter. At the moment, he is inclined to see it as an internal affair, but admits to having heard three different versions so far.

Conversation widens to those ECB funding talks and potential restructuring. Are all the minor counties as one on such matters?

'Yes, I think so. It's difficult in the different regions to please everybody, but that's why Nick [Archer, MCCA chairman] and myself go around talking to players, coaches, committees and other individuals through the year, to hear opinions. Nick and I played cricket and know a bit about it. People may think we are daft, but our heart is in the right place and hopefully we push it forward.' Visiting twenty clubs must churn up road miles. 'I've never managed to see everyone, my record is seventeen, but Nick has in his first full year in charge. His job is more amenable to getting around on Mondays and Tuesdays, but I'll still do fifteen this season.'

The MCCA secretary is 'a Suffolk boy, born and bred,' who came up through the ranks but, by his own admission, was: '...never good enough to play first-class. I just loved the game and took to it. I played twenty-eight years, fifteen as skipper, and had a thoroughly enjoyable journey, wouldn't change anything. I met a lot of good people playing and have done since, in the position I'm now in.'

His involvement with the Minor Counties Cricket Association began when: 'Funnily enough, a man from Cumberland stitched me up. A chap called Alan Wilson who, in his infinite wisdom, decided in 2009 that he'd had enough of being chairman of cricket, noticed my playing career was reaching an end and saw me as a suitable choice to take over. I never let him forget that he stuffed me out of sight.' He is joking, of course. 'It's actually nice to be able to put something back into a game you've enjoyed for so long.'

As the latest in a sudden barrage of fours sizzles by, a man with the look of a high school PE teacher explains how he then ended up as secretary. 'The position arose and someone had the bright idea that it might be good to have a younger face. I got voted in, perhaps due to my attitude and keenness for the game at this level. That was in 2016, start of 2017 – I've only been at it a year and a half, chairman of cricket was a bit longer. The previous incumbent, Geoff Evans, sadly passed away and it was suggested I combine the roles. I thought, well if the missus can put up with it, we'll give it a go.'

So actually he is doing both jobs? 'Yeah. From a chairman of cricket point of view, it's mainly going around talking to people and making sure we get feedback from those on and off the field as to how they feel about the game we've got currently. You listen to them, see if they've got different views and what have you, work things out and try to progress from there. From a secretary's point of view, it's much the same, but just dealing with admin – and there's a lot of it, especially with the ECB at the moment.'

Ah yes, the review process. How is it going? 'Nick's doing great work in the county partnership agreement [CPA] meetings we are having, which are about how we see the recreational game ... links with cricket boards ... bidding for the money we need to operate ... that sort of thing. The Minor Counties gets a very small proportion of funds and we need to ensure we are using them appropriately, to drive our level of the game forward. At the moment we think we are. We've just got to protect what we've got, try to move forward with it and continue to receive funding from the ECB.'

What does the future hold, especially for three-day games like these? There seems to be a lot of nervousness around. 'Indeed there is. We've got agreements for T20 and our knockout competition; the Championship is the one we are trying to nail down.' Then comes a crack of bat on ball. 'That's a very good shot and it's coming our way. We'll let that one go in the river.' Another six sails overhead and hits the far bank before rolling back into the water with a plop. A fielder dutifully trots over and is told that, unless he fancies a paddle, he is not getting that ball out either, so the call is sounded for another.

'We are fighting to retain six three-day games at the moment and get funding for it. The ECB seems to think it is costing them too much money to sustain this particular format. Which is fairly ironic when you think that we only get around £900,000 a year for twenty minor counties, whereas each first-class county gets £1.4 million for themselves. That's a bit lop-sided. But we've been asked to justify why we are running six three-day games and are hopefully going to be able to do that. It's difficult. ECB funding is tight as ever and they come up with arguments at every turn. I don't know, it's...' his breezy demeanour falters briefly. 'Personally, I think the Championship is really good value for money. There are 16, 17 and 18-year-olds that wouldn't have a chance of playing a longer format. Do well and they might go on to the first-class game. It also serves late-developers, not quite good enough to begin with. After a few years in the Minor Counties, they can have another go. What we achieve for what we get paid is a great effort, particularly when you recognise that minor county clubs represent some thirty five per cent of the cricket population. We are asking for a pittance in the big picture.'

The arguments are familiar, but Phil is at the sharp end of getting them heard. What is his feeling? Does he expect the MCCA to win the debate? At Penrith, Nick Archer suggested a more regionalised competition structure could be on its way.

'How long's a piece of string? I would like to think three-dayers will continue in some form or other. I don't want to see a reduction from six, however we might have to compromise on that. Personally,

I can't see the argument against it, but then perhaps I am a narrow-minded Minor Counties player, member, associate or whatever you want to call me, of many years standing who just thinks that what we have at the moment more than justifies the expense. Spectators are important too. In extremities like Cumberland, Devon and Cornwall, people wouldn't see the longer format at all without Minor Counties cricket. Large populations could be lost to the sport.'

Is Armageddon on its way? Are the ECB trying to kill off the Minor Counties competition completely?

'That's overly dramatic. I don't think it will happen, there would be such an outcry.' Clubs will though have to establish closer links with their local cricket board. 'It was new to everybody when introduced and people have their own little bits and pieces to protect in a way, but the sooner boards and clubs get along the better. Many have amalgamated already and it's working fine. The biggest problems occur in areas such as the two we are seeing here – Bedfordshire and Cumberland – who don't have a Premier League in the county. That causes huge problems. Players disappear to play the best cricket they can in neighbouring counties and Premier Leagues, which makes for issues with availability. Cumberland's go to Lancashire and North Yorkshire mainly, while Bedfordshire's go to Northants. It becomes harder to interest the locals then too.'

*****

During Cumberland's early collapse, Steve Sharp could be heard muttering 'be greedy... be greedy,' as one batsman after another threw away their wicket. Josh Boyne and Liam Watkinson have taken him at his word. Soon after president Wilson and his first lady arrive in mid-afternoon, Liam's latest boundary brings up the 250.

Alas, with some 30 overs in the day left, Boyney is stumped five runs short of a first Cumberland half-century. There were signs that nerves had taken hold, a steady run-rate slowing to a crawl. It also curtails an eighth-wicket partnership of 133, eight short of a fifty-year Cumberland record. His replacement Ben is then out lbw for 2 and suddenly the visitors have only one wicket remaining.

Adam Syddall is the man and when he comes in his side are 269 for 9. Can he hang around long enough to let Liam, on 91, notch his maiden Cumberland century? It is soon clear he intends to do just that, blocking every ball, even as superfast Hasan is reintroduced to the attack. Bizarrely, the fielding side doesn't bother to crowd in on him and pile on pressure. Instead, Syds is left to hold up an end as his batting partner advances to 99 before the landmark is passed with yet another heat-seeking boundary missile.

The hosts are leg-worn, weary. Only 70 overs have been bowled so far, such is the scoring rate, but the heat is merciless. It's clear Beds can't wait for a rest and, luckily for them, a chance to find shade isn't long coming. Liam mistimes a high one on 107 and Cumberland are all out for 286 before tea. That means 40 more overs can be bowled – a few wickets in the third session from a side fresh as the proverbial Cumbrian daisy and it could get interesting.

Slinging his kit down, Liam reflects further on his long absence since that 2011 debut. He'll be 27 next month and for a while looked likely to follow in dad Mike's illustrious footsteps, turning out for Lancashire's 2nd XI as an 18-year-old in the days when Toby Bulcock too dreamed of a first-class career. That was when those rumours Toby's dad Steve had hinted at in Wisbech began to circulate, of a mysterious figure sending images of Toby's bowling action to first-class clubs, allegedly to warn them off. Whatever the truth of that, both Toby and Liam have since had to be content with representative cricket of a still impressive if considerably lower profile.

Having grown up playing league cricket in Bolton and moving through the age groups with his home county, following his original spell with Cumberland Liam took himself off to Australia for six months and played in the state of Victoria. His return destination was Yorkshire, more specifically Leeds Metropolitan University, where between studies he spent three years playing for Leeds-Bradford. That added first-class fixtures to his CV, under an MCC scheme that sees six such institutes – Oxford, Cambridge, Durham, Loughborough, Leeds and Cardiff – play the major counties at the start of every season, and then each other. 'It's a way of getting your degree while developing your cricket,' Liam confirms.

That he is university educated comes as no surprise. Confident and eloquent, he also represented the Combined Universities in the 2nd XI Championship for a while, touring with them to Abu Dhabi. A PE teacher nowadays at the same school in Bolton he attended as a youngster, his only modern frustration is that he has to miss games at the start of every season due to the demands of school cricket. He was drawn back into the Cumberland fold during the knockout Trophy game at Oxton in May, by Edgworth teammate Syds. 'He just asked me if I wanted to do it.' Last week Steve gave him a call.

Despite today's long innings, after that injury earlier this year he now feels fit and well. 'I've had a good run-in with injuries, as do most seam bowlers,' he admits, chief among them a couple of stress fractures in his back, something else he has in common with Syds. 'Ankle impingements, rotator cuffs, side strains ... the lot. Touch wood, I'm all right now. I just get a bit stiff from time to time.'

Picking the side up here as he did was a splendid achievement, though he has the humility – or maybe absorbed media experience – to play it down. 'I just stuck to what I know, didn't take unnecessary risks and put the bad balls away.' Like just about everyone else in the side – with the exception of Boyney – cricket is part of the family, more so in his case. What was it like growing up with such a well-known father? 'Well when it came to playing, I had no choice in the matter,' he laughs. 'But it's good, I really do enjoy it. We are complete opposites personality-wise. I'm quite an extrovert, whereas my dad is an introvert. He needs time away from people to recharge his batteries. I need to be around them. You often see a clash when your dad is also your coach, but I enjoyed the coaching, the time he put in with me, and going to games. He'd retired by the time I really grew up, but I did get to see him. When I was very young we went to South Africa to watch him play for England and being around environments like that is a formative experience. Your knowledge improves and you get more experience of the game and its scenarios, which can only stand you in good stead.'

He was 'always the cheeky kid' who'd go into the dressing room and pick up everyone's bat, 'everyone' including such Lancashire legends as Wasim Akram, Neil Fairbrother and John Crawley. The roles of father and son though are these days reversed. 'We played together at Edgworth for a while, built a few partnerships, and still have all his memorabilia in the house. But nowadays he watches me.'

On resumption, Cumberland's start could hardly be better: opener Ben Mansell bowled Syddall, caught McGladdery, bat and pad in only the third ball, two runs on the board. Then Syds strikes again, helped by a great catch behind by Ben. Equally sensational is Slacky's take in the slips, batsman Liam now doing his bit with ball in hand, as a freak mini-tornado makes a weapon of an upturned patio umbrella at the river end. Fortunately, no one is impaled. Watched by his mother, Roxine, looking on from a little tent, fielder Sempy thwarts the 'dust devil', but Beds are in real trouble, 11 for 3.

The hosts' four and five are at the crease with not a run shared between them, essentially starting again as Cumberland's officials discuss dining plans. A Chinese restaurant, the Golden Cross in Great Barford, is the venue decided upon ahead of what is predicted to be an even hotter day tomorrow. With their otherwise debilitating fielding stint effectively cut in two, it's all going well for the visitors and their stand-in skipper Jacques. It was the perfect toss to win.

Seven runs are added and there's very nearly a run-out, Sempy's throw from the boundary almost a killer, but the batsman scrambles to safety. Both Syds and Liam are bowling superbly, getting through overs with pace and aggression. The new pair however weather the storm and Boyney comes into the attack with eight overs remaining. It heralds another breakthrough, the spinner bamboozling captain Andy Reynoldson with a twister Jacques does brilliantly well to nab. 'It's been a featherbed for the last hour-and-a-half, now it's a spitting cobra,' quips Neil, as another plane circles Luton airport.

There is still time for a dropped catch in the slips before a long and testing day's cricket concludes, Bedfordshire right up against it. Before heading off for his Szechwan chicken and cashew nuts, Neil confirms that he has spoken to Phil Caley and seems confident that the MCCA will agree to the matter being settled internally. 'Lessons have been learned,' he says, 'and now it's time to move on.' The two umpires, he adds, made no mention of the incident in their report.

He expects that Gary will resume the captaincy for the next Championship game against Northumberland at Jesmond, while conceding that the skipper really ought not to have played at all if he couldn't finish the game at Furness. Gary had though been in an invidious position. Previously, he has always put Cumberland first, but Richmondshire are this year insistent that he prioritises them and he isn't getting any younger. 'They pay his wages, don't they?'

As for last Friday's meeting in Kendal, no info is volunteered. Steve's manner when asked about it is guarded, suspicious even, the response of a man unused to being questioned on his motives. But then maybe few are at a level of cricket that most often exists under the radar. Either way, the issue of who knew about Gary's departure beforehand for the moment goes unanswered. Toby's future too is up in the air, whether or not this other dust devil expires harmlessly.

One last look at the wicket reveals that, despite the conditions, it is in pretty good shape still, bound by the tufts of unmowed grass left in place deliberately to keep it from disintegration in the heat. The outfield too has stayed surprisingly green, one gigantic fissure along the cowfield rope notwithstanding.

*****

Monday morning. Syds, in the shade of a large fir, fields in the deep, the only patch of field in shadow. A temperature of 30 degrees is predicted, hotter than yesterday, but when asked he enthusiastically takes the ball. Bedfordshire's number four, Sam Johnson, reaches his half-century and then Syds strikes, lbw, the hosts 110 for 5.

Alan, Eric and Neil discuss a suggestion from Sempy's mother, already back in her tent and settled in front of a camper van. Roxine rarely speaks to anyone, keeps herself to herself, occasionally exiting the canvas to go on a lap, alone. Or perhaps she only talks when she has something to say, in this case an idea for a charitable trust with which to fund more county development games. Neil says Roxine wishes to make a presentation at September's AGM.

'If the Cumbria board has two reps on it, make sure we have three,' says Alan, voting implications in mind.

'Once the facts are known, I'm sure we will have questions,' says Neil. Nothing is decided upon yet.

As for Prattgate, scorer Geoff Minshaw reckons that: '...people have been making mountains out of molehills. Gary shouldn't have done what he did, but he will be rapped on the knuckles and that should be it.'

Cumberland don't have a mascot, but in the absence of a green furry sausage Geoff, whose devotion to club and county is in his every West Cumbria syllable, comes closest. But then the same could be said of almost every scorer, that army of unsung sentinels who capture every no-ball, leg bye and six forever. Countless moments in so many real lives marked now by little dots. Think of it, the sheer volume of information that will neither be sought after nor ever needed again, pinned down for posterity anyway. A manifestation of humanity's urge to leave its mark.

Geoff was born in Maryport Cottage Hospital and raised in the nearby village of Broughton Moor, where 'mam and dad had a bit of a grocery shop,' in the triangle between Cockermouth, Maryport and Workington. It was in the latter town that he took up the game: '...but in them days there wasn't the level of junior activity there is now. Lads today are brought through all the age groups from under-11s upwards, play third team cricket, second team, 1st XI and then into this, the Minor Counties, if they are good enough. It's very structured. When I started at Workington, there was just under-16s, 2nd and 1st XI. To begin with, I did all right, batted and bowled a bit, but couldn't get into the second team, so started scoring instead.'

Not by himself though. Not to begin with.

'The club had an old scorer, Archie Gibbon, who looked after me. After finishing with the under-16s, I thought: "I want to be on a cricket field on a Saturday," so me and a mate used to travel the five or six miles on a bus and get there an hour before. I'll always remember looking in the local paper: "Wickets pitched at 2.00pm." We'd stay until the end and when he saw us Archie would ask us to put the tins up.' No electronic boards back then.

'I've still got a little scorer's book from 1978,' Geoff goes on, 'that I started filling in. The odd time Archie wasn't available I'd stand in. He used to go on at me: "Wait until I retire. I'll be able to garn watch cricket away." He worked in the steel industry, a big thing in Workington in them days, but when he did retire he died the following week. Poor old bugger.'

So Geoff got his start and enjoyed a first taste of associated glory. When a team wins a competition, as happened at Workington in 1983, their scorer gets a medal too. Three years later, though, he moved on to Whitehaven, scorer for the 1st XI until 1996. He still played the odd game then, mainly at the end of the season when sides were short of numbers, and once shared a last-man partnership of 70-odd with an opening batsman. 'A guy took a picture for the paper that I've still got. It has pride of place in my house. I didn't know at the time that it was my last game for Whitehaven. I ended up getting wed and moved to Cockermouth, eleven miles away, where I've been since.'

Coincidentally, the year Geoff was made club secretary, 2000, was when Cockermouth joined a breakaway as members of the now North Lancashire and Cumbria League. 'We had a players' meeting and a few were grumbling about having to travel to the south of the county ... it's going to cost money ... not gonna work ... that sort of thing. I said: "Listen. I've been in the North Lancashire League and that's where Cockermouth needs to be." Eighteen years I've been secretary since. We've won two premiership titles, something no one thought would happen.' Currently, Cockermouth are still riding high, third in the North Lancs and Cumbria table.

The Cumberland connection came about in the early noughties, when club professional Martin Lewis also skippered the county. 'It was him who told me they were looking for a scorer and asked if I'd like him to nominate me. I said yes and have been doing it for fifteen years now, enjoying every minute.'

Funnily enough, he debuted here in Bedfordshire, at Dunstable, in 2003. The captain was Steve O'Shaughnessy, Ashley Metcalfe and Graham Lloyd the professionals. 'We did well first innings. Lloyd and Metcalfe put on a then record fourth-wicket partnership. At the end of day one, me and Graham decided to go to the chippy, opposite our hotel in Luton. As we walked back through a little square this huge limousine – no word of a lie this, no word of a lie – came screeching around the corner. A guy leaned out the window, put a gun on us and said: "Get out of Luton, you white bastards." Honestly. I shouted to Lloydy: "Hit the deck!" So him and me dived to the pavement, fish and chips everywhere. That was my first ever game. Frightening. I tell it better when I've had a few beers.'

The highlight, inevitably, is the Championship-winning year of 2015. 'I feel as if I am part of the team,' Geoff says. 'I play every ball with these lads. Carlisle was pretty special, but even more so for me since I'm Cumberland born and bred. When I started, I used to watch Minor Counties matches and think: "Maybe one day I'll be able to score at this level." To now be able to do that is still an honour. I think of it as representing my county. It means a lot to me.'

It follows, therefore, that Geoff has appeared in scoreboxes up and down the land, hence his ready supply of often hilarious and on occasion dubious anecdotes. Yet one venue has thus far been denied his services – the self-styled 'Home of Cricket', Lord's.

'If that ever comes about it will be really nice, but if it doesn't I'm happy with what I've achieved so far. Yogi, from Cambridgeshire, has put some of the Minor Counties scorers in the frame there. Some have done Test matches and some one-day internationals, it's seen as a reward for their efforts over the years. I can't say whether it will come for me because I am the furthest north, people down south get more of a chance, but it is my long-term ambition. It would be in all the local papers, brilliant for my family and Cumberland cricket too. But whatever happens I've met loads of lovely people who you otherwise just wouldn't meet. That's a big part of it as well.'

A scorebox is also a great place to spot talent, if you know it when you see it. 'I scored for Cumbria under-17s and a young lad called Flintoff was playing for Lancashire.' In another game, Michael Vaughan turned out for Yorkshire. Arthur Brown was Cumbria team manager then, as he is now. 'I scored for them for about four or five years, so saw a lot of up-and-coming big names.' Including of course, Ben Stokes, who began at Cockermouth in the under-11s and turned out for the 1st XI while in the under-15s, before Durham enticed him away. That was in 2006 when Cockermouth won the league, Geoff tucked away doing the scoring. 'Who would have thought that a lad from our club would go on to play for England and be possibly the top all-rounder in the world?' It would make for a marvellous story if Stokes's old scorer should indeed be awarded a Lord's Test, or similar, and the pair's paths crossed again.

Conversation switches back to Gary, another man with whom Geoff is proud to have shared the ride. 'At this level of cricket you need people like him, with experience, to help the young lads. What Gary has brought to this club has been really important in my eyes. Since 2009, we've had nothing but success with him. The one-day competition in 2012 was the first thing Cumberland won for years; the side with him and Richard Gleeson in was a very special team.'

Does Geoff plan to continue scoring until he drops, just like Archie Gibbon? 'No! I'll carry on while I enjoy it, that's what I'll do. I 'd like to think I'd know when the time is right. Once my eyes start going and I can't see anymore … a big thing with scorers … although my eyesight is poor now to be fair; has been since being a very small boy. I can still make the players out in the middle. There is a scorer in the North Lancs and Cumbria League who is 73 or 74 and struggling, but cricket keeps him going, do you know what I mean?'

So, being 54 years old gives Geoff at least another couple of decades. 'Well, I wouldn't say twenty years ... three-dayers are tiring. You've got 110 overs in a day, three sessions of a couple of hours or more, but 50 overs on a Saturday isn't so bad. My first target is to score for Cumberland for twenty years and then let's see.'

In the here and now, following a flurry of boundaries another wickets falls, Ajay Singh Momi hammering one big hit too many down the throat of Sempy to give Josh Boyne his second victim. His third comes soon after, lbw, and Bedfordshire's men at the crease are again both on zero with the score 147 for 7. Josh's dad, watching from his fold-up chair, jokes that both teams were out together last night and shook hands on a draw. If so, Cumberland are reneging on the deal. Soon after, Ross chases and cuts off a boundary from the slips – 'Good work, Jesus,' yells Dutts – and Syds rattles another set of pads in front of the stumps with only seven more runs added.

At the start of another working week, the ground is surprisingly well populated, at least as many in as yesterday. When Slacky is given an over they see their quick bowler Al Muhad Hasan given a dose of his own medicine, caught Howarth, and it's 169 for 9. The only question now is will the last pair survive until lunch. They not only do so but by the fall of their last wicket soon after their feed – caught Sempill, bowled Boyne – have somehow moved on to a maddening 234 all out, just 52 runs short of the Cumberland score. Another opportunity to press home an advantage has been squandered.

'Sorry, we were delayed,' says the male half of a well-groomed elderly couple, greeting friends on the wooden decking.

'Not at all,' insists his opposite number. 'Can I get you a drink?'

'I'll get them a drink, darling,' the latter man's wife intercedes.

'Oh, thank you dear. Would you? We'll wait here.'

'What would you like?' she enquires of the new arrivals.

'Ooh a ginger beer, I think. Yes, a ginger beer, please.'

'A ginger beer?'

'Yes, please. A ginger beer.'

At 2.36pm, Helios riding high in the sky, Sempy and Ross walk out for the second innings. Time is on their side, wingèd chariots a distant rumour. Yet if long-form cricket is about filling your time pleasantly ahead of the dying of the light, three runs in the first five overs is a less than riveting echo of life's essential triviality.

As play drags on, even the fielders look bored. The Bedfordshire lads at cover and point embark on rock-paper-scissors. There is one very eventful over – Sempy apparently caught behind at the second attempt, but given not out; surviving an lbw appeal next ball; leaving a fast one that sails perilously close to his bails immediately after; and then edging through the slips for four. It isn't until the pair have crawled to 41 that his wicket is finally taken, caught at extra cover, but even then Ross and new partner Slacky paddle their way to 82 for 1 at tea, extending the lead to 134.

The breakthrough, if such it is, comes four runs after the restart, Slacky caught out and Marcus Stables coming in. The innings that follows doesn't quite live up to that debut century at Furness, but is nevertheless just what Cumberland need in the circumstances, a mature and measured occupation of the crease. The first target to be passed is Ross Zelem's half-century, deserved after such a resilient knock, after which the visitors' command of the situation is once again restored, until Marcus falls rather dubiously, lbw, for 30 runs and is replaced by Dutts before a couple more wickets fall without further score. Ross is first to go, skying a ball that was begging to be smacked out of the ground straight to a fielder, and his replacement Tyler is out via the finest of nicks to first slip for a golden duck. 'Don't destroy the changing room,' says Alan Wilson wandering by, but the banging and clattering inside suggest his advice has gone unheeded. The Bedfordshire and Flitwick officials are certainly not amused.

On the field, it's now 132 for 5 and in-comer Jacques would be fending off a hat-trick had Tyler's demise not come on the last ball of the over. As it is, Dutts faces it, happily nudging a single. When Tyler re-emerges, Steve Sharp sits and has a word with him. He has spent a lot of time among the players today, more so than usual.

With 20 overs left in the day, Dutts and Jacques forge another useful partnership, pushing Cumberland's lead above 200 in a running total of 149 for 5. Ian Smith, the Bedfordshire chairman, tells how Monty Panesar played here last year, apparently for a fee of £300 a day. That was funded by a dinner at which he, Monty, was guest speaker, though not many were impressed.

'What a waste of time he was,' someone chips in alongside.

Ian, the latest friendly face here among many, offers an enthusiastic shake of the hand: 'Hello. Chairman seven years. One victory. Very much looking forward to the second.' At the rate this is going, it's unlikely he'll see it tomorrow.

Bedfordshire, though, gain hope when Jacques misjudges a hook and the stand-in skipper is out for 37. Century-man Liam Wilkinson goes in and it is his single that puts Cumberland 250 runs ahead off the last ball of the 70th over, before Dutts then eases the scoreboard to 200 for 6. Flitwick's rounders team arrives, though shows little or no interest in the cricket. 'When does this finish,' one woman says aloud. 'Soon, I hope. We've got a game at seven.'

As overs dwindle, Jacques slopes off to sit in his car and lights a cheroot. 'They are lucky in a way, having Gary and me around,' he reflects. 'We have been in the professional environment and can pass it on.' He is not however sure of how Minor Counties clubs discover and develop talent. 'Is there an academy? Elite squads? These guys, in the winter, what do they do? Start working on things in January ... their technique ... drills ... what happens?' Or maybe he does know and is simply voicing his frustration. 'That's important. You've loads of lads with ability here ... Sempy, Slacky, Boyney. If they were given things to work on in a planned session once a week, you never know where they could end up. Get a contract with an academy, maybe, or wind up with a first-class county.'

What he is saying is that professionalism isn't just about money, but the expectation of high standards, both from individuals and organisations. It's clear he is not keen on going out on the lash in the middle of a three-day game, for example, sparking the memory of his voluntary late-night shuttle in Wisbech.

'The most important thing is man-management,' he says, when questioned on captaincy, and his enjoyment of it. 'Make sure they know what their roles are. Make sure you get the best out of each individual and work out what makes him tick. This year, I've had to take some time to observe everyone ... who is doing what, how do they work? Some are going through the motions and happy to do that, and it's easy for them to drag other players down. If they score runs they are happy, but if they don't, well, they don't ... It's important to keep standards high and lead by example, so I've always got to play bad cop really, telling these guys I expect better of them.' But of course respect is earned, not demanded. 'You don't get respect by drinking ten pints, then playing for the first hour and going back to bed in the field. You get respect by doing the right things and playing hard cricket.'

Back at the pavilion, Jacques reckons that tomorrow they will need a lead of 320 at least, so he'll maybe leave them with two and a half sessions ideally in which to chase that. 'It's one of those wickets where two batsmen can look good, then a wicket or two or three falls ... I'm quite wary of it.'

Bedfordshire's coach tips Jacques the wink. 'Are you going to bring them in yet?' he says. 'Reckon you've got enough.'

The day ends though with Dutts and Liam still out there on 33 and 11 respectively, 215 for 6. Cumberland are 267 runs ahead.

*****

On day three in Flitwick, the only Cumberland wicket to fall was that of Liam Watkinson, dismissed for 35, Dutts and Boyney not out on 65 and 6 respectively when Jacques waved them in with a lead of 331. In reply, Bedfordshire opener Ben Mansell retired injured after six overs on another sweltering morning. The skipper's catch gave Josh his side's first wicket just before lunch, whereupon Mansell resumed and Cumberland needed nine wickets in two sessions. But after 30 overs Beds had moved on to 95 for 1, Mansell on 30 and Ajay Singh Moni 43, by which time the smart money was on a draw. Then came the collapse. The bowler responsible was du Toit, contributing six for 35 in 18.3 overs.

'I noticed a bit of a ridge; if it hit that it was bouncing,' he later explained. 'All I was thinking was just bowl at it and something might happen. It's just about reading conditions and trying to turn them to your favour. It wasn't a bad wicket, just slow. As soon as one misbehaves people start thinking...'

First victim – quicker ball, batsman came down the wicket and yorked himself. That was Ben Mansell gone. For good this time.

Wicket two – the ridge was hit, the ball turned, bounced and Elliott Callis was caught by Boyney at leg slip.

Third victim – after a breather to allow Sempy to claim the first of his three wickets, Jacques took mid-on out, inviting left-hander Andy Reynoldson to play against the spin. The Beds captain tried to do that, his bottom edge ending up in the gloves of Ben Howarth.

Number four – having pouched his second catch of the innings off Sempy's bowling, Jacques had tossed down a slower one and Tyler caught the next man at midwicket.

Wickets five and six were lbws, either side of Sempy's third, and Jacques even had the luxury of seeing another chance dropped.

'On a wicket like that you try to mix your paces, a couple quicker, a couple slower,' he said. 'I'd meant to bowl Boyney. He is a proper spinner, gets it up in the air, whereas I bowl it into the pitch.' In the event, his superior experience and guile was so effective that Bedfordshire were 171 all out in a Cumberland victory by 160 runs.

With 48 points to play for in two remaining games, it wasn't – and still isn't – mathematically impossible for the Cumbrians to top the table and reach the final. Received wisdom is win four and you'll be there or thereabouts, although their defeat by eight wickets at Wisbech in June likely ended any realistic hope. After Flitwick, though, it had been suggested that Pratt would return to captain the side against Northumberland at Jesmond in a fortnight.

On the Tuesday preceding that game at Manor Park, Horsford, day three of Norfolk's Championship match with Hertfordshire is soon to be underway, the middle fixture in an annual three-game bash traditionally staged on consecutive July and August weekends. Here too Cumberland remains a ripe area for discussion, Herts being the wronged party at Furness after all.

The heatwave may be history. Day one was rain-affected, start delayed until 2.00pm due to a waterlogged outfield. Day two was interrupted by showers, play commencing an hour late on account of more heavy overnight rain. Today, though, the sun has once again got its hat on and East Anglia beams pretty as a picture.

Around here the Minor Counties Championship is news, one area of the country where it *can* make the back page. Even so, that people have heard of how Toby Bulcock has not been selected for Cumberland's penultimate clash on Sunday, despite having declared himself available, owes more to the MCCA grapevine than any such newspaper headline. It is however reported that home skipper Chris Brown has become Norfolk's second-highest wicket-taker ever.

Even so, these two sides are also unlikely to face the Western Division leaders in the final at Banbury in September. Last year, Norfolk and Hertfordshire sandwiched Cumberland on the Eastern Division ladder and are certainties for another middling finish this time, seventh and eighth in the table. Still, Norfolk games aren't like any other in the Minor Counties Championship. At Manor Park, there is always a sense of occasion.

In the 2018 *Minor Counties Annual*, committeeman and former umpire Keith Bray wrote: 'In August, the Norfolk faithful will gather at Manor Park to enjoy the Festival so admired by everyone. Good cricket and renewed friendships will follow, but I fear, it will never quite feel the same again. Someone is missing.' The gentleman to whom he referred was former MCCA secretary David Armstrong, a fixture and fitting here for so long, whose funeral was in March.

A visitor can immediately see why Bray considered this ground homely, if not holy. Along the car park side run seventeen white tents with space in each for three or four people, every one in use. They give it the feel of a medieval tournament, where Robin Hood might pop up in disguise to impress Maid Marian with his superior marksmanship and cock a snoop at nasty King John. Several tents have a wooden plaque at their rear bearing names of those entitled to sit inside: 'P.R. Hunt'; 'R.E. Laurie'; 'D.K. Wild'; 'K.E.G. Searle'; 'B. St. J. Dwyer' and, in prime position centrally: 'Mrs G.J. Armstrong'.

*****

Like death, the umpire's decision is final. Or so it was once supposed. Five months ago the bells of St Mary's tolled otherwise, summoning mourners up a mossy bank in Happisburgh – pronounced *Hayzbro'* around here – to the fifteenth-century churchyard on high.

A wet flannel of a March Monday morning had turned into a soggy and sombre afternoon, not helped by the funeral on the hill. In a lull between the 'Beast from the East' that had blown through the week before, and what the media had dubbed the coming 'Pest from the West', springtime rejuvenation was held in abeyance.

That said, hither and thither among angled slabs of memorial stone were daffodils, welcome daubs of yellow under gypsum skies, the day as if sculpted in marble. With 'Nunc Dimittis' sung and service done, the deceased's nearest and dearest would file out to the graveside later for interment and the last farewell, heads bowed.

On the Order of Service, David Armstrong (1936-2018), long-time servant of Norfolk CC, was pictured as a schoolboy chorister, smiling uncertainly in a cape and top hat, and already showing a respect for tradition he'd grow into absolutely. Below that was an invitation to join the family at The Lighthouse Inn, Walcott, 'for light refreshments' and 'the sharing of fond memories'.

Heavy oak doors muffled the organ music inside. Until struck by illness, David would have been playing those notes, but plenty had turned up to give him a send-off he'd have appreciated, a good-sized congregation. Mournful and insistent, the bells chimed on. The local paper said bright clothing was welcome, but aside from the club ties on view few had bought into that. As the music stopped, so did the chatter, only to resume when the organist did likewise, a false start. Then came a recording of King's College Choir, to whom Cambridge-scholar David had once belonged.

The service did have one non-traditional aspect. It was led by the Reverend Catherine Dobson, albeit from the *Book of Common Prayer*. Her acquaintance with David was short, she said and, by the sound of it, a female appointment may not have been to her late parishioner's liking, her tone one of wry and gentle understanding. 'I am the resurrection and the light,' she began, scripture concluding with an admission that this was in fact her first *Book of Common Prayer* funeral, followed by a revelation that surprised no-one: David had designed his own service. A favourite hymn was sung:

O thou who camest from above
The fire celestial to impart,
Kindle a flame of sacred love
On the mean altar of my heart.

David's brother Chris then delivered the Eulogy, fleshing out his sibling's life and personality in plummy tones swathed in echo.

David Armstrong, who died on 16 February 2018, aged 81, had his contradictions. A slow bowler in his playing days and honorary secretary of Norfolk from 1967 to 1983, an obituary in *The Cricketer*, a publication to which he regularly contributed, went so far as to claim that 'the continuation of competitive cricket at minor counties level bears testimony to him.' Made honorary secretary of the Minor Counties Cricket Association, he was able to extend that influence.

His adoption of that role – a paid job from 1985 – came during 'an era of great change', when counties who had previously played eight two-day fixtures per season in a largely *ad hoc* manner, found themselves split into two organised divisions – Eastern and Western – and playing six Championship matches, three at home and three away, together with a new-fangled one-day knockout competition.

More upheaval followed in the 1990s – this time existential – when the MCCA's future came under threat due to the MacLaurin Report, a radical streamlining proposal that, to many, knew the cost of everything and value of nothing. David Armstrong represented the MCCA on the ruling Test and County (TCCB) and England and Wales (ECB) Cricket Boards, standing up to such impudence until, with the assistance of such as Cumberland's Alan Wilson, the storm was withstood. 2001 saw the last innovation of his tenure, albeit one designed to strengthen the MCCA's traditional roots: a switch from two to three-day games. On his retirement, the job was split in two.

Also in 2001, Norfolk beat Devon to win the knockout Trophy at Lord's – as good a moment to go as any. Having written *A History of Norfolk Cricket*, he filled the club presidency from 2003 to 2007, recalling playing days as a member of the MCC and at school with *Test Match Special* legend Henry Blofeld. Back in 1986, a man who was also assistant secretary at Surrey and a schoolmaster led a Minor Counties tour to Kenya, where he met Sir Len Hutton. His marriage to Gail, assistant school matron, lasted 44 years, he and she living in a former farm-worker's cottage for all but four of those. This son of the manse, his father a vicar, was also a great-grandson of Benjamin Armstrong, a notable Victorian diary keeper.

As the congregation filed out to Elgar's 'Nimrod', it was clear that David Armstrong cherished order and ceremony. He was made for cricket and cricket was made for him – the traditional red ball variety that is. He cared not a jot for this white-ball nonsense.

*****

The coming season's *Minor Counties Annual*, published a few weeks later, had the unicorn logo of the MCCA on its cover and a picture of Berkshire's Waqas Hussain belting a four against Staffordshire. Inside, it called 2017 and 2018 'years of great change and challenges'.

In an introduction supposedly written on April Fools' Day, the main problem was said to have once again been justifying the role of Minor Counties cricket within the system. 'It seems each time there is regime change at the ECB, Minor County cricket, and the cost of it, comes under the microscope. The officers of MCCA have spent many hours at meetings highlighting the major benefits the 20 Minor Counties bring to the game.' Contributor 'Pip' August went on to explain how a recent ECB survey returned 'an overwhelming vote of confidence' in the three-day Championship. An objection that current levels of funding were already far short of every club's running costs for things like development teams was also raised, although no member would have needed the reminder.

As for 'change', having reverted to a straightforward knockout Trophy in order to make way for the new T20, this year's 50-over matches would be played with a white ball and in coloured clothing. 'This highlights MCCA's commitment to provide a major plank in the development pathway for young cricketers.' Further to that end, ex-professionals would act as mentors to the younger players. In 2017, all but one county had: '...received a full share of the Incentive Fee Payment for playing young cricketers.' Several members of England's U19 World Cup side in New Zealand over the winter had also played Minor Counties last season.

Kind words were shared about David Armstrong, a 'wonderful personality' who will be missed 'especially in Norfolk,' but by all who knew him. 'He was a great ambassador for Minor County cricket and the traditions of the game and was always splendid company.' 'PGM' recounted how he'd been: '...lucky enough to spend the day with [David] in September when Norfolk and Bedfordshire 2nd XIs were playing at Manor Park and his support for the young cricketers playing was total and the enjoyment he got from an exciting finish showed how much he loved the game.'

Complete with a wish that David was 'here to check my spelling and punctuation as was his wont,' ex-umpire Keith Bray's obituary went on: 'Many of you will know how wonderful his handwriting was, always with his beloved fountain pen. The ball point was not invented for David's benefit!' Bray continued: 'As the years passed, David found it more and more difficult to adapt to the ways of the modern game. The appealing and sledging were against all he held dear and he was often heard to say "I used to come to watch Norfolk play cricket, I now have to listen to them as well." Yet when wife Gail, then membership secretary, was offered the club presidency, he called it the proudest moment of his life.'

The Lighthouse Inn, venue for the post-funeral get-together, was like a scene from a BBC 1970s situation comedy, at the Rotary club do perhaps, when June has been given strict instructions from Terry to Impress The Boss. Blazers, cravats and bonhomie ahoy. And an hour before, eulogising his brother's stubborn yet generous nature and aversion to T20 cricket, Chris Armstrong had drawn a ripple of amusement from the Minor Counties' club representatives in the congregation, among them Cumberland president Alan Wilson on a pilgrimage down from Kendal, whose antenna is set permanently to the funny side. On this occasion, like the rest of his friends and colleagues, he had otherwise sat in respectful contemplation.

Geographically, Norfolk and Cumbria could hardly be less alike. The flat terrain here holds its secrets close to its chest, while England's far North West heaves and plunges through mountain, valley and fell. They do, however, share Minor Counties cricket and enough volunteers from instinctively insular populations to keep the unglamorous end of the game alive against stacked odds.

Cumberland patron Bob Bowman OBE had himself been such a figure, until his death, aged 84, five days before David Armstrong's. Was the universe trying to tell them something?

David certainly had been, given his choice of Psalm 39 for the reading, wherein his biblical namesake struggles to hold his tongue: 'My heart was hot within me; While I was musing, the fire burned...' – the musing in question on human fragility: '...every man at his best state is but a vapour...' And that had been followed by the Lesson, from the first Epistle of St Paul to the Corinthians: 'Let us eat and drink, for tomorrow we die...'

Minutes up the road from a sea frothing grey and forbidding at Walcott Gap, the family, friends and ex-colleagues of the dearly-departed took that advice to heart as, bang on cue, the sun at last broke through those bothersome clouds. People sat or stood in sociable little groups, taking bar orders, renewing acquaintances, by then chatting and guffawing too. A few leaned on walking sticks.

'Hello, how are you?'

'Very well, and you?'

It wasn't long before the subject turned back to cricket.

'David must be rolling in his grave,' said one chap, holding court, of a recent MCCA meeting at which the re-introduction of T20 this season had been inevitably confirmed. His objections were shared with an audience huffing, puffing and nodding sagely. 'Same opposition twice in one day?' he blustered, eyebrows crackling like wire wool. This 'lunacy' had not been adequately thought through.

In an otherwise empty beer garden, a younger chap had nipped out for a cigarette. 'Oh yes,' he reflected, exhaling a cloud of smoke. 'David was very much a traditionalist, didn't like the Twenty20 at all. He understood the value of what we already have, you see.'

Up from Hertfordshire and rolling his own, he spoke ruefully about the state of Minor Counties cricket more generally, an aspect of the game still precious to those involved, but about which the ECB no longer cared at all. 'They should build it up, but don't seem to value or want to fund it. The Minor Counties could be a feeder league for the first-class county system,' he said, 'but everything is about commerciality these days, isn't it?'

*****

On a roundabout near Norwich Airport, Manor Park is one of the few Minor Counties grounds signposted for traffic. Upon driving through a somewhat stately entrance, players and officials to the left, public right, a man bobs out of a little wood hut and tosses a 'Festival of Cricket' folded card on the dashboard, before requesting £7.50 for admission and parking. 'Hertfordshire have declared on 111,' he says, the start again delayed. 'Norfolk will try for 100, declare, and see if they can make a game of it. We begin at 11.00am.'

By noon yesterday, Norfolk had declared their first innings on an overnight total of 209 for 6 after 75.1 overs, Herts losing a wicket before scoring and then a second that left them 11 for 2 at one early stage. Wickets continued to fall cheaply throughout the afternoon and so a break for rain at 99 for 6 came as a relief. It was in the preceding spell, however, that Chris Brown got that all-important landmark scalp, bowling 'keeper Ben Cowell for one run, only for it then to be revealed that actually he was Brown's 501st Championship victim – he'd already bagged his 500th during the first match of the three-week festival schedule, against Staffordshire.

Not that the national media has noticed any of this, of course, swamped as it is by the start of the 2018-19 Premier League season. As Saturday's papers and online pundits obsess over José Mourinho's winning start at Man United, even Jimmy Anderson's five-wicket display against India at Lord's goes all but overlooked. 'Let this be a lesson,' tweets social media user Patrick Gearey. 'The second week of August is the bloody cricket season. Today England knocked the world's best side over for 107, despite missing half the day due to rain. But the headlines will be whatever Mourinho bleats on about...' It starts a thread that then meanders over familiar ground ... lack of terrestrial TV ... poor grass roots investment ... various ECB failures ... before a 'troll' interjects: 'Cricket [is] in the same bracket as darts. If you have to stop for tea and lunch, it's not a sport.'

You wouldn't get much agreement with that at what is widely held to be the Minor Counties' richest club; it certainly has a wealth of history. Set up in 1827, in those far off fledgling days Norfolk CCC was second only in reputation to the MCC, before cricket's spread to big city conurbations, north and south, on the back of industrial revolution brought an end to all that. The present day club – patrons H.M. Queen Elizabeth II and H.R.H. The Duke of Edinburgh – was formed in 1877, a founding Minor Counties member in 1895.

The roots of the modern-day festival lay in the first 'Norwich Cricket Week' in 1881. It remains unique in minor and first-class county competitions, looked forward to by hosts and visitors alike, especially when the sun shines. That has been missing so far in this game. Although the atmosphere is pleasant, when the on-field action resumes it will feel subdued. The players aren't exactly going through the motions, but you could be forgiven for thinking they were.

This is, in fact, the only dedicated 'county ground' in the Minor Counties Championship. Every other club, like Cumberland, is a band of travellers, whether through a desire to spread games around or out of sheer necessity. The value of having a place to call your own is immediately apparent – there is a sense of identity here unlike that of anywhere else, a feeling of ownership reinforced by the fact that the club actually has office space. Back in the 1920s, Norfolk are said to have considered going first-class, as Glamorgan did in 1921, but finances couldn't be made to stack up. Still, many a talent got a start in the city, most notably perhaps several members of the Edrich clan.

The club has, however, only been at Manor Park since 2000. During the one hundred and twenty-five years prior to that, Norfolk's home was in the suburb of Lakenham. A change in scenery seems to have done the trick. In 2002, they were joint-Championship winners with Herefordshire, their fifth and most recent appearance on the honours board, while three of the club's five one-day cup wins came in 2001, 2005 and 2009, also during their time at the ground.

It is not quite 11.00am and the largest marquee is already well populated with besuited and dolled-up types wetting their whistle with craft beer and sparkling Italian wine, 'sponsors and guests only'. Incongruously tucked into a corner of a boundary dotted with fold-up chairs whose inhabitants are here purely for cricket, the hubbub and giddiness is good-natured enough, though some of the touchy-feely flirting, as young women indulge the physical attentions of men old enough to be their grandfather, is verging on creepy.

Behind the sightscreens alongside are the football fields that give the ground an open aspect. Further around is another marquee, this one for the public, a brick pavilion, changing rooms and a patio clubhouse window protected by rubber netting, behind which lunch and tea will be taken. Damp underfoot, there are two piles of sand on the wicket; the sodden outfield has the consistency of malt loaf.

Hertfordshire gain early hope, Matthew Plater caught out and Norfolk are 10 for 1. Five runs later, Tom New falls, batsman number three, but if that vocalises an otherwise muted fielding side it is only briefly. They are soon driven back into their shell as skipper Reece Hussain uses eight occasional bowlers. Norfolk can declare for a second time after an unbroken 162 partnership sets Hertfordshire a target of 276 without further loss.

Before then, as the game edges towards lunch, its every titbit relayed to a good-sized crowd via the clear and precise delivery of a professional PA announcer, Norfolk's captain chugs on a 'vape' by the pavilion. Brown, stubble-chinned and baseball-capped, one eye on the pitch as a Herts fielder is hurt and a reserve summoned only for the victim to battle on, confirms this as his last Minor Counties campaign. Days away from his 44th birthday, this lanky and indeed former 'Lanky' off-spinner reckons that retiring as Norfolk's leading wicket-taker in three-day cricket makes sense, although he will continue to grace the local club scene. Impossible too, given his age, that he could ever reach or pass the all-round total of 690, taken by Michael Falcon between 1907 and 1946.

'I was on the staff at Lancashire between 1994 and 1997, when I got released and played for Glamorgan before going to Cheshire,' he says of his Minor Counties origins. 'Actually, we played in the last ever game at the old county ground, Lakenham.' He came to Norfolk when invited to do so in 2001, after Henry Blofeld presented him with a man of the match trophy in an ECB County Cup semi-final. That path led to coaching, a facet that most engages him still. Only this March, he worked with Zimbabwe in the Cricket World Cup Qualifier event in that country, won by Afghanistan, ahead of 2019's main tournament. He works in tandem with the Norfolk Cricket Board, as performance manager of an Emerging Players Programme from under-10s to 1st XI, part of the county's big-picture approach.

'We play all our fixtures here, some age group games too. The cricket board's offices are here. All these lads play in the local league – I've coached them through the system. Well, apart from Tom New, but everyone else, it's extremely close-knit. Norfolk is very much the county's team. You've only got to look in the *Eastern Daily Press*. Today it'll be Norwich City football club and this will be the next biggest thing. We get really good media coverage.'

He asks about and takes interest in events up in Cumberland, a club whose outlook could hardly be more different, but with whose personnel he is friendly. 'Herts were up there, weren't they? The other night when GP buggered off early.' So much for keeping it all in-house. Not wishing to stray further into a topic as boggy as the outfield, he sighs philosophically, predicts it will work itself out and by the end of the conversation is already back-tracking on his own decision to step away: 'Well, you never say never, do you ... but I'm definitely giving the captaincy up.'

Once upon a time, according to John Hurst's *Cumberland*

County Cricket Club – A History, umpire Arthur Stamper of Penrith stopped a cup-tie at Carlisle's Edenside due to the distraction caused by 'a low-flying jet aircraft giving a demonstration over the city.' As another plane goes overhead, one of several throughout the day and the odd helicopter too, you wonder what he'd have made of it here.

Further along, the offices spoken of are near the club shop and scoreboard, beneath which three wise men sit discussing past glories as the tins above tap like fingernails on a windowpane. Before them is a table laden with second-hand cricket books by authors long since dispatched to the great boundary in the sky, their impressions of a sport undergoing the latest revolutionary panic now dog-eared and forgotten within yellowing pages.

*****

For a spell before lunch, ugly rainclouds on the horizon look set to disrupt the game again before clearing off just as Norfolk leave the field, giving their opponents two clear sessions in which to chase down the total. The reason it is so damp, Chris says, is that the turf is mainly on sand and therefore any sudden deluge of water tends to sit on top, especially after such a prolonged dry spell.

Come the restart, there are no such fears, hospitality marquee throbbing as the bubbles and ale do their thing and the afternoon turns into a scorcher. 'Quite a generous declaration,' says one chap, filling in his scorecard. 'Not even four an over.' His friend politely agrees, though observes it will still take some getting on this surface. Outside the clubhouse, the non-batting Hertfordshire players are told that after a six-day trial Ben Stokes has escaped a charge of affray, after that nightclub incident in Bristol. Much wry chuckling ensues, but then attention switches to the middle where an opener hooks a short one for four and the chase is afoot. Indeed they go well until the first wicket falls with 45 on the board. Overheard in the gents, one retired-colonel type tells another: 'I gather this chap, Stokes, has been found not guilty. Don't like the look of the fellow. Covered in tattoos...'

Earlier, Norfolk CCC's chairman, Richard Wright, proffered a postprandial invitation to join him in his tent. It too bears a plaque with his name on it and, given the hierarchical layout, is positioned next to the president, in prime position on the halfway line were this a soccer stadium. Also squeezed in are Richard's substantive other half, Janet, and Dave Bowker, now in his tenth season as chairman of selectors. Richard, white-haired and amiable, has the air of a man who knows his way around a bottle of claret and would happily be your guide. He's been chairman for five years and must get on famously with Alan Wilson.

'I used to play a lot of cricket, but gave it up aged 55 and had a hiatus,' he says. 'Seven or eight years ago they asked me to come back, run the hospitality marquee and put me on the committee. A splendid chap who was chairman at the time, Graham Littlewood, moved down to Henley and I ended up taking the position. It's just a case of having taken a lot out of the game and now being able to put something back.' This annual festival is the epitome of another two-way benefit, the reviving of old friendships. 'Yes, it is more of an occasion than a cricket match. It goes into people's social diaries.'

For all its singularity, the Norfolk Festival of Cricket is not the oldest such event. That honour resides with Yorkshire's Scarborough Festival, which began five years before in 1876. But still, its presence in the calendar is for many a beacon of reassurance, especially since its first home at Lakenham is now a housing estate. According to Richard, it was formerly the sports club for Colman's, 'the mustard people,' who only this January announced that after 160 years they were moving production from their factory in Carrow. 'Its demise was inevitable,' he says, just as the players appeal loudly for a wicket that, once given, turns out to be Chris Brown's 502nd. 'Up until three or four years ago, we had to negotiate this, the middle fixture, and persuade someone we were due to play in early July to bring that forward and fill the gap. It always worked but then we had a bit of a dispute with somebody who didn't want to do that, so we went to the MCCA who formalised things. It's now in the fixture list that every ninth year someone has to play three games in a row for us.'

Dave joins the conversation. 'It used to be that there was only three counties on the cycle, but now each of the nine has to change once, every nine years.' It seems to be worth the sacrifice.

'Players love it because they are playing in front of a crowd,' says Richard, 'and our five-hundred-plus private members do too. With these little tents, you put your name on a list and when one becomes free it's yours. That dresses this side. The hospitality marquee doesn't make a lot of cash but it does make a lot of noise and is part of the atmosphere, one of the reasons people come here.' The bloke doing the man of the match award tonight is a local radio presenter, the suggestion it might be Alan Partridge laughed off. 'He has a tent and takes his holiday to coincide with the festival.'

Richard and Dave, like everyone here, are proud of the club's links with a tradition they see as being grounded, at least partly, in how Norfolk-produced talent is prioritised. 'Our committee has always foregrounded that and it gives us focus,' the chairman says. 'We have one pro' and everybody else plays locally. Some minor counties field four or five professionals and that's what they want, success. We want to watch local people. The only downside is we tend always to be playing for third, because if you are facing a couple of sides with three or four professionals you are pushing water uphill. But we wouldn't have it any other way.'

A helicopter clatters over and Richard looks to the skies. 'Ha! That is also part of the atmosphere ... the players don't stop though, they play through.'

'Not when the Red Arrows take off they don't,' says Dave.

'No, everybody watches the Red Arrows.'

The football ground at the far end is owned by Norwich City's community charity arm and known as the Nest, the name of the club's original ground before its move to Carrow Road. 'They coach disadvantaged kids, hold summer camps, that sort of thing. They bought it about eighteen months ago, re-laid all the pitches, and it's something Horsford CC is going to work very closely with as there's a reciprocity for parking spaces, hospitality and so on. Norfolk's arrangement here is that the club leases the ground on a 25-year basis, with a licence for us to use it for 18 days annually.'

And what of those apparently friendly relations with the county board, a partnership so fiendishly difficult to replicate elsewhere? 'Some counties are at odds with theirs, but we work very closely,' says Richard. 'Dave and I are both on the Norfolk committee and also directors of the cricket board. Chris is a director too. So while we are separate, a limited company and private members' club, we do have that link. At other counties, yes, it can be fractious. They are at war. Here, they basically run age group cricket to under-17s and then we go on from there, taking all the credit for what they have done.' The East Anglian Premier League, among the country's strongest, is also on the doorstep, servicing Norfolk, Cambridgeshire, Suffolk, Essex, Huntingdonshire and a bit of Hertfordshire too, with various feeder leagues below. 'Norfolk boys can be down in Frinton on Sea, Saffron Walden, Bury St Edmunds and places like that,' says Richard. 'Which is all very well until they're in a game with a half-seven finish and we have to play in Cumberland the next morning.'

Not that anyone at Norfolk is any less concerned about how things are going to pan out for the future of three-day cricket. 'For some reason, I don't think there's an entire understanding within the ECB of where the Minor Counties sit,' says Richard. 'We are very firmly entrenched in the pathway of player progression. I seriously believe three-day Minor Counties matches offer better competition than two-day 2nd XI county games. We provide a tolerable flow of young talent, which can't be said for a lot of first-class counties, who produce nothing and get a million a year for it. We get nowhere near that. There's the lack of recognition.'

A large part of that, though, must surely be down to how lacking in profile the Minor Counties Championship has come to be, presumably making events like the Norfolk Festival vital? 'We've not helped ourselves by calling it Minor Counties – that word, "minor". It's why we have tried to promote the Unicorns as a brand, which is still a bit of a non-thing... but, yes, our clubs also need to help themselves. We do get a lot of people here. Our PA system is excellent. Elsewhere, when people come out to bat you don't know who the hell they are. Little things like having a burger van that does chips. You get four or five hundred people here by lunch and they want chips! It's part of the experience.'

Welcome initiatives both, but hardly revolutionary. Is there a need for root and branch reinvention? The Minor Counties as part of the County Championship perhaps, beneath that competition but with no guaranteed pathway of promotion and/or relegation?

'I don't think we'd have that because no one could afford it,' says Richard. 'You saw what happened to Durham and all the money they had to spend. I don't really see movement between the minor and first-class counties because you are talking millions of pounds and our budget is £65,000 a year. That's difficult enough to manage.'

And anyway, he adds, in a sense they are already beneath the first-class game, aren't they? They don't need to be called, say, County Championship Division 3 (East) and County Championship Division 3 (West). 'I don't think you can have a division in the first-class game that you can't get into,' says Dave, anticipating some future rumpus.

Richard leans out of the tent and peers at the heavens, greying again. It can't make its mind up. 'Well, you are seeing us on a cloudy day and we normally attract a few more than this, don't we?'

'Yes,' says Dave. 'We'd double the crowd on a good day.'

Rain-affected or not, there is no doubt that the event comes over brilliantly, clearly well-organised. 'Yeah, but if you do it every year it becomes second nature – checklists and what have you.'

Dave interjects. 'I think it worth pointing out that it doesn't just happen though. A lot of work goes on behind the scenes. Planning starts for the next one in September, doesn't stop really. You have your meeting with the Minor Counties, then the fixtures come out and you can start your hospitality booking...'

'The actual layout of the ground, as you see it now, doesn't get going until a week before the festival starts,' says Richard. 'We have to pay rental on the big marquee, all these tents go up and then once its finished are taken down and it reverts to being a club ground.'

There are also, of course, games outside the Championship, such as that controversial T20 competition. If comments at David Armstrong's funeral were anything to go by, Norfolk folk aren't keen.

'We were totally against it, thought it a complete waste of time,' says Dave Bowker, with a chuckle. 'But now we're in the final so think it's the best thing since sliced bread. No, given the demographics of the membership, we've had fewer people for that. One hundred per cent honest? We didn't give it a lot of credence and concentrated on the 50-over knockout, compared to some other counties who had four or five warm-up games with former England internationals in their side like Sussex's Tymal Mills. He played against us, as did Somerset's Peter Trego. Yet somehow we've taken to it and won every game. We are looking forward to Wormsley in a fortnight.'

Again though, the taint of that word 'minor' brings problems. 'The MCCA felt they could get a significant sponsor who would pay for a website and still turn up £15,000 per club, but that has actually proved difficult. They had a demonstration T20 final at Wormsley last year and I don't think many attended that. It will be fascinating to see how this year's real one goes.'

So was a T20 competition a Minor Counties idea or the ECB's? 'The ECB wants more white ball cricket,' Richard says. 'We played the 50-over game as red ball, white kit; that's now gone white ball, coloured kit ... they want us to replicate the first-class game as much as possible. The Minor Counties sat down and thought: "Where can we be attacked? What can the ECB point to as no longer relevant?" We got our retaliation in first. Whatever we come out with at the end of this series of meetings between the ECB and MCCA, it will be better than had we not taken a degree of initiative early on.'

'And,' says Dave, 'just have a look at how many people playing in the Vitality Blast have come through the Minor Counties. Only last week, 59 players participating in first-class T20 had done that.'

On the field, Hertfordshire's third wicket falls before drinks, a contentious lbw from Yogi, last seen at Wisbech, umpiring today, temporarily halting the run chase at 99 for 3. For the hosts, the whiff of victory only ripens as tea is taken with Herts 111 for 5, a welcome further burst of early evening sunshine washing over the ground. With a target of 165 runs in the final session, an away victory seems too far-fetched and so it proves, despite a half-century in the middle order from Jamie Southgate. Instead, Horsford CC's own slow left-arm bowler, Ryan Findlay, enjoys his best Championship figures in four years and Norfolk win, with only four balls left, by 80 runs.

What was that Eric Cantona quote, about seagulls following trawlers? Had he played for Norwich he might have said tractors. Heading north, Norfolk, into which motorists are greeted by an image of Admiral Nelson, melds into Lincolnshire, whose welcome is their current tally of road deaths. At which point Mike Latham calls to say that Toby Bulcock has phoned Steve to ask if he'll be playing at Jesmond and was told 'no.' Asked when that would change, Steve is reported to have told him: 'Not while I'm at this club.'

*****

Ormskirk's Scott Lees remembers the good times. Having debuted for Cumberland at the end of 2012, he was destined to be part of the 2015 Minor Counties Championship-winning squad that included

Richard Gleeson, Gary Pratt and Toby Bulcock. Today Toby will play
for Ormskirk's opponents Leigh, in the Liverpool Comp.

'Hasn't he been ostracised by the Cumbria mafia?' Lees chortles
at a tidy venue surrounded by red-brick residential housing, as befits
an historic Lancashire market town. The club's own buildings aren't
so predictable. By the entrance, a mock Tudor clubhouse jostles with
a wooden structure that resembles an Alpine ski chalet. It holds the
changing rooms and has a raised viewing platform, only a pull shot
from Edge Hill University on the St Helens Road. He does a lot of
laughing, Scott Lees, a popular figure with everyone.

That ought to come as no surprise, given how as a kid he lived
about 400 yards away from Farnworth cricket ground, just up the
road from the original social club in Peter Kay's *Phoenix Nights*. His
step-dad, Ian, got him into the game until, aged 19, he moved on to
Southport in the Liverpool Comp, where he had five seasons, and
then in 2016 came to Ormskirk. Mainly a bowler, he can also bat,
scoring a century last year – against Leigh funnily enough – after
coming in at number ten. 'We still managed to lose the game.'

Lees got involved with Cumberland through a lad called Logan
Weston. 'He was an Australian trying to pursue a career in England
and was with me at Southport. He played a little for Worcestershire
seconds, Northants seconds as well, and then in the Minor Counties
for Cumberland. When they were a bowler short, Logan forwarded
my name to Mike Latham, who rang me up and explained things.
Without being rude, I knew nothing about Minor Counties cricket.'

All went well, although come the big year Lees hadn't actually
played in a Championship game until the final itself. 'I was studying
for my tax exams in Bolton, so didn't have time what with all the
Mondays and Tuesdays. One-day games were just on Sunday. Toby
rang me five days before, end of August, and asked me to play. I
asked what the team had been like all season and he said: "Oh forget
that, it doesn't matter. You did well for us last year and the year
before." To be honest, when it came to it, I didn't have the greatest
of games, but we absolutely rolled them. It was pretty one-sided.'

Yet the squad was still a work in progress. 'It was great. Mike's
work with the county and all his effort over the past three or four
seasons ... the group had togetherness. It wasn't just eleven or twelve
people getting together on a Saturday night – "all right, we've got a

three-day game coming up..." – these were people you actually called your mates. I'd known Toby through the Lancashire age groups ... under-15s to under-19s ... so five years at that point already. We were a well-knit side with incredible balance; very good top six, couple of all-rounders, four or five bowlers you could shove the ball to and they'd pick up wickets or keep it tight. Whatever the situation, we had a player in that side for it, which is what brought us success.'

Yet for all the promise, that high point was also the end of his Cumberland career. A flame that flickered for one brief moment, in the way that happens in sport and other collective enterprises, and went out before anyone so much as realised it had died.

For Scott himself, that again came down to having his time consumed by accountancy exams, although with those studies now all but done: 'I wouldn't say no, if they asked me again. I got on like a house on fire with Mike, because we both support Bolton Wanderers and know what cricket is all about. When he first handed me my cap, he said: "Cumberland will be the best days of your life." He wasn't far wrong.'

Ross Zelem is also here, awaiting play in front of the chalet with his Leigh teammates, not far from a plaque dedicated to Ormskirk's fallen in two world wars. Ahead of tomorrow's Cumberland match in Jesmond, he will drive up to Newcastle tonight, alone. Toby is still changing, but comes out to say hello. Last week, he took seven for 18 against Highfield, who were all out for 67. Beforehand, Toby told Ross he was sick of him only scoring 50s, not building to a century, and promised him a bottle of rum if he changed that. Ross, for his part, offered Toby a bottle of gin if he took six wickets. So Toby got his gin, but Ross also got his rum, finishing on exactly 100 not out in a total of 223 for 5 declared. When Leigh step beyond the picket fencing today, each wearing a Donald Trump-style red baseball cap, the first wicket falls quickly and Ormskirk – Cumberland chairman Neil Atkinson's first club – are already 9 for 1.

One youngster sits on a bench in front of the 'Tudor' pavilion, earphones in. 'Hello,' says a local, with a Scouse twang. 'Is your sister playing today?' He refers to a game on land around the back.

Yeah,' the lad replies, working one ear free. 'And me dad.'

This then is a family club and a well-organised, high-achieving one at that. They produce a printed matchday programme in which a columnist bylined 'Cover Point' details the influence of women on cricket, with a 19th-century contribution particularly in mind:

> Christina Willes and her brother John practised the game in the family garden. John preferred to bat, so Christina developed her own style of bowling. Underarm, the recognised method, her arm caught on her long skirt, causing the ball to deflect from the wicket. By lobbing the ball round-arm, her bowling was more accurate. Brother John, a keen cricketer, took note and tried the round-arm action himself. It was an improvement, so he introduced it in a match and was told it was illegal. He was not deterred and continued to bowl round-arm on every occasion, always no-balled.

Then, in 1822, while representing Kent against MCC at Lord's, John was no-balled once more, cycled off in a huff and swore never to play this stupid game again, though round-arm bowling was indeed written into the Laws six years later. 'Cover Point' reports that the headstone on his grave reads: 'I was first to introduce round-arm bowling to cricket,' his sister's contribution conveniently forgotten.

The match starts at noon to Liverpool Comp rules – essentially the batting side surviving if it can to 3.15pm and, after a half-hour break for tea, going on as long as they feel able, with bonus points worked out after 55 overs ... it doubtless makes sense to someone.

Whatever the mathematics, it continues to be about bat and ball and what follows is more than a little surprising, given the clubs' respective positions in the Premier League, with Ormskirk currently second and Leigh way behind points-wise in mid-table. The second wicket is claimed by Toby, lbw, and when Ross then takes a great catch in the slips, seen late, a third falls. Gary Knight – described by Scott as 'an exceptional wicket-keeper/batsman who will hopefully score runs for us today' – is another Cumberland link, in his case for one season only in 2016. The Longridge man does his best, but more wickets fall at the other end and Ormskirk are 59 for 5.

Last Sunday, they had the misfortune to lose to Nantwich in a National T20 regional final, denied progress to a televised ECB finals day at Derbyshire's Racecourse Ground. Tomorrow they meet Darwen in the semi-finals of the Lancashire Knockout Cup. A week tomorrow, Richmondshire are the opposition in the National Club Championship, so today they may be distracted. Plus they are missing a pair of key batsmen – Gavin Griffiths, on duty with Leicestershire, and Josh Bohannon, likewise away with Lancashire.

When Ryan Maddock's leg stump flies out of the ground it's 73 for 6. 'He had a game for Cumberland in 2016,' notes Mike, popping up on the boundary with Toby (the dog). 'Spent three days stood at third man in Staffordshire; face didn't fit with Gary.' Knight's innings culminates without further score, bowled by the splendidly monikered Finnegan Hulbert, one of his five victims on the day, the last via a superb catch at midwicket from Toby (the cricketer). The town of Ormskirk is said to be famous for gingerbread. The women here used to bake and then sell it in staging inns hereabouts, before taking advantage of a burgeoning new market with the arrival of railways in the nineteenth century. There may well be another lesson in there about adapting to change, but for now gingerbread serves dually as a metaphor for Ormskirk's crumbling batting order.

Skipper Nicky Caunce is in next. In 2012, during an emergency, he played for Cumberland at Workington. A former Lancashire 2nd XI player, he bowled well but didn't get to bat. Today, Toby bowling, he bags a duck. At number 11, Scott faces three balls without scoring and is not out as Ormskirk collapse for 84. At least Ross will get away to the North East in good time, although Steve Bulcock sounds a note of caution. 'It's important he stays in here or Leigh could go the same way,' he warns, while his son calls for a sweep of the wicket. Happily for Leigh, once play resumes, Zelem and Hulbert will do just that, foundation laid for an eight-wicket win by 2.45pm. Toby, though, is rattled, tossing the ball to an umpire before stomping off. And as the openers prepare, it's clear his thoughts are still at Furness.

'The game was coming to an interesting scenario and the captain absconded,' he says, during a chat that lasts precisely as long as Leigh's innings. 'Players are left in limbo, leaderless. No one has been directed to take over and in cricket, unlike many other sports, captaincy is vital. In football, it's pretty much a coin toss and the pick of an end. In rugby, the captain would get called over during an incident; that's as far as it goes. In cricket, the entirety of a fielding innings is directed and dictated by the captain. He sets the field, does the bowling changes, decides who goes where and when.'

As for prior knowledge: '...there were rumours Gary was going, though I didn't hear them. I'm convinced Eric Carter, Steven Sharp and the 12th man, Christopher Hodgson, were aware, though not sure how much detail Chris had. I'm fairly certain Eric and Steve knew where he was off to because, naturally, you would ask "why are you leaving", wouldn't you?'

Being the side's senior and longest serving member, to begin with Toby had assumed control. 'I thought the responsibility to do that fell on my shoulders. So I made a bowling change and was immediately over-ruled by Adam Syddall, a fellow senior player who had actually captained a game this season, so that was fine. What then ensued for the next hour and a half was two – no disrespect – weak batsmen putting on a century partnership, ninety minutes of torture. I bowled something like 37 overs in the innings, something daft, absolutely knackered. It was quite hot out there. I said to Adam: "Get me out on the boundary and let me simmer down." Obviously, it was a unique situation. The captain has absconded and no one knows what the hell is going on. Anyway, as I've reached the boundary, I've seen members of the committee and said to Mr Carter: "Where's the captain? Where's Gary?" He's directly ignored me, five feet away. So I repeated: "Eric. Where is Gary?" Ignored. Staring at his toes. I said, "Eric, listen to me. Where is Gary Pratt?" And finally he replied: "Well, he's not here, is he?"'

The chairman of cricket was next in line. 'I said: "Steve, where is Gary Pratt?" He said: "I don't know" and immediately jumped over the red-brick wall and scarpered up the stairs to the changing rooms. So I'm scratching my head, thinking where the bloody hell is he? At this point, I didn't know he'd left the ground. It was a totally bizarre scenario, firstly because the captain's fucked off. Secondly, nobody knew who were in charge and, third, people were unwilling to tell you where he was.'

So there Toby was on the boundary rope, allegedly ignored by the treasurer, while the chairman of cricket, so far as he was aware, tried frantically to find the skipper. 'Anyway, we comes off for tea at twenty past four and it looks like Gary has left at half past two, or something like that. Mike and Steve are stood on the stairs as we walk up and take me aside: "Listen Toby, we need you in this game. You've spent an hour and a half out now, had your rest. Come on, let's go and win this because it's looking like they will otherwise." We still needed four wickets and the team lacked inspiration, someone to bang the drum. Steve said: "I have absolutely no idea where Gary Pratt has gone. I've looked for him everywhere."'

According to Toby, that seemed okay at the time. 'So as we go back out, I give the lads a talking to. I spoke to Adam, the acting captain, and said: "Let me take the reins for this final session. I've a big part to play in this game. Let whether we win or lose be on my shoulders, because I'm happy with that responsibility." He said: "Yeah, absolutely fine, Bully. You take over from me, that's spot on."' So that's what he did. 'They've gone from looking like a raggedy bunch of tired players to a side with direction and drive. I don't want to take all the responsibility for that but, certainly, a stern word in the changing rooms and giving the lads a plan of action helped.'

And how about the rest of the side? What was their reaction? 'They were furious, absolutely furious. "Where's the captain? It's a fucking disgrace." I mean, what sort of example does it set to Marcus Stables, who goes out there and scores a 100 on debut and the captain fucks off on day three? How embarrassing. Or Tyler McGladdery making his second appearance, Sam Dutton on home turf ... I could go on. Can you imagine that happening in rugby or football? "Oh, I want to come off at half-time and go and play in another game for someone else..." It just wouldn't, would it?'

Victory in the bag and Hertfordshire hands shaken, Toby says he went up to the changing rooms and asked Steve Sharp and Mike Latham to come in, so they could be privy. 'I spoke wholeheartedly to the lads, thanked them for all they'd done, the effort they'd given, and said how we'd been severely let down. I then left them with these parting words: "What does playing Minor Counties cricket mean to you – because to me it means everything and I am absolutely disgusted," and left it at that. Steve Sharp then looked me in the eye and thanked me for my passion. Mike said something similar.'

The following Tuesday, though, Toby spoke to Gary at length. 'That was when it all came out. Gary and I are old friends. I'd played at Richmondshire with him and spent a lot more years under him at Cumberland as the main spinner. I ripped in. He's introverted, whereas I prefer things open. I explained how disgusted I was that he had kept me in the dark ... for someone like me, the way my mind works ... dark places are bad. I need blanket transparency from friends, otherwise it doesn't work. I felt he'd lied to me.'

Gary's position was that he hadn't, directly. 'But I felt like he had by hiding what he was up to. Had he made me privy I'd have said, well, who takes over in your stead? All these things would have been washed away. But keeping it from the lads caused a plethora of issues that could have been ironed out. No one I know has ever experienced anything like it and I know many people in cricket.'

Toby's unhappiness had been in evidence before the skipper's mistimed exit, however. There was his expenses-related ribbing of Eric, a situation unlikely to have arisen in 2015 when, according to Toby and Mike, every brother in the band received exactly the same. Though the skipper scarpering was hardly likely to lift his mood.

'I asked Gary directly: "Who did you tell?" Who were these relevant parties mentioned in his email to committee members? He said Eric Carter and Steve Sharp. I said: "Not any players? Don't they need to know the captain will be fucking off?" He said: "Well, I'd done everything I needed to in the game." Suddenly, things like young Marcus being unexpectedly moved up the order begin to look insidious, don't they? It's all become awful.'

In light of that, Toby made his call for an emergency committee meeting. 'Not an emergency general meeting, because that requires twenty-one days and you've to invite every committee member ... it needed sorting before Bedfordshire. On Wednesday, I managed to get hold of Rob Cairns, who arranged it for Stonecross Manor, seven o'clock, Friday. I finished work at half-four, half an hour early, did the M6 and when I got there four other people had turned up – Alan Wilson, president; Neil Atkinson, chairman; Rob Cairns, secretary; Steve Sharp, chairman of cricket. Not enough for a committee meeting, so it was instead termed a meeting of committee members, immediately watering it down.' As a result, everything said went un-minuted. 'In hindsight, I highly regret not stepping out of the room there and then, and walking.'

That, though, didn't happen. 'I said what I would have said at a committee meeting. I outlined what had gone on and said it had come to my attention that Mr Sharp knew [Gary had left], looked me in the eye and said he hadn't. He was so evasive that I asked him to stop avoiding my questions and to show humility and compassion towards the lads. I added that I felt his position was untenable due to lack of transparency. I'm on the committee too. We need to know what's going on, sing off the same hymnsheet and pull in the same direction. I said: "What you are doing is brushing things under the carpet. What does that do but breed problems down the line?"'

Before long, word was going around that Toby had been given his meeting and had plenty to say. 'Why would I call for a meeting and not have plenty to say? Fucking right I had plenty to say.'

Two days later, Steve asked if he'd be interested in playing at Flitwick. 'I spoke to him then about the hour-and-half after tea when Gary left, how it had all gone to cock very quickly, and realised that if someone was to lead it had to be me. So I said, I would be available, but with the condition I was captain. "Nobody is more experienced in playing for Cumberland than myself, no one knows the lads better than I do." He said: "Right, okay, leave that with me. Give me five minutes and I'll get back to you." He did so. "Sorry, Toby. Ringing to let you know you won't be captain. I won't be given an ultimatum."'

To Toby this sounded like a dictatorship: '...which is something I also queried at the Friday meeting. There is one man selecting the team, one man picking everything. Whatever happened to selection committees? Every other club I've been at has a selection committee. I told him: "What you need is an odd number, plural. Whether it's the captain, chairman of cricket or A.N. Other, vice-captain perhaps, you need disagreement or it doesn't work." The conversation got politically heated and I heard nothing for a while.'

Bedfordshire came and went. 'I wasn't there, so only know what Ross told me about it. It seems Liam Watkinson did well and I'd like it to be noted that I am pleased about that. Steve Sharp suggested I have bad blood about him playing for Cumberland, but I have absolutely nothing against Liam at all. He was my age group at Lancs and I was his captain throughout. No disrespect to him, but he was never quite there. A fringe player you might say, in and out of the team. But he's a nice guy and a good cricketer, as his century proved. There is no chip on my shoulder.' Toby says he is concerned that bits of his past are being dug up to imply that he is out of order.

'Steve also mentioned that various people were unhappy with my behaviour at Furness. "Unhappy with my behaviour?" I said. "You are aware that I was on the fucking field? What about the captain? What about his behaviour that is not being punished? But you are willing to punish me by leaving me out of the side." We're at Jesmond tomorrow, a big game at a top venue; good night out in Newcastle for the lads. I always look forward to Jesmond. But that's how it was and I've thrown the towel in with it, under the impression I will never be picked again.' Until last Tuesday when, simmering down a bit, he decided to reach out again.

'First time, no answer. Second time, no answer. Texted. "Ring me when you can Steve, thanks." So he calls back at 11.00pm, inappropriate because he knows I'm up at six for work. "Just out of interest, I'm wondering why I haven't been picked." He said: "It's nothing to do with your ability, Toby. Gary and I spoke when we put the side together and you've not been selected." "Am I likely to be selected for the remainder of the season?" "At this stage, no." "Any reason as to why?" "Yeah, because I'm chairman of cricket." I told him I considered it a great honour to play for Cumberland and asked what it would take to regain my place. "Me not being involved."

And it is there where the tale suddenly takes a rather bizarre turn. 'All of this, I feel, is bred of bad blood with Mr Sharp's brother, Ian, who once had a run-in with a certain Mr Latham.'

Like older brother Steve, Ian Sharp played for Millom. In fact he captained them and very successfully too, though he was never quite good enough to represent Cumberland. A decent club batsman, Ian was somewhat in the shadow of Steve, as anyone would be given how many good judges have his brother pegged as the most talented player ever to come out of Cumberland. Playing days over, Ian then became cricket manager at Barrow, before co-opted onto the county board, circa 2006, as team manager. Paths crossed in 2010 when Mike, a player agent and back then vice-chairman of the Northern Premier League, engineered a Cumberland debut for Blackpool's Richard Gleeson against Suffolk at Sedbergh, a match in which Gleeson struggled to make an impression. That led Gary Pratt to tell Mike: 'Don't bring me any more players,' a future leg-pull if ever there was one. Anyway, Ian got Mike involved with the Cumberland CCC committee, doubtless considering him a useful and influential acquisition. It wasn't long, however, before the pair fell out.

To impartial ears, the incident as related by Mike seems petty, however irritating it must have been at the time. When a game in

Cambridgeshire was rained off early on the third morning in July 2012, Ian Sharp nipped off to Newmarket to indulge his interest in horse racing. As team manager, of course, he had received travel expenses and given a player, Chris Miller, a lift down. Mike, by then a club official and an away game regular, was left to drive Miller home, some one hundred and thirty miles out of his way. After which, 'relations were strained.' Ian became secretary and was vice-chairman too for a while, while Mike, with huge success, became chairman of cricket. Grudges though have been borne ever since.

All of which makes Toby's 'water under the bridge' speech at Crooklands in March, when the prospect of Ian's return was mooted, even odder. 'That was a bit of politicking,' he says now. 'I knew he'd be out-voted due to Eric threatening to walk away.' According to Toby, this latest fuss, in which he and Mike, his agent, have found themselves firmly on the outer is, Toby says: '...an open door for Ian Sharp to come back and play happy families. All very insular and in pursuit of keeping it within their clique – and that's fine, if they want to do that. They can be world famous in Millom.'

There is zero evidence for this conclusion, of course, although it does typify the sort of destructive mistrust that can lay waste to any sporting organisation, large or small, in Cumbria as elsewhere.

Where does Toby go now? 'I started playing for Cumberland in 2011, one game. In 2012, we won the one-day comp with some fantastic lads. Really tight knit, great social side, people you would take to war with you. Weak of heart, weak of mind had no place there. What then ensued over four years – last year it began to go downhill – was something special. You couldn't wait to finish cricket with your mates on Saturday to go play with your other mates on Sunday. You got three days cricket and three nights out ... eight times if you were lucky ... which makes at least twelve nights out a year all over the country throughout the summer. It's not just about that, but it's a big factor – a happy team is a good team, isn't it?'

Nothing though lasts forever. 'People got a bit over-zealous and fell out of the fold, went to university, moved to London, got a job as a banker, a first-class gig ... for a plethora of reasons moved on. Minor Counties cricket isn't lucrative, the money's not there, so it makes sense. For me, it has served its purpose, given me all it can. I've taken 300 wickets in no time ... best one-day figures ... best three-day ... 8 for 8 ... 8 for 14 or something ... fastest to 100 wickets ... 200 ... 300 ... so I'm really happy with that, proud of it. But love has died this year. After the first day at Netherfield, I said to Gemma: "It's not the same. We don't have the heart. There's not eleven lads I'd take to war with me."

Away from the game, he was promoted at work this week. 'I'm 27 now, so I'll play on Saturdays and get professional gigs in club cricket for the next ten years. By which time I would like to be fully trained as an accountant and working towards something special.'

Is there a chance of playing Minor Counties cricket with some other side? Assuming the competition survives, that is. 'Watch this space. If the parameters and environment are right, there are two counties I'd consider.' The grapevine suggests Cambridgeshire with Yogi or Staffordshire with Phil Oliver, yet for all the bravado he can't keep his thoughts from returning to Gary who, despite his repeated efforts to make contact, remains so far unresponsive.

'His last words to me were that he didn't want this to affect our friendship. We were very close for a long number of years, but Gary now won't return my calls. At this point I'm fearing he's been told and believed more lies. He'd rather shun me than speak to me, along with the rest of a committee that won't stand up for what's right.'

*****

A day later, while Cumberland wait to face Northumberland an hour up the road, Richmondshire's ridiculously busy schedule is clearer. At Marton CC, they are to play in a Kerridge Cup final replay. Last Sunday's first go at settling the most famous knockout competition in North East cricket was a washout, but not before Middlesbrough were removed for 166, Gary Pratt taking a remarkable six for 26.

Those statistics however were expunged, both left to try again; hence the Cumberland skipper's unavailability after all. Similarly, Sam Wood, Matty Cowling, Bob Carr and Mattie McKiernan – picked at Derbyshire last Friday in a T20 match also rain-abandoned – remain out of reach. And while Mattie's six-week contract is now done, he and the rest of the quintet will be needed by Richmondshire next week in their ECB National Club Championship quarter-final tie with Ormskirk, Scott Lees and all, a fixture they'll win by 66 runs.

That will put them en route to victory in the final over Stanmore CC of Middlesex in September, a most impressive piece of silverware.

The Kerridge Cup isn't quite so distinguished or geographically diverse, but it is well worth winning. Richmondshire intend to do just that, though having been dismissed for 87 by Seaton Carew last week and fallen to third in the North Yorkshire and South Durham table, they can't take anything for granted. In fact, third is where they will stay, trailing eventual champions Barnard Castle and runners-up Great Ayton. With league hopes slipping away, the opportunity for a hat-trick of cups is all the more alluring. Seaton Carew are also the opponents in a game after the Ormskirk cup tie, the final of the now infamous Premier 15s that Gary left for, which starts at 5.45pm the same day. That will require a four o'clock finish to game one and immediate fifty-two-minute drive to Redcar. Some may see that as the price of success, others that shoehorning supposedly prestigious events in such a way is chaotic and crazy. It's certainly easy to understand how Gary would have felt pressured to get out of Furness in a hurry. Maybe it had even been worthwhile. Richmondshire are destined to collect the Premier 15s trophy too, by seven wickets.

Marton-in-Cleveland, a suburb to the south of Middlesbrough, has been wet, rainy and grey this Sunday morning, although the Met Office predicts it will be brighter later. Already, a strong breeze is persuading the clouds to tease patches of blue. Up on Tyneside, dampness overnight means play is yet to get underway, but down here the game will commence at 1.30pm as planned.

Tucked off Stokesley Road behind the Rudds Arms pub, entry costs £2 paid to one of a pair of gatemen, brick pavilion to the left fronted by a viewing area behind white picket fencing. To the right, the proximity of a social club lends a picturesque ground the feel of an enclosure, an impression heightened by the constant drone of the traffic flowing beyond a line of trees along the scoreboard end. The place is in its own little bubble, the ideal venue for a local final.

Last week's attempt had been well-populated, thanks in part at least to the fine Sunday lunch served beforehand. As is the way of replays, with a 'big day' vibe gone the turnout now is merely decent, as Cumberland's Carr and Pratt walk out to bat in blue and yellow tracksuits, having lost the toss. Middlesbrough, in black, ensure a slow start, the score after five overs 3 for 0, one of those runs a leg bye. They are helped in their endeavour by a pitch that is flat, green and slow. Carr survives an appeal for a catch at slip as he attempts a few shots. A fielder kicks a cap in the air, his high-fives and backslaps brought to a halt. The Beatles drift from an open dressing room window – *I think I'm gonna be sad, I think it's today* – before Bob does fall, caught and bowled, and it's 26 for 1. Midway through a 40-over tie Richmondshire have lost no more wickets but only added 52 runs, giving little warmth or distraction on a day when a jumper would be welcome. Enthusiastic fielding also does its bit to deny the spectacle before Gary – with a number 17 rather than his surname on his back – drives one down the throat of long-on, out for 24.

Richmondshire's Mike Layfield and Mattie – in at four – battle their way to a century, but it isn't long before Layfield, trying to get on with it, is caught in the deep just as spots of rain begin to fleck. The innings has been a crawl but ends in a flurry, as first McKiernan goes, clean bowled, and then the rest of his teammates tumble, all out for 146 with only Cowling, 15, in long enough for double figures.

'This pitch is horrible,' says Bob Carr, rehearsing his bowling action and insisting that 146 ought to be more than enough. Having moved to Richmond from Oxford as a 14-year-old and spent all his cricketing career here thereafter, at the end of the summer intends to take up a job in sports betting. 'I'm going to be the hero,' he winks.

Awaiting his call to the crease, Mattie had suggested similar. 'If we get 150 or 160 it'll be a good score on this pitch. The ball's spitting, keeping low. Four an over might be challenging.' If he is disappointed at how his spell at Derbyshire went, he isn't about to let it get him down. Ambitious, he's been on the county 2nd XI circuit for a while. Indeed a big part of his motivation in joining Richmondshire with Gary was to get under the nose of Durham, simultaneously travelling down to Hampshire in search of further opportunity.

'It's a complicated situation,' says a lad who has spent every year in the club game bar this at hometown Leigh, with whom he began as a six-year-old in the under-11s. 'My contract with Derbyshire has expired and they have just begun the process of appointing a new head of cricket. Once he's in place, I'll play it by ear and hopefully something will come from that.'

To begin with Mattie was primarily a medium pace bowler, before evolving into the leg-spinner he is now. As the years passed, his batting improved to the extent he can now fairly be viewed as a talented all-rounder, helped no end by the coaching in Lancashire sides from under-9s to the academy and 2nd XI. He has also twice wintered in Tasmania at Hobart Sandy Bay, intent all the while on improving his skill set, especially with the bat. His distinctive bowling style however is what most swiftly takes the eye.

'Yeah, I've got a slow approach,' he grins, 'quite low, arms and legs all over the place. It's just how you develop over the years, trying to find what works. I found the traditional leg-spinner's action, side on, fully rotated, didn't do it for me. Accuracy is one of my biggest strengths and that action helps.' One of his junior coaches said he reminded him of Jonny Wilkinson, steadying for goal.

Still, for all the advances he has made – and continues to make – this business with Derbyshire must have been frustrating, not least because it's severly restricted his Cumberland appearances this year, a set-up for which he has great fondness. 'Yeah, although it has also been understandable in that we had four international class bowlers in Lockie Ferguson, Wahab Riaz, Ravi Rampaul and Hardus Viljoen, so it was obviously hard to get a start with that line-up. Alex Hughes, the fifth bowler, has also had a good campaign and is the leading wicket-taker. Hopefully, I'll get another crack at it somewhere next year, if not at Derbyshire then we'll just see what the future holds.'

Last season, he goes on, '...was a bit of a weird one. I started it in Durham's second team and was going well until I got injured and missed two months' bowling. I played with Leigh and Cumberland as a batter only. By the time I was fit, Durham's contracted spinners were in their second team, so there was no room for me and I went to play for Leicestershire's seconds.' He did well, but due to squad sizes nothing more evolved until Leicestershire had a free week and Lancashire needed a spinner. 'I played in the second team final for them against Hampshire on the Isle of Wight. From that, Mason Crane moving towards the England set-up, their coach said come and finish the season with us. I played the last two games – or would have if the second hadn't been rained off! Against Glamorgan I got a hundred with the bat. I didn't bowl much as it was rain-affected.'

That's why, following three months in Australia, his pre-season this time was again focussed on the English south coast, where he at least played in a few more 2nd XI games. 'Unfortunately it didn't work out,' he says, but then came the opportunity at Derbyshire. Clearly, he's not averse to a spot of travelling, be it from Leigh to Hampshire, back to Leigh, over to Richmondshire, up to Cumbria or Derby or wherever else his determination to succeed might take him. It must be exhausting. 'Yeah, it can be. I was lucky enough to be given a car by Richmondshire, which is brilliant of them. The first three weeks, I did three thousand miles. It was just something I had to do. I'd go down on a Sunday afternoon, train Monday to Thursday night and come back. Did that for four or five months. I still live in Golborne, ten minutes from Leigh. Still travel a fair bit too, couple of hours to Derby, two hours to Richmond. It's all good fun.'

Tea ends and the Middlesbrough openers stake their claim just as rain begins to fall with greater regularity and vigour. Soon there are squalls, and the odd roll of thunder. Just four more overs are possible, the incomers amassing 10 runs and losing one wicket – a terrific catch by Mattie – before this 2018 Kerridge Cup final replay is also thwarted. They will have a third go on Sunday 9 September, by which time Cumberland's season will be over. Top scorers will be McKiernan and Cowling – 87 and 71 not out, respectively – in yet another cup-winning Richmondshire performance.

*****

Cumberland are unable to take the field until 3.30pm, but once they do so, having won the toss, swift progress is made. Northumberland are 76 for 4 at tea, Marcus Stables luring one batsman into a looping shot caught by Slacky at deep gulley, his debut county wicket. Syds, Liam Watkinson and Slacky himself take the other three, helped by catches from Ross Zelem, Ben Howarth and Jacques du Toit. Play is to be extended until 7.30pm, light permitting.

After a wet morning, the day here has dried up nicely. Seagulls whirl, finding rich pickings amid the cafés, bars and chic boutiques that line the streets of a well-to-do suburb north of the Tyne bridge. The cricket ground, on Osborne Avenue, is in a residential area with walls and white fencing to three sides and a white pavilion on entry, on which flags fly and flowers hang in baskets strung adjacent. Once this was a moneyed club, architectural morsels everywhere, like the remains of terracing in the upper-right-hand corner, hinting at past grandeur and popularity. Beyond that, tall trees and apartment-style buildings cast more shade, while the obligatory cemetery lurks here behind a wall that runs down from a two-storey scorebox opposite, in which Geoff Minshaw currently resides. Back at the pavilion end, another terrace has survived. Once upon a time it would have been heaving with people, as evidenced by the cover of *Northumberland – A History of County Cricket*, written and published in 1989 by one Harry Jude. In his foreword, the then club chairman, RW Smithson, hopes the book: '...will show yet again that in those parts of the country which are geographically away from the mainstream of the game, its followers are no less devoted and its roots no less strong,' having proposed that to most cricket lovers: '...the best known fact about Northumberland cricket is that alone among Minor Counties it has its own county ground.' This of course wasn't strictly true as, by then, Norfolk had been at Lakenham for more than one hundred and ten years, but Northumberland's bond with what was once the Constabulary Ground is, if not quite umbilical, certainly a defining feature. After formation in 1895 and entry to the Minor Counties Championship a year later (a competition they are still to win), the club's first fixture here was against Durham in June 1897. Almost immediately, Jude writes, the committee set about structural changes. 'One of the most far-reaching was the extension on the north side where, by kind permission of the City Corporation, the fence was moved back to the kerbstone on Osborne Avenue, thus extending the ground by approximately six feet.' Making use of the additional width, a single terrace some three feet above the ground was constructed for the benefit of spectators. 'Their wellbeing received further consideration with the construction of a double terrace on the east side, adjacent to the pavilion, which was a replica of a Swiss chalet built for the Queen Victoria Jubilee Exhibition on the Town Moor in 1887...' With a press box, telegraph boards, public refreshment bar and membership of four hundred, the future appeared to be set fair. And thus for many years was it so.

To date, Osborne Avenue has hosted some five hundred Minor Counties Championship matches, plus several MCCA Trophy ties. In 1965, what would now be the Unicorns representative side played a first-class match here against South Africa, a 243-run defeat. In 1974, Pakistan came to call, winning by five wickets. When minor counties featured in first-class one-day competition, Northumberland staged twenty games here, the last against Middlesex in 2005. But to compound the disappointment of losing such fixtures, the county was by then in financial strife, its days at the trustee-owned ground apparently numbered. Happily, some £30,000 was raised via a local campaign supported by such sporting luminaries as its patron Steve Harmison, Bobby Robson and Dennis Lillee. In the wash-up, the lease to the ground was taken over by Newcastle's Royal Grammar School, since when the place has been rented by Jacques du Toit's Newcastle CC, with Northumberland using what is still their official base on a more *ad hoc* basis.

Another benefit of the fund-raising was that personal stories were unearthed; memories of yesteryear intended to prove the venue special. The Newcastle club's website tells of how one unnamed lady in her 90s: '...remembered that the wicket roller used to be pulled by large horses wearing rubber boots over their hooves.' Ashes have been scattered on the site. In the here and now, Gilbert has indeed made the trip with his wife, John Patterson being back from holiday. Eric chats with a chap who has been to watch Newcastle Thunder beat Oldham in the rugby league – 'Good result, that...' – while Rob and Lesley sit next to Neil, as ever in club shirt and tie, before the pavilion. Assorted player family members are also here and there.

After tea a wicket falls almost immediately, caught behind off Slacky for 24, and it's 83 for 5. As the clock turns six, the scorebox numbers glow. 'He'll bring them off,' says Gilbert, 'if we keep bowling pace.' The words are no sooner out of his mouth than Slacky produces a sixth wicket, caught and bowled. He deserves a slice of good fortune, his car having burst a tyre on arrival at the ground.

Given recent shenanigans the make-up of the side was prone to speculation, but now settled it reads: Zelem, Sempill, McGladdery, Slack, Stables, du Toit, Watkinson, Boyne, Howarth, Hodgson and Syddall. One notable absentee – Bulcock, Pratt and Richmondshire boys apart – is Sam Dutton. 'He couldn't get time off work,' says Neil. Chris Hodgson's brother Matthew is 12th man, his duties to be taken over tomorrow by Gary. Of Steve there is no sign.

The visitors are made to work harder for their seventh wicket, the hosts reaching 123 before it falls, c. Boyne, b. Liam Watkinson. As the clock strikes seven though, Northumberland's middle-order batsman, Alex Simpson, completes a half-century and his side's 150 comes up six minutes later. The way he and newcomer Rob Peyton are knocking the ball around, light no longer seems to be an issue and, despite the late start, 50 overs are got through.

The partnership is broken the following morning; ten overs in, Peyton, caught Syds, Slacky's fourth and final victim of the innings. Jacques then strikes with a caught and bowled, but Northumberland enjoy a late flourish. The last tail-ender comes in with Simpson in his 90s, two balls left in the over. The newcomer blocks both, his mate at the running end taking the strike with relief and completing his maiden Minor Counties century with a six off Chris Hodgson. After which Simpson goes on a boundary rampage, Liam ending an individual contribution of 121 with a catch in the deep, 258 all out.

With yesterday's loss of playing time in mind, for Cumberland it's another innings that got away. Ross and Sempy will need to show resolve if a draw is to be achieved. Watched by fifty or so spectators, club officials and relatives mostly, they take that to extremes. As their teammates look on from the pavilion upper deck, the pair manage two runs in the first five overs. Absolutely nothing is happening.

Given the hemmed in nature of the venue, anyone attempting a lap at Osborne Avenue is met with an obstacle course, boundary jutting against walls and areas of architectural debris. Easier to stay put. But when the 'action' slows to such an extent, the urge to stroll is irresistible. At such times, the charge of boredom levelled at long-form cricket is understandable. As the seconds tick tick tick by, the graveyard behind prompts thoughts of wasted time ... all the stuff the observer might be doing at the start of another working week, matters useful and productive. And what does it say about these fixtures that they appeal most to those for whom time is in shortest supply, human brevity front and centre? Everyone likes to relax now and then, recharge the batteries and all that. But three-day cricket as a way of life, with no hiding place from the essential pointlessness of day-to-day existence? It's easy to imagine why cricket has so often impacted mental health darkly.

Three more overs pass with not a single run added, gee-ups and half-hearted clapping – 'C'mon, Sean...' – an effort to stay awake until Sempy livens it up by clipping an easy catch to square leg, out for a duck after facing 28 balls. With Tyler in the middle, Ross belts an immediate four, otherwise tedium endures. 'Even the bar is closed,' sighs a weary John Patterson, trudging by.

Gary Pratt is indeed on 12th man duty today, here with partner Leanne. Come Northumberland's second innings, will there be any Ricky Ponting-style run-outs to look forward to? He smiles and agrees to a chat on the ancient terrace banking at some stage. Chairman Neil isn't here, work calls, though Mike has made the trip without his canine chum, the venue hardly dog friendly.

Scoring remains sedentary before a leg bye off Tyler makes it 12 for 1, Ross having pitched in the rest alone. Lunch however is on its way and maybe it's that which prompts a burst of runs that guide Cumberland past the half-century. Food and chat are welcome after such a morning, although on the main table there are complaints – from both clubs – that the wine is only eight per cent proof and cost just £3 a bottle. No matter, as the second session commences, Ross and Tyler finally up the ante, motoring on to 113 for 1 by drinks – brought on to the field by Gary – both batsmen having registered 50s, in Tyler's case his first for the county. Play is scheduled to go on until 7.30pm and, upon resumption, the pair maintain their charge, two deft McGladdery fours taking the score to 158, exactly 100 runs behind, before his removal, lbw, for 74. A trio of seagulls on a chimney pot squawk in sympathy.

As the skies have dulled so the cricket has brightened. Ross is also out lbw, for 86, attempting a sweep at the end of what had evolved into a commanding stint and it's 187 for 3. Three runs later, it's tea, but not before fifth-man-in Marcus is bowled for a duck. Still, with Slacky and Jacques there on the restart further progress is made before a flurry of rain, not forecast, causes the umpires to up-sticks, presumably temporarily given how the storm just as swiftly abates with Cumberland 219 for 4. After an inspection, all looks fair for a 7.00pm restart and one last half-hour of action, until another brief downpour means the wicket is covered. At 6.45pm, those covers are removed but the light is murky and ground all but deserted, surely enough is enough? Not a bit of it. Moments later the umpires are out again, trailing fielders somewhat lacking in enthusiasm. 'Have you got your miner's lamp, bonny lad?' quips one local.

Seeking to force the issue, the hosts put a fast bowler on and the officials, upon conferring, duly offer Jacques and Slacky the light.

They decline, the South African hitting a four and then a six; he is certainly seeing it. The latter shot soars as far as the apartments at the western end, so more time is lost while they look for the ball. Bad light does stop play some 15 minutes early, when Cumberland are trailing, but now only just, on 235 for 4. Rob and Lesley Cairns, seated next to an old friend, are among a coterie that has hung around gallantly to applaud the teams off.

'Don't clap too hard,' Lesley says. 'You'll wake Arthur.'

*****

Gary Pratt has presence. Not charisma exactly, he is too reserved for that, although as companionable as anyone with a pint in hand.

Presence, yes. Even when he isn't around.

This Cumberland totem on and off the field since 2010 is again taking a day off work simply to watch the side and carry out 12th man duties, gratis. Pinning him down hasn't been so easy. When a game begins there is no wresting his attention from it and he emits a vibe of not being much given to introspection anyway. On recent events he seems bristly, however will now agree to a more general chat. So it is that as those on the field meander towards inevitable stalemate, he takes a seat amidst that crumbling section of Victorian terracing packed nowadays only with ghosts.

His career could have hardly begun with greater flash, bang and wallop. The spotlight could not have been brighter. Yet what of today? Here, in an all but empty ground, noticed by few on a damp and dreary day in Newcastle? There was a time when such a drop in fortunes would have rankled with a lad who by his own admission and that of those around him let fame go to his head. Frankly, he became a bit of a pain in the arse. Yet now he seems largely at peace with all that and has in many respects matured. The game itself is the thing, he has come to realise. The pleasure is in the doing and the watching. But then it really always has been, deep down.

'I didn't have much choice,' says a now 36-year-old who made his Championship debut in 2007 and has since played 120 games for Cumberland and counting, including Trophy and T20. 'My dad played cricket every weekend for Crook Town in Durham and my mum went to watch, it was a family day out.' Pratt Jr would go on to play for Crook too, though that was in Northern League football – another story. His cricket trajectory took flight at Durham City. 'My dad moved there in the later stages of his career. I was in the under-12s or under-13s, not there long.' Such was his precocity of talent that, at 14, he followed two older brothers into senior cricket with the Durham CCC Academy: '...which is what it was there for. My dad and another coach used to cover South Durham and they put players forward to advance.' As so often, parental encouragement and influence had secured a foot in the door. Once through it, only application and talent could do the rest. He batted ... he bowled ... the gift for captaincy emerged much later.

'I'd captained junior sides, but on the academy we were always under Geoff Cook; he just let the lads play. I didn't know I could do the job until Cumberland. They got me started with captaincy. In fact, it was only when I started with them that I began thinking about the game at all.' So handy a player was Gary that he became a regular England under-19s choice, sharing a dressing room with Monty Panesar and Ian Bell at the U19 World Cup in Sri Lanka. He signed professional forms at Durham soon after.

Following his 100th appearance for Cumberland in 2016, Pratt was interviewed by Nick Friend of Durham University's well-known student paper *Palatinate*. He was asked about the Ricky Ponting run-out, of course, but the piece also paints a picture of his route in and out of the first-class county game with Durham who, in a relatively short stint at that level since 1992, have developed some of England's fiercest modern competitors... Ben Stokes, Mark Wood, Paul Collingwood, Steve Harmison. In Gary Pratt, they had another maybe, although history records him as one who got away.

'We were a young side and didn't have any experienced players,' he tells *Palatinate* of his days on the playing staff, an era when it 'was not always plain sailing.' Twice relegated to Division Two during his spell, Durham finished eighteenth out of eighteen after a horrendous 2004 campaign, a year full of woe and frustration. 'Paul Collingwood was missing all the time, either through injury or being away with England. Overseas players kept on coming over and getting injured, we never had a stable side.' Harmison, also on national duty, missed the entire season. And yet Gary, having scored over 1,000 runs the previous year, was in an out of the team. New recruit Brad Hodge broke a thumb in the nets before game one. Nathan Astle, Martin Love and David Boon were largely past it and Shoaib Akhtar, although talented, was a law unto himself. At this distance it's easy to diagnose a lack of joined-up thinking, but a general mood of disorganisation and clarity cost young Gary dear.

Come 2008, a side made up of many of the same formerly youthful and now more experienced players, who four years before managed two wins in sixteen, would bag the first of two consecutive County Championships, although by then this teammate they had played with though the age groups had long since left the scene.

Given chance, he feels he too would have improved with age. 'The team that won the County Championship was basically all the same blokes, but at the right age for winning titles – around 27 years old.' Sitting here, he expands on that, recalling his first-class county debut, against Lancashire. 'It was at Old Trafford. They had a decent side with the likes of Atherton and Fairbrother, so a bit daunting for a young lad. You are on a Test ground against Test quality players and thinking: "Jesus Christ, it's a big step this..." but excited too.' Nor did he do particularly well. 'It was a let-down. I only got 11 and 17, something like that, but looking back you are nowhere near as good then as you are now ... which is even more disappointing. Even when I finished at Durham I still didn't know what to do really, as a batter. You don't know your own game until you are about 27 or 28 years old. I'm a much better player now than I was then.'

A big regret is that just as he was leaving, Durham brought in 'Mr Cricket', the Australian batsman and later coach, Mike Hussey. 'I didn't get the chance to play with him. From a Durham point of view, it would have been a beneficial thing to do, let me do that for a season as a left-handed opening batsman and learn a few things.' And his release in 2006 was all the more annoying because at the end of his impressive 2003 campaign Nottinghamshire had tried to lure him away. 'You just think: "Do I really want to rock the boat when I've had such a good year and everything is sweet and nice?" You are in your comfort zone and think everything is going to carry on in the same way. That's another regret, not going to Trent Bridge. If someone wants you, it counts for a lot.'

Especially when, a season later, he then had a poor run of form and was told to go away and get runs in the second team. 'I did that but still didn't get picked. You start to wonder: "What's going on?" You do everything they ask for, but it isn't enough. When they got rid of me, they just said they were going to give youngsters a go. I was, like, 23, and as I say, you don't really come into your own until you are 26, 27 or even later. Look at Mark Ramprakash. He must have been about 35 by the time he produced runs for England.'

The perceived injustice came as a shock and '...took quite a while to sink in.' It still rankles, by the look of it, especially as the incident that made his name, that Ricky Ponting run-out, may just have had a part to play in his release. To hear why is to gain insight as to the reasons for Gary's ambivalent attitude.

'In the 132 years that England and Australia have fought for the Ashes, some of cricket's most illustrious faces have competed for sport's smallest trophy,' writes Nick Friend, in the *Palatinate*, 'their names synonymous with this most famous of Test series. Bradman, Grace, Botham, Ponting, Flintoff, McGrath, Pietersen, Gower – cricketing royalty one and all. Yet among the unforgettable memories – Warne's ball of the century, the Edgbaston Test, Panesar and Anderson's heroic last stand, one sticks out for its sheer fairy-tale.'

'It's something that nobody can take from me,' Pratt straight-bats back. 'It's something people will always associate me with. You get one chance in probably the biggest game in England's history. I picked it up cleanly, threw it and the ball just hit the stumps ... to be part of that is pretty special.' There was a real bond too. 'When you were on the field, you were there as part of the eleven, not 12th man. Thankfully, I was able to contribute.'

In fact, he'd done the job since 2003 when, aged 21, he debuted with the drinks for England's Second Test with New Zealand at Headingley. Nowadays the host county provides subs, but back then it was normal for a national coach to bring people in to see how they reacted around big name players, how they mixed in, to get to know them. 'At the time it was my ambition to get into England's one-day side, but it didn't happen. There was an England tour I did well on, Ian Bell did too. He got picked to go to New Zealand after that. The place I was after went to Jim Troughton of Warwickshire, I think. I'd heard discussions they were keeping an eye out and once you hear that it gives you a boost, but then I started not getting picked for Durham. The ironic thing is that when you get chosen to do the 12th man thing for England, you are not playing well enough to play for your club, so it's a double-edged sword. It's good to be in that environment, around the players and coaches and see how they operate, but on the other hand you'd rather not be there and playing well. But, yeah, I did it loads of times and nobody realises, nobody would know ... who was 12th man in 2004? They've no idea.'

In 2005, the story goes that Duncan Fletcher was on the hunt for every possible Ashes advantage, seeking out the best fielders in the country. Hence Pratt getting the call, along with Trevor Penney, destined to become England's fielding coach, and Samit Patel. In his *Palatinate* interview, Pratt admits that routinely replacing England's fast bowlers between spells as they nipped off for a comfort break was indeed tactical. 'The plan was always for the guys to go off and get showered and freshened up – especially the bowlers – to come back out and have another spell.'

University scribe Friend makes reference to how 'the legitimacy of such tactics were somewhat blurred', but admits that Pratt makes 'a convincing case for the ploy's advantages.'

'I think the counties are missing out on it because it is good for the players,' Gary tells him. 'I learnt so much and gained so much confidence. I knew that I was meeting up with the squad and getting into that dressing room on merit – not just because I'd been plucked from the MCC Young Cricketers. Obviously, it didn't happen for me, but there's nothing to say that if they gave the chance to ten people to do the same thing over the years, two of them might make it and be back in that dressing room as part of the squad.'

Speaking now, he says that they were staying in a nice hotel in the middle of Nottingham, out of the way, 'a sort of tower-type place. It was odd, maybe about twenty rooms and only us in there. The way the lads operated was strange too. They spent so much time together playing that when they weren't playing they just did their own thing – went to the cinema on their own ... or shopping ... not really going out as a team. Whereas here at Cumberland we always go out as a team, have a few beers or a meal, that sort of thing.'

And the incident itself? 'I was used to running on the field by then and considered it a privilege to be part of what was a really big series, shown on national television and so on. Everyone is a fan of England, aren't they, and I was just fortunate enough to be a fan with a good seat. Anything I did on the field was a bonus.' But having come on to replace Simon Jones – receiving treatment for his right foot and destined, despite Ponting's protestations, for hospital – what Pratt also possessed was relative anonymity. On the county circuit, he was by then quite well known and batsmen pondering a quick single were wise to his antics. The Australians knew nothing of him.

'I'd been on at least two hours, maybe three, when the moment came. The first few times I touched the ball I was, like: "Fucking hell, I can't see it..." – it was hard to pick up sometimes against the crowd. But on the other hand you are thinking: "Go on, hit one to us, a catch or anything... then it just happened.' Damien Martyn called Ponting through for a 'horrific run' and 'what I remember clearest is that there was no-one backing up. I had a bit of a reputation for being a decent fielder, but hadn't hit the stumps all year. That was my first run-out of the season, so it was quite unfortunate for them.' Before long, the Barmy Army were noisily championing his inclusion for the return series down under, his status as a cult hero confirmed.

In 2016, Pratt, clean-cut and still with a look of dashing public school sporting hero about him, confessed to the *Palatinate* he found it frustrating. 'When people just associate me with that one ball, it does take away from the fact that I was a fairly decent cricketer,' he said. Did he wish it had never happened? 'It's a tough one. I'd rather it hadn't and I was still playing first-class cricket for Durham. I didn't play at all in 2005. I was away on 12th man duties and that then caused a problem, because Durham weren't too happy I was going away while they were paying my wages. I don't think it helped my case whatsoever in terms of getting a new contract. But obviously, at the same time, you're going away with the top players in the country. You're going to learn. You're around experienced players, experienced coaches. It can only be good for you. And that's going to be more beneficial to me as a player than playing second team cricket for Durham.'

But back to the Cumberland's skipper's memories of that run-out today: 'The wickets didn't seem to be any wider than usual,' he goes on, 'although I was never missing from the moment it left my hand. To be fair, there is always a bit of luck involved – pure instinct really.' Well, that and hour upon hour of fielding practice.

His teammates, of course, all went berserk. 'I was quite calm, thinking "hang on, it might not be out." But all the lads were reckoning he was miles from his crease and when it came up on screen the place went bonkers.' If that isn't a moment to lean back in your rocking chair and tell your grandchildren about, it's hard to know what would be. Yet there is still that nagging millstone.

Having come in, Mike Hussey had been made captain. 'When I got off the field that night I had a voicemail saying to give him a ring. So I rang back and he said: "You've to get back up here. We've got a game tomorrow and you are in the squad to play." I was like: "Okay, fair enough." I went back and they didn't pick us. You just think: "You bastards. Why would you do that?" That was the first time I thought there is something not right here. They were pissed off. Whether Hussey's had a call and they've said "Get him away," I don't know.' A bizarre attitude for sure, given all the publicity Gary's exploits brought to a part of the land where cricket is hardly the biggest game in town. 'I think they just felt I'd rather be off and away. But there I was, playing second team cricket, getting runs and still not picked. I might as well have been getting a bit of experience around the England set-up, hadn't I? They didn't like it.'

Ever since, with the arrival of every Ashes series, the telephone calls inevitably begin. 'Can Gary do this? Can Gary do that?' Mostly, he was happy to go along with it, before it all got rather tedious.

'I did the BBC TV *Sports Personality of the Year*, when Pele was on, which was quite a thing. Four of us went to that. I was asked to go on *The Weakest Link*, and did that. Anne Robinson was awful, didn't come to meet us, but she was doing about eight shows a day so you can see why she might get pissed off. We were last on; it was a cricketers' special.' He didn't win, but was at least not the very weakest link among Darren Gough, Allan Lamb, Graham Thorpe, Ashley Giles and Devon Malcolm. 'It was quite good fun actually, a charity thing, although the money you won didn't go anywhere near covering what they paid you to go on it.'

There were also after-dinner speaking gigs for rugby clubs and the like: '...but with a little question and answer thing, me on stage, which are better because people can get to know what they want.' Then there was Sky's *A League Of Their Own*, his tale being just the sort of caper they liked sending up. 'I'd seen Freddie [team captain Flintoff] somewhere and he said he'd get us on it. I was "...yeah, yeah, whatever..." but then I did get asked to go on it and we [Cumberland] had a game at Sedbergh. I just couldn't get to the studio when I was needed, so didn't do it in the end.' A shame. Ponting was a guest and lined up for Pratt to emerge suddenly and spark the usual volleys of banter. 'I have met him since, in Durham. He's actually a really nice fella. You can understand that it's not such a big thing for him – he only got run out really, didn't he? It just so happened to be their most important player and captain, which kind of magnified things.'

Well yes, that and losing the plot while walking off the field, which brings us back around to Pratt's departure from the first-class county scene. In his *Palatinate* piece, an impressed Friend concludes: 'To go from being an unsuspecting run-of-the-mill county batsman to the jubilation and fame that one throw from cover-point brought him; and then to be cast away from professional cricket – all in the space of twelve months, it shows a tremendous sense of perspective and strength of character.' How did Cumberland come about?

'I played at Bishop Auckland for a while, because it was my closest club and they wanted me. Then Barnard Castle got promoted and I went there as a pro, their first-ever professional. It was a village mentality though, where they didn't want you back if you didn't get enough hundreds, or Johnny in the second team got 70 not out one week, "why isn't he in the first team?" It's a bit like that still. But really, I should have gone to Richmond straight away. They wanted me, but I'd already signed for Barnard Castle. Richmond came back in 2012 and joining them is the best thing I've done; a good strong club. We're always in finals, have lots of good kids, always 16 or 17-year-olds pushing for first team places... doesn't happen often.'

Until, in 2007, a call came from Steve Sharp.

'He asked me to come and play and I said "yeah." It was a little different back then. There was no structure or anything, just kind of turn up on the day. You didn't know who was playing week in, week out ... "awright, nice to meet you" ... at least six strangers. Marcus Sharp was captain, good player, decent bowler, nice bloke, but not a captain. He had nothing about him to give a bollocking – it would just be "oh, unlucky, better luck next time." Leaders have to be willing to be disliked sometimes and if it's not in you, it's not in you. You just become a bit of a soft touch and that's what we were. It was quite frustrating watching it happen. So when Marcus finished it seemed natural I'd take it over. I had the best credentials, the only one playing in a high standard week-in week-out, enjoyed doing it.'

Winning the Trophy in 2012 gave Cumberland its first piece of silverware since 1999, the year of their second Championship victory. 'It was quite amazing really,' says Gary, the man who inspired that one-day success. 'The run-in was ridiculous. Cornwall in the quarter-finals and Dorset in the semis, both away from home. When you are meeting a coach in Oxford at one in the morning and getting there at half-four for an 11.00am start ... well, it's quite a good way to win it actually, the hard way. We were the best side by far.'

What had Scott Lees called them, a band of brothers? 'He did, did he? Yeah, he's one of those it's good to have in your team is Scott. He's got that aggression and is a funny lad. Sounds like Peter Kay. I'd like him still to be playing, but he has a lot of commitments at Ormskirk. They seem to be in a lot of finals, just like Richmond.'

Having served Cumberland for over a decade now, what are his thoughts on Minor Counties cricket more generally?

Presumably his opinion hasn't changed since he told the *Palatinate* a couple of years ago it's a standard of cricket 'criminally under-rated', with a host of 'untouched gems' like Richard Gleeson, at the time still to land his big break. 'He's 28, which is a shame because I've been saying for years that this guy should be playing first-class cricket. Everyone said you can't judge someone on a Minor Counties game. But you can't judge someone on a second team game either, because county 2nd XI cricket isn't as good as Minor Counties cricket.'

Sure enough, Pratt still detects a well of talent fit for a higher stage: 'There's lots of lads playing who are better [than many on the first-class county scene] but just can't get that chance. It's the same sport, same ball, probably on worse wickets, and they deserve a go. Lads like Mattie McKiernan, absolutely pissed about at Derby. They might as well have just left him where he was, playing for us, instead of taking him out and not even playing him. That seems harsh.'

As for his own captaincy style, if he has one it might best be labelled hands-off, until hands-on is necessary, certainly in terms of preparation. 'I would never ever say you must go and do this or that. I just let people get on with their own system. I know how it feels for someone to force you to do something, it's not a nice place to be.'

He's thinking once again of Durham. 'Our coach then was Martyn Moxon, who liked things his way – rotas, nets, who's bowling at who. Well, sometimes you don't want nets. Sometimes you just want to hit a few balls and that will do, but you were kind of forced into it because he was trying to justify his job ... the man-management wasn't there. We had a bit of a clash about it – it sounds like something similar is going on at Yorkshire now, actually.'

With a child on the way and the big '40' approaching, how long does he see his playing career lasting? It's impossible to imagine him doing anything other than play cricket, only marginally less vital to him than oxygen. He told the *Palatinate* he still had the game for the professional circuit, but that was in 2016 and in the unlikely event an opportunity was to arise, he wasn't sure he'd now consider it. 'I enjoy my life,' he'd said. 'I like playing for Cumberland and enjoy playing for Richmondshire. Life's treated me pretty well, so there's no reason for me to look for that anymore. I know what it's like, I've done it – it's not all that it's hyped up to be. It's all gone a bit too professional in the sense that guys won't finish a day's play and have a pint and just relax. Now they finish a day's play, go for a swim, have a protein shake and are in bed by 8.30pm, ready for the next day.'

He went on: 'Cricket's about playing, socialising and making new friends really. A little bit of that is getting lost.'

And in 2018? 'I feel fit as ever. I'm not one of these people who start to hurt and their body packs in, I feel exactly the same as I did ten years ago. Not as quick, but quick enough to get by. I'm 36, so maybe another five years ... I'm still as keen on Cumberland as ever. Obviously, I'm going to have to give a bit of time back to Richmond now, because they've been good to me and have just let me play these past ten years.' The obsession has a distance to run yet.

'I've had one Sunday off all year, but then you get one and don't know what to do. Leanne doesn't know any different. Fortunately, she enjoys cricket too.' And as predicted in Kendal, coaching is most definitely not on the agenda. 'Never. It doesn't appeal to me at all. I could see myself as a cricket manager, maybe. It's back to coaches justifying their position – sometimes doing nothing is better.'

*****

Ahead of a timely start on a wet outfield, Tuesday's talk is of the night before. The committee went for a Chinese, the players an Indian at a restaurant on the quayside. Odd Sock Night, they'd called it. Rule being: wear odd socks or buy a round. Despite this being a three-night stay, scorer Geoff, of course, only had one pair with him so ended up begging hotel staff for help. 'Anything in lost property,' he'd asked a lass on reception. Afraid not. She would have liked to assist, but wore tights. 'Can't you just cut the feet out?' he'd asked.

With a minimum 110 overs in the day and resuming on 235 for 4, Cumberland aim to reach 325 to collect the bonus points, hit a few more boundaries, declare, and hopefully engineer a collapse, Jacques in amongst it from the start with a huge six. That's followed by the majestic four that brings up his half-century in the fifth over and soon after, having been dropped in the deep, the 258 posted by Northumberland yesterday is passed. Two more sixes are smashed – one into a mesh fence guarding the cemetery, the other clearing the height of two pavilions to earn whoops and hollers from his comrades on the balcony – before he is eventually caught on the boundary for 76, Cumberland having progressed to 290 for 5.

Liam Watkinson is next in. He sweeps and is caught at square leg for a single run. The 300 comes up in only the tenth over, but Liam's replacement, Josh, is soon out for 7 after Slacky reaches his 50 with more runs in him yet. When Ben Howarth then falls, lbw, the visitors are 322 for 8, although the 'keeper is a little unlucky. The appeal was not dissimilar to one Jacques got away with earlier. 'They always give captains the benefit of the doubt because they fill in the umpires' appraisal form,' mutters one passer-by as Jacques and Liam put in a lap, the latter in fancy leggings. With three overs left in an allocated first innings of 90, Northumberland need another wicket for bonus bowling points, while Cumberland must reach 358 for a lead of 100. Slacky is middling every shot and the spin bowler kicks his own cap in vexation. It looks, though, as if the Wigton man will run out of time to reach his century, Chris Hodgson now at the other end. And so it turns out, the pair finishing on 82 and 8 not out respectively in a total of 356 for 8 – that's a 98-run lead.

Northumberland's second innings gets underway just before noon. 'I don't think we've got the firepower to bowl these out,' admits John Patterson, candidly. For a while there is spit in the air, but then

the day brightens up and turns muggy. Mike, here again, reports that
Toby (the cricketer) is feeling 'ostracised' as the hosts build well,
moving swiftly to 32 without loss before a sudden flurry of wickets
... 32 for 1 ... 33 for 2 ... 33 for 3 ... grips the attention and by lunch
only six more runs have been added. Before club officials follow the
players inside, on the boundary the atmosphere turns frosty as Mike
strolls towards a seated Gilbert and Eric.

'Here's the man who was never watching Cumberland again,'
mutters the treasurer.

Mike doesn't bite, although his expression speaks volumes.

'Stay with us, Mike,' is Gilbert's heartfelt plea.

'Well, I won't stay if I'm not wanted,' Mike replies and, ignored
by Eric, ignores him in return. 'This is down to the actions of one
person,' he offers, after a brittle silence. 'Not wanting them to spoil
a friendship with two of my oldest friends in Cumbria, you two.'

Gilbert is keen to make nice, wants all this unpleasantness to
go away. Mike, after all, is the person for whom he stood aside. He
admires a man who, he reckons, made the club more competitive.
The depth of bad feeling, however, is unambiguous.

At least the wine is now palatable. Rob as usual ensures none
of it goes to waste. Chairman Neil has driven east and as the table
empties talks modernisation 'going forward'. He has spoken to Gary,
whose responses will form part of a report requested by the MCCA.
Neil is keen to 'put procedures in place that will ensure this does not
happen again,' eager to show the issue is being taken very seriously.
To that aim, a meeting will be held between the end of the season in
a fortnight and the traditional debrief on Wednesday 26 September
at Crooklands, by which time any official MCCA sanctions ought
to be known. 'We have to be run more professionally,' Neil says. 'Any
repercussions will need a sense of proportionality and practicality,
but I see this as an opportunity for positive change.'

Despite the marketing speak, he means every word. Buzzwords
aside, accountability and a sharpening of the club's act would not go
amiss if the MCCA – and by extension ECB – are to be pacified.

Outside, Gilbert and John discuss how various actors have been
in the wrong or handled things badly, concluding that the issue does
need addressing. John suggests Gilbert should chat with president
Alan Wilson, although with his inside knowledge and list of outside

contacts, it's hard to imagine that 'Wils' isn't fully up to speed already. In the clubhouse bar, one group stares at a wall-mounted TV, on which day four of England v India is fought out in Nottingham. It's a game the tourists will wrap up tomorrow with a 203-run victory, drawing this quip from *Independent* sports writer, Jonathan Liew: 'Very decent crowd at Trent Bridge to watch 17 balls ... resounding endorsement of the ECB's investment in short-form cricket...'

Here, the Northumberland batsmen dig in and mid-afternoon are 75 for 3, just 23 behind. From nowhere, Syds removes another pair of bails in a four-wicket haul and a hunt that looked like stalling is on once more. Another couple of scalps now and there could well be an exciting run-chase later on. When the scoreboard reads 90, wicket five falls –James Thompson out for 32 – courtesy of a superb take in the slips by Ross Zelem. Whenever the game appears to be petering out there is a twist. The opener had been building a handy partnership with Cumberland's first innings tormentor, Alex Simpson, again in the runs with an eventual 61. This time he needs the support of middle order batsman Sean Tindale as, in the 43rd over, the Northumbrians move into credit, the team on 166 for 6 when Simpson's second stint finally reaches its end, caught Howarth behind the stumps, bowled Boyne, tea called two runs later. Tea over, Josh nicks another wicket, lbw, and it's 176 for 7. Cumberland are almost out of time if they are to steal victory. It's 5.00pm.

Sempy drops a tough one at forward short leg off Jacques, who against his ex-county teammates has been impressive on home turf throughout, and that seems to be that. There is still time for Tyler's first ball of the game to be half-volleyed to Josh at mid-off however – 197 for 8. A bizarre rain-affected fixture in which little has been at stake concludes in a blaze of early evening sunshine, as the umpires call 'last hour'. A result either way is now next to impossible, so the captains shake hands on a draw and head off for a cooling broon ale.

But what of the parish pump politics?

On the grapevine: Rob Cairns may be considering his position, unhappy with a wishy-washy response to the MCCA's request for an explanation. According to Mike, the club officials have already held a meeting, odd that Neil hadn't mentioned it. Steve, not at Jesmond, is apparently now saying that Gary may have told him he'd be leaving early, can't remember. If so, the story's changed. Will the MCCA buy it? On Thursday, word arrives that Cumberland have responded, the MCCA allegedly finding their explanation of events to be 'completely inadequate.' One high-paced individual says the reasons received for Gary's departure were twofold: Leanne felt unwell and the skipper had a sore knee, or foot, or something. No mention was made of a prior engagement to play in another fixture the very same night.

How anyone could think the MCCA wouldn't twig to what had really gone on is bewildering. The same source reckons they ought to have come clean from the start and admitted the error. Had Gary been reprimanded internally and suspended for a game, that may well have been that, an open and shut case. Now, however, the MCCA is 'very dissatisfied' with how the club has tried to conceal its faults, handling the affair poorly. Furthermore, Hertfordshire team manager Iain Fletcher also writes for *The Cricket Paper*, so he might well file a story, who knows? Evasion seldom ends well.

Still, life and cricket go on. By Thursday evening, in defiance of the rumour mill, Rob is still sufficiently on board to send a group email to every committee member, including the two from Cumbria Cricket Ltd, enquiring if lunch is required for the final game of the season at Edenside and, if so, on which days. Well, not quite *every* member. Mike Latham and Toby Bulcock aren't CC'ed.

Then, on Friday, the ultimate irony.

A trawl through the Minor Counties' regulations confirms that participation in two games – be they on the same day or on-going – is indeed forbidden. Reason being? In 2014, after complaints were raised when one Cambridgeshire player intended to turn out for Peterborough in a rearranged T20 game before joining a crucial Championship clash with Staffordshire on day two, the rule was introduced to ensure that a possibility said by one complainant to go 'against the spirit of cricket' could never arise again. And which club do you suppose had kicked up the original fuss?

Cumberland.

Lap Four

The Coastal Way

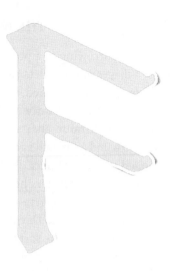

It's the last weekend in August and the Whoop Hall Inn and Country Club, near Kirkby Lonsdale, is taking bookings for Christmas. The Cumbrian coast too is way off in the distance, but on this Saturday morning the billboard flashing by contributes to a feeling of unease and dislocation. This final lap will take in haunts like Haverigg and Millom ... Seascale ... Egremont and onward north, bypassing such as Ravenglass, Muncaster ... places out on a limb with reputations.

Mike and Toby are otherwise engaged, so I am on this stretch alone, which hardly calms the 'naïve stranger in a horror film' vibe. Ludicrous, but leaving familiar country behind to head into territory that, while superficially benign, has a certain menace ... well, the tropes are certainly there. Weather vanes and windmills, tree trunks gnarled and twisted. Uplands are far as the eye can see built on yarns that will never be spun ... of field mouse, goat, hare and fox ... life forces once, twitchy and terrified, ancestral spirits now, in Mother Earth with the bones of Celts, Romans, Saxons and Normans whose modern descendants, sealed in horseless carriages, dart noisily by between roadside ditches overhead. The hills, pikes and windswept beaches to come will also have eyes – and folk tales of their own.

Fifty miles north west, the traffic on the A590 is back-to-back. Cartmel's ever-popular races are on. Once through that logjam the way clears to a breathtaking open vista. This stretch of road has seen over 1,500 fatalities in five years, a sign warns, the way undulating and then narrowing to a point where only one line of vehicles may pass. Villages and hamlets retreat into the rear-view mirror before Millom is finally reached, via a junction with a solitary flagpole bearing a limp and tatty Union Jack. Nudging into the cricket ground a half-hour after noon, there is no sign of any action, although a 2nd XI match against Lindal is soon to commence. I have arranged to meet 'Dinger' Bell, he of high reputation for the many talented young cricketers he has helped to develop down the years, several going on to bigger – and in one notable case stellar – things.

Dinger, real name David, sits waiting by the pavilion, a red ring binder on his knee. The sort of thing Eamonn Andrews used to hand over on *This Is Your Life*, although the events detailed within aren't of the sort a 74-year-old would relish leafing through as the curtain falls on an otherwise lauded coaching career.

'TO LANCE SPRINGS, LORD'S CRICKET GROUND,' [reads a stick-on label, inscribed in Dinger's own hand.] 'FROM D.I. BELL BSc (Hons), MRSC, CChem. SUBJECT: APPEAL AGAINST ACCUSATIONS MADE BY C.C.LTD. DATE: THURSDAY 24th Jan 2014.'

'We'll get to what's inside later,' promises a man who looks as if he has been through the wringer. Friendly yet edgy, he is keen to state his case. Prior to this, we've never met, though many a conversationalist this summer has mentioned Dinger in passing. His is the sort of name of which local legends are made. A celebrity in these parts, he is known to all, but that can have its downside. 'It's all in there,' he says, tapping the binder. 'I've written about what I've done and don't like doing that. It feels big-headed.'

Millom is Steve Sharp's club. Like him and brother Ian, Dinger too began here as a kid, although back in the 1950s. A 1st XI debut came at the age of 16 and by 1970 he was second-best bowler in the North Lancashire League in terms of averages, top of the pile three years later. In his late-20s, he also represented Cumberland nine times in the Minor Counties Championship, but it was on his retirement that he made most noise, turning his hand to coaching.

'It took over my life,' he admits. 'I played until I was 42, then realised I couldn't do what I wanted to and took my first coaching badge in 1979 with Ronnie Lindley at Vickerstown. I then took my senior coaching with David Lloyd and when my son, Robert, started playing, got involved with Cumberland schools. A lot of father/son combinations stay together while the son's playing, then the father clears off. That wasn't in my remit. I couldn't keep my hands off it. I was there for life, as far as I was concerned. Oh, it was brilliant.'

Best of all were the tours; life-changing experiences for lads up-and-coming. Most would flesh out the Cumbria leagues as adults, some still do. Others like Ben Stokes and Liam Livingstone were future headline-makers – and how about the three Clark brothers, Darren, arguably the most talented of the lot despite never playing first-class cricket, Graham and all-rounder Jordan, soon to sign for Surrey? 'They went away little boys and came back men,' says their former mentor. 'You gave them a bit of confidence ... let them go off for fish and chips or whatever, while keeping an eye on them like.'

Not that Dinger wants any credit. 'You couldn't, the good players were good already. There were more I think could have made it, but didn't.' Lads like Stephen Hindmarch, who went on to forge a career in professional football with Carlisle, Shrewsbury and others instead. 'When Dean Henderson came to us he hadn't played much cricket before but took to it, a fish to water. Manchester United signed him as a goalkeeper [most recently he was on loan at Sheffield United]. It's swings and roundabouts. You lose some, you gain some, but the ones I like coaching best are the ones who need it. I got a thrill if I could get someone who was really struggling to do something.'

Lots of coaches tell you what you are doing wrong but don't try to put it right, Dinger reckons. 'If I told a kid he couldn't do something, I'd spend hours with him ... throwing a ball ... no, no, no. That might seem negative to anyone watching, but it's about repetition, getting them to do it over and over and explaining why ... full bat on the line of the ball. Watch kids now and they go like that.' He makes a wafting gesture. 'Well, it's all right with contact, but it could go anywhere. If they play like that ... squarer ... or the cross-bat shots ...' Explaining technique, he is really in his element.

Before long, we head into the clubhouse. He has the demeanour of a man being watched and, who knows, maybe he is. It was Dinger who obtained the framed shirts, signed by Stokes and Livingstone, hanging by the bar. He would rather our discussion went unheard.

'Around 1997, I got headhunted by the Cumbria Cricket Board, who asked if I'd set up coaching courses. They'd had a few before, but nothing organised. I went all over the place doing it, bought a cheap car, as I didn't have one. Its windscreen wipers didn't work, which I didn't know until I set off to Wigton. Rained all the way there.' He also went to Carlisle, Workington, Whitehaven, Barrow, Kendal and Keswick. 'In each of these spots we set up a course and I'd just troop around. At Millom, we'd have two or three from each area, eighteen to twenty-four maximum, and I'd pick a 14 or 15-man county squad.'

This then, was the birth of the enterprise known only semi-humorously as 'Dinger's Academy,' of which people within the game still speak fondly. 'I got Ian Clark, Steven Sharp, all kinds of really good cricketers involved, and never took a penny because if I did it for nothing I could afford an extra coach. Magic. The coaches each got between £9 and £13 an hour, not a fortune, for four hours on a Saturday ... a labour of love for them really. If you are writing a book about Cumberland cricket, Bob Maxwell of Carlisle must get a mention. He was as keen as me. He'd come down on a Sunday and was never late, start at ten until twelve, an hour for dinner, one until three, then home. What a man he was. Always had stories to tell, brilliant with the kids. They all loved him. I'd say: 'You and you and you ... you're with Bob Maxwell.' And they'd go: 'Yeeeessss!' Don't know what they said about me like.'

The one thing people did complain about, Dinger recalls, is not being chosen. 'Very few complained who were in it – there was only the four who led to me being kicked out.' He is jumping the gun but goes on with the tale for now, speaking by way of example of a bloke who ran a pub in the nearby village of Kirksanton – '...lovely steaks, but he wanted his son...' Checking himself, he starts again. 'You see, the parents always have lads who play in junior club cricket, where they are opening bowler or batter. Eleven of those and it's hard to sort the order. I'd just say, right, you are going to open the bowling, but will bat ten or eleven. I wasn't too bothered about winning. What does a trophy mean at junior level? You've had a good team and were lucky to get it. I developed them so they could help a league to develop and then that would perpetuate itself ... that was my aim.'

'You know my son bowls as well, don't you?' parents would say.

'Yes and so do the other eleven,' Dinger would reply.

In a later interview, Ben Stokes called his junior coach blunt. 'I understand what Stokesey was saying,' Dinger says, 'because I did have to be blunt with him. He came to England with his dad, Ged, who was here to coach Workington Town when summer rugby league was just starting. Ian Clark told me: "There's a hell of a good cricketer [in Cockermouth], you'll have to see him." And I says, it's May, Clarky. I've got my team picked for the season; it's done. We've had final trials. He kept going on though, "You'll have to see him," so I arranged a County against The Rest game and put Stokes in The Rest. We'd a good side. There was Jordan Clark, Jamie Harrison, five or six top players, and the best captain I ever had, a kid called Hugh Gimber from Cockermouth. He's a businessman in London now [he says this with barely concealed pride], but his father keeps in touch. In actual fact,' he taps the binder, 'there's a letter from him in there. Anyway, we got 180 and I thought: "That's all right." Stokesey comes in, hits five fours and suddenly it's "bloody hell!" He was that good I thought he was going to win the game for them and that would make me look stupid, wouldn't it? He wasn't a particularly big lad then, but sent one miles up into the air. Fortunately, Jordan Clark was wicketkeeper. He caught it and they were all out for about 70.'

Afterwards, Dinger asked to see Stokes and his parents in the changing room. 'I told him: "Play the game my way son, don't give me any hassle and me and you will get on great. Let us down and you'll be out." His parents were dead chuffed with how I handled it; I think they knew even then he could be a handful. I never had any problem with him, although he never took to us. He was always wary because he maybe thought I was going to bollock him. I don't think it would have done him any harm.' He must be pleased though when any of his former lads go on to do well? 'I am, yes. This recent thing has made him grow up a bit. In his last Test, he applied himself – 50-odd in 150 balls, that's application. If they'd all done that... but he's one of the few good enough to play both ways.'

One other ex-junior-coach who came into regular contact with Dinger is Toby Bulcock's father, Steve. Chatting on the boundary at Ormskirk last week, he'd shared his thoughts on the character of a man who would ring him a night or two beforehand asking if Steve's Lancashire under-13s could bat first to ensure there'd be a full game. 'Dinger used to give his lads chance to shine in all the different areas,'

Steve had said, 'whereas at Lancashire we had a set of batters and a set of bowlers and train them that way.' On the whole, parents loved him. 'He turned up at Morecambe once and the bus was late. They'd taken a wrong turn, had a big contingent aboard and ended up being awful. No one seemed to mind. He gave his time voluntarily, but sometimes there'd be complaints: "Our lad's a batter and he's opening t' bowling today and batting at ten," that sort of carry on. He took all the pressure and stress away and just let them express themselves.'

In terms of coaching technique, Dinger was for going back to basics and letting natural ability do the rest, anathema you'd imagine to those who treat cricket as quasi-science, resolvable empirically to the nth degree, rather than the game of chance it essentially is. '"Stokes, belt it out the park," that was how he tended to operate. But he put together quite a strong side, hand-picked, and had success in a county without a lot of teams.' Until the Board got rid of him.

Steve Bulcock hadn't known why, though hazarded a guess. 'All these structures and coaching patterns were put into place. Did he have a coaching badge? No idea. He's just trying to pass on what he knows. If a thing had a solution it was usually simple: "Get on your front foot," or whatever. But if you spoke to the lads that were under him they'd hold him in high regard. He got them on the first step.'

In Millom, Dinger himself has more to say on the matter. 'If a kid travels all the way to Lancashire from Carlisle, he deserves to do something. Cricket's a terrible game if you've three or four dominant players and the other seven don't get a go. I went out of my way to avoid that. With me, a lad could take five wickets and not necessarily bowl the following week. I just wanted them to understand it isn't all about "me". Everybody wants a label – opening bat, opening bowler or whatever – but without the other ten helping you, you are nothing. I wanted to generate enjoyment of the game, not ego trips.'

Not that he decries technique. 'If summat's not broken, don't fix it is my philosophy, that's all. Take [ex-New Zealand all-rounder] Lance Cairns. If top coaches today had got hold of him, he'd have had to bowl a classical action. My own son was a "hopper", bowled leg spin. I tried to get him to bowl "properly", couldn't, and realised that what he did was natural to him. Look at Ben Stokes ... and by the way I'm not taking any credit for him, an all-time natural. His bowling action is far from classical ... head down a long way, very square on … but he'll be successful all his life doing it. These little idiosyncrasies are important. Some of the shots Viv Richards played, unbelievable. Clip off his toes, the swagger … you couldn't teach it.'

The thought cheers him to the extent that he is soon sharing anecdotes of trips to Lord's, where he used to take his boy, Robert, for coaching courses. It was there, one Easter, that he met legendary broadcaster Brian 'Johnners' Johnston. 'This beautiful melodious voice piped up: "Pleased to meet you, Dinger." We went back at Christmas and he walked in again. "Compliments of the season! Little lad still bowling leg breaks? Wonderful!" He remembered us eight months on.' Another nice memory was meeting John le Carré, author of such best-selling espionage novels as *Tinker Tailor Soldier Spy* and *The Spy Who Came in from the Cold*. 'His wife was there with their son, Nicholas, same age as Robert, on the same course. She said: "I've got pop off to Harrods for some skiing equipment." My missus said: "Oh, he'll be all right with us. You go off and have a good day's shopping." So we got Nicholas his dinner and when Mrs Le Carré came back she thanked us.' The fellow with her had a look of George Smiley. "John, this is David and Elaine Bell," she said. "They've looked after our son." He shook my hand. Everyone thought I was somebody, because I'd shaken John le Carré's hand.'

Everything went swimmingly with the Cumbria Cricket Board for the first few years and, in 2011, Dinger became director of schools cricket. 'I formed the under-11s county side in 1998, was assistant manager until 2010, co-formed the under-14s with Bill Barrington and managed that until 2012 … between 1998 and 2012 I took around one hundred and fifty boys on week-long tours … but you'll get all of this out of the binder.'

And now we are at the nub of it. How it all turned sour. 'Well, maybe I got too powerful. For them, it got to be about money, while I just wanted to expand it. That's about the truth. They preferred yes men.' It is certainly true that in Cumbria, as everywhere else these days, where junior development is concerned the clipboard rules, underpinned by corporate thinking. 'The Cumbria Cricket Board is now a limited company, Cumbria Cricket Ltd, affiliated to the ECB and fully engaged in chasing profit. Yet they won't be getting their cricket courses for the money we used to charge, that's for sure.' The actual break, though, was rather more dramatic, as Dinger relates.

'The under-13s were taken over by a bloke from Workington without anyone saying much to us and I'd gone back to under-12s. Communication isn't a strong point for Cumbria Cricket Ltd and certainly their disciplinary procedures need to be revised. Anyway, we set off with county trials, had a look, and I picked one lad who looked really good, a wicketkeeper and very mature. I made him my captain. The rest of the side weren't bad either, but we had a poor season and in seven or eight innings this kid scored 20-odd runs. His father started blaming me and a couple more pitched in ... why isn't my son opening...' Even the county welfare officer got involved.

The binder's contents lay out the case in detail, while leaving much to be deduced between the lines. His purpose in pulling it all together four years ago is, he writes: '...to appeal against the recent serious accusations' made against him. It's an attempt: '...to clear my good name and retire gracefully rather than in shame after thirty-five years coaching and managing Cumbria junior teams. As I am 70 years old next July, this will represent half of my life.'

Relieved in 2013 of any involvement at all with junior cricket in Cumbria, by then including the under-12s, he had previously hoped to keep it all low key, fearing things may turn 'acrimonious'. A year later, he still had no intention of going public with the 'harsh way I have been treated.' He intended to prove the allegations made against him were unsubstantiated, lacking in evidence. 'I have no intention of trying to manage a team again, but just want to leave with my head held high and look back on a job well done.'

To that end, the plastic sleeves are filled with biographical info, several letters of support from parents, Mark Davidson of Carlisle among them, opposition coaches and county and league officials such as Mike Latham, along with a testimonial for Dinger from 2010 by the Cumbria Cricket Board itself. He also includes a breakdown of events and correspondence surrounding the allegation.

On 21 July 2013, a parent reported his concerns to the Cumbria Schools' Cricket Association about Dinger's behaviour towards his charges, brought to a head by a round-robin message after 'an ignominious defeat' for the under-12s by Cleveland the week before. This parent felt 'that the email, whether directed at 11 or 12-year-old players or their parents, was particularly negative and intimidating.' The complainant went on: 'This is one of a sequence of such emails in a similar tone where the coach had described the squad as "the poorest he's had". A tour to Ipswich was imminent for which Dinger had pledged to bring in a new lad. The complainant also referenced language 'heard to be appalling and aggressive by an opposition coach and some parents' recently. 'Mr XXXX expressed concerns about letting his son attend the Ipswich Festival to endure five days of negativity and paying a lot of money to do so.' He had shared his feelings with other parents. The email last week was the final straw.

The text of that email, dated July 17, is also reproduced in full, wherein the team is indeed rebuked, mildly, if ill-advisedly: 'I hope EVERYBODY that played in last Sunday's match has been practising at least four hours a night ... getting beat by traditionally the weakest team we play by ten wickets is not acceptable, but to only bat 16.4 overs after winning the toss and batting beggars belief. When are we going to start playing like a team and not a load of very moderate selfish individuals.' It concludes: 'Please walk in when we are fielding. On Sunday nobody was walking in but when I shouted to walk in I got a sullen look. I am only trying to show you the correct way to play and hopefully make the game a little easier BUT if I can not get a response from you for something as basic as walking in with the bowler then my job is impossible.'

Two days after the initial allegation, the matter was referred to the CSCA's welfare officer who, together with Cumbria Cricket Ltd, concluded that Dinger ought not to be involved in a tour or match situation while such an allegation remained under investigation.

Speaking now, Dinger recalls: 'I'd gone home after the game and started getting everything arranged to go to Ipswich. It's a good minor-counties-type festival, you play the likes of Huntingdon, Cornwall, Lincolnshire, these types of teams. We were due to travel on the Sunday and I got a phone call on Thursday saying I couldn't go. I asked why not and they said "serious complaints".'

Dinger found two people to take his place and told them not to let this particular lad captain the side. 'Cleveland, bless their souls, had given us games year in and year out and we usually hammered them. But, you know, it's good to hammer somebody occasionally, because when you are playing Lancashire and Yorkshire the rest of the time you are getting plenty of leatherings yourself. Anyways, this particular day I'd asked our skipper what he was going to do and he said "bat". I thought he was joking. "That's a seamer's paradise," I said. "It will move all over." "Oh no, the ball will be wet." Anyway, we won the toss, batted – 31 all out. They knocked them off without loss, so we had a friendly to take up the rest of the time. It wouldn't have been worth them coming all the way over to Cumbria if we hadn't. I pulled the lad at the end; the CSCA chairman was with us. "Look, you are having a poor season mate," I said. "I think it's because you are doing too much." Captain, 'keeper and opening bat is a big ask for a kid, so I said I was relieving him of the captaincy. Oof! The shit hit the fan. I heard the tour went fine, but everyone was horrified. It was underhand.' His voice cracks, before he regains composure. 'I didn't have chance to fight back and wrote to Lord's, as I'd got no satisfaction out of Cumbria. Nobody seemed to back us, which was rather ... people were saying it's wrong, Dinger, yet no-one seemed to ... people with kids going through the system, they don't want to get involved ... it was that, I think. Everyone should have the right to appeal, innocent until proven guilty. Well I wasn't.'

Matters took another twist upon the intervention of one Arthur Brown, last encountered in the under-17s game against Scotland at Wigton. '28.07.13: Unsolicited Contribution from Arthur Brown Chair CCLtd, with reference to a previous referral to Lance Spring re David Bell,' as Dinger's timeline in the binder has it, in reference to an earlier 2009 run-in at an under-11s festival in Ipswich.

'Mr Brown is referring to a very minor disagreement between myself and Mr John Olpin [Norfolk's under-11s manager],' he writes by way of explanation. After his side failed to bowl what even Dinger admits was a 'dour Cumbrian team' out, the latter called Cumbria 'a boring lot' and was reproached for comments 'inappropriate and very near to a child protection issue. He took exception to what I said but neither of us was aggressive.' A year later at the same festival:

I was walking around the boundary, waiting for the game to begin, when I walked past the Norfolk camp and heard one of the more vociferous Norfolk parents saying: "Well done, John. I'm glad you've won the toss and put those boring Cumbrians in to bat." I turned around to discuss this sensitive topic with the under-12 manager who happened to be yet again Mr John Olpin. The Norfolk parents got in between me and Mr Olpin and I withdrew. He wrote a letter to Lord's describing me as a man who had come out of the pub on a Friday night after having 12 pints looking for a fight. I would like to stress that I have never had a fight in my life neither at school, in a pub or on a sports field. I have been non-violent all my life and intend to stay that way. The problem I have is one of perception. I am a big lump of a lad standing 6ft 3" and weighing in at 18 stone, so if I approach somebody they might perceive that I am approaching aggressively. I am a "Gentle Giant".

Bringing the matter up again, he says, was: '...an act of entrapment. The issue was dealt with fairly and closed off in 2010 by the CCB.'

There was also, in 2012, another email fuss that can now be seen to account for Dinger's drop from the under-13s to under-12s.

'In October 2012, I was first accused of sending out an inappropriate email to the team after an excellent victory over Nottinghamshire,' he tells Lord's, his response having been a further audit/survey sheet sent to all the parents, along with a copy of the offending missive itself. Their responses are in the appendix at the back of the binder. 'I was accused of bullying children and scaring women. These claims were unsubstantiated, although I was left in a state of shock. The meeting was over in effectively five minutes when I did not get a chance to appeal or defend myself. There was no incident report and no CC Ltd welfare officer present. I was however allowed to continue as manager of the CSCA under-12 team in 2013.'

That under-13s side, coincidentally, contained Cumberland's Marcus Stables, and the email Dinger sent read:

Dear All,
As you are well aware I am absolutely ecstatic and probably well over the limit (having supped 6 large glasses of white wine very quickly). I do not have to congratulate the top players as I am sure they will know by my reaction who they are but I want to bring the team game into perspective. [He then goes on to praise individual contributions ... '12 in 10 balls, what a difference from Wednesday' ... 'got out trying to score off the first ball but it was needed. We could not afford somebody to f_r_ around for a few balls when 6 an over was needed' ... 'Stick with me son and like

the Wizard of Oz I'll eventually give you a cricket brain' ... 'You were a slaughter to the cause but I hope you think it was worth it' and so on.] On reflection, we won [sic] a first-class county and not many Cumbrian teams know that (thank you Michael Caine) or do that ... beat a first-class county.

Enjoy the time because I will be back in your ear on Tuesday as if nowt has happened because Tuesday is another day and we have Derbyshire to beat. If we do lose at least go down with all guns blazing rather than that belch and a hiccup that we surrendered on Wednesday.

Dinger is a happy and proud man but do not forget the immense input my coach Mark Cameron is putting in for without him I could not do what I do. He does make a difference. In fact we are such a good team that Alex Ferguson and his team are –h–tting themselves. Celebrate tonight but I just hope I am sober by Tuesday.'

In accounting for it later, on a page headed 'My thoughts on the white wine email', he now thinks two glasses nearer the truth. He'd been using exaggeration to 'illustrate how happy and pleased I was with the overall performance of the team. It should be highlighted how positive I was in reference to the whole team, not negative as [has] been suggested by the complainant.' After which there is a stack of completed audits signed and completed by parents ... 'euphoric and amusing – in no shape or form offensive' ... 'Dinger's emails are always a joy to receive' ... 'anyone taking offence has not got to know him' ... 'excellent with kids' ... and so on.

Still, a year later in mid-September 2013, he was presented with a *fait accompli* by way of advice written by Cumbria Cricket Ltd and agreed by the CSCA and the head of 'ECB Safeguarding'. It read:

There is a concern shared jointly about your fitness or ability to coach, manage or be in a position of responsibility for children playing in an area or county cricket squads which we have responsibility for. It will be conditional on you, to be allowed to continue in such a role, to:

Attend a Safeguarding & Protecting Children course before being involved in any further coaching or managing of children in cricket.

Re-attend a level 1 (Cricket Activator or Coach Support Worker) cricket coaching course & be certified through that to be competent to coach.

On completion of this:

You will not be involved alone in the coaching & management of area or county age group cricket or any other children's or young person's cricket

You will not be involved alone in match day organisation

You will copy all team correspondence sent to players & parents additionally to a nominated representative of CSCA/CCL

Suggested timescale for this – 31 January 2014

The effect was devastating for someone who, since entering coaching in 1979, knew no other life. Whose list of pioneering achievements and life memberships as long as the Furness peninsula included an award for Services to Cumbria Sport in 2004. 'My father fought in the war and my Uncle Dick got killed fighting for freedom for the English Man,' he told Lord's, in conclusion, 'but if he is not allowed to have a fair hearing, then why did they bother?'

*****

Millom is a great little town. That's what Dinger reckons anyway, although even here he has had his spots of bother. 'Oh, that's another story,' he says, glancing around to see if anyone is listening. Deciding that the coast is clear, he proceeds.

'It was in 2007 or 2008. My lad and me had a night out, around Christmas time. You have your celebrations, don't you, and we were having one for winning the league. All the lads were there. Anyway, the two of us were just standing around when a woman comes out of there...' He nods towards a function room. 'There was some do or other, an 80th birthday party or something. "You've ruined my night, you've ruined my night, you've pinched from our buffet," she starts yelling. "What are you on about?" I says. Just couldn't believe it. Our Robert says: "Oh, shut up." He isn't normally fiery, but he'd had a drink and you're not reserved then, are you? "They are accusing us of stealing and we haven't." He was right, but I calmed him down.'

Later on, a committee meeting was called, during which the

woman's boyfriend spoke up. 'I travelled to work with this lad in a car pool and he had never said a word. I said: "You spineless bastard. Why couldn't you bring this up then?" He said: "My girlfriend is going to pull out her £25 donation to the club," and I said "I'll give you £50." "You can't do that!" he says. I says: "Why can't I? We weren't doing owt," got up and walked out. If they are going to do that to someone who has been a life member of the club since 1989...'

That's another of Dinger's achievements, by the way. 'I'm also a life member of the Barrow and District Junior Cricket League, Barrow District Table Tennis and the youngest ever life member of the North Lancashire and Cumbria Cricket League ... I'm one of them that gets involved, you see.'

But still, Millom is a great town. 'Everybody knows everybody. If you've got owt to say, you say it. I'd sooner have that than talking behind my back. Everybody seems to think I'm a thug because I come from Millom. I've an honours degree in chemistry from Liverpool University, where I studied from 1963-67, when university really was something to go to. Two people from this town went and I was one. I went to work at Sellafield. As I say, I've never had a fight with anyone – although I did get beat up in Liverpool one night.'

We head back outside where the game has begun. It's not what you'd call a high quality affair, but a smattering of people have now wandered in to watch. What are Dinger's memories of playing for Cumberland, selected after leading the averages in 1973?

'Oh, it was brilliant. I'd wanted to do that for a while, but when I came to bowl my first few overs it didn't feel right. I was that nervous and wanting to do well. It was one of the worst bowling spells of my life, but I still took 3 for 25. Then when we played Northumberland at Jesmond ... oh, what a wicket.' He turns dreamy. 'I'd never bowled on anything like it, one of the best spells I ever produced, ten or eleven overs, 2 for 15 and I got Mike Crawhall out, a Northumberland legend who scored 25,000 runs.' Lincolnshire came next. 'We played against Don Wilson. I tried to sweep him, didn't quite get it and a piece of my bat dropped off. "Hey," he told me, "you don't have to put it into the next field, a couple of inches over the boundary will do." Cricket is full of characters. That's what makes it, but I'm just sad there's too much of this these days.' He twiddles his fingers to indicate obsession with computer games, as someone might who has devoted his life to getting kids out into the open air. 'I honestly think that's one of the big problems. Kids don't want to play. Another one is travelling. They want to be home on Saturday for their night out, not spend two hours getting back from Carlisle. I'd have played forever. My lad was secretary for a bit.'

Not long ago, he actually went to see Cumberland, he says, at Cockermouth, but it got rained off. 'I watch cricket mainly on telly these days. It's good now as Jordan Clark and Liam Livingstone are at Lancashire and Graham Clark and Ben Stokes play for Durham. Liam Trevaskis is also there, isn't he? What a smashing lad. He wrote a nice letter thanking us once, after I helped get him sponsorship money for a tour. Kids don't do that these days. Their parents might, but he took time to do it himself.' Such signs of appreciation matter to a man, particularly when he hasn't been well, rushed into hospital three or four weeks ago for a cardiogram ... 'one of those echo jobs. I get the results next week. I feel okay now, but for a while...'

It's time to leave. Haverigg awaits, four minutes down the road, the most local of local rivals. As we say our goodbyes, another ex-Cumberland player, David Lupton – 'best bowler in the league,' says Dinger – walks through what was historically an ornate entrance, its turnstile now rusted shut where folk would once have paid to enter. In fact, Lupton's county debut was on this very ground in 1975, when he took 13 wickets against Lancashire's 2nd XI. Along the way sits another old boy, Don Weavers, also in that team of '75. The trio recall an amazing game when Millom skittled Workington for eight runs, and that after the visitors had been 8 for 0. Lupton took five wickets, Dinger three. It's good to see him laughing among friends, people who know him well, appreciate his qualities and forgive his foibles. Leafing through his binder, the following comments in a letter of support from one Gordon Lake, secretary and team manager of Cleveland Schools, will later jump out: '...to my chagrin, I am led to believe that the complaint made emanated from the game played against Cleveland at Milnthorpe.' Lake concludes:

> We have all made mistakes in dealing with youngsters, things said or written can be misinterpreted and taken personally, some of us older coaches are more often guilty of calling a spade a spade than the new methods demand, but it does not mean that

we are unable to coach a set of players in the finer points of the game, its techniques and technicalities, the motivation required to provide the best competition ... and most importantly, pay something back to the game that has been our life for so long. I know, and I suspect the powers in Cumbrian Cricket know, that hundreds of players over the years have been made better cricketers by listening to Dinger. I sincerely believe that, for whatever reason, a big mistake has been made – a man who should be cherished has been vilified – not because he does not care – more that he cares too much.'

*****

British folklore is rich with stories of isolated communities who, in Cornwall mainly, lure fishing vessels on to the jagged rocks and headlands of the Atlantic Coast by way of plundering salvage. Alfred Hitchcock's adaptation of Daphne du Maurier's novel *Jamaica Inn* (1936) is based upon such nefarious and parochial goings-on, as is Dame Ethel Smyth's opera, *The Wreckers*, first staged in 1906.

Haverigg is a good deal distant from Bodmin Moor, but it too feels like somewhere the locals may be inclined to throw a blanket over a lighthouse beacon, or where an outsider, just passing through, might come to realise what's really going on. Driving in, all eyes turn.

Those onlookers gather outside a pub next to a cricket ground in a village whose population, at the last count, was just under 2,000. Dinger's son Robert played cricket here and, according to his dad, enjoyed it more than at Millom. Distracted by stares and thereby missing Haverigg CC, a three-point turn is soon required in the fishing harbour around the corner, reached via a bridge that crosses the censorious River Lazy, on its way to the sea. And it wouldn't be fair leave unacknowledged how a spot on the Duddon estuary, hemmed in and protected by sandbanks, does have a certain charm.

Family groups make the most of what may be the last of the summer sunshine, picnics on the dunes. The ocean breeze is chilly, from which seagulls swoop, squawk and loot. Haverigg is Old Norse for 'the hill where oats are grown' apparently, a surprisingly rustic derivation in a place so obviously nautical. Thirty-odd miles south of our ultimate destination Whitehaven, however, the area's greatest claim to fame may be its Category C low security prison, one of the fictional settings for HMS Slade in the BBCTV sitcom *Porridge*.

Tucked away like Norman Stanley Fletcher, Haverigg CC is a distinctive presence back over the bridge, where the visitors are Wigton, Cumberland's Michael Slack *et al*. A patch of raised land acts as a car park bordered by the top of a compound cinder wall, over which six leaning backs can be seen, strung out like crows on a telegraph line, their owners viewing the game from outside as if disinclined – or afraid – to commit to going in. Wigton are batting, Slacky taking strike. His teammates await their turn at the pavilion end of a strip of benching that spans one entire length of the ground, scorebox opposite. This seating backs on to a long wall punctuated by a pair of green wooden styles – swifter exits, perhaps, should the natives grow restless – with a range of hills inland to the east.

Maybe it's over-vivid imagination, but the atmosphere is again more suspicious than friendly, certainly the least welcoming venue of the summer so far, though lap one at Furness ran it close, twenty-five miles away below the estuary. Perhaps they are just not used to casual visitors, especially those of a ground-hopping persuasion who might snap pictures here and there, or stand around taking notes.

'It's gin o'clock,' says a woman in the clubhouse, by a temporary bar festooned with bunting. It confirms a sign over the men's urinals advertising 'Gin Day', alongside another one imploring: 'Please put chewing gum in the bin behind you.' As racing from Goodwood booms out of the telly, Haverigg's Minister for Confrontation strides up with intent. 'What are you doing taking photos?' He is told. 'Oh, that's all right then. It's just with kids about and what have you...' Which might sound eminently reasonable were the average age of everyone in there not something in the region of 50 years old.

Outside, Slacky hits a single to complete his half-century in a running total of 118 for 1, and with a long drive ahead up miles of twisting coastline and other games to see, it seems like a good time to brave more glares from the Harbour Inn and bugger off. The B-road out is a zigzag affair, a bone-rattle over cattle grids and railway line – barrier up, thank goodness – before a double back to cross the same track further on, just as the fugitive is congratulating himself on having escaped. Seascale – who Jeeves, as informed as ever, has warned won't be at home today – are third on the schedule.

On such a Saturday afternoon in August, your average stretch of English coastline would likely be crawling with traffic, much of it heading to or from the beaches. Eskdale is all but deserted, hardly a motorist in sight, as fields roll by and dip toward the sea, pylons and wind-farms jostling for position with salt marshes to the west and, to the east, the copper and verdigris crags and screes fronting distant visions of Scafell Pike and the edge of a Lake District teeming with tourists. According to the map, Swinside Stone Circle and Muncaster Castle are up there somewhere, beyond Britain in Bloom-winning Bootle and its pretty if incongruous palm trees, Ravenglass (which, *The Guardian* reports, has a smell of 'seaweed and woodsmoke') and finally Drigg, whose rugged dunes hide a low-level nuclear waste dump that one report in 2014 claimed is 'virtually certain' to leak radioactive waste at some point. On foot, you could risk it and walk along the beach here to Seascale. At the wheel, the most pressing threat is a herd of cows led over the road by a nonchalant farmer.

As predicted, the cricket club is deserted, although a game of bowls goes on peacefully, next door. The ground looks forlorn and not just because no one is in it. A piebald outfield dips and rises like the equally empty skateboard park behind a sightscreen so lacking in slats as to be see-through. Rough wooden retainers fight a losing battle on a boundary crumbling to sand, a couple of well-maintained benches, displaying plaques for dear-departed members, the only contemporary touch. As settings go, it's bleak, so off to the sea we go, beneath a railway bridge and down to the front where the sun shines in a clear blue sky even as the wind begins to gust. Suddenly there are welcome signs of life – and a monument to its opposite.

Seascale is where, in June 2010, taxi-driver-turned-gunman Derrick Bird killed for the last time during a spree in which twelve lives, other than his own, were lost and eleven people injured, one of the most brutal and to this day unexplained crimes of its kind Britain has ever seen. The story is a haunting one of random acts of violence, a fruitless police chase and trail of devastation. Beginning by shooting his twin brother, David, eleven times in head and body in the village of Rowrah, he then went and did likewise to the family solicitor, Kevin Commons, in nearby Frizington, before sparking carnage in the streets of hometown Whitehaven among taxi-rank colleagues, one of whom, Darren Rewcastle, was slain, as witnessed by unfortunate pedestrians. Manhunt on, the public of neighbouring Egremont and Seascale were soon warned to stay indoors. A number of victims, whether murdered or left with life-changing injuries and trauma, were merely out walking, such as Susan Hughes, returning from the shops, and pensioner Kenneth Fishburn. Some, under the mistaken impression he was asking for directions, were called over to his car and shot in the face. Jennifer and James Jackson, a couple on a farm in the village of Wilton were next to be killed, before Isaac Dixon, a mole-catcher, was shot dead as he chatted to a farmer in field near Carleton. The rural trail of horror continued in another field outside a pub in Boonwood, near Gosforth, when former semi-professional rugby league player Garry Purdham lost his life while working with his uncle on mending a wire fence. After which, the mass-murderer then continued in the direction of Seascale.

It was heading here that Bird claimed his tenth fatality, Jamie Clarke, 23, shot in the head after being waved past like several other motorists as the killer began to drive more slowly. Harry Berger, having stopped his own car before courteously waving his attacker through the narrow passage beneath the railway bridge I just drove under, was shot twice in the arm, though thankfully survived. Cyclist Michael Pike was not so lucky, shot in the head at the second attempt along Drigg Road. Moments later, Jane Robinson was hit in the neck and head at point-blank range, after which Bird sped off towards his own doom, later found dead by his own hand in Oak How Woods, near Boot, after injuring four more innocents horrifically.

Next to a free municipal car park, there is a playground where children play with their families. Joyful. Alongside, the monument referred to, a castle turret of sorts in a little stone-built area complete with black cannon, a trio of flags and a commemorative plaque:

In Memory Of
All The Victims Of The
WEST CUMBRIA
SHOOTINGS
2nd June 2010

When built, there were complaints in the local press that, given the circumstances, the style was inappropriate, though time appears to have eased that controversy as evidenced by the fact it still stands. Going by the laughs and squeals of children enjoying a day at the seaside, time is doing its thing in other ways too. The ghastliness of that day is receding into what will fast become ancient folklore, the complexity of every life lived and ultimately wasted summed up with but a name and single line; the one true reality here and now.

With or without such tragedy, this is a coastline to stir thoughts morbid enough to unsettle anyone, yet Seascale has a melancholy beauty to it also. Apparently, it is often possible to see the Isle of Man from here, out across the sea haze, though not today. Nor from this spot anyway can the chimneys of Sellafield – the world's first commercial nuclear power station – be detected, the region's largest employer further up around the headland. When Bird went on the rampage, the afternoon shift was told to stay away as a precaution, until the coronavirus in 2020 the plant's only ever lockdown.

A site that in the early seventeenth century was home to seven tenant farmers was in the twentieth century chosen, with the coming of the Cold War, as an ideal spot on which to produce the plutonium required for atomic bombs. Known as Windscale from 1947-1981, the first big scare there came a decade later when a fire broke out in Reactor 1. Catastrophe was averted only by the filters insisted upon by chief engineer and future Nobel-winning physicist John Cockcroft, limiting the radiation spewed out into the atmosphere. Fast-growing unease about the dangers of such energy led to a 'consumer-friendly' rebrand back to Sellafield before, in the 1990s, reprocessing plants were built and environmental concerns acknowledged, issues of low, intermediate and high level nuclear waste clearance taking centre stage. To do such a subject justice would require many more chapters than we have remaining, if not an entire library. And anyway, while the site can boast its own shops, laundry and postal service, it has no cricket team. And so past all of those disquieting miles of fencing and armed guards on the gate we must go, bound for the marginally less harrowing if certainly far less apocalyptic market town of Egremont.

I jest. It's a pleasant little spot, unchanged in layout since the 12th century according to the scribes, with a ruined Norman castle and marketplace at one end of a busy main street. Sadly, we are three weeks early for the famous Crab Fair, held annually here on the third

Saturday in September. And that's a shame, since among its attractions are Cumberland and Westmorland wrestling, greasy pole climbing and, best of all, the World Gurning Championships, set to be won this year by Adrian Zivelonghi, aka Adrian from Coventry. 'I can't believe it. It's bizarre,' he will tell the *Whitehaven News* once his gums descend from his forehead, framed by a leather horse collar. Best woman gurner for the fourth time running will be Claire Spedding, 31, a local who'll dedicate the title to Anne Woods, also of Egremont, twenty-eight time winner before passing away in 2015.

As for cricket, there is not much happening in that line either, Egremont CC adjoining a rugby pitch, also inactive, on a little road leading to Gillfoot Park, behind a high-meshed fence that protects a busy roundabout from balls round and oval. In the cricket section, a couple work from the back of a car and trailer. They are assembling a marquee ahead of a concert tomorrow night – star turn Holborn Hillbillies, from Millom. 'They'll be here with their banjos,' says the male half of the duo. 'Mind, they all play those down there.'

It comes as a relief therefore to find an actual game taking place at the next spot on the itinerary, Cleator, who have a 2nd XI fixture with Ulverston. 'Jeeves' Latham had warned that even this may be scrapped as 'Ulverston seconds call a lot of games off,' but no. At a tiny and picturesque spot two miles inland, the scorebox reveals a home total of 157. After three overs, Ulverston are 4 without loss.

That this is second-team stuff is clear both from the standard and age-disparity on view – either bus pass or GCSEs. And the JD Campbell Memorial Ground is so well disguised as to verge on covert, flanked by trees, a grassy slope and fields of dandelion, cats ear, ribwort and yarrow. To leave the main road and drive on a track by a church, before crossing a decidedly shaky bridge, is to inhabit one more part of Cumbria where time has stood still. A horse grazes without prejudice in its pole-and-barbed-wire enclosure.

Cleator, as seen on our earlier laps, are doing well in the North Lancs and Cumbria League, challenging the leaders Cockermouth, where today the 1st XI will lose by four runs. Punching well above its weight, this is a small but well-run club that, as recently as 2013, went so far as to win the National Village Cup at Lord's, beating Rockhampton of Gloucestershire with only eight balls remaining in a real thriller. But all of that is a far cry from this.

At the crease, a grey-haired pensioner exhibits the most bizarre stance of the summer, and batting style to match – one part golfer chipping from a bunker, one part metal detectorist sweeping for treasure. His audience amounts to four men, one woman and a dog; the neighbouring nag taking no interest whatsoever. It's a low octane route to an eventual total of 61 all out and the moment soon comes to press on via a boundary marked not by rope but cast iron bollards.

*****

After such a journey, dropping into post-industrial Whitehaven – with the faded grandeur of its Georgian architecture and views of the salty ocean – feels simultaneously grounding and uplifting.

Its cricket club though lacks visual appeal, taking up a wide and unremarkable patch between a couple of supermarkets and a sports centre car park. Appearances, however, can be deceptive. This is a spot with a great historical tale to tell, as good a way in as any to the study of sport and culture in the Victorian era and beyond.

Richmond Terrace is in the oldest area of Whitehaven and today's visitors are Haverigg's 2nd XI who, according to the concrete scoreboard opposite, posted 83 all out. The home side's innings does not seem to be going any better, their running total is 37 for 8. As this game is no great shakes, let's beat a retreat to that glorious past.

One of the oldest sporting venues in Britain, 'The Playground' has hosted cricket since May 1838, although Whitehaven CC itself was formed in 1824. Today, a much different looking site is shared with the town's rugby union club, who have two pitches either side.

Back then, Whitehaven was a prosperous place, the principal seaport in Cumberland, no less, with a population of around 15,000, second only to Newcastle-upon-Tyne in coal trade eminence. Ahead of the opening, in the year of Queen Victoria's coronation, the town band paraded the streets before a crowd of 12,000 saw the Earl of Lonsdale perform the official ceremony with a presentation silver key, made by Mr Spittall, a jeweller in the Market Place.

A newspaper report dug up by you-know-who sets the scene: 'An enclosure about six acres in extent, approached from Howgill Street, surrounded by the Castle Gardens, the enclosure attached to the factory of Messrs Bell, and a meadow, that abuts upon Preston

Street and the Rope Walk of Messrs Hartley and Company.' The new ground was: '...a kind of amphitheatre, the New Houses forming a sloping side on the west, the Castle with its superbly wooded park on the east, the lofty buildings on the north and the shady sycamores on the south completed the picture.' Having moved in, Whitehaven played All England four times at The Playground in the 1850s and '60s, while Warwick Armstrong's 1921 Australian tourists would go on to play Cumberland here, quite a thought on an afternoon like this. Yet as the 20th century advanced, the combined deprivations of unemployment, economic depression and war did their worst, leaving the venue's high status reputation to sink into the realms of memory. Crowd numbers fell and wider interest failed.

Today, a family group, mainly elderly, sit before the ground's only real structure on white plastic chairs, a single-storey rendered clubhouse with bars on the windows behind which changing rooms are likely found. Otherwise, apart from the teams, this playground is all but deserted. Before long, it is time once again to depart.

If Whitehaven was an otherwise welcoming sight, the drive east via Bassenthwaite, Keswick, Thirlmere and Grasmere, home to Dove Cottage and the Wordsworth Museum, and then Rydal Water is akin to spiritual cleansing. In fact, so heartening and majestic are the views that an additional stop seems in order, at Ambleside, where that town's team moves towards the close of a Westmorland Cricket League fixture with Arnside.

As I swing in off the main road, the setting sun prepares to dip behind the spectacular ridge of Loughrigg Fell. I am welcomed by a chatty little group, none of whom I know. Each is revelling in a game that threatens a late run-chase, acknowledging their good fortune in having such a beautiful setting from which to watch it unfold. The visitors got 121 for 9 in their 45 overs; Ambleside are 56 for 8 with 17 overs left. They are destined not to get there. In fact they are soon all out for 69, not that it will ruin anyone's good humour.

The scorer is a young mother, two children at her feet, multi-tasking yet amiable as the rest, content to follow the cricket among friends in the open air, no scorebox required. An elderly chap in a baseball cap leans back contentedly, drinking it all in. 'On a gorgeous day like this,' he smiles, 'there is no better place to be.'

And so afternoon slips into evening.

CHAPTER NINE
THE FINAL TEST

Arriving in London by train, an American senator is shocked to hear local after local bemoaning the sad and sorry state of a once proud nation. 'I tell you, England's finished,' a ticket inspector tells him. 'She hasn't got a ruddy chance.'

'Little Hope for England,' reads the *Daily Mail*.

'England May Collapse Today,' reads the *Daily Express*.

It's only when he hails a taxi that the truth dawns. England in this context is a cricket team and, what's more, they are up against Australia today at the Oval. He tells the driver to take him there.

Pressing his way into a busy stand, he finds himself seated next to a fellow who resembles a youthful Richard Wattis. That's because it *is* Richard Wattis, playing a bespectacled toff, in suit and tie. Said toff studies a team-sheet intently as he awaits play, all the while side-eyeing this intrusive Yank with suspicion.

'Ought to be an exciting day,' says the senator (Canadian actor Stanley Maxted), by way of polite small talk.

'I hope not,' Wallis replies. 'All I want is to see the boys pile up the runs quietly and not get out. Don't want any excitement, thanks.'

'Pardon me, sir,' the senator goes on, 'but as a stranger in these parts, may I ask a question?'

'Go ahead.'

'This, I gather, is the fourth day of this particular game. I also

356

gather that during the past few weeks there have been other games, each of five days, between these same teams?'

'Correct.'

'I also gather that this particular game cannot possibly decide anything, whichever team wins.'

'That's right.'

'It is also, I'm told, likely that neither side will in fact win this game.'

'Well, let's hope so...'

'Now, looking around this field, I'd say at a rough estimate there are 30,000 people here?'

'Oh, about that.'

'Now, your hope that there will be no excitement is, you would say, a fairly general view among all these spectators?'

'Of course, if they're English.'

'I see. [He doesn't.] Yes, I see...'

'So what was your question?'

'There's plainly no point in asking it.'

Thawing a little, Wattis then briefly explains the state of play on the scoreboard before: 'Oh lord. There is something happening...'

'What?' says the American.

'They are taking the rain covers off.'

*****

The film is *The Final Test* (1954), its director is Anthony Asquith and the screenplay is by no less a dramatist than Terence Rattigan. Its two stars are Jack Warner, the following year to find fame in *Dixon of Dock Green*, the long-running BBC TV police serial, and the never less than delightful Robert Morley. With cameos from cricketing legends Len Hutton, Denis Compton, Alec Bedser, Godfrey Evans, Jim Laker, Cyril Washbrook and others, it's a shame Carlisle aren't showing it in the clubhouse as Cumberland and Lincolnshire wait for the predicted morning dew to clear, so they can begin their last Minor Counties Championship match of the 2018 season.

A film of no little charm with a surprisingly philosophical bent, *The Final Test* was on Talking Pictures TV last night, comical viewing before a fixture that, for the Cumbrians anyway, means absolutely nothing results-wise. Their opponents, however, top the Eastern Division table, thanks to a winning draw with Suffolk a fortnight ago in Ipswich, as Cumberland were sharing a stalemate by the Tyne.

There being no action yet, thoughts drift back to Jack 'Evening all' Warner's performance as a bloke romancing a barmaid at least half his age, while holding her to the highest moral standards. In the film, he plays a famous fictitious cricketer preparing for one last Test match, as per the title, thereafter to retire following a glittering career in a country thoroughly obsessed with cricket. Sadly, his son Reggie is obsessed with poetry and takes no interest in his dad's achievement, preferring to compose verse in his bedroom rather than attend the old man's glorious swansong.

Robert Morley is in top form as renowned poet and playwright Alexander Whitehead, hero-worshiped by young Reggie. So much so that he opts to meet his hero rather than see his father's innings. Conversely, cricket-loving Whitehead has little interest in another wannabe before he discovers he is the illustrious batsman's son. At which revelation, off they tear in Whitehead's motor to Kennington.

En route, Reggie makes his feelings about cricket known: 'The fact of the matter is, I find it so frightfully dull.'

'Frightfully dull?' says Morley, astounded. 'Well of course it's frightfully dull; that's the point. Any game can be exciting. Football, dirt-track racing, roulette ... the measure of the vast superiority cricket has over any other game is that it steadfastly refuses to cater to this boorish craving for excitement. To go to cricket to be thrilled is as stupid as to go to a Chekhov play in search of melodrama.' Chekhov and cricket, the poet concludes, share great similarities: 'Same sense of shape and pattern, form and design, each time with that superbly satisfying art which conceals art, having the same passion for the beautifully inconclusive.'

Certainly this interminable wait at Edenside is proving to be inconclusive, beautiful or not. On the drive north, the early morning drizzle enveloping Tebay had cleared come Shap. Penrith woke to hazy sunshine. In Carlisle the drizzle resumed, the city's cricket pitch damp and bejewelled under a faerie-woven carpet of gossamer.

September's constellation: Cygnus. The swan. One was spotted on the way here, a flash of white in a patchwork field striped by hay harvests piled high on rumbling tractors. Birds have begun to migrate with summer on the wane, northern vistas otherwise active now surrendering to the lull between seasons.

Inevitably, the planned 10.30am start was delayed and although the rain lifts all but completely within an hour, conditions underfoot remain precarious. None of which stops a handful of Lincolnshire players kicking a football about by the nets, as four Cumberland lads wander back to a pavilion bustling with amateur climatologists.

Once again, Cumberland lack key players, not least the captain, Gary Pratt. Last Sunday, Richmondshire were to play two games in a day – that ECB National Club Championship quarter-final with Ormskirk, kicking off at 10.30am in Richmond, and the final of the Super 15s in Redcar, the start there 5.45pm. Heavy rain thwarted that, although there had been a result of sorts in the first. The early start meant they could each get ten overs in, Ormskirk winning the toss and coming to regret it. The hosts swiftly belted a remarkable 158 for the loss of two wickets, the only batsmen being Cumberland players. Pratt was bowled for 14 and Matty Cowling 11, but Mattie McKiernan hit a mammoth 100 not out – including ten sixes – in only 34 balls, Bob Carr making 26 not out. In reply, Ormskirk managed 92 for 5, not bad but not good enough. Ex-Cumberland pair Gary Knight, on 23, and Scott Lees on 14 were the two visitors with wickets intact. It set Richmondshire on course for a semi-final today with Northern, meaning no Pratt, Wood or anyone else could be here. Cumberland, the county side, was weakened yet again.

The rain that Sunday also pushed the all-new Minor Counties T20 finals day to a reserve date – Bank Holiday Monday 27 August. And having dispatched Devon and Norfolk respectively in the semis, Berkshire it was who celebrated a six-wicket final win over Cheshire seen by a couple of hundred in belatedly sunny Buckinghamshire. The following day, the Minor Counties' rep side, the Unicorns, fell to a four-wicket defeat by the MCC at the same venue. Adam Syddall was in the side, not so Toby Bulcock. On Wednesday 29 August, also at Wormsley, Cheshire beat Devon by a mere two runs in the final of the Knockout Trophy, their first such success in 22 years, as Yorkshire staged its first County Championship match in 128 days, the tide against long-form cricket most definitely turning.

Four days later in Carlisle, the expected morning dew. Why did they ever stage a Championship final here, as happened in 2015, when Cumberland famously won it? Mike Latham, chairman of cricket then, is here with Toby (the dog) and explains. 'That was when one of the competing teams used to host it and there was nowhere else available. We were lucky with the pitch for mid-September, only four months before the floods.' Doubly lucky, given how it was over just after lunch on day two. Coming north expecting to win, Oxfordshire took one look at the ground and were beaten before they started. 'The MCCA were pissed off. They had all booked into the Crown Hotel [in the picturesque village of Wetheral] and liked a good trip away.' So fed up were they, in fact, that every final since has been held at a neutral venue. Common sense, really.

Ben Howarth's dad too is here. 'The umpires are pissing about,' is his opinion, the day now overcast and muggy. 'They do that. Look at Northumberland, no need to be off four hours that morning was there? Then on ... then bring them off for a spot of rain ... then, when it's dark, back on again...' At Blackpool yesterday, he watched Richard Gleeson take 7 for 43. Gleeson's game with county side Northants had only lasted three days, so they said he could go back to his club. 'He would have played for England this year if not for his injuries.'

Geoff Minshaw sits in the scorebox alone. He reckons they will have lunch at 12.50pm and start after that, the covers tentatively removed as he speaks. Cockermouth also won yesterday, in their case against 'this lot', Carlisle, and now need only five points to be certain of the North Lancashire and Cumbria League title. 'The problem today isn't dew,' is the Minshaw verdict. 'It rained here last night, that's what all the droplets are. It'll be a spinner's wicket.' The floods here left the wicket soft. 'It's been a good season this summer, I've enjoyed it,' he reflects, the prince of all he surveys.

There will be two changes from Jesmond. Ryan Maddock, the fast bowler from Ormskirk, replaces Liam Watkinson, back on term time tomorrow, school holidays over. Marcus Stables is on a beach somewhere overseas, so Carlisle's Ben Davidson comes in for him, his brother Jonathan 12th man. 'It's a family affair,' says their father, Mark, busying around the clubhouse ... tea and coffee available, England's Fourth Test v India on a propped-up tablet by the boiler, the tourists struggling on 17 for 2. 'Nothing wrong with the wicket,' Mark sighs, meaning the one outside. 'The umpires have to keep it fair to both sides, I suppose.' Fair enough, although today's visitors certainly seem keen to get on with it. And why shouldn't they be, with the Eastern Division title and a place in the final at stake?

Cumberland chairman Neil is here, as is John Patterson, while Eric chats with one of the umpires who'd been in charge at Furness, still talking, obviously. As another India wicket falls – 22 for 3, chasing 243 – John, business head on, speaks of how Workington would have handled the scandal: 'Proper meeting ... clear the air ... move on.' He is still not on the committee here and has no intention of joining. Come season's end, though, he'll be persuaded otherwise.

The toss comes after lunch, won by Lincolnshire. Needing to force the pace, they bat first. Play commences at 1.30pm and Syds takes the first over, outfield still wet in parts, drops of water on every blade of grass. There is still no sign of Steve Sharp. Gilbert is here, of course. The application has gone in for the return of his driving licence, he tells Chris Hodgson and family, now awaiting a decision.

Along the giant benched hill, Rob and Lesley Cairns hawk their teamsheets, though the market is small. After a hearty Sunday lunch in a pavilion that resembles the sort of railway station waiting-room Will Hay or Arthur Askey might haunt, the players belatedly emerge to an audience of around fifty. Like Ben's dad, some watch from parked cars lining the road by the riverside, on the way in. It's from just such a vantage point, towards the end of his life, that Bob Bowman used to spectate; nowadays he has a lounge in his name at the rear of the clubhouse. It is there that Neil Atkinson agrees to an informal debrief re the campaign about to pass.

The chairman is in good spirits by the look of it, owing much to how Penrith have survived in the Northern Premier League by beating Garstang yesterday to avoid relegation. Greg Hall, moved up the order, contributed 57 runs. 'It was a relief. We couldn't afford to go to Blackpool for the last game because they look like being champions. We had to win and did so.' Greg isn't playing today. He's a teaching assistant and so back at school himself. 'He wouldn't have been selected anyway. We've gone like for like with replacements.'

Considering the number of players used, he reckons a bottom-half finish for Cumberland has been okay. 'There have been good opportunities for young players to come in... which shows that if they are prepared to put themselves out they will get a chance.' A transitional year, he calls it: 'Cumberland face challenges that other counties don't, such as the weather. It's wetter in the west than in the east.' And then of course there was Prattgate at Furness, the outcome and potential punishment from which he says the club is still awaiting. 'Whatever the decision, obviously we'll go with that.'

And from a personal perspective? Did his first year as chairman live up to expectations? 'Since we spoke at the start of the season in Cheshire, about what the role would likely involve, I'd say my views have evolved a little,' he chuckles. 'We had a few situations the county hasn't had to deal with in previous years, but that said, as a club we are stronger for it. As I said in Newcastle, we need to look at the structure and how we make changes that will benefit us all. I'm excited about how things are going to pan out. If we can keep the nucleus of the team together and bring in new players as opportunities arise, we are in a good position.'

What about the chairman of cricket, Steve Sharp? Where is he? There is still no Toby Bulcock either. Or Sam Dutton.

'Steve has been away to Italy and is back now. We've got the season debrief at Crooklands at the end of this month and those structural issues will be discussed there, among other things.'

It ought to be an interesting meeting, that one.

'I think it could be,' he laughs.

*****

To begin with, the game holds little fascination. The wicket is too slow, outfield slower, and by the 14th over Lincolnshire have only amassed 20 runs when their first opener falls. Jacques du Toit gets down sharply in the slips, off the bowling of Maddock, one of four wickets the Lancastrian takes in the innings. Lincolnshire's second victim tumbles just six runs later, to Chris Hodgson's 50th ever wicket for Cumberland, an admirable milestone given a lack of game-time this year. Shortly after drinks, the spinner strikes again to leave the visitors 54-3, aided by a Ben Davidson catch at mid-off that does for batsman number four.

Third man Louis Kimber ploughs on and it is largely thanks to him that Lincs settle and have reached 143 for 5 when his wicket goes for a personal haul of 68, he and the batsman before also falling to Hodgson, lbw and caught Josh Boyne respectively. Kimber's last partner at the crease, Daniel Freeman, then takes the reins, moving his side past 200 before he's out for 45 in an eventual total of 231 for 8 declared. The back end of all that, however, takes place another day. At the close of day one, Lincolnshire will still be 182 for 5.

The afternoon has its moments, entertainment-wise, but the tale is one mainly of frustration, gloomy here as the rest of the nation bathes in late-summer sunshine. At one stage, former sports shop owner Dicky Spruce, the ex-Cumberland wicketkeeper last seen at Keswick and Penrith, embarks upon a lap with his walking stick and a man not yet spotted this season, namely Langwathby-born former goalkeeper, cricketer and egg-farmer Graham Monkhouse.

Sporting a jaunty salmon pink shirt and holding forth with an eloquence that betrays familiarity with a boardroom table, Graham retired from first-class cricket in 1987, aged 33. His team was Surrey and he'd gone there as a 24-year-old in 1981, from a county he played with since the age of 17 – another on the list of late-starters forged in Minor Counties cricket. His first Cumberland game was a defeat to Durham in South Shields. First-class career over, he had a further year with Cumberland but found he was no longer up to it. He continued to play club cricket, however, until he was 40 in fact. 'A lot of pro-cricketers just quit,' he says now. 'Not me, I loved playing.'

So how did he land the 'job' of Cumberland CCC patron and what exactly does it involve? 'Alan Wilson rang me up,' he says, as a hint of music from the last day of the Carlisle Fringe drifts in over the trees. 'I played for Cumberland with Alan, so know him really well. He has called me a couple of times about taking on a role, but I'm heavily involved with the MCC, so it's difficult to find the time.'

Graham, a more than handy all-rounder in his day, right arm bat and ball, is in fact on the main committee at Lord's, in the eye of the storm you might say. He has been an MCC member since 1982, playing around 150 times for them over the years, and can also boast of having been a professional goalkeeper at Workington and Carlisle when those clubs were in the Football League, before a knee injury as a 22-year-old ended those ambitions. As for farming, he is semi-retired now, he says, and lives just outside Penrith. His job with the MCC came about on the back of a golfing trip with Mike Gatting.

'The MCC were going through a lot of disruption due to redevelopment of the ground, I won't bore you with the details, and

Mike said they were very keen to get more cricket-orientated people in positions of responsibility on the main committee. That's the only one that is elected by members – you have to be invited, proposed, nominated and then say your little piece. There are 18,000 members of the MCC who have to vote you on.' The term of service is three years and Graham began his three years ago, meaning he leaves next month. 'But I was also co-opted on to the cricket committee, which carries on for another three years. Then I can put myself up for re-election to the main committee again, but have to have a year off.'

It is apparent that his real value these days – for Cumberland and indeed every minor county – is as a well-placed champion in high places. It must be handy to have a supporter in the corridors of power, able to point out the odd home truth now and then, Lord's also being home to the England and Wales Cricket Board of course, the sport's national governing body since 1997. How does the club patron see the all-important MCCA discussions panning out?

'I'll be very surprised if they remove funding,' he says. 'The difficulty is, if they reduce and keep reducing it then it becomes incredibly difficult for counties to continue. And I don't just mean Cumberland. There is a limit to sponsorship, a limit to membership, and in the grand scheme of thing the Minor Counties has a place. I wouldn't have played first-class cricket if I hadn't played Minor Counties cricket. I know there isn't a huge pathway but the difficulty now is everything's about academies, Premier Leagues ... though there aren't too many Premier League lads coming through.'

Are Cumberland and friends right to feel under threat? 'Yes they are, if the funding keeps being reduced. It's got to be tough.' He is less a voice in the wilderness, he goes on, than an educator with regard to what the Minor Counties brings to areas like this, Carlisle, among other things. 'In London there are hundreds of opportunities to further a career thereabouts ... Essex, Surrey, Sussex, Middlesex, Kent, Hampshire ... that's not the case in Workington, Whitehaven, Penrith and Carlisle. This has always been an area where it is very important to step up from club to minor county. They have a friend on the MCC board, for sure. I still see this as an integral part of the make-up of cricket in England and Wales.'

Long may it prosper? 'Yes, and it's important too to remember that not everybody wants to play first-class cricket. For some people, this is the level they want to play at. It's not all about the Roots and the Stokeses and the Andersons ... the ECB is supposed to be about representing the whole of cricket.'

Graham still hasn't really revealed, however, what his patronage will require. 'To be honest, I'm a little bit in the dark myself, as I've only just taken it on. Sadly, this year I've not had the best of health so have not been able to get to as many games as I'd have liked. I suppose, without being arrogant, I see myself as being a bit of a figurehead, someone well known around the county scene here, contributing what I can and helping to promote the club. When I'm down in London, that will be a second string to my bow, won't it, patron of Cumberland? It's a club I'll always have happy memories of because it's the club that gave me a chance to further my career.'

A minute before tea, drizzle returns and not just on the lemon cakes. On the tablet, India have moved on to 142 for 5, needing 103 to win. Outside, ominous clouds gather stubbornly overhead. At just gone 4.00pm it's getting dark and, after the umpires confer in the middle, a decision is taken to continue despite the murk and complete the remainder of an eventual 78 overs.

Elsewhere, Richmondshire advance to the ECB Club final after victory over their Crosby-based opponents, Gary Pratt helping himself to a half-century and three wickets. At least there can be no clash with Minor Counties fixtures now. And down in Haverigg, Furness CC too have lots to celebrate – beating Workington in the Cumbria County Cup. During a highly competitive final, Sam Dutton scores an unbeaten 59 and is named man of the match.

*****

Monday morning, drizzle returns. Constant drizzle of the sort that will wipe out a morning session, necessitate an early lunch and then refuse to shift all day. The only action is the inaugural Cumberland Football Tennis Championship, as orchestrated by Josh and Slacky, which the duo win, 5-2, beating Ben Davidson and Ryan Maddock in the final. After which, they all go for a swim before the day is abandoned at 3.30pm. In the evening, the officials and players – apart from 12th man Jonathan, banned by his brother – go for a meal at Adriano's Italian restaurant, not far from the Crown and

Mitre, their hotel in the city centre. 'Roosevelt stayed there in 1910,' says John Patterson. 'It's still got the same décor.' The waiters are told it's Geoff's birthday, so they bring him ice cream, which he asks if they'll save until February.

Today came an official Met Office announcement that 2018 has been Britain's joint-hottest summer since 1910, when records began, a tie with 1976, 2003 and 2006. By Tuesday, sunshine has returned, blue sky over the Toby Carvery swinging in off the M6, though cloud soon gathers, the outfield again wet, raising fears that the game may be abandoned completely. Thankfully for Lincolnshire, those worries are alleviated and the teams walk on at 11.15am.

By then, it has become clear that if there is to be a result here there will need to be some sort of contrivance. The option agreed to is a double declaration, Lincolnshire first setting a target and gaining a batting point maybe, before Cumberland chase that total in their 'second' innings, having forfeited their first. It's suggested that stand-in captain Jacques may refuse to go along with this, as is his right. According to chitchat, the visitors have a reputation for not helping others out in similar circumstances. The plan though is agreed to.

Carlisle secretary Mark Davidson and chairman Mike Rayson are up to their arms in soapsuds, doing the washing up. Word also comes in of a sensational nature: Steve has resigned his position and did so last week, reveals one connected contact. 'Fallen on his sword,' is the quote. Odd then how no one has yet mentioned the fact, even when questioned. The contact goes on to say that the MCCA is 'very angry' about the club's 'clear duplicity.' Gary Pratt will be banned for two games at least next year and the club is to be punished too.

Lincolnshire intend to target 225 runs – which would actually reap a couple of batting points – before declaration, Cumberland already having two bowling points via their five wickets taken so far.

A little down the hill on the way in is a wooden pavilion that has seen better days, in which currently the juniors get changed. A plaque reads: 'Jimmy Little Memorial', the chap in question a Carlisle legend of the 1970s, famed for bowling quickly in jam jar-bottom spectacles. 'He played football in 'em too,' says Mike Rayson, who, washing up finished for now, wanders over with Mark Davidson to shed more light on those Roman remains referred to when passing through earlier this season. If this bit of the ground is re-developed as the club would like, rather than let Jimmy vanish to history they will memorialise him somewhere else in the venue.

But first, talk touches on Dinger Bell, nursing his grievances at Millom. Both of Mark's sons played under Dinger, so it is natural he would have insight. 'His ways are old school,' the Carlisle secretary says, 'but, generally, people wanted him to carry on in some capacity. Look at his record for the sort of cricketers produced ... his methods clearly had merit. A fraction of parents didn't like the way he was and some of the comments in his letters were non-PC, you might say, by today's standards. But ask my lad, Ben, and he'll tell you... "I've set off at half-past-seven on a freezing January morning to go down to Millom and would do it again."' After the fuss, they played a county game at Arnside and Dinger wasn't allowed anywhere near. 'He stood in a field over the road, watching it from there. Very sad.'

As for these Roman bathhouses – a 'once in a lifetime find,' according to one archaeologist – the club unearthed them and much else while trying to relocate their clubhouse to higher ground after Storm Desmond did its worst in 2015. Nowadays they are re-buried and backfilled with soil and rubble under a blanket of weeds, nettles and unsightly vegetation. But let Mike Rayson tell it.

'The floods were sixteen-foot deep,' the chairman says. 'We decided to move the pavilion, had all the reports done, the last one being an archaeological survey. It was decided to dig three pits. Pit two found the side of the bathhouse we are literally on top of now. Turned out it's very significant – it is the bathhouse of Ala Petriana, the most feared legion in Rome, and it belonged to the largest fort on Hadrian's Wall. They were sent to this area to deal with the Picts, the Scots, who were very aggressive and needed putting down.' Not only that, but on a site thought to be around 1,600 years old, various items of weaponry, coins, pottery and even a piece of carved stone upon which was carved a reference to the wife of Emperor Septimus Severus (193-211 AD) were discovered. 'It was a Eureka moment for the archaeologists and a bit of a pain in the arse for us.'

Now to a casual observer, that may seem flippant, not to say a miserable response to such a phenomenal historical find. After all, with a little creativity, it could be the making of the club. Imagine ... glass walkways ... tourists galore ... a goldmine. Suddenly, Carlisle CC is a site of national importance. Except that, well, that was exactly what they'd thought, to begin with. 'It could be a golden egg,' agrees Mike, 'or it could be a millstone.' In its earliest stages, the development was said by one councillor to offer an opportunity to 'do for Carlisle what the Jorvik Viking discoveries did for York.' The club was certainly open to working with whoever they needed to, in order to preserve the finds properly and seek an alternative dryer location for its long-suffering clubhouse. 'At the moment, Historic England are holding us back and it has cost us two years.'

The latest theory is there's likely to be an imperial villa down there too, three tennis courts wide – an apt means of measurement since much of it is also beneath a disused tennis court. Cavendish Tennis Club now play further up the hill, forced out after the floods by lack of sufficient insurance funds to pay repair costs of £32,000.

'Under one old rubble pile there were all these vaulting tubes ... hypocaust plumbing ... behind us is a kiln where they'd walk in and put their stuff.' Historic England, Mike says, are concerned by the river being so close, there may be seepage. 'They think water will come underneath when its in spate, but have done no reports. The flood that got us was the first in five hundred years to touch this part of the ground ... they're talking rubbish. We know a civil engineering company that would basically block it off and make sure no seepage comes through, but they won't even look at that or reply to emails. They want it underground. The council's desperate to get it out and we are desperate to get it out too. Really and truthfully, we need the pavilion built. It may not look like it, but we are stood three metres higher here than we would be over there.' He points to the current clubhouse opposite, down in the bowl. 'We had all the levels done.'

Still, the dream of what this place might one day be persists and the process has at least been an education. 'I can now tell you what a pilae stack is,' Mike says. It was 'one of those things where you had to come down and have a look. My 23-year-old son was fascinated. It looked like something that had just been built.' And wherever that new pavilion goes, it will almost certainly have a museum aspect. 'We've got so much stuff. What I said about the Ala Petriana ... they were sort of mystical ... a bit like the SAS in the 1980s. No-one knew who they were, but if the Petriana turned up, you had a problem. Until now, no-one could quite pin them down, just knew they were "up there" somewhere. It is a massive, massive find.'

*****

Edenside: maybe once an actual – as well as natural – amphitheatre. As they sit on hillside benches among the spirits of legionaries, auxiliaries and other long-dead citizens of the Roman Empire, at least the 21st-century spectators who are here today can finally see some cricket, ritual slaughter having thankfully gone out of fashion.

Joining them is a trident of gladiators from Richmondshire, Bob Carr, Sam Wood and Gary Pratt, here for the denouement of Cumberland's year, if not yet their own. Having at last tasted victory in their Kerridge Cup final with Middlesbrough, and a week ago beaten Seaton Carew in the competition that caused all the fuss, three weeks from now they will meet and vanquish Middlesex side Stanmore by five wickets in the final of the ECB National Club Championship at Bristol. No one could call them idle.

President Alan Wilson puts in an appearance, natty in club tie and blazer, and Pratt's partner Leanne has a hug and kiss for Gilbert, her growing bump now keeping her awake: 'Doesn't want to sleep,' she says. Gilbert has come by bus. His grandson got on at Aspatria, so he'd budged up to let grandma and grandson have a good chat. There is a last-day-of-term feel to proceedings, helped along by the old fellow's anecdotes. 'I used to live in Carlisle. Coming home once, I turned the corner on our street and what was sticking out the front door but a horse's arse!' His daughter had parked it in the hall.

With weather and cricket brightening, out front of the pavilion is a nice place to be this fine September afternoon. The season's cast is here in not far short of its entirety, Steve and Toby the most noteworthy exceptions. 'Steve's working,' says Eric.

On one bench, the parents of Ben and Josh chat happily, Boyne junior off to Australia this winter, as are a few of his teammates. Rob and Lesley – seldom far apart – sit contentedly with at least one glass of red to hand, and chairman Neil leans on a gate by a white picket fence, before taking a solo lap.

On the back row, old-timers wax nostalgic with Gilbert, as Gary, leaning on a rail, talks to a member of the opposition on a raised area outside the changing rooms. Alan Wilson meanwhile discusses travel arrangements with an elderly bloke who is about to head out to Sri Lanka. 'All taken care of,' the man tells him, 'jabs and what have you. Little prick in the bottom...'

'I don't think you were looking for those words,' Alan says.

Mike Latham and dog too are here, while Adam Syddall's parents and wife push the baby in a pram. Roxine Beaumont-Sempill, Matty's mother, sits alone in her little tent next to the sightscreen, as usual, while the Eden meanders ceaselessly behind. Eric, a natural organiser, busies about in conversation with everyone. This is who he is. Couldn't change if he tried.

Every one of them, like their observer, is captured in a snapshot of time.

Wicket! Having made sure and steady progress, Lincs are 204 for 6, Freeman out to Ben Davidson's second catch of the game, the first of three Maddock scalps at a cost of two runs. Lincolnshire's 'keeper Carl Wilson is next, caught behind by the slightest of nicks after a bag of sand is brought on amid concerns about the ball. Curtis Free is the last of the trio, stumps scattered to an extent that suggests this 'slow pitch' must yet contain pace. The batting side's bonus point is under threat. Mobiles out, the progress or otherwise of Lincs' Eastern Division rivals is eagerly sought on social media.

They needn't have worried. Alex Willerton, Lincolnshire's next batsman, hammers a six off Josh Boyne to bring that self-imposed target a chunk closer. In the flurry that follows, the title hopeful then dispatches three sixes and a four in one over, allowing Lincolnshire to declare on 231 for 8. As the players depart the field, Neil wanders off on a lap with Gary, having shown him a text message presumably just received. Eric and Alan share a confab behind the pavilion.

Cumberland require 232 runs from 60 overs remaining in the day, the sky azure and increasingly glorious. A target of four an over, then, which may not sound like much but will be a tall order on a pitch as large as this one, outfield still damp and funereal. At the end of over nine, Ross and Sempy have amassed only eight runs between them. Lunch is a refreshing salad whose preparation somehow sets off the clubhouse fire alarm just as, equally mysteriously, a portrait of HM The Queen suddenly drops with a clatter from the wall.

'Lovely day for it,' a passer-by says to John Patterson, when play resumes. Pleasant conditions indeed in which to close a campaign.

'You lads from Kendal have brought the sunshine,' John replies.

Slacky's family too are in attendance and have in their ranks another sporting member of the clan, his cousin Sara McGlashan, a New Zealand international women's cricketer from Hawke's Bay. Soon, she too will head to Australia, part of the Sydney Sixers squad in the Women's Big Bash, a wicketkeeper. Through this summer, she has played in the Kia Super League with Southampton's Southern Vipers. The Cumbrian scenery is very much like New Zealand, she says, happy to talk while supporting her kin.

When Sempy is caught behind and Tyler McGladdery bowled, the hosts are struggling on 41 for 2. Sara's cousin comes in and for a while he and Ross settle to the task without every really looking like quickening the scoring rate sufficiently. Then Ross – whose cousin Katie Zelem will this month score in Manchester United's first-ever Women's Super League match, a 12-0 defeat of Aston Villa – is clean bowled for 24. Fours on other grounds are hard-run threes here; it's a pitch big enough to host two games at once – and has done so.

With 30 overs remaining Cumberland are still 167 behind, Lincs bowling as well as they might, given what is at stake. Slacky's batting partner now is Ben Davidson who, after a much-needed drinks break, drags his side past 100 with a four that only just makes it to the rope. That though is followed by Slacky's demise via a ball that stands up to be hit, but is dispatched only as far as the hands of square leg. Ben loses his off-stump, no score added, and in the box Geoff Minshaw immediately changes the tins to read 106 for 5.

There are enough overs remaining in which to reach a target of 126, far from impossible normally, especially with Jacques du Toit and Josh Boyne at the crease. The South African survives a scare, the ball clipping a leg-side pad and not snicked to the 'keeper. Lincs doubtless see him as their last threat. Shortly after tea, with only nine runs added between them, Jacques, frustrated, skies one so high the fielder beneath it has time to nip off and brush his teeth. That may be it, especially when Josh falls, lbw, one run later. His replacement, Ben Howarth, is then judged similarly, out for a golden duck, carbon copy. At 126 for 8 it is all over bar the handshakes.

Or at least it should be. Chris Hodgson survives the hat-trick ball – just – as it whizzes through to the 'keeper, before contributing a handy 12 runs while Ryan Maddock increasingly takes charge at the other end. But when he too falls lbw – perhaps the umpires, like

Gilbert, have a bus to catch – last man Syds comes in and no-one is expecting very much there. At which point Eric and Neil wander over to report that the MCCA has awarded the club a 16-point deduction. Instead of fifth bottom, they'll finish fourth-bottom. Gary Pratt has indeed been banned for the first two matches of 2019. Neither appears disheartened. It seems a relief more than anything.

Out in the middle, the gallant last pair slog on, with heart if not bat, before Maddock is finally gone, caught after 33 hard-earned runs in a loss by 53 runs, Syds 4 not out. Lincolnshire are elated. Despite one-time favourites Staffs hammering Northumberland, and Suffolk beating Cambridgeshire in the hope of a first divisional title in thirteen years, the Eastern Division title is theirs for a third successive season. They will now face – and in a fortnight's time be beaten by – Berkshire, eventual victors by an innings and 32 runs in the 2018 Minor Counties Championship final at Banbury.

The Cumberland batsmen, meanwhile, repair to a beer on the balcony, where their non-batting colleagues have seen the campaign seep inevitably away. As with much of the rest of the season, with a little more vim and vigour – more oomph – from the outset, here was another game there for the taking, rain-affected though it was. No-one seems overly bothered, this being 'a year of transition.'

Alan Wilson, Dicky Spruce and the latter's trusty walking stick meanwhile complete what may be one of the slowest lap of all time. Back in the traps, Alan shares his farewells.

'See you next season, Dicky.'

'Well, you will if I'm still alive,' his old clubmate replies.

'Oh, don't you worry about that,' says Alan, kindly. 'Only the good die young.'

CHAPTER TEN
CHARITY BEGINS AT HOME

Mist descends on Goat Gap. October under a week away, nights are drawing in. On the descent through Nook and Cow Brow, a pair of hamlets on the A65, cosy firesides are reflected in passing cottage windows as intermittent brake-lights glare an angry red.

It is Wednesday 26 September, evening of the season debrief and a lively occasion it promises to be. As with its March equivalent, the venue is again Crooklands, the roadside hotel on the way to Kendal, although this meeting is in a different room: the 'Hayloft'.

Normally its whitewashed walls and beamed ceilings host private parties and 'an award-winning Sunday Carvery'. Tonight they are in the service of Cumberland CCC. Tables are pushed together in a rectangle, seats positioned around the outside. By the top table, a screen stands upon which a power-point presentation is soon to be projected, Roxine Beaumont-Sempill and son grappling with the settings. On Sunday, Sempy flies to Melbourne.

The pub's rabbit-warren feel comes into its own at this time of year, accentuating its Dickensian air. One alcove contains a pair of porcelain pigs. In another, a stuffed owl glowers with indeterminate menace from within a glass box. On a chimney breast hangs the head of an old stag, fireplace purely decorative nowadays, home to a pair of scales rather than, andiron, scuttle and nutty slack.

Several committee members are absent, among them the fall-out-averse Geoff Minshaw, Alan Wilson (on holiday as promised), and most significantly Steve Sharp. Gary and Leanne Pratt are most definitely present however, as are Toby Bulcock and Mike Latham.

To begin with, the mood is chatty and relaxed. John Patterson and Eric went to see Gary and Co in their ECB club final last week, a victory that earns a round of applause. Introduced by chairman Neil Atkinson, Roxine then kicks off proceedings, her 25-minute presentation an array of surprises. 'No heckling at the back,' she says, as her son embarks upon his shared duties. Uncomfortable as he is, Sempy hauls himself through. The slide goes in:

Cumbria Cricket
Charitable Trust &
Talent Support

Heard in respectful silence, a proposal is presented for just such an organisation, with lots to take in. Detailed costings of what will be needed 'to support cricketing talent in Cumbria' are distributed, while year-on-year projections are outlined and there is a character portrait of the chap apparently prepared to underpin the scheme – Richard Roberts, son of former Cumberland 'publicity officer' Ted, who features so prominently in John Hurst's 1982 history of the club. It's then that Roxine commands the floor, speaking with an ease that might not have been anticipated given her usual preference for sitting alone in her tent. The gist of the spiel is that of the current 20 minor counties, nine have charitable trusts, Cheshire's reportedly having raised £15,000 in 2016 alone. Wealthy Roberts Jr, it appears, is keen to fund similar progress on his father's old stomping ground.

Then comes the snag, anticipated at Flitwick. If it's to happen, it will have to be a combined effort. 'We'd need a representative from your board, a representative from Cumbria Cricket Ltd and neutrals like myself ... the Board have been talking about a charitable trust for a while.' Bob Simpson, it seems, has already been approached.

'I knew Ted very well,' says Eric.

Richard it turns out is Ted's only child and the owner of a national firm of solicitors, head office in Grange-over-Sands. 'He also lectures at Durham University in Law, a busy chap,' Roxine says. 'His legal expertise includes setting up trusts. He has led a hedonistic life and is a fairly wealthy man. He would have been wealthier still if he hadn't been divorced from two husbands, but never mind.'

That brings a distinct rumble around the table.

'Now he's turned sixty, about to retire, and would like to devote the rest of his life to raising money for charity, especially cricket in Cumbria because it was such an important part of his father's life.' Richard's introductory email referred to some significantly wealthy Cumbrians '...who may be interested in a properly thought out and cohesive plan.'

One idea raised at his recent lunch with Roxine and Matty at Armathwaite Hall, Keswick, was to set up the sort of academy as might be found at first-class counties such as Durham and Lancashire. 'The trouble is in Cumbria, wherever you put it, they'd want it somewhere else. If you put it in Barrow, they'd want it in Carlisle. And it could also turn into a white elephant because they are quite expensive to run. We didn't think – and you might disagree – that was necessary. Between getting his email and meeting, we prepared a project proposal with photos of the Cumbria development side and Cumberland CCC on the cover. Before we even sat down, Richard took one look at that and almost cried. He was absolutely delighted.'

The ballpark figures to be raised are astronomical. 'For a ten-year project you want about forty-five grand a year, roughly a million will need to be raised to keep it going in perpetuity.' As eye watering as such sums are, however, he has done his homework, working out the costings down to winter nets with a level three coach and one extra development match – £1,500. 'He knows lots of worthies, such as the widow of an ex-MCC chairman, Lady Someone or Other. He'd mentioned the idea and she said: "Dear Richard, how much would you like?" He says Durham university raised a million for their new library in about a fortnight, just by asking their alumni for £25 each.'

That first meeting was a few weeks ago, by when he'd already met the Cumbria Community Foundation, who manage hundreds of trusts. 'Some big, some small. Egremont got £5,000 from it for their clubhouse. Richard is a trustee so he's asked them to agree to manage this as well, which would be useful. So, he said he loved our proposal and would get a business plan to me on Sunday, although it hasn't arrived yet. He has just suffered two bereavements.'

Would he deliver? Roxine didn't know. 'That's the simple answer. But Ted Roberts, when he was at Penrith CC, said he would get Sir Len Hutton to come and do a presentation and they thought, "yeah, right", but he did. Ted organised all sorts of fund-raisers, like Penrith versus the Black and White Minstrels, fully made up. Not sure they'd get away with that today.'

'Only allowed in Cumbria and Suffolk,' Toby chimes in.

'But Richard did have some great ideas, like a best cricket teas competition; he knows Mary Berry. All sorts of people would buy tickets, not for the cricket, but because they want to see Mary Berry. He's also got an arrangement, in principle, to bring a Gay Male Voice Choir up from London to perform in Penrith church, which seats two hundred. He's also organising a match down south, not for us, between a local side and some drag acts. So he does have big ideas.'

After which – 'Matthew has been like a condemned man all day,' says his mother – Roxine and Sempy pack up and go, leaving Neil to ask for everyone's thoughts. 'Is it workable?'

Toby reminds everyone that the club's sponsorship role is still open and Richard Roberts would be the ideal candidate.

'Also,' says Neil, 'there's no doubt we need to be working more closely with Cumbria Cricket Ltd. Given they have an active interest in this as well, it would be another step in that direction.'

'If he is an influential person, it opens it up to different funding sources than we are able to tap into,' says Mike. 'It's a model lots of clubs in other sports follow, there are plenty of advantages, but when you see these figures it's beyond our comprehension, isn't it?' Neil asks for interest in being Cumberland's rep on the Trust committee. 'It's good of you to volunteer,' Mike retorts. 'Yourself or Rob really.'

'I have indicated I'd be prepared to do that initially,' says secretary Cairns, 'but if anyone else...'

Neil: 'I don't hear a stampede of feet.'

*****

Apologies for absence completed, formerly reluctant John Patterson is proposed and seconded onto the committee by Messrs Atkinson and Latham respectively, as the meeting proper gets going. The minutes of March's meeting are circulated and ploughed through a point at a time. Neil asks for comments – none arise – so he proposes they are a true and correct record.

Among matters arising, the relationship with Cumbria Cricket Ltd. 'We've got to drive some cohesion, haven't we?' says Toby. 'It's apparent we are going to be obliged to coalesce at some stage.'

'Fair comment, Toby,' says Neil.

'Would it not be advantageous,' says John, 'to have one of them on our board?' They already are, he is told. Lee Conroy has again sent an apology. Neil says he will contact Bob, telling him they have seen the presentation, are broadly in favour of a joint-approach, but that it would be useful to get his feedback before they respond.

Correspondence? Nothing of note, although congratulations ought to be sent to Berkshire, Mike suggests, for winning the Minor Counties Championship. As Steve's not here, his chairman of cricket report is circulated with no official word on whether or not he has left the role as rumoured. Mike does however point out that if this single sheet of A4 is the basis of his report for the yearbook he edits, then something a little more substantial would be appreciated.

After a few more grumbles about matters sundry ranging from the pitch in Workington to Barrow's enthusiasm to be readmitted – 'Best teas in cricket,' says Toby – it's on to the financial report, Eric reckoning they will break even this year, or maybe a very small profit or loss either way. That's 'quite good' given how they've been forced to manage without the £2,000 donated by late patron, Bob Bowman. The shortfall has been in large part made up by record takings in the raffle – £1,268. 'Well done, Rob,' says Toby. There has been £700 taken in match sponsorship too. 'And well done, as ever, Eric.'

There remains however an elephant in the room unobscured by Chris Hodgson's development update – 'We've had lots of young players come through this year ... Marcus ... Boyney ... Tyler.' Or the latest sponsorship progress. Or the cost of yearbook advertising: 'I'm sure Steve Sharp's sister will advertise again.' And with every quip from Toby, Gary sinks further into his seat. Two more subjects to go and there will be no escaping it. Any other business.

Item number 12: Working with Cumbria Cricket Ltd.

'We've covered that off,' says Neil. 'I'll write to Bob...'

'Well,' says Mike, 'it's a two-way street, Mr Chairman. I'm not aware that they attended any of our fixtures this year. They didn't attend either Myerscough development game. Their behaviour at the meeting we had with the ECB was very poor, as I think Steve reported at the last meeting. It will be incumbent on us to work more closely, that's evident with the way the Minor Counties is going, but they've got to show willingness too and I haven't seen any.'

'Okay, Mike,' Neil says. 'It's disappointing that there has been no representation, either in an official or unofficial capacity, but let's contact them in a spirit of co-operation.'

Item number 13: MCCA meetings, none to report since the last one, covered here in February. 'Oh, there's one thing,' says Toby. The Unicorns rep side has been disbanded, losing a clear route between the Minor Counties and representative cricket. 'Around fifty-seven players in the last ten years have played for the Unicorns and then gone on to play for first-class counties,' he adds. 'Not too bad.'

Eric: 'The only plus is that each county will gain another couple of thousand pounds.'

Toby: 'That's good, but you lose a pathway, don't you?'

Neil: 'And once you've lost that pathway, it's all the harder to resurrect.' The Minor Counties' days do seem to be numbered.

Nor is the evening's final topic likely to cheer anyone up.

*****

'Okay,' says Neil Atkinson. 'Any takers?'

The offer is met with silence you could drive a roller through, until Toby – who else – speaks first, calm and deliberate. He brings up his meeting in Kendal with Neil, Rob, Alan and Steve, before adding by way of understatement: 'At Furness, there was an incident on and off the pitch that has led to a little bit of controversy. This might be the time to decide how we put it right.' And slides in some corporate gobbledygook: 'Moving forward is inevitable as the world will spin, but it's how we go about that to future-proof reoccurrence and keep everybody in an area with blanket transparency.'

Neil straightens his pen and papers before injecting a measured response of his own. 'Okay, well, the MCCA have reviewed the incident you are talking about and it's common knowledge that Cumberland have received a 16-point penalty, deducted this year. Gary received a two-game suspension from the start of next season, however representation has been made because Gary hasn't played for Cumberland since and has actually got written confirmation that he wasn't considered for one of the remaining Championship games, the other a verbal conversation. Whether or not the MCCA take that into account or add two games to what the club has already applied, we don't know. The MCCA have said they will consider that and let us know after the next meeting at Edgbaston.'

And that may – or may not – have been the end of it had Gary himself not piped up.

'Can I just say that it wouldn't have gone this far were it not for people around this table. It should have been an in-house thing. If we are all together as one team, we don't chuck anybody under a bus. That's how it should be.'

Toby: 'It's been done. You can't undo something; you can't unsay something. But, yeah, it calls for future–proofing. How do we avoid this happening again going forward? We are unanimous and on the same page in respect of having the best for the county at heart; moving forward is important to me and I'm sure everybody else. I totally agree with what you are saying Gary and it's because of that blanket transparency is called for.'

Rather than take an opportunity to air his grievances, in his desire to be reasonable Toby is in danger of letting the moment pass, enabling what, to an outsider, sounds like an agreement to formalise how such cover-ups will be better co-ordinated next time. The fact that MCCA rules were broken is largely brushed to one side.

'I think you are right, Toby,' says Neil. 'The matter should have been handled in-house. It was difficult as well, insofar as I don't think we'd ever been in such a situation before. We had no infrastructure within the committee to support how we were going to deal with that. My suggestion, which I have spoken with Eric and Steve about, is that if we have an issue of a similar type in the future, we should have a sub-group. You would have three officials [who] would have the authority to deal with it as an internal matter, as they see fit.'

Nor does it seem to have dawned upon anyone that the club has a responsibility to be open and accountable to its admittedly few followers and the county it represents. Again there is blurred focus regarding just what exactly Cumberland CCC is supposed to be – a private or public sporting organisation? Are tonight's minutes destined to be read like the posthumous papers of Cumbria's very own gentlemen's club? Or will the committee recognise that far greater transparency is required in a competition with ambitions to raise its national status and profile? The former, it seems, until Mike Latham joins the fray: 'Can I ask who is responsible for selection?'

'This season,' says Neil, 'selection has been by the chairman of cricket [Steve Sharp], Gary and Syds.' He glances in the direction of Gary. 'Has Jacques had any involvement?'

Gary: A little bit, yeah. When he's been captain.'

Mike ups the ante. After the third match of the season, Toby, a committee member, asked the chairman of cricket why he wasn't selected for the next one, he points out. Having asked what he would have to do to change that he got the answer: 'Me not be involved.' Does that, Mike wonders, mean that while Steve is chairman of cricket, Toby won't be selected for Cumberland? And if so, does Neil, as chairman, condone that?

'That comment does contradict one made at the meeting I sat in at, and at which Rob sat in too,' Neil replies. 'I asked the specific question about Toby being considered for selection and the answer I got was "yes".'

Toby, thus emboldened, now switches tack and shares a stream of consciousness account of his own, thus paraphrased: 'Our call was on the Tuesday after that Thursday meeting. Steve didn't pick me for Bedfordshire and that's fine. He decided not to pick Gary too, unavailable anyway. It then turned out there was availability for someone and I suggested Sam Wood, who bowled so well at Furness. If you want to leave Gary and myself out due to the controversy fine, but I don't think you should prevent Sam, who won us the previous game essentially, from playing and representing. It so happens that his replacement, Liam, got a hundred. Fantastic. More power to him, you don't speak ill of the lad who's filled in. But what I'm saying is that there was no consideration and I think I used the word "dictatorship". It was upsetting. On the phone Steve's actual words were: "You were considered for selection and we didn't select you." I asked: "What do I have to do to get back in the team?" He said: "Me not be here." He then said: "As long as I'm chairman of cricket, you'll not be involved at Cumberland." Words direct from Mr Sharp. I think it stems from me calling him a liar at the meeting with yourselves; I think it upset him, as being called a liar by anybody does. But when you lie to somebody you're a liar, there's no getting around that. Again, I called for blanket transparency there and I do again here. I'd like to see it minuted this time around.' Were Steve here in person, of course, he may well have been able to shed a different light on Toby's version of events. But he isn't.

'You've got the details there, haven't you, Rob?,' says Neil. 'Okay, to answer your question, Mike, that's a matter I'll take up with Steve.'

Mike though isn't finished yet. 'The president told me that Steve Sharp had resigned as chairman of cricket. Is that correct?'

'Steve Sharp has offered his resignation, yes,' Neil nods, again a development one might have expected to be disclosed earlier, given that this is billed as a post-season debrief. 'It hasn't been accepted, pending a discussion after the end of the season. Initially we were looking at early November, when I was going to sit down with Steve and decide whether he's had his fill and is stepping back as chairman of cricket, or whether there is a way to take things forward ... what his views were, having had a couple of months to reflect on recent events and general cricket matters. Following that, Steve has given me reassurance that he will make a final decision as to whether or not he continues and, if he does, on what basis.'

Toby: 'On that note... I'm just wondering how many games of the six, how many of the 18 days, was Steve present at? I only ask because I've a feeling something there wasn't right and it's destroyed the second half of my season, from a personal standpoint, and...'

Gary Pratt (*sotto voce*): 'Your attitude has contributed to that.'

Toby: 'Pardon?'

Gary: 'Your attitude has contributed to that.'

Toby: 'In what respect, Gary?'

Gary: 'In that it's shit.'

Toby: 'Okay, well I called a meeting, to which you guys [he nods towards Neil and Rob] were privy. I think you can both vouch for me when I say that I conducted myself well. I always try and conduct myself in a professional manner when I can. The only time you could argue that I have not conducted myself in a professional manner was when faced with a scenario that no-one present at the meeting there – and no doubt here tonight – has faced, in what happened at Furness. You can speak ill of attitudes and suchlike, but I'm a professional cricketer who makes my money to pay the mortgage and put food on the table by playing cricket. That was diminished by one man and his unwillingness to select an available player. I will finish talking now by saying that I've got every intention of remaining part of this group. I want to play cricket for Cumberland. I have every intention and every passion to play cricket for Cumberland. I have no intention and no passion to play for another minor county. However I really hope that people can see I'll be wanting to play Minor Counties cricket next year, so I'd like to hear a reasonable and honest, for once, answer from Mr Sharp on why I'm not likely to be selected. If not, and not just to spite anyone here, I'll have to do that for my personal betterment and opportunities, monetarily speaking.'

Neil: 'I understand that, Toby. You are entitled to understand where you fit or don't as the case may be. Rob, if you minute it that I will be meeting with Steve in November and then we'll come back and let you know exactly what the outcome of that discussion was.'

Toby: 'I just hope we can let this water pass under the bridge and move forward. If there's no way of moving forward then changes need to be made and I understand that. But there's no moral high ground for anyone because, unfortunately, we've got to face the reality that we are disgraced – 16 points deducted because of broken rules – and we've got to hold our hands up and face that.'

Neil: 'Mike, anything to add?'

Mike: 'Yeah, I wasn't able to attend the meeting at Kendal, but wrote a detailed email that put forward my thoughts. And I'm quite happy to say that they are unchanged. I thought that Gary's actions as captain were against the spirit of cricket. I thought he should apologise to his teammates and committee for what he did and I thought the committee members referred to in his email, who he'd told what he was going to do seven days prior, should also apologise and then we could have all moved on. I still hold those views. Instead it's driven a rift between people who were previously good friends and made for an unpleasant atmosphere amongst everyone, which no one really wants because we are all here for enjoyment.'

Gary, face a rockslide, though quietly-spoken as ever, responds. 'I don't know when you started to become anti-Cumberland, at what point? You were one hundred per cent for us and all of a sudden we were dropped like a stone. Then you wanted to get back involved. You don't need to look at Toby. I'm speaking to you.'

Mike: 'I am not anti-Cumberland. I was appointed chairman of Leigh Centurions and didn't feel I could do both, with rugby league being a summer sport. I was chairman of cricket to the end of 2017, and during that season wasn't able to commit as much as I'd hoped. Of the 22 available days' cricket I went to 12, which I didn't think was enough – so that's why I resigned as chairman of cricket and Steve Sharp took over. I still tried to support the county as best I could, by doing the yearbook, which takes a lot of time – I've nearly written the 2019 one – and attending games. So I attended ten days' cricket out of 22 in the current season. I've helped Steve with players I recommended who went on to play for the county, Josh Boyne and one or two more like Ben Howarth, who I introduced the previous year. Tyler McGladdery ... a number of others, the Blackpool opener Matthew Houston, who played in the development team ... there's probably a couple more. I'm in no way anti-Cumberland. I support the county as best I can.'

Gary: 'Are you anti-me then?'

Mike: 'I'm not anti-you at all. I've always been supportive of you, but felt your actions at Furness were against the spirit of cricket. I felt if you'd just apologised we could have all forgotten about it. Unfortunately it's reached another level now where...'

Gary: 'How did it reach that level?'

Mike: 'It reached that level by calling me poison, which...'

Gary: 'How did it reach the level of getting to the Minor Counties though?'

Mike: 'In the world of the internet, if you play in two games in one day people are going to find out about it, because your scores...'

Gary: 'Not necessarily, Mike...'

Mike: 'So you think it's perfectly acceptable to tell an umpire that you've got a sore leg, leave the ground, allow a 12th man to come on the field and three hours later play...'

Gary: 'At the time, yeah.'

Mike: 'Well, I don't think it's acceptable and I don't think it's acceptable for the captain of Cumberland to do that, because you are lying basically.'

Gary: 'Oh, and you don't do that, do you?'

Neil: 'Come on chaps, listen...'

Gary: 'You are just a snake, that is the bottom line.'

Mike: 'Well, so that's where we are at then, isn't it?'

Gary: 'So, all those times when you're telling me ... you're laying the law down to me there ... did you tell Toby about when you told me to get rid of him at Richmond because of his attitude?'

Mike: 'I've always supported you. Do you remember when we had a problem at Netherfield?'

Gary: '...and you said he should be banned?'

Mike: 'I said he should be taken off the field. I've told Toby that.'

Gary (to Toby): 'Did he tell you that he told me to get rid of you at Richmond?'

Toby: 'He didn't, but what we need to do is take this down [a notch] and say, well look...'

Neil: 'Okay, we are getting into areas here that are unrelated to this matter...'

Mike: 'No, it's perfectly clear. I am not anti-Cumberland and I am not anti anyone in the room. And I think a simple apology would have sufficed.'

Gary: 'Why do people need to go telling people like Yogi then?'

Mike: 'Well, why lie to the umpires?'

Leanne: 'Why didn't you go and see Gary?'

Gary: 'Yeah.'

Mike: 'You weren't there, were you?'

Leanne: 'No, but afterwards. Yogi wasn't there either, or whoever at the MCCA. But perhaps speaking to Gary might have been the right route...'

Gary: 'That should have been how it went.'

Toby: 'This is a conversation that needs to be had, because air needs to be cleared, and it doesn't hold a place here. However, what I would say is that I've been accused of throwing you under a bus. I've been accused of X, Y and Z. There's an awful lot of mistruths been told, and I can tell you that other minor county committee members have been lied to by our committee. People here have lied to other committees about how things have gone. Other committees have asked: "Why isn't Toby playing?" and been told: "Toby demanded to be paid," "Toby demanded to be captain" and "Toby demanded to pick the side." All three of those things are untrue. All three of those things are twisted words. I'd suggested to Eric that expenses needed to be looked at in the AGM. I also suggested to you, Steve and Alan Wilson at the meeting we had that there ought to be a selection committee because at that moment in time it was a dictatorship. There was one man picking the side, because Gary wasn't available for selection. Mr Sharp was doing it all by himself. I offered the suggestion of Sam Wood playing. He denied it. I said, well then, it's a dictatorship if you're not willing to take on another person's opinion. One man doesn't select an entire county side. The third one was that I picked the team and I think it follows along the same lines.'

Toby takes a breath, but only a short one.

'Those are three lies that have been told to other minor counties on my behalf. The very integrity that had me personally call a meeting regarding the issues at Furness, so we could get over this, so that we could move forward, so that Gary could apologise to the committee and we could just carry on – was the aim of that meeting. That's how it adjourned. I was happy. You were going to meet with Gary, he was going to give his apologies and that would be that.'

Neil: 'And Gary has given an assurance that the situation would not arise again, correct?'

Gary nods.

Toby: 'Now, moving on from that, two weeks down the line and we've got another game. *Quelle surprise*! I'm not selected.'

Gary: 'I don't think your attitude's helped, Toby, to be honest. I think that is the reason why there was a cooling off period.'

Toby: 'Half a year is a long time...'

Gary: 'I've had ten years with you and you've not been much different.'

Neil shifts ever more uncomfortably. 'We have to look at this in terms of how we take it forward. We can look back in hindsight and say, okay, we could have done this and we could have done that, the bottom line is we've done what we've done. What we need to try and do now is have a framework that enables us to deal with situations in the future, which is what we've talked about, but equally there has to be a clearing of the air.'

Toby: 'Yes.'

Neil: 'From your perspective, Toby, in terms of playing cricket for Cumberland, I will come back to you. I am going to be speaking to Steve, who may or may not be part of the process going forward, and if he is to be part of the process going forward, on what basis...'

Gary: 'We had two people picking the side when Mike did it...'

Toby: 'It is wrong, though, because there needs to be an odd number and I mean plural odd. Two people out-weighs one, that's how committees are.'

Neil: 'In the past, the team manager always used to have input. Is that correct, Mike?'

Mike: 'Well, it worked well when Gary and me did it. You got the team you [Gary] wanted really, which is fine because you're the cricketer and I'm not. I just found cricketers who were available and it worked. We won the Championship. Things have slightly changed since, but I agree, if you are happy to move on in these circumstances, contrary to what Gary might think, I don't bear any of you ill. The county is far more important than individuals. So if you are all happy with the current situation and plans you've got in place to safeguard the county going forward and whatever, that's absolutely fine. He might not believe me, but I don't bear Gary ill. What he's achieved with Cumberland, his dedication and his service, is beyond...'

Toby: 'I think he's the only captain ever to win both the Championship and Trophy...'

Mike: '...and the dedication he's shown over the years, playing as an amateur and everything he's done, is absolutely fantastic. So contrary to what you might think, I've got every admiration for you and what you've achieved. I'm just sorry that an incident happened that has driven a rift between us that will never be repaired.'

Gary: 'You know me, Mike. I just like being straight.'

Mike: 'Yeah, and so do I. I thought that you and the committee members should have apologised and then we could have faced the punishment or whatever between us. Unfortunately it didn't happen. I've been to games and people have ignored me, been called names, so that's the way it is. Passions run deep. It happens in all sports.'

Neil: 'The nature of sport is unpredictable. People react differently in situations. It's not necessarily that they are conspiring against you...'

Mike: 'Look back at 2012. We won the one-day, had those trips to Cornwall and Bournemouth and won the league in 2015. It was like a band of brothers. I've been involved in sport a long time, they are the best memories I've ever had. I'll always be indebted to you for that. Leanne has been a personal friend, as has Eric, so no-one is more gutted than me about what's happened. All I will say is that I wish you all well. Eric, yourself, Leanne. I wish you well with the baby and I wish you well in your future career, but unfortunately it's quite clear that I can't be part of it.' His voice begins to crack. 'What's done is done. I'll come to games, support you, but leave you all to get on with it and then you can do what you like.' Addressing Gary again: 'Just take it from me that I hold you in the highest regard for all you've achieved in the game, what you've done for me personally and what you've done for the county. I mean that honestly.'

Toby shuffles in his seat. 'It's about repairing on a personal level now and that's not for here, is it?'

Neil: 'I will report back with what Steve's decision is, and then obviously that will have implications for where we go next season.'

Mike: 'Yes, and if you could just minute that I'll be resigning from the committee too please, Rob. I'll carry on doing the yearbook unless anyone else wants to. If Gary goes on to become the highest run-scorer in Cumberland history no one will be happier than me.'

Neil: 'Okay. That just leaves date and time of next meeting.'

EXTRAS

A year is a long time in cricket. Three days after Dinger Bell's protégé, Ben Stokes, led England to an unlikely series-levelling Ashes win at Headingley, and six weeks since his outstanding contribution to his adopted nation's victory in the 2019 World Cup, Cumberland have somehow reached the final of the last-ever Minor Counties Trophy.

At the Wormsley Estate, Buckinghamshire, on Wednesday 28 August, hard on the heels of a new 'hottest late August Bank Holiday on record', the side to face Berkshire is made up of familiar faces. Opening the batting are Sam 'Dutts' Dutton (who in the interim has launched the club's official Twitter account – @CCCCumberland #Sausages) and Toby Mowat. In at three, Gary Pratt, still captain and as pivotal as ever. Thereafter: Michael Slack, Matty Sempill, Jacques du Toit, Alex Grainger, Liam Grey, wicketkeeper Ben Howarth, Toby Bulcock, Adam Syddall and Ben Davidson. Nothing has changed, it seems, and yet in the bigger picture everything is about to change.

After one hundred and twenty-four years, following the last ball of this season, the Minor Counties will be 'minor' no more.

Thereafter, its twenty clubs will make up the National Counties Championship, set to commence in April 2020, when Cumberland will meet Cheshire – 'weather permitting' – at New Brighton CC in group one of the National County Cricket Blast, a rebranded T20 tournament organised along the lines of 2018.

As for the Trophy, of which this is the culmination, it too will be renamed the National County Cricket Trophy, while going on pretty much as before – group stages followed by semi-finals and a final. But now the top two in each regional group will qualify for quarter-finals in which the group winners earn home advantage.

The big change, though, is to come in the Eastern and Western Championship divisions. Each of these will become two leagues of five, meaning a reduction in the amount of three-day matches from six to four, two home, two away, together with the introduction of promotion and relegation. Every 'national county' will also stage a 50-over 'showcase' game against a first-class county, Lancashire in Cumberland's case, to ensure the same amount of fixtures overall.

What is it they say about the best-laid plans?

No-one on this glorious August morning in 2019, of course, has heard of Covid-19. The only clouds on the horizon are those forecast to bubble as the day progresses. Yet by December in China, the first few cases will emerge of illness from a virus that will cut a swathe through every sport on the planet – large and small – to devastating effect. Bats will be blamed, though of a different variety.

Reports that the MCCA would soon become the NCCA broke shortly after the 2018 campaign concluded, followed by a vote of confirmation the following February. ECB board member and one-time Bedfordshire CEO Martin Darlow told *The Cricketer* that, having been minded at the outset of the review to abolish the Minor Counties Championship altogether – 'I was one of the people who raised the question, is the competition still doing what it should be doing?' – he was persuaded it is: '...so long as we restructure it.'

Darlow went on: 'I was told by some people that we would never get a name change through. It's been the Minor Counties Cricket Association forever – it's legacy, it's history. But in the end there was no iota of opposition to the name-change.' The first-class counties wished to change it too, feeling 'awkward' about using the word 'minor'. Some counties had found attracting sponsorship tough for something thus branded. 'It's self-defeating. We need to make all counties viable for sponsorship.'

Age and qualification regulations are to be introduced, with counties penalised for 'too old squads', the aim being to develop locals rather than 'ship' players in. Eight must come from the region in teams with an average age of 25 and under. Yet for a county club as geographically isolated as Cumberland, that brings issues quite apart from where sufficient quality is to be found. Assuming there is enough talent in Cumbria – and that it has passed its driving test – is it fair to expect young and perhaps inexperienced drivers to play into the early evening on a Saturday and then embark on a journey of several hundred miles to participate in one-day Trophy and T20 fixtures, before making the return journey in time for work or college on Monday morning? And what about those from outside the county, or over the age of 25, who aspire to play at this level?

Such issues and others like them are unlikely to disappear if the comments of ground-hopper Tony Hutton, in his online blog in January 2019, are anything to go by. He regrets:

> ...less three day cricket, to make way for nonsensical T20 games involving sides travelling long distances for one day contests that many of the players do not want to play in and would prefer playing for their club sides. I suppose all good things come to an end and [I] should feel grateful that I have been able to watch county cricket for a period of seventy years. I cannot help feel an element of sadness that such a great sport is apparently destroying itself with no regard whatsoever for the people who have supported it for so long.

On the up side, a four-division system ought to mean the strongest sides compete at a regularly higher standard and, where necessary, lads need take only eight days off work, not twelve, unless of course they work Sundays. First-class 2nd XI Championship matches have been promised not to clash with those of the new National Counties.

Chairman Nick Archer, a member of the review group along with the now NCCA secretary Phil Caley, told BBC Sport: 'These changes will make [the Championship] far more competitive. There will be no hiding place.' The best will play the best. 'In the past, there have been too many occasions when, with only six games played in a ten-team league, you can finish top maybe not having played the three best other sides. Now, with more availability of players too, the best team will win it.'

According to Martin Darlow in *The Cricketer*, the all-important funding is not only to be maintained but in real terms will grow, one-day games and T20 cheaper to organise than three-dayers, though with distribution from the same £10million pot already allocated to non-first-class cricket in its entirety. Darlow would like to see more counties develop charitable foundations. To put all that in context, however, the ECB has increased the funding it gives to first-class counties to £75million, each club set to receive in excess of £4million-per-year until 2024 at least.

When the NCCA Championship does get going, Cumberland are to join Northumberland, Bedfordshire, Buckinghamshire and Hertfordshire in Eastern Division 2, thanks to a 2019 chairman Neil Atkinson calls 'patchy'. In front of a vast hospitality tent at what must be one of the most beautiful cricket venues in the country, he sums up a campaign that may nevertheless end in unlikely glory. 'This season has had its issues,' he says. 'Our Championship game with Suffolk, meant for Sedbergh, was switched at the last minute because the school made the pitch unavailable, replaced by a one-innings game at Netherfield on the Tuesday.' That was no fun for Suffolk, who arrived at 03.00am expecting a three-day fixture. And in the end it will thwart Cumberland, being one of the three draws, along with a victory and two defeats, that are soon to leave them sixth and condemned to the lower reaches. As we speak, that single win hasn't yet happened. It will be achieved in next weekend's game against Buckinghamshire at Tring – thereby avoiding a first season without a Championship victory since 2006.

In some ways, though, luck has been on their side. After all, it is due to another hurriedly-relocated fixture, a 'bowl-off' in the nets at Penrith, that they are here today. For that was when Jacques du Toit's steely nerve got them through against Staffordshire, 3-0, after more flooding at Carlisle wrecked the original 50-over semi-final.

This, though, will indeed be the end of an era. 'When the new rules come in next year, the team will be forcibly broken up,' says Neil. So this may well be the last they see of Pratt, Syddall, du Toit and Bulcock. 'It's all a bit sudden. Especially as, in Cumbria, given the weather, less club cricket is played than is the national average, so players tend to develop later.' Slacky (26), Dutts (27) and Chris Hodgson (31) for example. 'Even the older locals are under threat.'

One of those old-timers, Syds, will remain involved off the field, having taken over as chairman of cricket from Steve Sharp, whose resignation was confirmed after that stormy Crooklands meeting. A round-robin email in November 2018 made Steve's reasoning clear, and put forward his own version of events re Toby. On holiday when the draft minutes were released, he had now looked them over and felt 'some defence of my "dictatorship" is required.'

Re "Mr Bulcock"'s non-selection in the final three games of 2018, Steve wrote: '[Versus] Bedford away, Mr Bulcock was selected to play by me, Mr Bulcock's reply was that he would only play if he was captain. After a couple of hours mulling over the "offer" I came to the decision that no individual should put forward that proposition and told Mr Bulcock of my decision. This was confirmed by Mr Bulcock at the meeting at Kendal the Friday before the Bedford game, Rob, Neil, Alan please correct me if I'm wrong.' He continued: 'At the Kendal meeting it was agreed that Mr Bulcock would be considered for the last two games. For Northumberland Mr Pratt and I considered Mr Bulcock's selection and agreed not to select him. For the last game I was not involved in selection having already tendered my resignation.' That decision, he said, was predominantly sparked by 'a lack of appetite with what is coming with the changes within the MCCA and the CPA over the next couple of years.' Wishing the club well for 2019, Steve offered to continue managing the Cumberland CCC development team, an offer the committee willingly accepted.

Also in 2019, Cumberland implemented a selection committee structure, in which Syds and skipper Pratt made their choices in co-operation with a vice-captain: Toby Bulcock (T20), Sam Dutton (Trophy) and Michael Slack (Championship), effectively giving the club an Australian-style 'leadership group'. Out of which sprang 'few disagreements and a great deal of consensus,' according to Syds in his *Cumberland County Cricket Yearbook* report, published at the start of a – for the moment – virus-free 2020. He went on:

> Team successes and outstanding individual performances were too numerous to mention, however we were treated to memorable Championship hundreds from elder statesmen Jacques du Toit (101 not out) at Netherfield and Gary Pratt (114) at Tring. Ben Davidson, Matthew Sempill and Michael Slack

strangely all managed Championship top scores of 86! Special mention should also be made of Sam Dutton's extraordinary display in the two T20s against Northumberland, where he scored 167 runs over the two games off 88 balls without being dismissed.'

After today's encounter, Jacques, unavailable at Tring, will leave the club having led 'a young and inexperienced side to one of our most memorable and celebrated wins in recent history,' that of the quarter-final defeat of favourites Lincolnshire at Bourne CC en route to the Trophy final. In all, Syds writes: 'Twenty-four players pulled on the Cumberland jersey in 2019 over the three formats ... it was also pleasing to see so many Cumbrians take the field. Their selection was based on merit alone, rather than any ECB/MCCA directive.' Unacknowledged, however, is that in terms of Championship alone, while twenty-one different players were fielded, only seven of those were from Cumbria.

In closing, the new chairman of cricket added how: 'Those of us who were born and play our cricket outside the county have always felt welcome and have been equally proud to represent the county as honorary Cumbrians. I find it sad that in 2020 there has been found a need for imposed restrictions and selection criteria and I can only hope that a level playing field has been created for all counties and recreational cricketers throughout the country. My instinct tells me otherwise. That said, we are well placed to succeed, despite these impositions.'

*****

Wormsley, on the outskirts of Stokenchurch, Buckinghamshire, is a magnificent place to watch cricket, and an even better spot, you'd imagine, in which to play it. Nestled into a rolling Chiltern landscape on a private estate whose country house and walled gardens have been owned by the Getty family since 1985, its bucolic beauty flirts with caricaturing what a Minor Counties final ought to look like.

At the lower end of a ground whose entry point is a mile-and-a-half into the estate, chap with a feather in his cap waving everyone in, is a quaint little scorebox redolent of Hattytown. Looming high at the other, a thatched pavilion is the dominant feature. With a red telephone box to the rear, its walls are hung with cricketing *objet d'art*, paintings of old Test matches and such, between a couple of hospitality marquees. The pitch between is immaculate, managed by a full-time team whose magnificent work somehow disguises how it stages forty games per year – including some Buckinghamshire Minor Counties clashes, village matches and visits from tourists and other notable sides like the MCC and Sir Tim Rice's Heartaches XI.

Purchased by Sir Paul Getty, the American multi-millionaire philanthropist who died, aged 70, in 2003, his extensive renovations to an estate whose existence is traced back to the 12th century were completed in 1992. That year also saw the inaugural cricket match here, watched by among others HM The Queen Mother, John Major, Freddie Trueman, Denis Compton and Michael Caine. Since when many a famous cricketer has trodden its turf, either for or against the Sir Paul Getty XI ... Andrew Flintoff, Brian Lara, Graham Gooch and Imran Khan among them. Its website claims Mick Jagger turned Getty on to cricket 'over cups of tea whilst watching Test matches on television in the 1960s,' naming the man who then persuaded him to consummate that love affair with a ground of his own as legendary *Test Match Special* commentator Brian Johnston. So posh is it here that a visitor can't even tread in cow pats. Deer shit, maybe.

Gary Pratt may not have reached the heights of some of those names, but he most definitely has a place in history. It is good to see him, Toby and the rest of the Cumberland squad back where they belong, on the field before a prestigious game. Retained as skipper, Gary missed the opening two Championship games of the season through suspension, as prescribed, and would feature in only three overall, but that will be more than enough to accumulate the 188 runs that see him reach 4,385 for Cumberland in the Championship, second in the all-time list behind the great Bob Entwistle (5,708), who sadly passed away in 2019. Gary's club side Richmondshire, meanwhile, this time fell to Scott Lees's Ormskirk in the quarter-finals of the ECB National Club Championship, that title going to Norfolk side Swardeston, who completed a unique double with the ECB T20s. The Richmondshire club will, however, soon be crowned North Yorkshire South Durham ECB Premier League champions.

As for Gary's former nemesis Toby Bulcock, he too moves up

the Cumberland rankings, his 270 wickets putting him third behind Marcus Sharp (344) and Malcolm Woods (275). And despite the apparent demise of the Minor Counties' representative side at the end of 2018, a man who, by the look of it, is as ebullient as ever somehow regained selection for the Unicorns v the MCC in 2019.

Toby has spent this summer too with Leigh, while Sam Dutton, opening here with Barrow captain Toby Mowat, left Furness CC as promised to join Josh Boyne and Ben Howarth at Blackpool, a club from whom another youngster made his Championship debut this year, 21-year-old Matthew Siddall. In the weeks to come, Blackpool will fail to retain their Northern Premier League title, however, that honour this year going to Leyland. And after having escaped the drop in 2018, Neil Atkinson's Penrith will be relegated on a dramatic final day. Having lost at home to bottom side Barrow by 54 runs, they will soon look on in horror as fellow relegation candidates Kendal get one over on hated local rivals Netherfield – 92 all out – to pull off a last-gasp great escape.

Of the rest of today's Cumberland line-up, Michael Slack went from Wigton to Carlisle as club professional, joining Ben Davidson, and led the way with 508 runs and 50 wickets in a side destined to finish champions of a renamed Cumbria Cricket League – reference to North Lancashire ditched – Carlisle's first such title since 1982.

Elsewhere in the now CCL, Matty Sempill and Alex Grainger of 2018 winners Cockermouth will have to make do with third this time, though with Alex as the league's top scorer (702) at an average of 58, Sempy contributing 504 runs himself and man of the match when Cockermouth beat Wigton to lift the Meageen County Cup. In the 2019 final of the Higson Cup, meanwhile, Furness beat Keswick at Haverigg. Carlisle's 2nd XI are to finish runners-up to winners Caldbeck in the Eden Valley League, while Carnforth will once again come top of the pile to retain their 2018 title in the Westmorland League.

Further afield, Jacques du Toit began his 2019 season with a switch from Newcastle to South Northumberland; Liam Grey lined up with Northern in the Liverpool Comp; and, to complete a circle, Adam Syddall took himself back to Bolton and played for Lostock CC. Further afield still, in a cast unrelated to today, when the season is done ex-Cumberland pair Richard Gleeson and Liam Livingstone will have helped Lancashire to gain promotion from the second division of the County Championship, Gleeson the leading wicket-taker with 47 and Livingstone, having resigned the captaincy, scoring 599 runs at an average of 46. Livingstone also wintered in the lucrative IPL for Rajasthan Royals with Ben Stokes, who will complete a summer of achievement by being made freeman of the town he grew up in, Cockermouth.

Mattie McKiernan finally won his professional contract, but his first full-time season has been ruined by a stress fracture. He will, though, make his first-class debut for Derbyshire later, upon making a big hundred for their 2nd XI. Ex-Cumberland lads Liam Trevaskis, Graham Clark (both Durham), Luke Procter (Northants), Stephen Parry (Lancashire) and Jordan Clark (Surrey) feature in the first-class county set-up too, while Lincolnshire all-rounder Azeem Rafiq, Wiltshire captain Ed Young and one-time Shropshire skipper Richard Oliver are just three of some ninety current and former Minor Counties players to be included in an inaugural draft for 2020's The Hundred.

What was that about 'best-laid plans' again..?

But back to Wormsley where a good crowd has turned up, certainly larger in number than were here to see four clubs battle it out on the inaugural T20 finals day last summer, albeit those games delayed a day by rain. The scene now, as then, is pretty as a picture when Berkshire's openers jog down the pavilion steps, favourites by a considerable distance. Previews have called it a battle of David v Goliath proportions and there is no doubt which county is which.

As with last year's T20 games, there is no sign of anything so vulgar as face paint or bouncy castles, but then the Trophy is a variety of cricket with longer lineage. A kestrel circles and then hovers on high; one doing similar in 2018 was frightened off by a drone. In a corner of the upper boundary, the Cumberland party, flag draped proudly, has established base camp. Margaret and Vera, in charge of Eric and Gilbert, are generous in dishing out sarnies, pies and assorted picnic goodies. Rob and Lesley Cairns sit side by side, as ever, Rob with a plastic 'glass' of red in his seat cup-holder. 'Ah, room temperature,' he sighs, contented. BBC Cumbria is here too, their table and gear pitched next to a hospitality tent that president Alan Wilson and his friend Derek, the Wing Commander, will before long find a use for. It isn't long before the radio boys have drama to relay – eighth over in fact.

Berkshire pair Jack Davies and Archie Carter are weathering the combined pace of Adam Syddall and Liam Grey nicely, having reached 29 without loss before opting for a quick single. And who should be lurking for just such an opportunity? Gary Pratt, of course, whose Ricky Ponting-like throw ends a promising partnership. Three overs later, it is Syds's turn to strike – twice – next man in Dan Lincoln lbw and batsman four, Richard Morris, bowled. Enter Toby Bulcock, who has lost a bit of weight by the look of it. His left-arm spin soon adds England under-19 player Davies to the list of fallen, caught Sempill for 31, in his very first over.

With the scoreboard reading 60 for 4, Cumberland tails are up and, as ever in such circumstances, human dynamo Toby is at the heart of it. Two overs later, he claims a second scalp, James Morris, caught behind, and adds a third, Euan Woods, ex-England U19, lbw. Looking at 81 for 6 with 25 overs gone, these underdogs have hope.

Ten runs more and Jacques gets a seventh, another lbw decision going Cumberland's way. However, the Cumbrians let the pressure slide, Chris Peploe and Tom Nugent's partnership moving their club past the century mark and on to 131, before Grey this time steps in and Peploe flashes one through to Ben. The end, when it comes, arrives quickly. Nugent is also run out – Toby B showing that anything Gary can do ... but on his hands and knees. When Grey adds his second, Luke Beaven lbw, Berkshire are 144 all out, with 3.2 of their overs going unused.

If anything deserves another of Vera's buns it is that, although with a little more killer instinct the outcome might have been still more encouraging. And when Dutts is then caught Davies, bowled Beaven, with the very first ball of Cumberland's reply, confidence dips. Irrepressible when in form, he now looks forlorn, trudging off and up the steps, decapitating imaginary dandelions with his bat. Gary, meanwhile, heads the other way, a task on his hands.

To begin with, it looks doable. The skipper and Toby Mowat get the tins moving with a shared 16 runs, but then Toby is lbw for 7 and, with Michael Slack in tow, it is all to do again.

This time the pair do make inroads, Slacky with fine shots en route to a personal 26. It seems he may end up as Cumberland's top scorer when Gary is then caught behind for 17, foreshadowing a middle order collapse and a few spots of rain. 'Aww,' says Leanne, on crutches after a leg operation and watching among Cumberland's mini-army. Less interested is the couple's recent arrival, Freddie, a bobby-dazzler now safely delivered and fast asleep in his pram. Has he had a cricket bat in his hands yet?' 'Not yet,' she says. It surely won't be long however. He has just begun to crawl.

Come the 25th over, the Cumbrians have lost 7 wickets for 65, which is 11 runs short and one wicket more than Berks at this stage, the further victims being Sempy (1), du Toit (1), Grainger (3) and most latterly Slacky himself, after a fifteen-minute break for a sudden afternoon shower. The spine of the side is snapped. Yet although it may appear that way, the game isn't quite over yet.

Enter the lower order. As Slacky departs and sunshine returns, Liam Grey is yet to get off the mark. Joined by Ben Howarth, he does that and the new pair hunker down. 'If we win this, I'll run around the pitch naked,' says Lesley Cairns.

'Everyone will close their eyes,' warns Rob.

'You speak for yourself,' says Gilbert.

'You just called her a rottweiler!' Rob counters.

'Well, they're not bad dogs,' says Gilbert.

Neither Liam or Ben will make a huge score, but they use up more overs and show a bit of resistance before being felled for 12 and 18, clean bowled and lbw respectively, to move the side to 121 for 9. Suddenly, an innings that looked as if it was dwindling away, gets interesting. Berkshire are just 23 runs ahead.

Toby Bulcock – coached unheard on a hill by his dad, Steve, in a fold-up chair – was motoring along with 18 notched already when the finger went up for Ben. Joined by Syds, the number 11, through judicious runs and crease management the target edges tantalisingly closer. One good ball – or one mistake – and it's done. But the good ball or error doesn't arrive and the old-stagers begin to enjoy – while their followers endure – an increasingly thrilling moment on the big stage. Before long, helped by a timely Bulcock four, the duo somehow need 'only' 10 runs for victory from the last 14 balls. Will Berkshire buckle? Like the champion side they are, they will not. Thanks to a combination of tight bowling and wise field positioning under pressure, instead they hang on – but only just. With 50 overs bowled and Cumberland's potential match-winner Toby prevented from taking the strike, the favourites win on the last ball by one run, both batsmen left with stumps intact.

Bearing in mind Berkshire's five pieces of silverware in the last three seasons – and how they are on course for a fourth consecutive Championship final – perhaps no-one ought to have been surprised that they have clawed their way over the line today. In 2020's *Cumberland Yearbook*, new editor Chris Gore will call it a 'fantastic effort' and so it has been. But they still lost the game, didn't they?

Whether or not that matters, of course, gets to the heart of Minor Counties cricket. Berkshire certainly seem to prefer victory. Their Championship final one-wicket victory over Staffordshire in September is also set to be the last under the Minor Counties moniker, even as the club sets its sights on Devon's four successive titles, a record set in seasons 1994-1997.

For most clubs, however, despite the new name, the song will largely stay the same. And when real change inevitably does arrive, as it must, with any luck moving from minor to major, must that necessarily be so terrible?

From acorns, giant oaks grow – a cliché, but nevertheless true. It was shown clearly in the July 2019 edition of *The Oldie*, a magazine to which many a Minor Counties devotee doubtless subscribes. In his column 'Profitable Wonders', James Le Fanu wrote of how that most English of trees – 'the boast and bulwark of the British nation', as 18th century arborist William Boutcher had it – owes its prevalence on these islands to William the Conqueror: '...whose expropriation of large tracts of forest, transformed into open woodland parks for deer hunting, created the ideal habitat for the oaks' growth and maturation.' In other words, laid the groundwork for exactly the sort of venue we have enjoyed today.

And without that development, Le Fanu continues, the nation would likely not have had enough wood to build *HMS Victory* and the fleet that won the Battle of Trafalgar before the arrival – in such as Barrow and elsewhere – of iron and steel for shipbuilding.

The Minor Counties is dead.

Not so the wicket men.

Cumberland's 2019 Trophy final squad: *Back*: Geoff Minshaw (*scorer*), Ben Davidson, Sam Wood, Liam Grey, Toby Bulcock, Toby Mowat, Michael Slack, Gareth Wade. *Front*: Ben Howarth, Jacques du Toit, Gary Pratt, Adam Syddall, Sam Dutton, Alex Grainger, Matthew Sempill

Photo: Lesley Cairns

ACKNOWLEDGEMENTS

At Buckinghamshire during the last Minor Counties Trophy final, Cumberland's quietly modernising chairman, Neil Atkinson, let it slip that the club may be destined for a name change – to Cumbria.

'We are meeting in October for a vote to confirm it,' he said, adding that the club constitution was also 'being looked at'.

Nine months after that reported get-together – as the world continues to grapple with a coronavirus pandemic few if any nations saw coming – it seems that the vote must have gone the other way.

If so, it is still bound to happen one day.

The re-branded National Counties T20 has been scrapped for one year at least. As has the Knockout Trophy. On Thursday 25 June, the ECB formally announced that 2020's new National Counties Championship, upon which so much hope had been pinned, already delayed, would not go ahead at all; nor would the 'Showcase' fixtures with first-class counties. Four weeks later, the idea of a late-summer T20 or 50-over comp was knocked back, 11 votes to 9. Discounting a couple of World Wars, this would be the first year since 1894 that a Minor/National Counties competition had not been contested.

In the wider world, wherein Carlisle's favourite Prime Minister, Boris Johnson, called a cricket ball 'a natural vector of disease', other events have been similarly disrupted. In July, England's series with the West Indies was staged behind closed doors and recreational cricket began late and with restrictions. However, as lockdown kicked in, the heavily-trumpeted Hundred was postponed until crowds are allowed into stadiums again, in its case no earlier than 2021.

Whatever future form cricket takes in what is being sold as 'the new normal', it will essentially be the same game, forged in ceremony and inevitably obsessed with what went before. It will be built on people too, many of whom made writing *The Wicket Men* a delight.

Most of those were at Cumberland of course, where, from field to committee to boundary rope, the welcome could not have been warmer. I am especially grateful to each of the boys in green for reaching a final in 2019, so I could avoid an unhappy ending!

Alan, Neil, Eric, Rob and Steve – across the board – could not have been more accommodating with their time and knowledge. A big thank you to Gilbert, for statistical assistance and entertaining tales. Geoffrey Minshaw was a champ in the latter department also.

I must of course send up the old two-gun salute to Jeeves – aka Mike Latham – whose original idea this book was some three years ago, though he doubtless envisaged it in different circumstances. I could not have done it justice without his invaluable heads-ups and supply of Milnthorpe pork pies. What-ho to Toby (the dog) as well.

My gratitude to everyone – well, *almost* everyone – at every club we visited on our laps around Cumbria, a county of vast and breathtaking beauty that is truly one of a kind. Pay a visit today!

The hospitality of those in the Minor Counties across the rest of the country too was appreciated; a fraternity more congenial it would be hard to find. I hope you enjoy having a light shone on your level of competition, so undervalued by the sporting world at large.

There is little doubt that the popularity of long-form cricket is not dwindling so much as plummeting right now, a fate perhaps shared with meandering books like this one, in an age when if the majority bother to read at all it is for information or a quick thrill, rather than the slow simple pleasure of watching a story unfold.

Yet can't a journey be every bit as captivating as its destination?

As I hope this book has shown, there are few places better than Cumbria – or Cumberland, if you'd prefer – in which to surrender oneself to what will always be a glorious summer folk ritual.